WHAT IS RACE?

WHAT IS RACE?

Four Philosophical Views

Joshua Glasgow

Sally Haslanger

Chike Jeffers

Quayshawn Spencer

OXFORD
UNIVERSITY PRESS

OXFORD
UNIVERSITY PRESS

Oxford University Press is a department of the University of Oxford. It furthers
the University's objective of excellence in research, scholarship, and education
by publishing worldwide. Oxford is a registered trade mark of Oxford University
Press in the UK and certain other countries.

Published in the United States of America by Oxford University Press
198 Madison Avenue, New York, NY 10016, United States of America.

Library of Congress Cataloging-in-Publication Data
Names: Glasgow, Joshua, author. | Haslanger, Sally Anne, author. |
Jeffers, Chike, 1982– author. | Spencer, Quayshawn, author.
Title: What is race? : four philosophical views / Joshua Glasgow, Sally Haslanger,
Chike Jeffers, Quayshawn Spencer/
Description: New York : Oxford University Press, 2019. |
Includes bibliographical references and index.
Identifiers: LCCN 2018053834 (print) | LCCN 2019007102 (ebook) |
ISBN 9780190610210 (Online content) | ISBN 9780190610197 (updf) |
ISBN 9780190610203 (epub) | ISBN 9780190610173 (hardback) |
ISBN 9780190610180 (paperback)
Subjects: LCSH: Race—Philosophy. | Race relations—Philosophy. |
BISAC: PHILOSOPHY / Political. | PHILOSOPHY / Metaphysics. |
PHILOSOPHY / Movements / General.
Classification: LCC HT1523 (ebook) | LCC HT1523 .G643 2019 (print) |
DDC 305.8001—dc23
LC record available at https://lccn.loc.gov/2018053834

To our children,

Samantha Rose Glasgow-Shulman, Aminata Lilla Jeffers, Ayo Jelani Jeffers, Aza Katherine Ida Jeffers, Julian Buo-Hon Spencer, Quentin Buo-Yi Spencer, Isaac Amazu Haslanger Yablo, and Zina Siyasa Haslanger Yablo,

in the hope that their generations will find a more just world.

CONTENTS

ACKNOWLEDGMENTS

The theories presented in this book are derived from articles and books that we have previously published. Numerous people helped us as we developed those earlier publications. We would like to reaffirm our gratitude for their help.

With respect to the present work, we gratefully acknowledge the following:

Sally Haslanger would like especially to thank the other authors of the book, Joshua Glasgow, Chike Jeffers, and Quayshawn Spencer, for their ongoing work, helpful conversations, and friendly collaboration in putting this book together. In addition, she would like to thank Lawrence Blum, Jorge Garcia, Adam Hosein, Karen Jones, Lionel McPherson, Megan Mitchell, José Jorge Mendoza, Deborah Mühlebach, David Plunkett, Laura Schroeter, Francois Schroeter, Greg Restall, Tommie Shelby, Isaac Yablo, Stephen Yablo, and Zina Yablo for ongoing conversations on the topics discussed.

Chike Jeffers would like to thank Linda Martín Alcoff, Veromi Arsiradam, Tiffany Gordon, Tyler Hildebrand, David Ludwig, Tina Roberts-Jeffers, Katie Stockdale, and his coauthors Sally Haslanger, Quayshawn Spencer, and Joshua Glasgow for their feedback on drafts of his chapters in this book. He also presented versions of Chapter 2 at the University of Memphis and at Northwestern University. He is thankful to all who were present and especially to those who provided feedback on those occasions.

Quayshawn Spencer is thankful for feedback from Mariana Achugar, Linda Alcoff, Elizabeth Anderson, Luvell Anderson, Robert Brandon, Liam Bright, Mazviita Chirimuuta, Haixin Dang, Michael Devitt, Brian Epstein, Patrick Forber, Justin Garson, Joshua Glasgow, Michael Hardimon, Sally Haslanger, Jay Garfield, Chike Jeffers, Saul Kripke, Meena Krishnamurthy, Edouard Machery, Lionel McPherson, Charles Mills, Sandra Mitchell, Jennifer Morton, Albert Mosley, Wayne Norman, Sumeet Patwardhan, George Smith, and Daniel Wodak. He would also like to thank the faculty and students in the philosophy departments at the following universities for allowing him to receive feedback on drafts of his chapters at a colloquium talk: Carnegie Mellon University, College of the Holy Cross, CUNY Graduate Center, Drexel University, Duke University, the University of Michigan at Ann Arbor, Smith College, Temple University, Tufts University, University of Maryland in Baltimore County, and Virginia Polytechnic Institute. Also, Spencer would like to thank the participants of the University of Pittsburgh's Summer Program in Philosophy of Science for Underrepresented Groups in 2017 for all of their useful feedback on Chapter 3, and he'd like to thank the Center for Philosophy of Science at the University of Pittsburgh for providing two opportunities to present and receive feedback on Chapter 3. Finally, he'd like to thank the participants at the 2015 Metaphysics of Social Categories Workshop at the University of Colorado at Boulder for offering helpful feedback on work that would become part of Chapter 3, and the participants at the ninth annual Ida B. Wells conference at the University of Memphis for offering helpful feedback on work that would become part of Chapter 7.

Josh Glasgow is thankful for the help of Shani Long Abdallah, Paul Bloomfield, Matt Ingram, Robert Ingram, Esa Díaz León, Dan López de Sa, and audiences at the University of Barcelona and University of Geneva. He is also grateful to Sally Haslanger, Chike Jeffers, and Quayshawn Spencer for both their collaboration on this project and their ongoing work. Finally, he'd like to thank Rani Bagai for conversation about Vaishno Das Bagai, Kala Bagai Chandra, and events surrounding the *Thind* decision.

INTRODUCTION

Historically, efforts to make sense of human diversity led to classifying humans by where they live, by culture or custom (including language or religion), by family or ancestry, by appearance, by personality type or temperament, by physical and intellectual capacities, and, of course, by race. But what, if anything, is distinctive of *racial* groups? A race is not just a group of people linked by a common ancestry. While this may account for the idea of the *human race*, since all living humans share a common ancestor (so-called Mitochondrial Eve, who lived about 200,000 years ago), it also would make any group of people who are biological siblings a race, which is not how anyone talks about race. Nor is a race just a group of people linked by a common geographic origin. If that were true, then African Americans and Afro-Caribbeans would be American, instead of Black, because both of these groups of people originated in the Americas, not Africa. And it is difficult to unpack race in terms of shared skin color, since people of different races can share the same skin color and people of the same race can have different skin colors.

So, how should we understand what a race is supposed to be? This is the question we address in the chapters that follow.

One might think that the best way to answer the question is to consult current biology. However, whether *race* is essentially a biological thing is controversial, as this book demonstrates. For that matter, there is not even agreement among biologists. In one recent survey, 45.5% of American biology professors believed that "[r]ace is biological," 50% believed that "[r]ace is not biological," and the remaining 4.5% were uncommitted (Morning 2011, 111). Moreover, the term 'race' has been used in multiple ways over the centuries, and in some uses, it clearly does not function as a biological term (Herzog 1998, Ch. 7; Stevens 1999, Ch. 4). Don Herzog (1998) characterizes the problem:

Take Coleridge: "Men of genius are rarely much annoyed by the company of vulgar people; because they have a power of looking at such persons as objects of amusement, of another race altogether." A race of vulgar or stupid people: is that a genuine or merely metaphoric race? Does a concept as nefarious and slippery as that of race admit of a genuine or innocent or primary usage and then parasitic and metaphoric usages? Or are there no clear core cases to which it applies? If there is a clear core, does it have to do with something revolving around blood or genetics? Or, as Coleridge seems to suggest, around hierarchy and contempt? (290)

Each of the four authors included in this book proposes a different account of race. Quayshawn Spencer (Chapter 3) is a naturalist about race and believes that there are racial groups distinguished by biological features (e.g., shared genomic ancestry), but that the biological features in question do not justify any social hierarchy among the races. Chike Jeffers (Chapter 2) and Sally Haslanger (Chapter 1) argue in different ways that races are socially constructed groups. Jeffers holds that the cultural aspect of racial difference— that is, the ways in which races are groups differentiated by distinctive ways of life—is underappreciated in its importance to the past and present and is the centrally important feature when thinking about how we might continue to construct races in the future, past the end of racism. Haslanger, by contrast, argues that races are first and foremost sociopolitical groups, marked by bodily features, that function within a dominance hierarchy. In the case of the current social structure in the United States, the dominance hierarchy is White supremacy, but races are formed within different hierarchies that aren't organized around Whiteness. Joshua Glasgow (Chapter 4) maintains that the concept of race includes, as a necessary condition, that there be a set of visible features that are disproportionately held by each race. If this condition is strongly interpreted to require that visible-trait groups are supposed to be legitimized by biology, then, Glasgow argues, there are no races (racial anti-realism); but if, instead, this condition is weakly interpreted to mean simply that there are differences between humans, then race is arguably real in a non-biological and non-social way (basic racial realism).

After laying out the fundamentals of our views in the first four chapters, we each reply to our coauthors in Chapters 5 (Haslanger), 6 (Jeffers), 7 (Spencer), and 8 (Glasgow).

We don't consider our four views to exhaust all of the plausible metaphysical views one can have about what race is and whether it's real, nor do we think that our particular ways of defending the metaphysical views represented are the only ways to defend these views. For instance, the arguments over whether race is biological cover a wider terrain than we survey here. And it's possible that race is, essentially, a social grouping of people without necessarily being a cultural grouping of people (à la Jeffers) or a political grouping of people (à la Haslanger). For example, Ron Mallon and Daniel Kelly (2012) have argued that race is a socio-psychological grouping of people.

These limitations notwithstanding, we aim for this book to highlight some central themes and compelling arguments in a difficult and contested debate. The history of sorting out the nature of race has been fraught, implicated both in oppression and in efforts to liberate from that very oppression. Our hope is that by focusing on some promising lines of argument, analysis, and inquiry, we can facilitate understanding and progress.

References

Herzog, Don. 1998. *Poisoning the Minds of the Lower Orders*. Princeton, NJ: Princeton University Press.

Mallon, R., and D. Kelly. 2012. "Making Race Out of Nothing." In Harold Kincaid (ed.), *The Oxford Handbook of Philosophy of Social Science*. New York: Oxford University Press, pp. 507–532.

Morning, Ann. 2011. *The Nature of Race*. Berkeley: University of California Press.

Stevens, Jacqueline. 1999. *Reproducing the State*. Princeton, NJ: Princeton University Press.

TRACING THE SOCIOPOLITICAL REALITY OF RACE

Sally Haslanger

1.1. Methodological Preliminaries

The question before us is: What is race? When we pose questions of the form "What is X?" there are a variety of ways we might go about answering them. For example, if, pointing to a small wiggly thing in the corner, I ask, "What is that?" I will probably want someone to help me figure out the species of insect it belongs to, as determined by entomology. If you tell me it is a silverfish, I might also pose a question about the kind of thing (e.g., "What is a silverfish?"). Plausibly I am asking how silverfish, as a group, are classified: what features something must have to count as a silverfish, what to expect of silverfish, and how they are related to other sorts of creepy crawly things.

These sorts of questions seem to presuppose that we have a well-developed science that will provide us with empirically based answers. However, sometimes our "What is it?" questions take us beyond what science has figured out. For example, if in the seventeenth century someone pointed at a burning log and asked, "What is that?" a straightforward answer would be "Fire." But if the speaker already *knew* that and proceeded, "But what is fire?" the question is probably attempting to probe features of fire that aren't apparent from our ordinary familiarity with it; and it would (and did) take substantial empirical research and future scientific theory to reach any answers.

In the sorts of contexts just considered, it would be, at the very least, odd to answer the questions by consulting our linguistic intuitions.[1] Our judgments about when to use the term 'silverfish'

---

1. Some parts of this section are repeated and developed more fully in Haslanger (forthcoming).

don't tell us what a silverfish is. However, there are a variety of "What is X?" questions that many philosophers seem to think can be answered by discovering the meaning of the term(s) substituted for X, as determined by our disposition to apply the term(s) in question (e.g., 'knowledge,' 'moral worth,' 'justice,' 'a person,' 'causation'). In some of these cases, one might think that this a priori methodology is warranted because the boundaries of these kinds depend in some way on us and our practices. Perhaps moral worth, justice, personhood, and the like, don't exist independently of our judgments of what counts as moral worth, justice, and personhood. So, of course, we should at least begin by investigating our judgments and putting them in order. (This is more plausible in some cases than in others; e.g., the answer would have to be more complicated in cases such as 'causation' or 'intrinsic property.')

But the idea that (some) philosophical kinds somehow "depend on us" is not entirely clear; nor is it clear why our a priori (linguistic) reflections should be sufficient to provide an adequate theory of them—for example, "What is a sheriff?" Even if you are a competent user of the term 'sheriff,' you may not be able to tell me what a sheriff is. A full answer would presumably require information about the jurisdiction of sheriffs, what their responsibilities are, how they are chosen, etc. as determined by law. We might need to consult experts in civics to get answers (and the answers will depend on what country we are in). We can't just depend on common sense or linguistic intuitions. But surely what counts as a sheriff depends on us—there are no sheriffs outside of a humanly constructed system of government.

In the case of 'sheriff,' there will be a well-defined role specified by statute, and someone who knows the relevant statutes will know the answers to our questions. But there are also social phenomena that in some sense "depend on us" but are not stipulated or planned by us. Such social phenomena range from macro-scale economic depressions, globalization, urbanization, and gentrification, to more local social practices and relations (e.g., within a town, religious congregation, or family). These phenomena call for explanation, and the social sciences (broadly construed) endeavor to provide theories that enable us to understand them, usually identifying kinds of institutions, economic relations, cultural traditions, social meanings, and psychological predispositions, to do so. The kinds in question are social kinds, in the sense that they are kinds of things that exist in the social world (and so, in some sense, depend on us). But we discover these kinds through empirical inquiry, just as we discover chemical kinds through empirical inquiry.

For example, accounts of gentrification often make reference to the "urban pioneer," sometimes characterized as artists and "bohemians" who take advantage of low rents in poor neighborhoods. When single people who share rent enter a neighborhood, businesses (such as cafés and pubs) take interest, and landlords see opportunities to raise rents, which drives out the locals. *Urban pioneers* are a functional kind that identifies a particular role in an evolving real estate market. The term 'pioneer' is chosen due to the perceived parallel with pioneers who "settled" the western United States, displacing the local population. If someone were to object to the term 'pioneer'—perhaps thinking that it carried an overly positive connotation—this would not undermine the explanatory claims.[2] The adequacy of explaining gentrification by reference to singles moving into an urban neighborhood does not depend on our linguistic intuitions about applying the term 'pioneer' to them. The choice of terminology was intended to illuminate a parallel; if the terminological choice doesn't work, then another term could be used as a substitute.

However, insofar as philosophical kinds such as *justice* and *personhood* "depend on us," it is not in the sense that we stipulate what they are (like *sheriff*), or in the sense that they serve in explanations of social phenomena (like *urban pioneers*). Rather, it is something along these lines: the adequacy of our theory is not to be judged simply by reference to "the facts," but also by its responsiveness to our prior understandings. In the case of *sheriff*, you might think that there aren't any independent facts we're trying to accommodate. Oversimplifying, we simply create sheriffs and then talk about them. In the case of *urban pioneer*, the prior understandings of 'pioneer' are not crucial to the explanation provided by the theory. But in the case of *justice*, there is something we are aiming to understand that is not simply constituted by what we say, but at the same time, our conclusions cannot float completely free of the discursive tradition in which we are aiming to understand it.

How might we explain this? Note that in the philosophical cases, we are not situated as anthropologists trying to understand the social life of the "natives." Nor are we legislators specifying new practices. We are seeking an understanding of practices in which we are currently engaged as participants. The practices are not fully understood, however. And they are open-ended, revisable, possibly self-defeating. In making sense of them, we are making judgments about how to better understand what we are doing, and how then to go on. This is not primarily a linguistic exercise: we aren't just deciding how

---

2. Metaphors and analogies can play an important and even ineliminable role in theorizing and can aid in explanation. My claim here is only that the choice of terminology for the functional kinds in the proposed mechanisms of gentrification (specifically the influx of singles) is not essential to the success of the model for some purposes (though it may be for others).

to use existing terminology, but how to collectively orient ourselves toward the world and toward each other. Language provides tools to achieve this. But language is a practice within practices and is itself a proper target of philosophical inquiry: meanings are not simply constituted by what we believe, yet we are situated within a tradition of linguistic practices that have already shaped our meanings and our world; so ignoring those practices would be a mistake. We are situated inquirers, and the question is how we should go on, given where we have been, where we are now, and where we are trying to go (Lear 1986).

1.2. What Is the Question?

The question arises, then, what sort of question is at issue when we ask, "What is race?" Is it an empirical question that we should answer using the methods of biology? Or should we use the methods of empirical sociology or history? Is it a question about what 'race' means? And how might one determine the meaning of 'race'? Do we get to stipulate the meaning? Are we seeking a philosophical tool for explanatory purposes? Or is the question best understood as arising for us as participants in racializing practices?

I don't think there is one right way to pose the question, "What is race?" In fact, I think it is useful to ask different versions of the question in order to understand the phenomenon, and different forms of the question, raised in different contexts, will call for different answers.[3] In my own work (e.g., Haslanger 2012, Ch. 7), I have explored the question as a critical theorist. There are multiple ways of characterizing critical theory, but for our purposes here, I will draw on Tommie Shelby's characterization of a social critic:

> There is also the discourse of the social critic, which is identical with neither everyday discourse nor scientific discourse. Social critics don't merely systematize common sense or popularize scientific findings. Social critics seek to inform, and possibly shape, public opinion with clear and careful thinking, well-established facts, and moral insight. They will of course draw on and engage both common sense and

---

3. I embrace an "eretetic" approach to explanation that takes explanations, and theories more generally, to be answers to questions. So the first task of any theoretical project is to clarify the question being asked. Apparent disagreements can sometimes be resolved by noting that the parties to the disagreement are answering different questions (see Garfinkel 1981; Risjord 2000; Anderson 1995).

scientific thought, but they do so without taking a slavish attitude toward either . . . [In the context of debates over race and racism,] the principal role of the philosophical social critic, as here conceived, is to shed light on the most fundamental conceptual and normative issues that race-related questions raise. (Shelby 2014, 63)

Plausibly, all inquiry is situated. Inquiry begins with questions, and all questions have presuppositions. And any serious effort to answer a question relies on a method that is taken to have at least some epistemic credentials. I've been suggesting that certain forms of philosophical inquiry are situated in an additional sense; that is, the project is not simply a descriptive or explanatory project, but aims to shape or guide our thinking and acting. Social critics take this even a step further: we are situated as critics of ordinary social practices and offer tools and understandings that are designed to improve them (Fraser 1989; Marx 1843). The social critic embraces the normative dimension of philosophical theorizing, and also relies crucially on empirical research. The idea of *race* is already embedded in our customs, practices, and institutions, and facts about its role in our lives are crucial to the critical project. Such empirical information and normative concerns are also important, on some accounts, for adjudicating linguistic meaning, and so, in particular, for understanding what 'race' means.

1.3. The Semantic Strategy

Quine (1953) has taught us that if we are engaged in an ontological debate about the existence of some kind of thing, say, *races*, we should semantically ascend. In other words, instead of asking directly whether races exist, we should ask whether the term 'race' picks anything out in the world, and if so, what. This is an especially helpful move if parties to the debate don't agree on what the term 'race' means, for if, say, a racial realist and a racial anti-realist have different understandings about what 'race' means, then the conflict between them may be only apparent.[4] It may be true, for example, both that *biological races* don't exist and *social races* do exist.

---

4. I assume for the purposes of this discussion that a racial realist believes that at least some statements involving the term 'race' are both truth-apt and true. Anti-realists disagree. Anti-realists may hold that all statements involving the term 'race' are not truth-apt (they are "noncognitivists" about race talk), or they may hold that race talk is truth-apt, but false (they are "error theorists" about race). In this book, Spencer, Jeffers, and I are all realists (though we disagree about what makes race talk true); Glasgow is either an anti-realist error theorist or a "basic" realist that allows 'race' to refer, but to uninteresting groups. (Other anti-realists include Appiah [1996] and Zack [2002]; Blum [2002]; Hochman [2017].)

Ron Mallon (2006, 527) considers this "semantic strategy," widespread in the race debate, and argues, however, that it is not helpful. The problem is that different parties to the debate seem to adhere to different theories of meaning. So the controversy is just pushed up a level. For example, the realist and anti-realist, it would seem, don't agree on how we might determine the meaning of the term 'race.' When the realist claims that 'race' refers to a social kind, and the anti-realist says that 'race' does not refer to anything, they haven't established a basis for debate because they are committed to different theories of meaning or reference. As a result, there is a risk that the race debate just collapses into a debate in the philosophy of language. Given the unlikelihood that we will be able to settle on a theory of reference any time soon, it looks like the race debate is left hanging.

However, Mallon suggests that there are important questions that should be asked and whose answers shouldn't depend on a metaphysical or semantic theory. His proposal is that we take up a normative approach to race. The important question isn't the metaphysical one (i.e., whether races exist or not) or the semantic one (i.e., what 'race' means, if anything). Rather, the question is normative: how we should think and talk when it comes to matters of race.

> While there is (or should be) a wide basis of metaphysical agreement on the expanded ontological consensus, there is profound disagreement over the practical and moral import of 'race' talk. Resolving this disagreement requires a complex assessment of many factors, including, the epistemic value of 'race' talk in various domains, the benefits and costs of racial identification and of the social enforcement of such identification, the value of racialized identities and communities fostered by 'race' talk, the role of 'race' talk in promoting or undermining racism, the benefits or costs of 'race' talk in a process of rectification for past injustice, the cognitive or aesthetic value of 'race' talk, and the degree of entrenchment of 'race' talk in everyday discourse. The point is that it is on the basis of these and similar considerations that the issue of what to do with 'race' talk will be decided, not putative metaphysical or actual semantic disagreements. (Mallon 2006, 550)

I am sympathetic with Mallon's (2006) suggestion that resolving the issue depends on normative and empirical considerations.[5] However, as he frames

---

5. For a parallel argument concerning gender terms such as 'woman,' and 'man,' see Saul (2012) and Kapusta (2016).

it, the questions we must answer still concern "race talk." But recall that, by hypothesis, the different parties to the race debate disagree about what 'race' means because they embrace different accounts of meaning. What counts, then, as "race talk?" It can't be identified by talk *about* race, for we don't agree on what race is, or even whether there is such a thing as a race. And we can't just consider talk that includes linguistic items pronounced as English speakers pronounce 'race,' for we use that sound also for boat races, running races, and the like. Although Mallon is right that we need to ask a wide range of epistemic and moral questions of the sort he lists, his characterization of the task retains too much of the semantic strategy. What's at issue isn't just our talk and thought, but racial structures and practices of all sorts—linguistic, cultural, medical, political, juridical. We begin our theorizing already situated in these practices. What we are trying to do is understand how they work, what is salvageable (if anything), and how to go on.

Consider a comparison with the notion of moral worth. We begin with our practices of distinguishing the worth of an action from its consequences. We seem to be prepared, at least sometimes, to commend an action as good, even if it has unfortunate consequences, and to condemn an action as bad even if it has good consequences; yet we don't have a clear idea of what moral worth is. For example, if I bring my new neighbor a bouquet of flowers, not knowing that she has severe allergies, and she suffers as a result, my action was nevertheless kind and thoughtful, and seems to have moral worth, even though it had bad consequences. When we ask, "What is moral worth?" we consider a full range of cases, the presuppositions and effects of this practice of attributing moral worth, and what function it has. The point is not to look at "moral-worth-talk," since the language of 'moral worth' is rather rare in common parlance. We are attempting to capture a set of practices of moral evaluation. After careful scrutiny, we may find that the feature that seems to distinguish worthy actions isn't as valuable as we thought, or the worthy feature is more rarely present; and this justifies a revision to the practice. If we are consequentialists, we may find that the practice isn't justified at all and we may recommend discontinuation.

As mentioned before, ideas of race are "woven into" many of our everyday practices (i.e., racial distinctions seem to play a role in so much of what we do, where we go, with whom we associate, in what resources are available to us and what is required to access them). This is not to say that race is explicitly and intentionally functioning in these practices. But our lives are shaped by a racial geography. As in the example of moral worth, we begin by collecting a full range of apparent examples, consider their presuppositions and effects, and consider what function they have. What is it, if anything, about these practices that makes them "racial"? In the contemporary "post-racial" climate, some will no doubt argue that there is nothing specifically "racial" about them (e.g., they are to be understood in terms of class). But there is also plenty of evidence that racial distinctions, racial assumptions, and racial identities continue to structure our lives together (and apart).

1.4. Representational Traditions: 'Water' as an Example

Laura and François Schroeter (2015) offer an account of meaning that not only seems to be compatible with the spirit of Mallon's suggestion, but also situates our linguistic activities within our broader social practices. They focus on the example of 'water,' and suggest that to determine what 'water' means, we should undertake an inquiry into what water *is*. But how do we do this? We cannot assume from the start that this is a task for the chemist, for when the chemist says that water is H_2O, she may be using the term in a technical sense, in which case it would not provide an account of what the ordinary person means by 'water.' (Note that the same might be said of the biologist's use of 'race.') But neither can we just undertake reflection on linguistic usage or common sense.

> Before you explicitly reflect on the question of what water is, your own assumptions about the topic are bound to be heterogeneous, incomplete, and partially contradictory—and this heterogeneity is only exacerbated when you take your whole community's views into account. Thus justifying an answer to a 'what is x?' question is nothing like slotting some missing values into an implicitly grasped formula. Your goal in rational deliberation is to find some principled way of prioritizing and systematizing your own and your community's commitments about water, so as to identify the appropriate normative standards for evaluating the truth and acceptability of beliefs about the topic. (2015, 430)

The broad idea is this: when we deliberate about what X [water, race, freewill, moral worth . . .] is, we have to start with *something*. In the sorts of cases we are considering, we can take ourselves to be situated within a broad representational and practical tradition concerned with X. We are not starting from scratch and stipulating the meaning of theoretical terms. And we may assume that the tradition has a certain epistemic ambition, so we may "take our words and thoughts to represent genuinely interesting and important features of the world—not just whatever happens to satisfy our current criteria" (Schroeter and Schroeter 2015, 436). So scientific inquiry, although not definitive, is relevant, since it discloses some parts of the world that are important for many of our purposes. But where do we begin? The Schroeters (2015, 426) give a sample of inputs to deliberation in the case of water (the examples are theirs):

- *Particular instances*: there's water in this bottle, in Port Phillip Bay, Lake Michigan, etc.;
- *Perceptual gestalts*: the characteristic look, taste, odor, tactile resistance, and heaviness of water;
- *Physical roles*: water's rough boiling point, its transformation into steam, its role as a solvent, the fact that it expands when it freezes, etc.;
- *Biological roles*: water's necessity for the survival of plants and animals; how it's ingested; the effects of water deprivation; etc.;
- *Practical roles*: the roles water plays in agriculture, transport, washing, cooking, surfing, etc.;
- *Symbolic roles*: water is strongly associated with cleanliness and purity, it plays an important role in many religious rituals, etc.;
- *Explanatory roles*: water has a non-obvious explanatory structure, which explains many of its characteristic roles; water is composed of H_2O;
- *Epistemology*: water is easy to spot but hard to define; our beliefs about water may be mistaken or incomplete; observation of instances of water grounds induction to unobserved cases.

Our aim is to answer to the "What is X?" question. The project is not semantic but *meta-semantic*; that is, we are not trying to find what the X-term means. Rather, we are trying to determine what the kind X is. The inputs just considered help us narrow down the kind so we can investigate it further. As we proceed, we may find that some of our background beliefs are false and our theoretical efforts misguided. It is only the result of our investigation that gives us the meaning of the term. But what do we do with these inputs? How do we balance various considerations? Schroeter and Schroeter (2015) propose that

> . . . ideal epistemic methods for answering 'what is x?' questions hinge on rationalizing interpretation of one's representational traditions. You need to diagnose the most important representational interests at

stake in a representational tradition with 'x', and you should identify the correct verdict about the nature of x as the one that makes best sense of those interests. (2015, 430)

A rationalizing interpretation, on their view, is not determined by reports of beliefs and intentions of participants in the tradition, nor is it a causal explanation of the tradition:

> From the deliberative perspective of a rational epistemic agent, the interests that are relevant to adjudicating 'what is x?' questions are those that help justify or rationalize that tradition. Ideal methods for adjudicating 'what is x?' questions don't simply construe representational practices as meeting psychologically or causally fixed representational interests. Our interpretive methods construe them as meeting representational interests that help make sense of our practices—that help construe them as having a point or rationale. (2015, 435)

In the case of 'water', there are at least two candidates. One set of interests served by our attitudes toward and talk of water are explanatory, another set is practical. These two interests may come apart; for example, our practical interests do not require that we identify water with H_2O, for liquids that are mostly H_2O but contain other ingredients (harmless trace chemicals, fluoride) are fine for most purposes (drinking, bathing, swimming, etc.). However, scientific inquiry enables us to explain the properties of water—and how it can actually serve our practical interests—by reference to its chemical structure. This divergence of possible interpretations of what's at stake in the tradition leaves us with two candidate answers to "What is water?" and so two candidates for the meaning of 'water.' Water is H_2O, or water is the watery stuff found in lakes and rivers (etc.). It might appear that this leaves the term 'water' as ambiguous, or perhaps with no determinate meaning.

On the Schroeters' (2015) view, there is a best interpretation of the representational tradition, where the scope of that tradition is determined by commitment to *de jure* sameness of reference and shared linguistic and epistemic practices (428). (We all take ourselves to be referring to the same thing in our thought and talk and are engaged in talking and thinking together.) What I mean is not just a function of what I think water is, or any old interpretation of our representational tradition: I can get the meaning wrong if I don't do adequate justice to the interpretive task. For example, if I decide that, given our interests and collective uses of the term, water is the alcoholic beverage also known as 'beer,' I would be wrong. I would have failed to capture a reasonable interpretation of our representational tradition. But I could also be wrong if I miss what is worth talking about:

> As rational epistemic agents, we normally take our words and thoughts to represent genuinely interesting and important features of the world—not just whatever happens to satisfy our current criteria. When asking about the nature of water (or free will, color, etc.), we don't assume that we (or our community as a whole) already implicitly know the right answer. (2015, 436)

We postulate ambiguity or opt for an error theory only as a last resort.

The Schroeters' view seems to me to provide a kind of middle ground between adopting the "semantic strategy" and moving entirely to normative considerations. Recall the previous suggestion that in undertaking at least certain kinds of philosophical inquiry, what we are doing (roughly) is interpreting an indeterminate tradition and deciding "how to go on" with our practices. In doing philosophy, we are both interpreting and recommending. However, they seem to suggest that there is one "best" way to rationalize the representational (and practical) tradition, and so just one way to go on. I find this implausible and unnecessary.[6] Different communities may highlight different parts of the tradition because of what is important to them, what practices they are committed to, what questions they ask, and how the world around them pushes back (e.g., what else they come to know).

1.5. Representational Traditions: 'Race'

Does the Schroeters' model give us resources to make progress in understanding what race is? The case of race is clearly more complicated: there are substantive disagreements about the different roles the idea plays in our representational tradition, and the tradition has clearly changed over time. This is something we should take into account. Moreover, there are significant differences in how the idea of race functions in different cultures; for

---

6. Botchkina and Hodges (2016) defend a view similar to theirs, but that allows for multiple reasonable interpretations. Moreover, the Schroeters' view is more individualistic than my own. On their view, a primary normative constraint is to provide a rationalizing *self-interpretation*, i.e., to make sense of one's own beliefs and practices (linguistic and otherwise). I see this as a more collective project. See also Haslanger (forthcoming) for an elaboration of the idea that conceptual amelioration through such reflection is possible.

example, which racial group one belongs to may differ depending on the country one is in, and the background beliefs about races may differ. In the case of *water*, there is a basic human interest in being able to refer to the stuff in question, and at least most languages will have some way of talking about it. This is much less obvious in the case of *race*. So the idea that there is a single best interpretation of *what race is*—across languages and cultures—is not entirely plausible.

For example, the United States has relied—sometimes implicitly and sometimes explicitly—on a rule of hypodescent (i.e., assuming a racial hierarchy, the child of individuals of different races is assigned the "lower" race of the two parents).[7] However, social scientists have found a variety of other rules for assigning race in the case of "mixed" offspring. In some societies (such as Hawaii, at least before statehood), "mixed" offspring are fully included as members of both races (Davis 1995, 116). In other societies, children of differently raced parents constitute a separate group that, depending on the case, may be considered inferior to, superior to, and or between the racial groups of the parents. In parts of Latin America, the race of "mixed" offspring does not depend simply on ancestry, but also on "economic and educational achievements":

> Whites are at the top of these class structures and unmixed blacks and Indians on the bottom. Blacks are defined as only those of unmixed African descent. Although the many rungs on the long status ladder are indicated by terms that describe the highly variable physical appearance of mulatto and mestizo individuals, this racial terminology can be quite misleading. These are actually class systems in which lifestyle is much more important than racial ancestry or physical traits. "Money whitens" as the phrase goes, and a person who rises in educational and economic status is identified by whiter racial designations. (Davis 1995, 119)

And finally, in some cases, there is a possibility of assimilation, so that after some number of generations, "mixed" offspring can become members of the superior or dominant race. Thus, at least currently in the United States, individuals who are, say, one-eighth Asian and seven-eighths White may count as White with an "Asian" heritage (Davis 1995, 120). The practices of racial identification are also evolving.

---

7. https://www.encyclopediavirginia.org/Racial_Integrity_Laws_of_the_1920s

So when I suggest we consider "our representational tradition," what do I have in mind? For the purposes of our discussion I will be focusing on what race is in the United States, keeping in mind that the goal is to provide an interpretation of what has plausibly been at issue (though not always clearly at issue) "all along," as evidenced not only by what we say, but what we do, such as the practices we engage in, the laws we pass, and social scientific explanations of these. Given the history of the United States, the representational tradition draws upon some historical uses of the term and practices in Europe as well. In the following I've made a start on the relevant inputs to deliberation about what race is within this tradition. Inputs include both ideas that I take to be broadly shared in the United States, ideas from both natural and social sciences, and normatively relevant ideas, as the model recommends, though some will be controversial. I will use the term 'race$_{us}$' to designate what I take to be outputs of deliberation about this representational tradition. I hope that in interpreting our own tradition we will gain insight into related ones.[8] I also use an initial upper-case letter for the names of purported races.

- *Particular instances*: When we say that Martin Luther King, Jr., is Black, Hillary Clinton is White, Che Guevara is Latino, Sacagawea is Native American, and Aung San Suu Kyi is Asian, we are classifying each as belonging to a different race. Everyone belongs to at least one race, possibly more than one. The criteria for racial membership varies depending on context and is not consistent: the US government relies primarily on self-identification; epidemiologists and demographers sometimes rely on self-reports, but also on birth certificates, mother's birth certificate, death certificates, doctor's (or other's) attribution of race (Root 2001, 2003, 2009). Generally, however, one's racial designation is confirmed or disconfirmed by facts about whether one's ancestry derives from a particular geographical region or regions. It is possible for someone to belong to a race without knowing that they do, e.g., an illiterate Kayin peasant from Myanmar is racially Asian, even though she may know nothing about Asia

---

8. I have found it challenging to judge which instances of the word 'race' should include the subscript '$_{us}$'. My goal has been to leave the subscript off when we are considering candidate inputs to the deliberation—allowing that they may or may not be aptly considered a core part of the phenomenon and may be simply associations or related phenomena—but adding '$_{us}$' when drawing conclusions about the US phenomenon we're aiming to track. I'm not sure I've been wholly consistent in this because it isn't obvious, to me at least, what occurs as part of deliberation and what occurs as a result. My apologies for any confusion this may cause.

as a continent or US racial practices. There is disagreement about whether Latino(a)s are a race (Gracia 2007).

- *Perceptual gestalts*: Members of different races can usually be distinguished by physical features such as skin color, hair texture and color, eye shape; it is sometimes difficult to identify the racial makeup of mixed-race people, so perceptual gestalts are fallible, and some individuals do not have the distinctive features associated with their race (and so may intentionally or unintentionally "pass" as a member of a different race).

- *Biological roles*: People inherit their race (though the criteria for inheritance have been contested and variable over time, and seem to differ, depending on the race at issue). Race is correlated with differences in life expectancy, various diseases, etc. Historically, it was thought (and some, but not all, people continue to believe) that one's race is part of one's nature, and at least in the case of some races, it is passed along to biological offspring (though Whiteness, apparently, is not always passed on, though Blackness is, according to the system of hypodescent!). Scientific research suggests that there isn't a meaningful biological basis for racial distinctions, sufficient to postulate racial "natures" or essences, though it is currently a matter of controversy whether there are minor biological differences among groups roughly corresponding to the most commonly assumed racial groups (Black, White, Asian, Native American, Pacific Islander) (see Spencer's Chapter 3 in this volume; also Andreasen 2000, 2004; Kitcher 2007).

- *Historical roles*: Attributions of race have played a major role in world history. For example, the trans-Atlantic slave trade and European colonization across the world were justified on the basis of beliefs about race. The most common racial divisions have been based (roughly) on appearances that differ between continents, but there has not been unanimity on what races there are (Bernasconi and Lott 2000; Herzog 1998, 288ff), and arguably we are in a historical moment when those of (apparent) Arab descent, having been White, are being re-racialized as non-White (Jamal and Naber 2008). US federal and state law has restricted the civil rights of members of non-White races, and there have also been attempts at legal remedies, e.g., affirmative action. Race continues to be a matter of heated social, political, and legal debate. The history of science reveals ongoing scientific attempts to justify claims about racial differences, especially in intelligence and character.

- *Practical roles*: Race is a significant factor in the organization of social life, e.g., in patterns of association, housing, religion, employment, crime, athletics. It is also an important part of many people's identity and sense of solidarity with others, and contributes to shaping their life plans and political views.[9]

- *Symbolic roles*: Race is strongly associated with cultural norms, artistic traditions, and forms of life; historically it has been associated with character traits and degrees of moral worth.
- *Explanatory roles*: Race is used to explain a broad range of differences between social groups, including educational attainment, patterns of arrest and incarceration, health outcomes, social history, etc. It is also used to explain different interests, cultural and artistic tendencies, and political affiliation. These explanations vary in their form. Some purport to be biological explanations, others sociological explanations.
- *Epistemology*: A person's race is usually taken to be evident based on widely accepted perceptual gestalts; however, race has been hard to define, and many assumptions about race have been undermined by scientific inquiry; our beliefs about race may be mistaken or incomplete; nevertheless, observation of racial regularities grounds induction to unobserved cases.

Given these inputs (I don't mean for these to be exhaustive—this is just a sample), the task is to provide an interpretation of our representational tradition.[10] What are we doing when we divide humans into different races? What interests are being served? Is there an interpretation that rationalizes or justifies the tradition? If not, then should we reject the idea of race completely?

One might argue that, as in the case of 'water,' there are several different reasonable ways to go here. A first option is to note that the representational tradition concerning race includes a history of drawing distinctions between groups of people on the basis of certain bodily features (skin color, hair texture, eye shape, and the like) and postulating racial "natures" underlying these observable differences to explain further cultural and behavioral differences

---

9. There is a broad literature on the content of racial identities, and African American or Black identity in particular. A helpful philosophical snapshot may be found in Gooding-Williams (1998); Appiah (2002); Shelby and McPherson (2004); Shelby (2005); Gracia (2007); Kendig (2011).

10. As I read Quayshawn Spencer's (2014) argument for a modest racial naturalism, he could agree with the Schroeters' approach that has us trying to make sense of a representational/practical tradition; he chooses to place great weight on the federal discourse around race as regimented by the census. I don't think his choice of emphasis takes sufficient account of the many functions of race in our ordinary discourse and places too much weight on the role of the state; but as I make clear in my reply, our priorities are different.

and to justify unjust treatment of non-Whites. The tradition was in the material and cultural interests of Whites and continues to play a role in many Americans' thinking about race. The Schroeters are clear, however, that the best interpretation of the representational tradition must capture what we have been thinking and talking about "all along."

> The method we have sketched precisely aims at determining what's interesting and important relative to the subject's own past representational tradition. So from the point of view of a rational epistemic agent, these pragmatic meta-cognitive methods are ideally suited to getting us closer to the truth about the interesting and important topics that we were thinking and talking about all along. (2015, 436)

It is reasonable to claim that our linguistic forebears were thinking and talking about races distinguished by racial natures or essences. Yet at this point we know that there are no racial "natures," (i.e., a set of properties that a member of a race has necessarily, by virtue of which they are a member of the race, and that explains their characteristic behavior and abilities).[11] If the point or purpose of the tradition was to attribute racial natures to humans, and there are no such racial natures, the representational tradition has failed and we should give it up. In short, we should be anti-realists about race$_{us}$, more specifically, error theorists.

One need not think that our representational tradition is invested in racial *natures,* however, in order to account for the inputs to deliberation about race. Michael Hardimon (2017; also 2003) has argued for a minimalist account of race according to which:

A *race* is a group of human beings

(C1) that, as a group, is distinguished from other groups of human beings by *patterns of visible physical features,*

(C2) whose members are linked by *common ancestry* peculiar to members of the group, and

(C3) that originates from a *distinctive geographic location.* (2017, 31)

---

11. I prefer the term 'nature' to 'essence' in this context because of the complexities in the historical and contemporary use of 'essence,' though 'essence' is the more commonly used for this postulation. Think of something like the nature of a tiger—each tiger has a set of properties necessarily by virtue of which it counts as a tiger (tiger is its *kind*), and this set of properties explains its behavior and abilities, e.g., it is by nature a feline, a carnivore, etc.

Hardimon argues that there are groups that satisfy the minimalist race concept, and so races$_{us}$ exist. Given the simplicity and plausibility of Hardimon's conditions, it would seem that his account is an excellent candidate for an interpretation of the inputs regarding race. Should we take this view to be sufficient and the task to be complete?

Joshua Glasgow (2009) rejects a minimalist view such as Hardimon's. He maintains that according to the "ordinary concept of race" (i.e., the one that has the most currency in the contemporary United States), "while an *individual's* particular race might depend on social factors, each racial *group* is, as a conceptual matter, defined only in terms of its visible, biological profile" (2009, 123) (see also Alcoff 2005). The condition Glasgow isolates, however, is not satisfied: human appearance falls on a broad spectrum, and the supposed visibly notable and biologically relevant clumping that would be required by the condition does not occur.[12] Glasgow concludes that "since these groups' putative distinctiveness is not, as a point of fact, legitimated by the biology, there are no races" (2009, 123). So the term is vacuous, and statements employing the term are false.

I agree with Glasgow (2009) that there are no existing human groups that meet the condition that there are inherited visible features that demarcate the races. Note, however, that an error theory about race$_{us}$ has substantial costs, given that we are attempting to give an interpretation of the inputs described earlier. Not only would we have to claim that our attributions of race to individuals are false, but that the historical, symbolic, explanatory, practical, and epistemic roles of race are all founded on illusion. We would need to give up the idea that race explains certain group differences (from artistic traditions to health outcomes); we would need to give up the idea that race provides reasons for certain practical, historical, and symbolic choices. We could potentially replace these claims with the suggestion that false racial beliefs about racial groups explain the broad range of racial formations. But this is to take a substantive stand on difficult explanatory questions in the history and sociology of racial practices, racial institutions, and the like.

Although false beliefs about racial groups may be the best explanation of early forms of racial hierarchy (though I find even that questionable, given the economic and other forces at work), it is implausible that such beliefs are the best explanation of ongoing racial injustice, including the perpetuation

---

12. An extension of this argument is also relevant to discussion of Quayshawn Spencer's (2014) minimal naturalism (see Chapter 3 for details).

of economic and political injustice, social segregation, and cultural stigma (Haslanger 2016, 2017a). For example, the waning of racial essentialism is not sufficient to undermine the legacy of economic deprivation because belief in racial essentialism—or racial naturalism more generally—is not what runs the economy; nor does correcting false beliefs about race correct the legacy of centuries of legal and political wrongs. So an error theory about race needs to be supplemented with alternative explanations of apparently racial phenomena, including our abilities to deliberate about race, perform induction on racial regularities, and find meaning in racial identification.

Consider an analogy. For centuries, philosophers have attempted to provide necessary and sufficient conditions for being a person. Candidate necessary conditions have included the following:

- X *is a person* only if X has a soul.
- X *is a person* only if the stages of X are psychologically continuous.
- X *is a person* only if X occupies a continuous living human body.

There are compelling examples suggesting that accepting any of these conditions fails to capture what we mean by *person* due to a mismatch between what the condition requires and the cases we judge to be persons. Should we conclude that there are no persons and be error theorists about person-talk? Surely not! For ordinary cases, we do fine in judging whether an individual is a person or not. There are hard cases and our practices in these cases are contested, but we usually have rules or laws for settling them, at least for the time being. The question remains whether these rules or laws for the controversial cases are appropriate or justified, and they are open to revision based on actual cases that need to be settled. Our practices are evolving: new technologies and medical discoveries have forced us to answer questions that never had to be faced before. Such open-endedness and revisability do not show that there are no persons, that person-talk is vacuous, or that we should discontinue practices that rely on a background idea of persons.

In discussing the example of *person*, I am relying on the methodology I have recommended: given the function of language to guide and coordinate our ongoing practices, we should investigate what something is by providing an interpretation of the representational (and practical) tradition that helps us make sense of the new and challenging cases. Admittedly, there may be circumstances in which the tradition cannot or should not be sustained. But holding fixed one condition on the application of a concept that actually serves multiple purposes is not a sufficient reason to reject or eliminate the concept. Communication in a context does not require a rigid representational tradition that anticipates every empirical discovery and every technological change. We make do with rough overlapping understandings of phenomena that concern our shared practices, and update as life goes on.

A third option for interpreting the inputs sketched in the preceding would be to turn to a social constructionist account of race$_{us}$. When the representational tradition was historically postulating racial natures, the point was to provide an explanation of the striking observable differences in human appearance, behavior, and culture found through voyages of exploration and conquest. The explanations that were ready to hand at the time were based on biblical interpretation or neo-Aristotelian biology (Stocking 1994). These explanations of human differences, we have found, are faulty. But there were and continue to be differences among the groups that were then designated as races that call for interpretation and explanation. A better approach looks to social formations.

A social constructionist account (e.g., sociopolitical account or cultural account, to be discussed more fully in the next section) proposes that the conditions for being a member of a racial group are to be given in social terms, rather than in physical, biological, or other non-social terms.[13] Consider, for example, *slaves*. Aristotle seems to have thought that there were natural slaves (*Politics*, Bk. 1): natural slaves are individuals who are incapable of sufficient practical reason to lead an autonomous life. Natural slaves, on his view, were justifiably owned by others and were better off as a result. But the idea of a natural slave is badly mistaken. Slaves are a social category, that is, to be a slave is to be owned by someone according to the laws or customs of one's social milieu. A social constructionist account of slaves is an improvement on the naturalistic account that defines slaves in terms of their cognitive capacities. There are many other cases in which social constructionists have challenged naturalistic accounts, for example, of sex, gender, sexual desire, disability, parenthood, family, and race.

How does attention to social relations and social structures help us understand the observable differences among human groups? There is overwhelming evidence that differences between racial groups in educational attainment, health outcomes, incarceration rates, and the like are due to the looping effects of social structures that impose a racial hierarchy. Many

---

13. Social constructionism about race takes many forms. For other examples, see Omi and Winant (1994); Mills (1997, 1998); Gooding-Williams (1998); Sundstrom (2002); Mallon (2003); Taylor (2004); Alcoff (2005).

of the great achievements and cultural traditions of different races are also a product of living within such structures (Taylor 2016). This social structural hierarchy is partly a product of a history of false beliefs about races and racial natures, but such beliefs are systematically linked to cultural and material factors that are equally important in accounting for the systematic nature of racial differentiation and racial injustice; false beliefs are a small part, maybe even an eliminable part, of what sustains the system. For example, it is insufficient to explain racial differences in educational achievement simply in terms of false beliefs about the abilities or "natures" of Whites and people of color. Additional factors include the racial patterns of wealth and poverty, patterns of housing segregation, the dependence of school funding on property taxes, the expense of university education, hiring discrimination, and the social meaning of intelligence and education.[14] Such social phenomena do not depend entirely on the psychological states of individuals (Epstein 2015; Haslanger 2017b).

This second, social constructionst, approach gains further support from the parallels with other scientific advances. Early explanations of many natural phenomena have been rejected over time and have been supplanted by better explanations without disrupting our representational traditions. Hippocrates was aware of and treated cancer, though he thought it was caused by an excess of black bile (thought to be one of the four humors) in the body; it is plausible that Hippocrates is part of our representational tradition concerning cancer (he is credited with the origin of the word *karkinoma*), in spite of the fact that some of his core assumptions about cancer have been thoroughly rejected. The idea that empirical hypotheses about the nature of a kind are analytically entailed by our use of a term would make scientific inquiry difficult (this is an old point made by Quine, Putnam, Kripke, and many others). If we could not substantially revise our understanding of kinds, then as we develop new hypotheses about a phenomenon, we would not be improving our understanding of a poorly understood kind, but investigating a new kind, thus obscuring the dynamics of inquiry.

One might argue, however, that shifting from a "natural" to a "social" kind is more than meaning can bear. But shifts across different categories of explanation are not uncommon. For example, medical conditions that were once

---

14. There is a huge social science literature on racial health gaps, educational achievement gaps, etc. For a glance at the numbers in 2014, see Irwin et al. (2014). An important approach to explaining this is offered in Mills (2017, Ch. 7). See also Anderson (2010) and Haslanger (2014).

thought to have been the result of God's punishment, or evil thoughts, or anxiety, have been shown to have straightforward physical causes. Various caste, class, and ethnic divisions have been thought to be established by divine law or nature, but are now understood in terms of the workings of social systems. For example, monarchs were once thought to gain their political legitimacy from God. To be a monarch is to have sacred power, invested in the family lineage. This explanation of a monarch's legitimacy was eventually rejected, and yet we did not give up the idea of a monarch. Instead, alternative social accounts of monarchy were supplied.

A social constructionist account of race$_{us}$ will also face challenges in accommodating some of the inputs to deliberation listed in the preceding. For example, it is commonly thought that race is inherited. But social position is only inherited metaphorically; one usually occupies a similar social position to one's parents, not by virtue of "blood" but by virtue of social conditions and pressures. I mentioned earlier, however, that there are multiple ways of "tracing" race through ancestry, hypodescent being only one of them, even in the United States. This suggests that a commitment to the idea that race is inherited is not a fixed point. Moreover, the use of ancestry to track race is a phenomenon that an error theorist will also need to explain. Any account of race$_{us}$—whether realist or anti-realist, naturalist or constructionist—will need to include details that make sense of or explain away the complexities of representational and practical tradition. So there is much work to do.

1.6. What Is Race?

Even if the representational tradition concerning race allows for a social scientific analysis of the explanatory interests being served, two questions remain:

(i) How exactly should a social constructionist capture what *race* is?
(ii) Are our current interests served by continuing with the representational tradition concerning the term 'race,' or should we replace race with another term, e.g., 'racialized group'?

I will consider (i) in this section and (ii) in the next.

Two forms of social constructionism about race have been proposed in the literature. One is the *sociopolitical account*, the other is the *cultural account*. The two accounts agree on many points, for example, that the current dominant races$_{us}$ emerged in a particular historical context of White racial domination; that members of races are "marked" as having a particular appearance;

that the "marking" is taken to be evidence of where, geographically, the group mostly lived at a key moment in time; that racial groups function differently within the contemporary sociopolitical structure, and are positioned on a hierarchy. The primary differences between the two accounts are (a) the cultural account requires that races, as a group, share a culture,[15] whereas the sociopolitical account does not, and (b) the sociopolitical account takes the sociopolitical hierarchy to be a defining feature of race, whereas the cultural account does not. I defend the sociopolitical account. Chike Jeffers (2013) elaborates and defends the cultural account.

In my earlier work (2012, Ch. 7), I argued that critical theorists should adopt the following core account of race, and use this to explicate other racial phenomena, such as racial identities, racial norms and traditions, racial narratives, racial oppression, racial justice, and the like.[16]

Social/Political Race (SPR): A group G is *racialized* relative to context C iff$_{df}$ members of G are (all and only) those

(i) who are observed or imagined to have certain bodily features presumed in C to be evidence of ancestral links to a certain geographical region (or regions)—call this "color";

(ii) whose having (or being imagined to have) these features marks them within the context of the background ideology in C as appropriately occupying certain kinds of social position that are in fact either subordinate or privileged (and so motivates and justifies their occupying such a position); and

---

15. A cultural constructionist view does not require that every member of the group participates fully in the culture; rather, a group does not count as a racial$_{us}$ group unless it represents a particular form of life. DuBois is often taken as offering a paradigm of the cultural account, suggesting that a race is "a vast family of human beings, generally of common blood and language, always of common history, traditions and impulses, who are both voluntarily and involuntarily striving together for the accomplishment of certain more or less vividly conceived ideals of life" (DuBois 1991[1987], 75–76), also quoted in Jeffers (2013, 405). In other words, the set of conditions that make a group a *racial*$_{us}$ group may include reference to a form of life, but the conditions for being a member of a *racial*$_{us}$ group may not include this condition; e.g., the condition could simply be that one's parents are a member of the group. So, for example, the Jewish people have a particular form of life, but not all Jews are observant. Nevertheless, one is a member of the Jewish people by virtue of being born of a Jewish mother (or in some forms of Judaism, a Jewish mother or father, or by conversion), not by virtue of observing the practices of Judaism.

16. Note that the term 'iff$_{df}$' is sometimes used to indicate that the biconditional is offering a definition of a word or a concept, I intend it here to indicate that I'm answering a "What is X?" question or "What is it to be X?" question, i.e., to give what is sometime called a "real definition." See, e.g., Rosen (2015).

(iii) whose satisfying (i) and (ii) plays (or would play) a role in their systematic subordination or privilege in C, that is, who are *along some dimension* systematically subordinated or privileged when in C, and satisfying
(i) and (ii) plays (or would play) a role in that dimension of privilege or
subordination.[17]

The idea is that races$_{us}$ are racialized groups, that is, those groups demarcated
by the geographical associations accompanying perceived body type, when
those associations take on evaluative significance (or social meaning) concerning how members of the group should be viewed and treated, and the
treatment situates the groups on a social hierarchy.

Thus, to say that Martin Luther King, Jr., is Black$_{us}$ is to say that he is a
member of a group that meets these conditions, and in particular, that he is
marked in the United States as having relatively recent ancestry from Africa,
and this situates him as subordinate in the social hierarchy of the United
States. Moreover, to say that Whites$_{us}$ have higher educational achievement
than Latinx$_{us}$ is to say that a group that is marked as having recent ancestry

---

17. There are several aspects of this definition that need further elaboration or qualification.
First, the definition does not accommodate contexts such as Brazil in which membership in
"racial" groups is partly a function of education and class. This is because my project here is to
capture what race is in the contemporary United States, i.e., race$_{us}$. However, a related racial
phenomenon can be found in other representational/practical traditions and another version
on which appropriate "color" is relevant but not necessary might be captured by modifying the
second condition:

> (ii*) having (or being imagined to have) these features—*in combination with factors
> such as economic and educational status*—marks them within the context of C's cul-
> tural ideology as appropriately occupying the kinds of social position that are in fact
> either subordinate or privileged (and so motivates and justifies their occupying such
> a position).

The first condition already allows that the group's members may have supposed origins in
more than one region (originally necessary to accommodate the racialization of "mixed-race"
groups); modifying the second condition allows that racialized groups may include people
of different "colors" and may depend on a variety of factors. Second, I want the definition to
capture the idea that members of racial groups may be scattered across social contexts and may
not all actually be (immediately) affected by local structures of privilege and subordination. So,
for example, Black Africans and African Americans are together members of a group currently
racialized in the US, even if a certain ideological interpretation of their "color" has not played
a role in the subordination of all Black Africans; there are parallel phenomena in the case of
other races. So I suggest that members of a group racialized in C are those who are *or would be*
marked and correspondingly subordinated or privileged when in C. Those who think (plausibly) that all Blacks worldwide have been affected by the structures and ideology of White
supremacy do not need this added clause; and those who want a potentially more fine-grained
basis for racial membership can drop it.

in Europe and that is situated as privileged, as a result, has higher educational achievement than those marked as having recent ancestry in Latin America and who are disadvantaged as a result. This claim reveals a correlation between certain forms of social subordination/privilege and outcomes. It does not itself make a causal claim. A relevant causal claim might be this: those who are marked and privileged as White$_{us}$ have higher educational achievement *because* of their racially marked privilege. This is not a tautology, nor is it a vacuous explanation: a group with racial privilege could have educational success due to other causes. However, the explanation is far from being complete, for we would want to know how the privilege is more specifically related to the achievement.

The proposed *SPR* account also helps us explain certain aspects of racial meanings, artistic traditions, and cultural norms. On my view, races are distinct from ethnicities. An ethnicity is a cultural grouping—involving shared language, customs, social meanings, cultural formations—that typically (but not always) relies for its existence and coherence on geographical and genealogical connections, and sometimes carries (defeasible) presumptions about appearance. So Germans, Italians, Basques, Armenians, Berbers, Croats, Fula, Hausa, Gujarati, Icelanders, Kurds, Luo, Manchu, Mongols, etc., are ethnicities. Ethnicities are often positioned hierarchically within a society or broader sociopolitical formation. On my account, the hierarchical positioning of an ethnic group within a broader society (or broader political formation) is a process of *racializing* the group. The ethnicity may predate the racialization, and will (hopefully) continue after racialization has ended. Moreover, multiple ethnic groups may be racialized together as a single race; this may result in what Yen Le Espiritu (1992) calls *pan-ethnicities*. So, Asians are considered a racial group, but include many different ethnicities (e.g., Bamars, Bengalis, Gujarati, Han Chinese, Hindustani, Hmong, Hui, Japanese, Kashmiri, Khmer, Konkani, Korean, Manchu, Marathi, Mongols, Napali, Sinhalese, Tais, Telebu, Tibetens, Uyughur, Vietnamese, Zhuang, to name a few). Such ethnic groups do not share a form of life, and may have long-standing conflicts over land, religion, and politics (see also Alcoff 2000 on the different ethnic groups considered Hispanic or Latinx). The cultural differences between the ethnic groups does not prevent them from forming a race, however, because racialization is not in the first instance a matter of identity or shared culture, but of an imposed (ascribed) position in a sociopolitical formation.

The Africans who were forcibly brought to the United States came not as "blacks" or "Africans" but as members of distinct and various ethnic populations. As a result of slavery, "the 'Negro race' emerged from the heterogeneity of African ethnicity" (Blauner 1972, 13).... Diverse Native American tribes also have had to assume the pan-Indian label in order to conform to the perceptions of the American State. . . . Similarly, diverse Latino populations have been treated by the larger society as a unitary group with common characteristics and common problems.... And the term 'Asian-American' arose out of the racist discourse that constructs Asians as a homogeneous group. Excessive categorization is fundamental to racism because it permits "whites to order a universe of unfamiliar peoples without confronting their diversity and individuality (Blauner 1972, 113)." (Espiritu 1992, 6)

The development of a pan-ethnicity may emerge, for example, among Asian immigrants in the United States, but is an accomplishment, not a given. And such pan-ethnic identities do not necessarily extend to communities of origin; "group formation is not only circumstantially determined, but takes place as an interaction between assignment and assertion. . . . In other words, panethnic boundaries are shaped and reshaped in the continuing interaction between both external and internal forces" (Espiritu 1992, 7). Thus, Asian American may be a pan-ethnicity because Asian immigrants to the United States, and their descendants, form a sense of shared Asian American culture. This suggests that there are three relevant types of groups: ethnicities, pan-ethnicities, and races. Ethnicities have distinctive cultures. Races typically consist of people from multiple cultures. Pan-ethnicities emerge when multiple groups are racialized and treated as one group, and form an identity and way of life as a result.[18] So Hmong, Japanese, Khmer, and Korean are ethnicities. They are all treated as Asian in the United States, and *Asian Americans* form a pan-ethnicity. Some individuals living in Asia may come to see themselves as Asian in response to the racialization of Asians in the United States (and elsewhere), so there may be a group larger than just Asian Americans who are members of the pan-ethnicity; we might call these the *pan-ethnic Asians.* But this does not make the group of people living, or with recent ancestry, in Asia who are "marked" as Asian, a pan-ethnicity. The large heterogeneous group does not have a shared culture. Asian is not recognized as an identity by those living outside of a process of Asian racialization; nonetheless, it is, or has been historically considered, a race. Plausibly also, *Black* is

---

18. See also Alcoff (2000) on *ethno-race*, and Gooding-Williams (1998).

not a pan-ethnicity, even if African American, or Diasporic African, is. This is a central difference between the *SPR* account I support from a cultural constructionist account that takes shared culture to be a defining feature of race (Jeffers 2013).

I agree with Jeffers that often identities and cultural practices associated with races (e.g., "African American" or "Asian American" or "Latinx") offer creative (and protective!) resources for those who have been racialized (2013, 422) that go well beyond a response to oppression; and a pan-ethnicity such as "White" offers other creative opportunities, in addition to resources for domination—or even more often, escape from subordination. Pan-ethnic groups share at least some minimal culture. How this works will vary from context to context. At one time the ideology invoked racial essences to justify the differential treatment of different "colored" groups, and conceptions of the essence or spirit of a people was a basis for identity; ideology has also linked racially marked people with cultural traditions, histories, and talents. People so marked have shared experiences, and some have bonded together in celebration and resistance. This has resulted in racially identified artistic movements, cultural norms, and forms of association. I do not claim that racially inflected culture is all about the position of the group in a hierarchy. Culture is dynamic and relatively autonomous from, and so not determined by, economic, political, or historical factors with which it is always manifested (Sewell 2005). But such pan-ethnicities are not races, or so I would argue. An individual ethnic Hmong living in China or Laos is, I would maintain, Asian$_{us}$, even if there is nothing distinctively "Asian" about Hmong culture, and she does not identify as Asian (and maybe has not even heard of the designation). That she counts as Asian$_{us}$ is clear, however, by how Hmong are viewed and treated within the United States (Fadiman 2012), and how she would be viewed and treated if she came here.

Although I believe that *SPR* is a reasonable interpretation of the representational tradition concerning race, there are also reasons to resist it. This is to be expected, given that I embrace the idea that we can reasonably draw different conclusions about what is crucial to our representational and practical traditions, depending on the questions we ask and the purposes we bring to the inquiry. For example, some definitely take their racial identity to be an important part of who they are, and it is offensive to them to regard it as a response to racial subordination or privilege. It is important to note, however, that it does not follow from *SPR* that a racial identity must focus on facts of subordination or privilege, and nothing I have said entails that it is wrong or illegitimate to embrace an identity or the distinctive way of life that has emerged with the pan-ethnicity. In fact, I believe that many forms of racial identity are important, valuable, and in some cases even inevitable responses to racial hierarchy. As I see it, a racial identity is a kind of know-how for navigating one's position in racialized social space (Haslanger 2012, Ch. 9). The apt content for a racial identity, then, may be positive, affirming, and empowering, even if the racialized social position one occupies is oppressive.

There is a key normative difference, I think, between the sociopolitical account of race and the cultural account that becomes clear when one asks why hierarchy is built into race according to the *SPR*. Why not say that races are groups who are "marked" by reference to ancestry and geography, where this marking has implications for the group's social position, without claiming that the social positions in question need be arranged hierarchically? If I drop the hierarchy condition, then the account comes much closer to the cultural account, on the assumption that those who occupy the same social position are likely to share some non-trivial practices that would amount to at least a thin "way of life." Jeffers argues that we should adopt an account of race that does not have the result that race is eliminated once racial hierarchy is eliminated. He suggests:

> From the cultural perspective, though, a situation in which racial groups persist but in a state of equality rather than socioeconomic and Eurocentric cultural hierarchy, respecting and mutually influencing each other while remaining relatively distinct, is a coherent and admirable goal. (Jeffers 2013, 421)

I worry, however, about the extent to which we should embrace cultural groups marked by ancestry and appearance *in the long run* (of course in the short run, they are necessary to achieve justice). Currently, ethnic groups carry a presumption of shared ancestry, appearance, and geography, but this is merely a presumption. At least many cultural groups (understood as groups sharing a way of life, a language, a religion, a set of common practices) have porous boundaries: one can marry into them, convert, immigrate, look very different from other members, not originate where other members originated. Jeffers emphasizes the benefits of racial cultural unity, but not the costs of racial segregation. As I see them, the costs include tendencies to cultural norming and authenticity tests of those with a "marked" racial appearance (this results in the arguably slurring racial terminology of 'oreo,' 'banana,' 'twinkie,' 'apple,' 'coconut,' and 'egg'). It also suggests that those without the right physical and ancestral credentials don't belong in the culture, shouldn't participate in the way of life, and are suspect when they build strong alliances with and take up the practices of those who satisfy the racial conditions. Living, myself, in a mixed-race (Black-White) and cross-cultural (Jewish-Christian) family, I may be overly influenced by the huge contemporary challenges posed by racial (ancestry and appearance-based) membership criteria in cultural practices and cultural communities. These challenges could—and I think *should*—subside under conditions of justice. I find problematic the idea that a just world is one in which cultural groups can restrict their membership on racial grounds. I embrace, instead, a model of multiple coexisting cultures that are mutable, flexible, and creatively tolerant around issues of ancestry and appearance.

Clearly there is more to be said about the ways in which *SPR* does or does not make sense of our representational tradition concerning race. I believe, however, that it is an excellent candidate, given the Schroeter-style method, for determining at least one thing race is, and so at least one thing we can mean by 'race.'

1.7. Going On: The Normative Dimension of Racial Classification

I think it is unquestionable that *SPR* captures an important set of social groups. They are those groups that have been racialized. Drawing on the Schroeters' methodology, I have also argued that there is a good case to be made that *SPR* is a reasonable interpretation of our ongoing representational tradition and social practices with respect to the idea of race. However, I do not want to be committed to there being a single best interpretation of that tradition, nor do I think that how we should go on with our representational practices depends entirely on what our past practices have endeavored to identify as an important matter of shared concern. Even if the best interpretation of the tradition shows that it is *semantically permissible* to use the term 'race' along the lines that *SPR* suggests, that does not settle how or whether we should continue to use the term. In other words, even if we can isolate a set of social groups that are reasonably considered races, we could still decide not to use the term anymore, or to use a new term.

So the question remains whether our current interests are served by continuing with tradition of using the term 'race.' For example, some theorists have chosen to reject the term 'race' because of its problematic history in justifying racial injustice, and have opted instead for terminology that echoes but does not maintain the term (e.g., 'race' is replaced by 'racialized group'; Blum

2002). As mentioned at the start, I enter this debate as a social critic, and believe we can criticize our past practices and recommend changes to them. This includes changes to our linguistic practices.

On my view, this is a practical and political issue that is best answered by well-informed activists at a specific historical moment. As Mallon suggested, there are empirical and normative considerations that matter, for example, "the epistemic value of 'race' talk in various domains, the benefits and costs of racial identification and of the social enforcement of such identification, the value of racialized identities and communities fostered by 'race' talk, the role of 'race' talk in promoting or undermining racism, the benefits or costs of 'race' talk in a process of rectification for past injustice, the cognitive or aesthetic value of 'race' talk, and the degree of entrenchment of 'race' talk in everyday discourse" (2006, 550, also quoted earlier). How we go on also depends on the sources of solidarity that unify and empower a movement, and the importance of consistent demographic information across time and domain. These are clearly not questions that can be addressed a priori, and depend enormously upon context and moment (Shelby 2005).

To say that the issue is best addressed by well-informed activists, however, is not to relinquish philosophical input. Suppose we find reasons to think that the racialization of groups is a bad thing and that society would be better if we were to acknowledge and respect ethno-cultural differences but cease to think and act in racial terms. (I think there are compelling reasons of this sort, and briefly discussed this in the previous section.) It would be unrealistic, I think, to suggest that we can achieve such a society simply by ceasing to use racial terminology, by becoming "color blind," or by denying that races are real. This is because racialization has caused tremendous social and economic harms, and reparative justice is required. But how can we go on, if on the one hand, it would be wrong to continue our current racial practices, and on the other, it would also be wrong to ignore the legacy of what's been done?

One strategy mentioned earlier is to employ a new term for the groups that have been racialized. But there are two risks here. First, most neologisms don't catch on. Second, racial identity has a deep and pervasive grip on Americans. It is very difficult to cast off an identity without offering another in its place, for identities shape our relations to others, the practices we engage in, and the possibilities we imagine. A second strategy is to offer a debunking account of race. Debunking accounts aim to shift our understanding to reveal how our prior thinking is false or misguided. The point is to disrupt our ways of thinking, to motivate a new relationship to our practices. This is the sort of account I think *SPR* provides. The hope is that if we can see that what we are tracking with our racial classifications is something captured by *SPR,* then we will begin to see the importance of disrupting race and organizing ourselves on different terms.

Note, however, that debunking accounts are employed strategically; whether they are apt is highly sensitive to contextual factors. The goal, recall, is to challenge our investment in certain unjust practices whose injustice is occluded or masked. The debunking attempts to highlight features of the practices that make it hard for those of goodwill to continue enacting them. Yet there are different kinds of racial practices, and people engage in them with different degrees of awareness. Some practices we enact routinely, mindlessly. Others we enact in spite of knowing they harm us or others, for they define the broad shape of life in our social milieu. And others are recuperative practices that offer counter-hegemonic understandings and opportunities. Because debunking has an epistemic and political aim, it may not be necessary if the harm or wrong of the practices are transparent, or if the practices have already been turned toward justice (Botchkina 2016). In defending the SPR account, I offer it as an option to be taken up, or not, as a tool in moving forward toward racial justice.

1.8. Conclusion

It will become clear to the reader that my methodology for answering the question "What is race?" is different from that of my coauthors. According to all of them, we should be seeking an understanding of what we are ordinarily talking about when we talk of race, and with caveats mentioned earlier (i.e., that it isn't all about our talk), I agree with that. But how do we determine what that is?

In answering the question "What is race?" there are semantic constraints on us. It would not be reasonable to answer, "Race is a type of furniture." But the semantic constraints don't determine how we *must* go on. There are different epistemic and pragmatic standards that may guide our interpretation of the representational tradition. And there are normative considerations about what practices we should continue and the best route for maintaining or discouraging them. I have argued that the *SPR* account is semantically permissible, and that in some contexts it is morally and politically valuable, depending on the practices that are being targeted and the epistemic position of those engaged in them. One of the important functions of language is to highlight features of the world that matter for coordination; the function of

SPR is to highlight—in the relevant cases—how our racializing practices and identities contribute to injustice.

References

Alcoff, Linda. 2000. "Is Latina/o Identity a Racial Identity?" In Jorge Gracia and Pablo DeGreiff (eds.), *Hispanics/Latinos in the U.S.: Ethnicity, Race and Rights.* New York: Routledge, pp. 23–44.

Alcoff, Linda. 2005. *Visible Identities: Race, Gender and the Self.* Oxford: Oxford University Press.

Anderson, Elizabeth S. 1995. "Knowledge, Human Interests, and Objectivity in Feminist Epistemology." *Philosophical Topics* 23(2): 27–58.

Anderson, Elizabeth S. 2010. *The Imperative of Integration.* Cambridge, MA: Harvard University Press.

Andreasen, Robin. 2000. "Race: Biological Reality or Social Construct?" *Philosophy of Science* 67(3): 666.

Andreasen, Robin. 2004. "The Cladistic Race Concept: A Defense." *Biology and Philosophy* 19(3): 425–442.

Appiah, K. Anthony. 1996. "Race, Culture, Identity: Misunderstood Connections." In A. Appiah and A. Gutmann (eds.), *Color Conscious: The Political Morality of Race.* Princeton, NJ: Princeton University Press, pp. 30–105.

Appiah, K. Anthony. 2002. "The State and the Shaping of Identity." In *The Tanner Lectures on Human Values*, vol. 23, ed. Grethe B. Peterson. Salt Lake City: University of Utah Press, pp. 234–299.

Bernasconi, Robert, and Tommy L. Lott. 2000. *The Idea of Race.* Indianapolis and Cambridge, MA: Hackett.

Blauner, Robert. 1972. *Racial Oppression in America.* New York: Harper & Row.

Blum, Lawrence. 2002. *"I'm Not a Racist, But . . .": The Moral Quandary of Race.* Ithaca, NY: Cornell University Press.

Botchkina, Ekaterina. 2016. "Issues in Objectivity and Mind-Dependence." Ph.D. thesis, MIT.

Botchkina, Ekaterina, and Jerome Hodges. 2016. "Objectivity and Conceptual Change." Unpublished manuscript.

Davis, F. James. 1995. "The Hawaiian Alternative to the One-Drop Rule." In Naomi Zack (ed.), *American Mixed Race.* Lanham, MD: Rowman and Littlefield, pp. 115–131.

DuBois, W. E. B. 1991[1987]. "The Conservation of Races." In Philip S. Foner (ed.), *W. E. B. DuBois Speaks: Speeches and Addresses 1890–1919.* New York: Pathfinder, pp. 73–85.

Epstein, Brian. 2015. *The Ant Trap.* Oxford: Oxford University Press.

Espiritu, Yen Le. 1992. "Ethnicity and Panethnicity." In Espiritu, *Asian American Panethnicity.* Philadelphia: Temple University Press, pp. 1–18.

Fadiman, Anne. 2012. *The Spirit Catches You and You Fall Down*. New York: Farrar, Straus, and Giroux.

Fraser, Nancy. 1989. "What's Critical about Critical Theory? The Case of Habermas and Gender." In Fraser, *Unruly Practices*. Minneapolis: University of Minnesota Press, pp. 113–143.

Garfinkel, Alan. 1981. *Forms of Explanation*. New Haven, CT: Yale University Press.

Glasgow, Joshua. 2009. *A Theory of Race*. New York: Routledge.

Gooding-Williams, Robert. 1998. "Race, Multiculturalism, and Democracy." *Constellations* 5: 18–41.

Gracia, Jorge J. E. 2007. *Race or Ethnicity? On Black and Latino Identity*. Ithaca, NY: Cornell University Press.

Haslanger, Sally. 2012. *Resisting Reality: Social Construction and Social Critique*. Oxford: Oxford University Press.

Haslanger, Sally. 2014. "Studying While Black: Trust, Opportunity, and Disrespect." *DuBois Review* 11(1): 109–136.

Haslanger, Sally. 2016. "What Is a (Social) Structural Explanation?" *Philosophical Studies* 173: 113–130.

Haslanger, Sally. 2017a. "Racism, Ideology, and Social Movements." Res *Philosophica* 94(1): 1–22.

Haslanger, Sally. 2017b. "Failures of Individualism: Materiality." Presented at the First Annual Critical Social Ontology Workshop, St. Louis, MO.

Haslanger, Sally. Forthcoming. "Going On, Not in the Same Way." In Alexis Burgess, Herman Cappelen, and David Plunkett, (eds.), *Conceptual Engineering and Conceptual Ethics*. Oxford: Oxford University Press.

Hardimon, Michael. 2003. "The Ordinary Concept of Race." *Journal of Philosophy* 100(9): 437–455.

Hardimon, Michael. 2017. *Rethinking Race: The Case for Deflationary Realism*. Cambridge, MA: Harvard University Press.

Herzog, Donald. 1998. *Poisoning the Minds of the Lower Orders*. Princeton, NJ: Princeton University Press.

Hochman, Adam. 2017. "Replacing Race: Interactive Constructionism about Racialized Groups." *Ergo* 4(3): 61–92.

Irwin, Neil, Claire Cane Miller, and Margo Sanger-Katz. 2014. "America's Racial Divide, Charted." *New York Times*, August 19. https://www.nytimes.com/2014/08/20/upshot/americas-racial-divide-charted.html

Jamal, Amaney, and Nadine Naber. 2008. *Race and Arab Americans before and after 9/11: From Invisible Citizens to Visible Subjects*. Syracuse, NY: Syracuse University Press.

Jeffers, Chike. 2013. "The Cultural Theory of Race: Yet Another Look at Du Bois's 'The Conservation of Races.'" *Ethics* 123(April 2013): 403–426.

Kapusta, Stephanie. 2016. "Misgendering and Its Moral Contestability." *Hypatia* 31(3): 502–519.

Kendig, Catherine. 2011. "Race as a Physiosocial Phenomenon." *History and Philosophy of the Life Sciences* 33(2):191–222.

Kitcher, Philip. 2007. "Does 'Race' Have a Future?" *Philosophy and Public Affairs* 35(4):293–317.

Lear, Jonathan. 1986. "Transcendental Anthropology." In Philip Pettit and John McDowell (ed.), *Subject, Thought and Context*. Oxford: Oxford University Press, pp. 267–298.

Mallon, Ron 2003: "Social Construction, Roles, and Stability." In Frederick F. Schmitt (ed.), *Socializing Metaphysics: The Nature of Social Reality*. Lanham, MD: Rowman and Littlefield, pp. 327–353.

Mallon, Ron. 2006. "'Race': Normative, Not Metaphysical or Semantic." *Ethics* 116(3): 525–551.

Marx, Karl. 1843. *Letter to Ruge*, Kreuzenach, September. http://marx.eserver.org/1843-letters.to.arnold.ruge/1843.09-ruthless.critique.txt

McPherson, Lionel, and Tommie Shelby. 2004. "Blackness and Blood: Interpreting African American Identity." *Philosophy and Public Affairs* 32(2): 171–192.

Mills, Charles W. 1997. *The Racial Contract*. Ithaca, NY: Cornell University Press.

Mills, Charles W. 1998. *Blackness Visible*. Ithaca: Cornell University Press.

Mills, Charles W. 2017. *Black Rights/White Wrongs: The Critique of Racial Liberalism*. Oxford: Oxford University Press.

Omi, M., and H. Winant. 1994. *Racial Formation in the United States*. New York: Routledge.

Quine, W. V. O. 1953. "On What There Is." In Quine, *From a Logical Point of View*. Cambridge, MA: Harvard University Press, pp. 1–19.

Risjord, M. W. 2000. *Woodcutters and Witchcraft: Rationality and Interpretive Change in the Social Sciences*. Albany: State University of New York Press.

Root, Michael. 2001. "The Problem of Race in Medicine." *Philosophy of the Social Sciences* 31(1): 20–39.

Root, Michael. 2003. "The Use of Race in Medicine as a Proxy for Genetic Differences." *Philosophy of Science* 70(5): 1173–1183.

Root, Michael. 2009. "Measurement Error in Racial and Ethnic Statistics." *Biology and Philosophy* 24: 375–385.

Rosen, Gideon. 2015. "Real Definition." *Analytic Philosophy* 56(3): 189–209.

Saul, Jennifer M. 2012. "Politically Significant Terms and Philosophy of Language: Methodological Issues." In Sharon L. Crasnow and Anita M. Superson (eds.), *Out from the Shadows: Analytical Feminist Contributions to Traditional Philosophy*. Oxford: Oxford University Press, pp. 195–214.

Schroeter, Laura, and Francois Schroeter. 2015. "Rationalizing Self-Interpretation." In Chris Daly (ed.), *The Palgrave Handbook of Philosophical Methods*. New York: Palgrave-Macmillan, pp. 419–447.

Sewell, William. 2005. "The Concept(s) of Culture." In Gabrielle M. Spiegel (ed.), *Practicing History: New Directions in Historical Writing after the Linguistic Turn*. New York and London: Routledge, pp. 76–95.

Shelby, Tommie. 2005. *We Who Are Dark*. Cambridge, MA: Harvard University Press.

Shelby, Tommie. 2014. "Racism, Moralism, and Social Criticism." *DuBois Review* 11(1): 57–74.

Spencer, Quayshawn. 2014. "A Radical Solution to the Race Problem." *Philosophy of Science* 81(5): 1025–1038.

Sundstrom, Ronald. 2002. "Race as a Human Kind." *Philosophy and Social Criticism* 28(1): 91–115.

Stocking, George Jr. 1994. "The Turn-of-the-Century Concept of Race." *Modernism/ Modernity* 1(1): 4–16.

Taylor, Paul. 2004. *Race: A Philosophical Introduction*. Cambridge: Polity Press.

Taylor, Paul. 2016. *Black Is Beautiful: A Philosophy of Black Aesthetics*. Hoboken, NJ: Wiley-Blackwell.

Zack, Naomi. 2002. *Philosophy of Science and Race*. New York: Routledge.

2

CULTURAL CONSTRUCTIONISM

Chike Jeffers

Human races are social constructions. What I mean by this is that, while there are aspects of racial diversity among humans that may be studied by natural science, the fundamental factors making it the case that races exist are sociohistorical in nature. Racial distinctions have come to be and continue to exist in the present as a result of the ways that we as humans have interacted and organized our affairs over time. To believe this, as I do, is to be a social constructionist about race. Like Sally Haslanger in the first chapter of this book, one of my aims in what follows is to explain why this is the most attractive position on the metaphysics of race. More distinctively, however, I want to argue that it is important to distinguish between two kinds of social constructionism, which I will call *political constructionism* and *cultural constructionism*. In contrast with Haslanger's political constructionist account of race, I will defend a cultural constructionist account.

The first section of the chapter provides a framework for comparing theories of race and then offers critiques of biological realist and anti-realist positions on race, delivered from a perspective that is neutral between the two kinds of social constructionism that I will differentiate in the chapter's second section. In the second section, once I have distinguished political from cultural constructionism, I discuss why political constructionism might be seen as the default position for a social constructionist. The third and final section then provides an explanation and defense of my version of cultural constructionism. Among my tasks in this section will be spelling out the normative underpinnings and implications of my view.

2.1. Why Social Constructionism?

People have used and still use the English word 'race' and its etymologically related cognates in other languages in a variety of ways. This makes it important to achieve some clarity about the subject matter to be dealt with before fruitful metaphysical discussion can take place. For example, people sometimes treat the terms 'race' and 'ethnicity' as completely interchangeable. It seems necessary to me, though, that we avoid paying too much attention to this kind of usage if we are to see any reason for debating whether races are real and what races fundamentally are. Few people debate whether ethnic groups exist and, although saying what they are might be slightly more contentious, most experts would agree that we are talking about a kind of social category. Thus, if races were nothing other than ethnicities, there would be little reason to debate whether they exist and whether they are fundamentally biological or social. We get closer to understanding debates about the nature and reality of race, though, when we acknowledge the widespread assumption that people of different ethnic backgrounds can be members of the same race (e.g., white people may be Irish, Italian, Russian, something else). This belief is commonly held among those who agree that race is real, even if they disagree about whether race is biological or social in kind, and those who do not believe that race is real can be expected to agree as well, though they might be more careful to say that this is a matter of what *would be* the case if races were real. Shared assumptions of this sort evidently suggest that there is some common ground, some useful starting point for discussion, that we can isolate before going on to investigate why and how people disagree about the nature and reality of race.

The most helpful attempt at making precise what this starting point is, in my view, would be Michael Hardimon's account of the "logical core" of the concept of race.[1] Hardimon claims this logical core can be summarized as follows:

(1) The concept of race is the concept of a group of human beings distinguished from other human beings by visible physical features of the relevant kind.

(2) The concept of race is the concept of a group of human beings whose members are linked by a common ancestry.

---

1. Michael O. Hardimon, "The Ordinary Concept of Race," *Journal of Philosophy* 100 (September 2003): 441.

(3) The concept of race is the concept of a group of human beings who originate from a distinctive geographic location.[2]

Each subsequent thesis here can be seen as building upon and explaining what comes before it. People possess visible physical features of various kinds for various reasons (their sex, their lifestyle choices, etc.), but the kind of physical features that distinguish them as members of races are inherited from their parents, as races are groups whose members are linked by common ancestry. These features at least somewhat reliably indicate where in the world the ancestors of group members lived, as races are groups who originate from a distinctive geographic location. Regarding this last point, Hardimon notes: "[t]he aboriginal habitat of common-sense and conventional races is fixed by the location the ancestors of the members of those groups occupied immediately prior to the advent of European oceangoing transport, which is to say around 1492."[3] Thus two Canadians, both of whose heritage in Canada goes back many generations, may nevertheless be obviously racially different because the physical features of one are indicative of ancestors located in Europe at the time Hardimon suggests is relevant, while the features of the other indicate ancestors located in sub-Saharan Africa.

According to Hardimon, "[o]ne of the most striking results of our account of the logical core of the ordinary concept of race is that race turns out to be relatively unimportant."[4] One way to explain what he means by this is to say that, if one sees a man who happens to be Chinese and rightly guesses on the basis of his appearance that most of his ancestors in the fifteenth century lived somewhere in East Asia, it is not clear that one has recognized anything of great significance. It is certainly the case that, historically, in the West, recognizing someone as "Oriental" was often thought to license various inferences about the character and capacities of the person in question, but Hardimon argues that the three theses at the core of the concept of race do not, by themselves, necessarily imply that we can learn anything of interest about people merely by noticing the connection between their appearance and their place of ancestral origin.

One useful way to compare metaphysical positions in the philosophy of race is to see them as diverging with regard to what significance, if any,

---

2. Ibid., 442, 445, 447.

3. Ibid., 447–448.

4. Ibid., 451.

they accord to the differences in human appearance and ancestral place of origin underlying racial categorizations. The dominant view about race from some time in the early modern era until at least the latter part of the twentieth century has been a biologically essentialist realism, according to which we inherit, along with racial membership, a set of distinctive traits broader than the particular physical features that indicate this membership, including mental and behavioral tendencies, moral and intellectual talents or deficiencies, and physiological characteristics beyond a distinctive appearance as well. Thus we have a long tradition, especially in the West, of taking appearance and ancestry to be very significant indeed. More recently, some philosophers have jettisoned the essentialism of the past while maintaining that there are nevertheless biologically significant divisions of the human species that we can describe as races (a view that will be defended by Quayshawn Spencer in Chapter 3).

An anti-realist about race, on the other hand, would take Hardimon to be begging the question when he says he has revealed race to be unimportant, for, insofar as he is describing something real, it is not clear that it should count as race. It is impossible to deny that there are some regularities in how we look that relate to where many of our ancestors lived, but anti-realists deny, first of all, that these regularities are significant in the way they have traditionally been taken to be significant and, second, they hold that to deny this implies the nonexistence of races. They hold, in other words, that it is only if there is some systematic and more broadly relevant significance to appearance and ancestry of the type imagined by biological essentialists that we have reason to affirm that races exist. From this perspective, which will be defended by Joshua Glasgow in Chapter 4 of this volume, to discuss biologically defined groupings of humans in the non-essentialist manner of some more recent biological realists is to leave the topic of race behind.

In contrast with both of these positions, social constructionists about race take appearance and ancestry to be very significant, not as a matter of biological reality that we discover by looking at the world, but as a matter of social reality that we produce and maintain through widespread patterns of thought and behavior. The remainder of this section will consist in arguments for rejecting biological realism—whether essentialist or not—and anti-realism, along with explanation and defense of the social constructionist alternative.

Reasons for dismissing traditional biological essentialism have by now become familiar to many. Simply put, the view is baseless: the ways in which it connects differences in outer appearance and ancestral place of origin to imagined inner differences—differences in our blood assumed to cause systematic variation in how we think and act—are not currently and arguably never could be supported by scientific research. Paul Taylor aptly notes that, from the essentialist perspective (which he refers to as "classical racialism"), the result of two races mixing can be compared to "diluting a potion."[5] This idea that each race's blood is like a potion, with the special characteristics of the race being the powers of the potion, is at odds with (1) our overwhelming genetic similarity as a species, (2) our genetic distinctness as individuals, and (3) how much we still do not know, even regardless of race, about how genes interact with each other and the environment to cause character traits. With regard to this last point, whatever we learn as our understanding of the relationship between genes and personality increases, it is extremely unlikely that it will validate the traditional essentialist ascription of stable sets of hereditary traits to the wide and somewhat arbitrarily demarcated swaths of humanity that common sense racial groupings are.

But what about non-essentialist biological realism? Whatever it is, it is not baseless. Take Robin Andreasen's cladistic account of race, which would have us understand races as reproductively isolated breeding populations whose biological relationships with each other can be depicted as an evolutionary tree, the branches of which constitute different races.[6] As evidence that we can construct such a tree, Andreasen points us to the work that geneticist Luigi Luca Cavalli-Sforza has done, with others, to map the history of human evolution by measuring the genetic distance between populations. Cavalli-Sforza's work, while not without controversy, is credible scientific research. Andreasen's proposal for how to understand what races are thus leaves behind biological essentialism's implausible claims about character traits while making use of fascinating evidence from the field of genetics.

But should we see groupings of humans like those represented by the branches of Cavalli-Sforza's tree as races? Anti-realists and social constructionists agree that we should not.[7] Note, first, Andreasen's finding that the tree appears to explode our normal idea of East Asians as a group, as Southeast and Northeast Asians appear on "two distinct major branches."[8]

5. Paul C. Taylor, *Race: A Philosophical Introduction*, 2nd ed. (Cambridge, UK: Polity, 2013), 50.

6. Robin O. Andreasen, "A New Perspective on the Race Debate," *The British Journal for the Philosophy of Science* 49 (June 1998): 199–225.

7. Cavalli-Sforza himself also disagrees with calling them races, but I accept Andreasen's claim that we should not take this disavowal as decisive. See Andreasen, "A New Perspective," 213.

8. Andreasen, "A New Perspective," 212.

Southeast Asians branch off of a division that also includes Pacific Islanders, New Guineans, and indigenous Australians, while Northeast Asians branch off of a division that includes the indigenous peoples of the Americas, Europeans, and "Non-European Caucasoids."[9] Thus, according to Andreasen, it would be more accurate to represent Koreans as sharing a race with Germans and people from Thailand as sharing with a race with Fijians than to represent these two somewhat similar-looking peoples of eastern Asia as sharing a race with each other! Note, second, something that Andreasen does not explicitly address: the categorization of South Asians as "Caucasoids." This does receive mention, however, in Quayshawn Spencer's recent work arguing for biological realism. Spencer's argument relies on noting the overlap between the racial categories of the US Census and what he takes to be a biologically significant division of the human species into five genetically clustering partitions of populations, but he notes that one obstacle to complete overlap is the lumping in the Census of "South Asians with Asians and not with whites."[10]

Anti-realists and social constructionists hold that these kinds of discrepancies between common-sense racial classifications and biologically respectable accounts of how we may subdivide our species demonstrate that biology ultimately undermines, rather than supports, our talk of races. There is, of course, the option of seeing these discrepancies as a matter of natural science correcting misconceptions in our common-sense classifications. Consider, however, the way that such discrepancies lead us to abandon the core notion that race involves how appearance is linked to ancestry, and think also of the confusion this may engender. Imagine a young woman, born in England to parents from Bangladesh, whose dark brown skin has marked her for her whole life as a minority of foreign origin. What should she make of the idea that it would be accurate to classify her as being of the same race as the majority? Faced with a choice between describing herself in relation to white people as racially different in recognition of how her appearance has generated a particular experience and describing herself as racially the same on the basis of the broadness of "Caucasian" or "Caucasoid" as a category, should she see both options as equally reasonable? The anti-realist will reject both options as misleading while, as a social constructionist, I would deem the first

---

9. Ibid.

10. Quayshawn Spencer, "A Radical Solution to the Race Problem," *Philosophy of Science* 81 (December 2014): 1031. See Chapter 3 in this volume for Spencer's most recent expression of his view.

option more illuminating. Either way, the point about the second option will be that it conflicts with common sense in a way that is best addressed by giving up the idea that it counts as a description of race and choosing to phrase its insight into our development and diversity as a species in other terms.

If we therefore put aside biological realism as an approach to race, how do we decide between anti-realism and social constructionism? Anti-realism certainly has much to be said for it. There is good reason to think that it is hard to separate talk of race from traditional biological essentialism. Even Hardimon, while asserting that the concept of race at its core is logically independent of essentialist ideas, admits that, as a historical matter, the concept came into general usage already laden with essentialism. He adds six theses, which he calls the "racialist development" and which amount to biological essentialism, to the original three theses in order to give us what he calls "the ordinary *conception* of race," and he acknowledges that "[w]hen the logical core first entered the historical scene, it was *already articulated* by the racialist development."[11] If essentialism is thus a heavy historical legacy to be overcome, it should furthermore be acknowledged that we are by no means yet near to overcoming it. Many think that the fact that people today often dress up essentialist ideas in talk of 'culture' rather than 'race' only extends the power of such thinking. Lawrence Blum gives us an example of this kind of talk: "These people (Jews, whites, Asians) just are that way (stingy, racist, studious); it's part of their culture."[12] It seems clear, from an anti-realist perspective, that we will not defeat this insidious tendency to essentialize by encouraging continued belief in and talk about races as real. We should instead expose all such belief and talk as mistaken or confused (not to mention, in many cases, hateful and oppressive).

---

11. Hardimon, "The Ordinary Concept of Race," 451, 453. According to the six additional theses, a race is "(4) a natural division of the human species into a hierarchy of groups that satisfy the conditions specified in (1)–(3); (5) a group of human beings satisfying the conditions specified in (1)–(3) which is characterized by a fixed set of fundamental, 'heritable,' physical, moral, intellectual, and cultural characteristics common and peculiar to it; (6) a group of human beings satisfying the conditions specified in (1)–(3) whose distinctive visible physical features are correlated with the moral, intellectual, and cultural characteristics that are common and peculiar to it; (7) a group satisfying the conditions specified in (1)–(3) that possesses an 'essence' which explains why it is that the group has the distinctive visible features that it does, why it is that the group has the particular moral, intellectual, and cultural characteristics it does, and the correlation between the two; (8) a group of human beings satisfying the conditions specified in (1)–(3) whose members necessarily share its "essential" characteristics; (9) a group of human beings satisfying the conditions specified in (1)–(3) whose essential characteristics constitute the essence of its members." Ibid., 452.

12. Lawrence Blum, *"I'm Not a Racist, But . . .": The Moral Quandary of Race* (Ithaca, NY: Cornell University Press, 2002), 134.

Despite the attractions of anti-realism, however, I reject it. When evaluated as a position on the significance or insignificance of appearance as related to ancestral place of origin, I think it fails to accurately describe and explain reality. Think once more of the Englishwoman of South Asian descent. How she looks as a result of where her ancestors are from has indeed been very significant, not because of differences of character rooted in her blood, but because of the social situation of South Asians in England. While anti-realism helps us appreciate ways in which differences of appearance and ancestry are not significant, only social constructionism redirects our focus toward ways in which they really are. Racial difference, it should be noted, is not wholly unrelated to that which we may study by means of natural science because it is partly a matter of physical, biological, and geographical differences: it involves how distinctive physical appearances indicate biological connections of descent that tie us to particular geographical regions of the world. It is, however, only through social and historical processes that the particular physical, biological, and geographical differences that we recognize as racial have come to gain some relatively stable significance. It is only because racial distinctions are, fundamentally, significant social distinctions that we can say, in spite of the falsity of biological essentialism, that racial difference is not an illusion.

One might object, from an anti-realist perspective, that we have here the same problem we encountered with non-essentialist biological realism: namely, the problem of changing the subject. I claimed earlier that anti-realists and social constructionists alike see the mismatches between common-sense racial categorizations and those invoked by non-essentialist biological realists as evidence that what those biological realists are discussing is not, in fact, race. The question then becomes why anti-realists cannot make a similar charge against social constructionists, given that they too are at odds with common sense. According to common sense, how we look and where we are from determine our race, regardless of social and historical conditions. It also remains to a great extent common sense that people of different races naturally inherit different characteristics or tendencies in thought and behavior. If social constructionists deny all this, why should they be seen as still talking about race?

The first thing to be said in response is that it matters that the divergence from common sense in the case of social constructionists does not involve racial categorizations, as in the case of non-essentialist biological realists. Social constructionists accept common-sense racial categorizations, precisely because it is only by looking at what people as a matter of sociohistorical contingency widely accept that we can determine what races there are from a social constructionist perspective. The pattern of overlaps and divergences in categorization that we see with non-essentialist biological realists suggests that they are talking about a kind of distinction that is similar and perhaps closely related to racial difference, but not the same thing. The lack of divergence in categorization by social constructionists, on the other hand, suggests that what is at stake from this perspective is the same distinction that is at stake in ordinary talk of race, despite the fact that social constructionists offer an alternative and disruptive understanding of the nature of this distinction.

As an analogy, compare, on the one hand, the divergences between the known facts of a real-life murder case and the plot of a film loosely based on the case, and, on the other hand, the divergence or shift in understanding brought about by a new piece of evidence that appears to exculpate the person convicted of the murder. The murderer in the film may be similar to the person we take to be the murderer in real life, but they are not the same. By contrast, the person convicted of the murder is the same being even after we come to believe that he is innocent. Social constructionism about race involves this kind of shift in understanding what something is, not a change in subject matter.

In relation to this same objection, though, we should also note that anti-realists are generally not so obtuse as to deny that there are significant social distinctions that people normally discuss using the language of race. They claim, however, that to speak clearly and accurately about these social distinctions, we must admit that there are no such things as races and use a different term to refer to the socially differentiated groups we wish to discuss. Thus Kwame Anthony Appiah at one point held that there are no races but there are *racial identities*, and it has remained Blum's position that races do not exist but *racialized groups* do.[13] Conceptual moves such as these allow anti-realists to claim that the social constructionist confuses rather than clarifies things by continuing to use the term traditionally associated with biological essences when referring to a social and historical phenomenon.

---

13. See K. Anthony Appiah, "Race, Culture, Identity: Misunderstood Connections," in Appiah and Amy Gutmann, *Color Conscious: The Political Morality of Race* (Princeton, NJ: Princeton University Press, 1996), 30–105, and Blum, Chapters 7–8 (131–163). Appiah has not made the same distinction in more recent work and has thus drifted toward social constructionism. See, for example, Kwame Anthony Appiah, "Does Truth Matter to Identity?" in Jorge J. E. Gracia (ed.), *Race or Ethnicity? On Black and Latino Identity* (Ithaca, NY: Cornell University Press, 2007), 19–44, and *Lines of Descent: W. E. B. Du Bois and the Emergence of Identity* (Cambridge, MA: Harvard University Press, 2013). For Blum's continued commitment to his position, see Blum, "Racialized Groups: The Sociohistorical Consensus," *The Monist* 93 (April 2010): 298–320.

What would make switching terms most appropriate, however, is a belief that everyday talk about races is talk about some nonexistent stuff that must be distinguished from the real social groups worth discussing. If, as I have already suggested, the best account of the social construction of races would have us acknowledge the existence of the groups referred to in everyday talk but then provide a different account of their nature, then it is, in fact, a matter of clarifying things to continue to use the same term, while it would be at the very least unnecessary and possibly even misleading to switch terms.

Everyday talk about black people, for example, is best understood as referring to a real group to which one can belong, even if such talk often involves false assumptions about what comes naturally to people of recent sub-Saharan African ancestry. What needs to be recognized in order to properly transform everyday understandings of this group is that it is distinct as a group not merely because some of us have ancestors who, in the fifteenth century, lived in sub-Saharan Africa, but rather because being visibly of this ancestry or in some other way being known to be of this ancestry has, particularly since the sixteenth century, been socially significant. Through, among other things, the horrors of slavery, the injustices of colonialism, and, contrastingly, the activism of movements promoting black pride, to be black in our world has been to belong to a meaningfully distinct category of human beings. When we recognize this as a social and historical phenomenon that forms one part among others of the larger global story of race, I believe we describe and explain reality in an informative manner without indulging in essentialist myths, without taking detours through respectable biology toward a separate subject matter, and without mistakenly suggesting that talk of race is talk of nothing real.

2.2. Political versus Cultural Constructionism

I would not be so bold as to assume that the account of what races are in the previous section would receive assent in its every detail by all who would call themselves social constructionists. Details may be disputed, and perhaps major features of the account as well. Nevertheless, the account in the previous section is neutral between two different kinds of social constructionism, and it is my view that the divergence between these two is highly significant. Fruitful philosophical discussion of race going forward, I would argue, will require serious attention to and critical comparison of these two positions so that their potential merits and disadvantages may become clearer and those participating in the debate about race may develop views on why to prefer one or the other.

One way to begin introducing the difference between the two views is to note that there is a certain vagueness in saying that race is socially constructed. What kinds of social relations, processes, or states of affairs are involved in the construction of racial reality? One answer is that race is made real wholly or most importantly by hierarchical relations of power. I call this *political constructionism*. Stated abstractly, the position need not commit one to any particular understanding of history, but, as a matter of fact, social constructionists who think this way generally believe that the specific hierarchical relations of power that make race real are those constituted or brought about by European imperialism and the various social structures it created—in other words, the global sociopolitical system of white supremacy. Taylor, for example, conceives of races in the modern world as "the probabilistically defined populations that result from the white supremacist determination to link appearance and ancestry with social location and life chances."[14]

Let us look now at Haslanger's view of race, as she is especially explicit about offering a form of what I have called political constructionism. She gives us this account of what a race is:

A group G is *racialized* relative to context C iff$_{df}$ members of G are (all and only) those:

(i) who are observed or imagined to have certain bodily features presumed in C to be evidence of ancestral links to a certain geographical region (or regions);

(ii) whose having (or being imagined to have) these features marks them within the context of the background ideology in C as appropriately occupying certain kinds of social position that are in fact either subordinate or privileged (and so motivates and justifies their occupying such a position); and

(iii) whose satisfying (i) and (ii) plays (or would play) a role in their systematic subordination or privilege in C, that is, who are along some dimension systematically subordinated or privileged when in C, and satisfying (i) and (ii) plays (or would play) a role in that dimension of privilege or subordination.[15]

---

14. Taylor, *Race*, 89–90.

15. Sally Haslanger, *Resisting Reality: Social Construction and Social Critique* (New York: Oxford University Press, 2012), 236–237. Note that Haslanger, unlike Blum, treats "groups that are racialized" as synonymous with "races."

Note, first, the relationship between (i) and Hardimon's three theses. Haslanger, like Hardimon, takes race to involve visible features that relate us through ancestry to a certain part of the world, although there is the interesting difference here that Haslanger speaks also of *imagined* features and *presumed* ancestral links, rather than simply observed features and actual links.

We see in (ii) and (iii) Haslanger's commitment to social constructionism. She does not take the connection between features of the body, ancestral relations, and ties to particular geographic regions to be sufficient for racial membership. In order to amount to something distinguishable as such, these attributes must furthermore figure in widely shared patterns of thought about how different kinds of people can be compared with one another, and they must moreover serve as the ground for actual differences in how people in society position themselves and find themselves positioned in relation to one another. As she puts it, adapting the classic feminist explanation of how gender relates to sex, "race is the social meaning of the geographically marked body."[16]

But Haslanger will not count just any kind of commonly drawn distinction and associated relationship between different groups as racial. She holds that these distinctions in thought and patterns in group relations must be matters of subordination and privilege. This is, in fact, what explains why imagined and presumed attributes count just as much as accurately perceived ones for her. If you are not actually linked by descent to the place where many guess that you have roots, but the mistaken perception that many have regularly results in your experience of advantage or disadvantage comparable to that which is experienced by people who are actually linked by descent to that place, then Haslanger aims to capture your social reality in her account of what it means to belong to a race.

Haslanger's approach is distinctive and, in several respects, controversial, but I take her to be representative of the norm among social constructionists in being a political constructionist. If I am right about this, one irony is that what many take to be the pioneering philosophical account of race as a social construction rather than a natural kind is, in fact, *not* a political constructionist account. In 1897, at the first meeting of the American Negro Academy, W. E. B. Du Bois presented a paper entitled "The Conservation of Races," in which he attempts to answer the question of "the real meaning of race."[17]

---

16. Ibid., 236.

17. W. E. B. Du Bois, "The Conservation of Races," in *The Oxford W. E. B. Du Bois Reader*, ed. Eric J. Sundquist (New York: Oxford University Press, 1996), 39.

Du Bois argues that natural science has failed to clarify and distinguish the criteria for race membership, but that it remains the case that "subtle forces" have divided us into "races, which, while they perhaps transcend scientific definition, nevertheless, are clearly defined to the eye of the historian and sociologist."[18] Having thus committed himself to the view that races are fundamentally sociohistorical, he goes on to define a race as "a vast family of human beings, generally of common blood and language, always of common history, traditions and impulses, who are both voluntarily and involuntarily striving together for the accomplishment of certain more or less vividly conceived ideals of life."[19]

With its emphasis on differing "traditions" and "ideals of life," I would classify this definition of race as a form of *cultural constructionism*. For the cultural constructionist, participation in distinctive ways of life, rather than positioning in hierarchical relations of power, is what is most important in making race real. As I have argued elsewhere, Du Bois can be seen not merely as offering a cultural theory of race, but also as explicitly distancing himself from the political approach.[20] Writing in the wake of *Plessy v. Ferguson*, the US Supreme Court case that cemented the system of Jim Crow segregation, Du Bois identifies his *purpose* in thinking about the nature of race as political but claims that, when seeking the *substance* of race, we will have to look beyond political conditions:

> It is necessary in planning our movements, in guiding our future development, that at times we rise above the pressing, but smaller questions of separate schools and cars, wage-discrimination and lynch law, to survey the whole question of race in human philosophy and to lay, on a basis of broad knowledge and careful insight, those large lines of policy and higher ideals which may form our guiding lines and boundaries in the practical difficulties of everyday.[21]

As this passage suggests, it is not only of theoretical but also practical significance for Du Bois that he arrives at his cultural definition of race. He ends

---

18. Ibid., 40.

19. Ibid.

20. Chike Jeffers, "The Cultural Theory of Race: Yet Another Look at Du Bois's 'The Conservation of Races,'" *Ethics* 123 (April 2013): 403–426.

21. Du Bois, "The Conservation of Races," 39.

up arguing that the advancement of civilization has been a matter of the pursuit of different ideals by different races, and then claims on that basis that it is incumbent upon African Americans to proliferate institutions that will help them to develop black culture and thus contribute something special to world, rather than buckle under the pressure of American racism by devaluing and seeking to be rid of their racial distinctness.

Cultural constructionism is thus an alternative to political constructionism with a long history. It has sometimes been recognized and discussed as an alternative, even if not by the name I have given it, as when Taylor describes the "racial communitarian" as believing that "we construct races by creating cultural groups."[22] Taylor offers arguments against this position, which I will consider in the following section. More often than not, though, cultural constructionism is simply ignored as a distinct option. The reason for this, I think, is that political constructionism is such a common position among social constructionists that many seem not to consider the possibility that one might be a social constructionist without being a political constructionist. While unfortunate, this is not, in my view, mysterious. Indeed, I think there is much that can be said in explanation of why, to many, it seems just *obvious* that political constructionism is the right way to think about the social construction of race.

Note, first, that political constructionism appears to offer the best way from a social constructionist perspective to understand the historical development of racial difference. While biological realists may be willing to envision races becoming distinct from each other as much as tens of thousands of years ago, social constructionists tend to treat races as products of the modern era (that is to say, the last five centuries or so), and the most obvious way to explain how they came about given this assumption is to point to the hierarchical social structures created by European imperialism. Taylor is notably flexible in being willing to see "race-thinking" in a broad sense—defined as "assigning generic meaning to human bodies and bloodlines"—as already existing in the ancient world, but he sharply distinguishes what existed before from "modern racialism," or the system of thought and practice that "relies mainly on skin color, facial features, and hair texture to divide humankind into four or five color-coded groups—black, brown, red, white, yellow."[23] His

---

22. Taylor, *Race*, 100.

23. Ibid., 16, 18. One form of pre-modern "race-thinking" that Taylor does not say much about is that which can arguably be found in medieval thought, especially that of the Islamic world. The most convincing philosophical account of how modern racialism differs from that which

willingness to recognize antecedents does not prevent him from saying that "modern Europe invented the concept of race," thus emphasizing that however old the process of assigning meaning to bodies and bloodlines may be, modern Europeans "developed a vocabulary that highlights certain aspects of this process" and then "refined it, exported it, tried to make it scientific, and built it into the foundation of world-shaping . . . developments in political economy."[24]

That last part is, of course, hugely important. The standard social constructionist story is that Europe's colonization of most of the rest of the world, with all the voluntary and involuntary movements, new assortments, and reorganized institutional relations of peoples this entailed, brought it about that differences of appearance and ancestry gained significance in the modern era in a systematic and global manner unlike anything that came before. This is why, as we have seen, Taylor argues for the current reality of races by defining them as populations distinct from each other not merely in appearance and ancestry, but also in probabilities of social location and life chances, with the distinctness in these latter regards being directly or indirectly the result of modern European efforts to establish the supremacy of white people over all others.

What alternative story might a cultural constructionist tell about how races as we know them came to be? Unfortunately, it will not help to look to "The Conservation of Races." Du Bois tells a tale of nomadic groups settling in cities and beginning to specialize in different ways of life, followed eventually by the coalescing of cities into nations that constitute racial groups and which are characterized by "spiritual and mental differences."[25] As fascinating as this story may be, it is frustratingly vague on matters of chronology and geography, making it hard to evaluate, much less accept. Du Bois is specific only when he gets to the modern age, congratulating "the English nation" for its role in developing the ideals of "constitutional liberty and commercial freedom," the "German nation" for "science and philosophy," and the "Romance nations" for "literature and art."[26] Note here also that, while Du Bois recognizes "whites" as constituting one of two or three "great families

---

precedes it must, in my view, pay serious attention to this part of the world's intellectual history. For a starting point, see Paul-A. Hardy, "Medieval Muslim Philosophers on Race," in Julie K. Ward and Tommy L. Lott (eds.), *Philosophers on Race: Critical Essays* (Malden, MA: Blackwell, 2002), 38–62.

24. Ibid., 19, 20.

25. Du Bois, "The Conservation of Races," 41.

26. Ibid., 42.

of human beings" from a scientific perspective (along with "Negroes" and "possibly the yellow race"), he disaggregates them into smaller families, including those just listed, when differentiating between sociohistorical races as he understands them.[27] Given that it was in his time and remains in our time socially significant to be white, we might even say that the charge of changing the subject as evidenced by leaving behind common-sense racial categorizations—leveled by anti-realists and social constructionists against non-essentialist biological realists—applies also to his view. A political constructionist explanation of white distinctness as resulting from the white supremacist construction of social hierarchies based on appearance and ancestry thus seems clearly preferable.

Secondly, political constructionism appears most persuasive in explaining how race is made real socially, partly through the impact of racial categorizations on personal experience. Consider a young black man in the United States who has grown up as the adopted son of white parents in a nearly all-white suburban community. Depending on how he was raised and the interests of his friends, such an individual may feel culturally quite disconnected from black people as a group and rather continuous with those around him. This fact, however, may have little bearing on his feeling that his appearance and ancestry are very significant because of how often he is looked at suspiciously by strangers, how store owners sometimes harass him, how encounters with the police go differently for him than for his friends, etc. This would seem to suggest that cultural difference may be unimportant to one's experience of race, while social hierarchy is essential or at least especially deep in its impact given its connection to our ability to feel respected and valued in our social context.

Another way we can make the foregoing point is by considering, in sharp contrast, how race might be experienced by some as having little to no impact on their life. The concept of white privilege, for example, is the concept of a condition of which it is characteristic that having it makes it more likely that one will be unaware of its existence and unaware that one has it.[28] Many white people living in social contexts characterized by racial multiplicity nevertheless go through much of life reflecting comparatively seldom upon matters of race, and it can seem particularly unimportant to their sense of who they are as individuals. This is best explained from a social constructionist perspective

---

27. Ibid., 39.

28. In this respect, it is similar to some but not all mental illnesses. I thank Tina Roberts-Jeffers for this point.

not by accepting that race has done little to shape their lives and identities, but rather by noticing that it is precisely one aspect of how race may shape us that one's whiteness may be systematically hidden from view even as the relative privileges flowing from said whiteness are enjoyed. The enjoyment of white privilege is not merely compatible with but, more importantly, facilitated by a lack of consciousness about race.[29] Recognizing how an imperative to justification may come along with the conscious possession of privilege thus helps clarify much about how many white people experience their whiteness, and this is best explained as a matter of social hierarchy rather than simply as cultural difference.

Finally, moving from personal experience to consideration of the social landscape at large, political constructionism can seem best attuned to how race matters socially in terms of major events and trends. As I first wrote this during the summer of 2016, some of the ways in which race had been a prominent feature of current affairs in the recent past included: growing attention to police violence against black people and the corresponding growth of the Black Lives Matter movement; the racism associated with Donald Trump's campaign for presidency of the United States, especially in the form of xenophobia directed at Latinos and Muslims; concern about the role of racism in the Brexit vote in the United Kingdom; concern over the role of racism in the water pollution crisis in Flint, Michigan; racist reactions to Syrian refugees in various Western countries; and activism and turmoil concerning racial justice on university campuses in the United States and South Africa. At issue in all cases, arguably, was the problem or response to the problem of the classification of non-white people as less valuable and, in many cases, as particularly threatening to a social order. If this is how race matters, how could it not be clear that race is fundamentally a matter of social hierarchy?

2.3. Why Cultural Constructionism?

I do not find it strange, then, that political constructionism has been taken to be the default position among social constructionists. So why would I choose to defend cultural constructionism? The first thing I should say in order to clarify my position is that I take race, at present, to be *both politically and*

---

29. Charles Mills has famously addressed this by developing the epistemological concept of "white ignorance." For the most focused expression of his view, see Mills, "White Ignorance," in Shannon Sullivan and Nancy Tuana (eds.), *Race and Epistemologies of Ignorance* (Albany: State University of New York Press, 2007), 13–38.

culturally constructed. If the only way we could make sense of the distinction between political and cultural constructionism were viewing the former as denying that race is in any way culturally constructed and the latter as denying that race is in any way politically constructed, I would deny that we have to choose one or the other and reject both positions as false. Happily, I think many other social constructionists who I would normally identify as political constructionists would agree with me on this point.

Charles Mills, for example, when explaining his popular model of the system of white supremacy as a "Racial Contract," clarifies that this contract should be understood as "creating not merely racial exploitation, *but race itself* as a group identity."[30] This point about hierarchy not merely being based upon but rather generating racial difference is, of course, characteristic of political constructionism. Still, many of Mills's efforts at exploring the various dimensions of white supremacy include insightful attention to cultural difference. For instance, while imploring political philosophers to take seriously how race brings up questions of personhood, he encourages reflection on ways in which personhood is linked to cultural membership. First, he notes: "Colonization has standardly involved the denigration as barbaric of native cultures and languages, and the demand to assimilate to the practices of the superior race, so that one can achieve whatever fractional personhood is permitted."[31] Resistance to racism thus often involves affirming the worth of indigenous languages or, as in the Caribbean, creoles that deviate from the imperial standard. In the United States, Mills argues, "the construction of an exclusionary cultural whiteness has required the denial of the actual multiracial heritage of the country," which means that white people "appropriated Native American and African technical advances, language use, cultural customs, and artistic innovations without acknowledgment, thereby both reinforcing the image of nonwhites as subpersons incapable of making any worthwhile contribution to global civilization and burnishing the myth of their own monopoly on creativity."[32] As Mills sums up this discussion, he suggests that thinking about race necessarily requires thinking about cultural difference:

Culture has not been central to European political theory because cultural commonality has been presupposed. But once cultures are in

30. Mills, *The Racial Contract* (Ithaca, NY: Cornell University Press, 1997), 63.

31. Mills, *Blackness Visible: Essays on Philosophy and Race* (Ithaca, NY: Cornell University Press, 1998), 115.

32. Ibid.

contestation, hegemonic and oppositional, and linked with personhood, they necessarily acquire a political dimension.[33]

If thinking about race requires thinking about cultures in contestation, it seems clear that Mills believes race involves both differential power relations and participation in different ways of life.

Assuming I am right that it is common among social constructionists to recognize that both of these kinds of difference are somehow involved in race, one might begin to suspect that distinguishing between 'political constructionism' and 'cultural constructionism' is misleading and unnecessary. I think this suspicion is wrong. What is required for the distinction to be useful is that there be some social constructionists who think that differential power relations are somehow most fundamental in the social construction of race and some who, by contrast, accord that status to participation in different ways of life. Mills, like Taylor, Haslanger, and others, fits the first description.[34] I have already suggested that those who fit the second description are less common, but, among those who have been prominent in debates about the metaphysics of race, one example would be Lucius Outlaw.[35]

Let us consider more carefully, then, what might be involved in treating politics or culture as more fundamental to the social construction of race. We can define a maximally robust political constructionism as a view that takes politics, in the sense of power relations, to be what matters most for the reality of race in all of the following ways: (1) differential power relations are what first brought racial difference into existence and are thus fundamental in being the *origin* of races; (2) differential power relations count as *most important in the present* to the reality of race, which is to say that properly understanding any event, process, or state of affairs that involves race always requires understanding how power relations are at stake, whereas there is nothing else

---

33. Ibid.

34. That politics is more fundamental than culture to the social construction of race for Mills is especially clear in his "Multiculturalism as/and/or Anti-Racism?" in Anthony Simon Laden and David Owen (eds.), *Multiculturalism and Political Theory* (Cambridge, UK: Cambridge University Press, 2007), 89–114.

35. See Lucius T. Outlaw (Jr.), *On Race and Philosophy* (New York: Routledge, 1996), especially the Introduction (1–21) and Chapters 6–7 (135–182). Outlaw's position is unique because he not only treats culture as fundamental in the social construction of race, but also takes race to be both social and biological in nature in such a way that races are appropriately called "social-natural kinds" (7). The opposition between social constructionism and biological realism that I depicted in the first section thus leaves out his distinctive view.

that must similarly always be understood; and (3) differential power relations are *essential* to race, making it the case that if an egalitarian state of affairs in which appearance and ancestry do not correlate with positions in a hierarchy is achieved, race will be no more. I think many social constructionists are robust political constructionists according to these criteria.

A maximally robust cultural constructionism would, by contrast, hold that (1) the origin of racial difference is to be found in divergences in ways of life; (2) only cultural difference must always be understood in order to understand the reality of race in the present; and (3) cultural difference is essential to race, such that the end of distinctive ways of life would mean the end of race. Confrontation between this bold position and political constructionism as I have described it would perhaps be the most exciting way for things to go in the rest of this chapter, but, unfortunately for those awaiting such excitement, this is not a version of cultural constructionism I would defend. Indeed, I disagree with each of these three points, which might lead one to think it doubtful that I could deserve the title of cultural constructionist!

The reason I take on the title, in spite of not holding the maximally robust version of the position, is because I reject political constructionism in a way that is, I think, best expressed by calling my view a form of cultural constructionism. Before explaining how and why I reject it, however, let me first acknowledge the crucial respect in which I do not challenge the political constructionist account. I completely concede the first point about the origin of race. In other words, I take European imperialism and the hierarchical social structures it created to be what gave rise to racial difference as we know it. If admitting this were all it took to be a political constructionist, I would have to identify as one.

I disagree, however, with the second and third points of the robust political constructionist account for reasons involving my belief in the significance of cultural difference to race's existence and functioning as a social distinction. I reject the claim that politics is more important than culture at present. I hold that they are of equal importance and, though I do not go so far as to claim that culture is more important, this disagreement nevertheless already commits me to putting additional emphasis on the significance of culture in opposition to the political constructionist's relative disregard. I also reject the claim that the end of social hierarchy based on appearance and ancestry would mean the end of race. Race as a social construction could live on past the death of racism, in my view, given that racial groups could continue to exist as cultural groups. Here too we see how my disagreement with the political constructionist allows me to uphold culture as particularly significant.

While the political constructionist sees the end of racism as a potential future transition from social reality to nothingness, I see the potential for a transition from cultural difference being one component of a social reality to being the entirety of that reality.

To see most clearly why it is useful to call my view cultural constructionism, though, it is necessary to pay attention to the role of values and ideals in thinking about the nature and reality of race. The more we try to draw a very sharp distinction between ethics and metaphysics, the less reason there will be to say that my metaphysical stance should be described as centering culture more than politics. Race is fundamentally social, in my view, but I do not take either politics or culture to be more fundamental in the sense of being what is essential for the social reality of race. Culture cannot be essential in this way if, as I hold, race is political at its origin. Politics cannot be essential if, as I believe, a future in which race is merely cultural is possible. This comparison seems, however, to leave the two equal in status.

Think now, though, about the fact that getting rid of unjust social distinctions clearly ought to be our shared goal as human beings in society. We therefore have a duty to work toward the end of race as a social reality insofar as it is constituted by a hierarchy based on appearance and ancestry. It is not so clear, by contrast, that we have any duty to work toward ending the existence of different cultures. People differ in how permissible and valuable they take the perpetuation of cultural distinctions to be, but I am among those who value cultural diversity and think that, at least in many cases, the preservation of distinctive cultural traditions is desirable and admirable. The continued existence of racial diversity as cultural diversity after the end of racism is therefore, in my view, something good. As a result, one normative implication of my position on race is that we should be orienting ourselves in the present toward the eventual achievement of a world in which races exist only as cultural groups. This vision for the future and the concern for valuing the cultural aspects of race in the present that it entails makes it sensible to say that culture is indeed fundamental, on my view. Thinking of cultural constructionism as including perspectives according to which *we ought to actively continue constructing races as cultural groups* makes applying that label to my view perfectly apt.

I will provide in the remaining space of this chapter a preliminary defense of my version of cultural constructionism. I mentioned earlier that Taylor criticizes cultural constructionism, and I will first consider the trilemma he devises in order to do so. Responding to Taylor will be useful for establishing the basic coherence and plausibility of my position. Second, I will say more about how and why my position contrasts with a robust political constructionism, allowing me to defend the superiority of my view. Further development and defense of my position will then come in Chapter 6.

Taylor's trilemma is aimed at what he refers to as the "strong communitarian" view that races are groups "composed of people who share or have some claim on a common culture," with the normative implication that these groups "deserve a certain kind of reverence or commitment from their constituent members, such that the people who don't participate in the culture ought to do so."[36] This is, as he also calls it, a "cultural-nationalist account of race."[37] The question that arises in relation to this view is this: How might the claim that races are made up of people who share not only a similar appearance and ancestry but also a common culture be justified? Taylor imagines three options for how the cultural constructionist (as I will refer to his target) could reply, and deems each option unsatisfactory.

First, the view might be that it is simply how nature works that, just as members of races inherit common physical features, they inherit common cultural tendencies as well. But this is classical racialism (i.e., biological essentialism), and so it must be ruled out as an option. Second, he imagines that a non-essentialist version of the position might take as its starting point the plausible idea that "people who are treated in similar ways might do well to join forces to resist their common oppression."[38] From there, one might reasonably conclude that people oppressed on the basis of their common racial categorization will be aided in their struggles against oppression by cultivating togetherness through a sense of cultural community. The problem with this "practical cultural nationalism," as Taylor calls it, is that it is a prescriptive view about what members of races ought to do, not a descriptive view concerned with what races are, and thus it is irrelevant to the debate over the nature and reality of race.[39] Finally, if the cultural constructionist is not being prescriptive but rather is, in fact, making the descriptive claim that races are, like ethnic groups, made up of people associated with a common culture, then the view is "simply incorrect."[40] Races and ethnic groups are not the same things.

---

36. Taylor, *Race*, 100–101. Taylor takes Molefi Asante's Afrocentrism to be an example of a view of this sort.

37. Ibid., 101.

38. Ibid.

39. Ibid.

40. Ibid., 102.

Taylor thus treats cultural constructionism as untenable because it is either empirically baseless (because essentialist), irrelevant (because prescriptive, not descriptive), or a confusion of two distinct categories (races and ethnic groups). It is already obvious that I would reject the essentialist version of the identification of races with cultures, so the question becomes whether my position is captured by either of the two non-essentialist options and, if so, what I might say in response to Taylor's criticisms. Let us first notice what is strange about Taylor's conception of a practical cultural nationalist. In order for his criticism of irrelevance to work, he must imagine the practical cultural nationalist as refraining from describing races as being presently cultural groups, even while prescribing that the members of at least some races work to change this situation. But cultural nationalists, as a rule, argue for the preservation and cultivation of a culture that they believe already exists, at least in some shape or form, and this is true for those whose cultural nationalism is racial in scope as well.

Take Du Bois. In "The Conservation of Races," he exhorts African Americans to lead black people as a whole in making a distinctive cultural contribution to civilization. This is a prescriptive, future-oriented view, but Du Bois clearly suggests that the cultural contribution to come will build on contributions that have already been made. As "members of a vast historic race," he claims, his people have brought unique gifts to America, for their "subtle sense of song has given America its only American music, its only fairy tales, its only touch of pathos and humor amid its mad money-getting plutocracy."[41]

The position Taylor depicts is certainly not logically impossible, but given the goal of evaluating what has actually been held by proponents of cultural theories of race, we should note that, in practice, prescriptions of the type he is discussing are almost always inseparable from an understanding of the race being exhorted as already a cultural group in some sense, whether this understanding is biologically essentialist or not.[42] Thus Taylor's second option is not really worth distinguishing from the first and third options. Given

41. Du Bois, "The Conservation of Races," 44.

42. Whether Du Bois should be viewed as relying on biological essentialism in "The Conservation of Races" is a famously controversial question among philosophers of race and Taylor, as a matter of fact, is one of the major contributors to this debate who have written in defense of Du Bois. See Appiah, "The Uncompleted Argument: Du Bois and the Illusion of Race," *Critical Inquiry* 12 (Autumn 1985): 21–37, and Taylor, "Appiah's Uncompleted Argument: W. E. B. Du Bois and the Reality of Race," *Social Theory and Practice* 26 (Spring 2000): 103–128.

that the first option has been ruled out, the crucial question is thus whether my view is, as Taylor's trilemma suggests, a simple confusion of race with ethnicity. This would, of course, be an ironic result, in light of the fact that the need to avoid treating 'race' and 'ethnicity' as synonymous in order to think productively about race was among the first things I asserted in this chapter.

Before responding, I should clarify how Taylor takes these two terms to differ in meaning. According to him, both terms refer to groups based partially on descent, but "'race' points to the body while 'ethnicity' points to culture."[43] In other words, while races are groups distinguished at least in part by shared ancestry and distinctive physical appearances, ethnicities are groups distinguished by shared ancestry and by cultural factors like language and religion. I happen to think that this is a very reasonable way of differentiating between race and ethnicity, so it will not be my strategy to say that Taylor has failed in drawing the distinction. It is compatible with and, I would say, important to my view that physical appearance plays a key role in racial difference that it does not by necessity play in ethnic difference. Taylor seems to suggest that recognizing races as cultural groups involves contradicting that point, but this is not the case. Culture is not displacing the centrality of the body, in my view, but rather serving as a key factor in explaining how the body is socially meaningful in cases of racial difference.

Consider examples of people feeling cultural pride in both their race and their ethnicity, where these are not the same thing. One can feel a sense of cultural allegiance to the black race as a whole, for instance, while also proudly identifying as a member of an ethnic group that is but a small component of the race or one that overlaps multiple races, as in the cases of those who identify ethnically as Latin American or Arab. An Afro-Cuban individual may love being a Latino and yet simultaneously take great pride in being of African descent, with the result that she feels a strong sense of kinship and shared cultural ownership when witnessing or participating in forms of culture originating in sub-Saharan Africa or in places in the African diaspora outside Latin America. This example fits well with Taylor's claim that ethnic belonging need not be associated with a shared physical appearance, given the diversity of ways Latin American people can look, while racial membership is linked with visible continuities, as in the case of those whose features indicate sub-Saharan African ancestry.

---

43. Taylor, *Race*, 53.

We can, however, go a step further in demonstrating the lack of confusion between race and ethnicity on my part by recalling my agreement with Taylor and other political constructionists that the origin of races as we know them is to be found in the construction of white supremacist social hierarchies. What this means is that, on my view, when the Afro-Cuban I described feels culturally connected to other black people, the pride she experiences involves valuing black bodies and their activities in the face of their historical devaluation, a devaluation that was part of the colonial projects that made being of this particular descent a salient shared identity in the modern world in the first place. Adding this historical specificity to the account helps to make it obvious beyond a shadow of a doubt that race is not being confused here with ethnicity or any other social category. This pride is racial pride, and it can be felt without having a biologically essentialist understanding of racial identity, for our Afro-Cuban friend may well recognize the historical contingencies upon which her feelings of belonging within a larger whole rest, whether with respect to her race or her ethnicity.

Cultural constructionism thus need not be seen as necessarily empirically baseless, irrelevant, or confused. There is a coherent and plausible idea here. In order to make it clear why it should be seen not only as plausible but also as preferable to political constructionism, I will now systematically contrast my position with the three tenets of the robust version of that view. As mentioned multiple times now, the first tenet of the view is one I accept: races emerged out of political conditions that divided people into groups unequal in power. What I would add, though, is that as soon as you have races emerging in this way, you have social categories shaping the identities of those who are included in them in such a way that these members may plausibly view these categories as culturally significant.

The cultural significance of races can be seen as coming about in at least three ways (and I mean all of these ways, not just any or some). First, the emergence of racial categories is itself a cultural shift, and thus a social context in which people are viewed as being of different races is in that way culturally distinctive. This is a point that may seem subtle but which is ultimately somewhat obvious. I am not yet describing how individual races might differ in their respective ways of life. I am describing instead how being socialized into a world where people conceive of each other as racially different means being socialized into a particular way of life. If we think, for example, of the difference between, on the one hand, someone growing up in a West African village in the fifteenth century in an area where it was common to be aware only of what we would now think of as ethnic differences and, on the other hand, an enslaved descendant of this person on a Caribbean island a couple of centuries later who is acutely aware of her place in a racial hierarchy, we are noticing a difference in the cultures that shaped these two related individuals. The social construction of race is therefore, from the beginning, a cultural process, and race can accurately be described as being from the start both politically and culturally constructed, even if we acknowledge that, at the point of origin, it is the political circumstance (e.g., the social hierarchy of slavery) that gives rise to the cultural condition of racial identification being common.

Second, there are the novel forms of cultural difference between groups that arise in the wake of the development of racial difference. Once people are being socialized into worlds in which they inhabit different racial categories, it is a necessarily common occurrence that these social distinctions lead to inhabiting relatively different worlds and thus participating in different ways of life. As people of different African ethnicities came in the Americas to inhabit the category of 'Negro' or 'black,' for example, their new cultural creations were products of *black culture*. They could not be products of the distinctive ethnic groups of old as these distinctions faded. One might associate them with particular territories, calling jazz a product of the United States, samba a product of Brazil, calypso a product of Trinidad, and so on, but to say this alone is misleading, for no explanation of these musical cultures that fails to acknowledge their initial development primarily by those of African descent is adequate.

Third, we should not let the novelty that comes along with social orders and relations brought about by colonialism cause us to miss the ways in which racial groups are also shaped culturally by historical patterns and events preceding racial formation. It is true that there is some level of anachronism in an African American boy alive today learning about Great Zimbabwe, the large city whose ruins we can still visit, that served as the capital of a flourishing kingdom from the eleventh to the fifteenth century, and experiencing this as a moment of pride in 'black heritage.' On a social constructionist view, we have reason to deny that the Shona people who lived in this place at that time were part of something we can call the black race (in contrast with Shona people today, as the development starting in the late nineteenth century of Rhodesia as a settler colony and the struggle against white rule leading up to Zimbabwe's independence in 1980 make it *especially* obvious on this view that they are black). But there is also something clearly right about him describing his experience in that way. He is engaging in the common cultural practice of taking pride in the past accomplishments of one's people, but what enables him to count those who constructed Great Zimbabwe as his people is an ancestral connection to Africa made significant by the social reality that being black is significant. Note how whiteness as a cultural reality has been similarly shaped by pride among Europeans and those of European descent in the accomplishments of ancient Greeks and Romans.

It might be thought that, while it makes sense to call this boy's feeling a case of taking pride in black heritage, the accuracy of the description does not mean that the practice itself makes sense. This boy's ancestors in Africa were likely to be found in West Africa, not the southern part of the continent where Great Zimbabwe is. With no known connection to Zimbabwe, how could Shona people be his people? There is much that could be said in response, including the political constructionist point that a world shaped by white supremacy is a world in which it makes sense for this boy to see himself as in the same group as others with a similar appearance and sub-Saharan African ancestry. An important point about culture that should be made in response, though, is that to scoff at the idea that West African ancestry could allow a sense of cultural connection with people from what is now Zimbabwe is to wrongfully assume that geographic distance automatically means a lack of cultural commonality. We can relate this to Kwame Gyekye's complaint about some of Appiah's work. Gyekye claims that Appiah expends great energy emphasizing Africa's cultural diversity at the expense of recognizing common "threads visible in the cultural tapestry of the African peoples."[44] Without denying Africa's "pluralism," Gyekye points out a number of "horizontal relationships" (i.e., similarities) between traditional African cultures in metaphysical, epistemological, moral, and sociopolitical matters.[45] We can discern premodern horizontal relationships in other racial groups as well, and this is best understood, of course, not as the result of inborn impulses, but rather sociohistorical processes. Think, for instance, of how we can tell the story of Buddhism arriving from India in East Asia and gradually spreading throughout the region, centuries before East Asians were classed together by Westerners as "Orientals" or the "yellow" race.

These three forms of cultural significance—racial consciousness itself as cultural, racial consciousness as facilitating new cultural developments, and racial consciousness as shaped by prior cultural developments—are key

44. Kwame Gyekye, *An Essay on African Philosophical Thought: The Akan Conceptual Scheme*, revised ed. (Philadelphia: Temple University Press, 1995), xxx.

45. Ibid., 195–210. His examples include: an ontology including a Supreme Being and ancestral spirits; divination, witchcraft, and spirit mediumship as sources of knowledge; and communalism in social thought and practice.

aspects of a proper account of the social construction of race, on my view. They are not central to standard political constructionism. That being said, it is not clear that the committed political constructionist has reason as yet to deny anything I have said. As long as I admit the political origin of race, my talk of cultural significance arising in the wake and as part of this process of origination may be seen as helpful detail, rather than harmful challenge. A maximally robust cultural constructionism might claim that premodern cultural commonalities represent in themselves the origin of racial difference. I would not claim that. Cultural commonalities across large expanses are not hard to find, and if one tried to divide up the world on that basis, many different sets based on alternative choices of how to divide would be possible. Premodern commonalities matter in the case of races only because they accord with divisions based on appearance, but given the various continuities in how we look, there are different sets based on alternative divisions possible on this basis as well. Races as we know them, on my view, are appearance-based groups that initially result from the history of Europe's imperial encounters.

Where cultural constructionism as I conceive of it moves from offering a change in emphasis to seriously challenging the dominant view among social constructionists, then, is in its opposition to the second and third tenets of a robust political constructionism. I reject the idea that cultural difference is less important than differences in power relations for understanding racial phenomena in the present. This forces me to address what we should make of hypothetical examples like the adopted young man who experiences little cultural attachment to blackness but whose experiences of social inequities nevertheless render his blackness very significant. Does this not show that the political constructionist is right and I am wrong about what is important?

The mistake here is the expectation that the cultural construction of race would involve a uniformity of experience across individuals, whereas this is the case neither for race's cultural nor for its political aspects. For any particular way in which disadvantage can be experienced within a social hierarchy, one cannot assume that because a person is non-white that he or she has personally experienced that form of racism or racism's effects. This is why Taylor's political account of race is structured around probabilities—around the fact that, in the United States, for example, "non-whites are *much more likely* to be unemployed, to commit and become victims of violent crime, to receive substandard medical care, and to live in inadequate housing."[46] To point out

---

46. Taylor, *Race*, 82–83. Emphasis mine.

a non-white individual in the United States today who is employed, who has not committed or been a victim of violent crime, who has received quality medical care, and who lives in a very nice house does nothing to disprove his theory.

Similarly, it is not my claim that all members of races have uniform cultural experiences. Indeed, there is no such thing as uniformity of experience within cultural groups, especially when the group in question is large and geographically dispersed. In any group that can be described as a cultural group, it will be normal for some individuals to be more familiar with certain aspects of the culture, less familiar with others. Once we are talking about groups that are associated with cultures but whose members are also connected by other ties—such as descent in the case of ethnicities, or citizenship in the case of countries, geographic location in the case of regions, and so on—then there can be not only differential familiarity with various aspects of the culture, but also the common occurrence of some group members having little to no investment in the group's culture. What makes it the case that there is a culture of the group to speak of is not *all* group members being equally invested and engaged in reproducing a specific set of customs, but rather there being *many* group members whose identification with the group is connected with investment and engagement in practices that they take to be distinctively related to the group's existence, which is a state of affairs compatible with a significant amount of diversity in what is taken to be distinctive and in how invested and engaged group members are.

I have provided an argument, then, against taking cases of individual experience as evidence that politics is more fundamental than culture to race, but this defensive move is, of course, not enough to show that politics and culture are, at present, equally important to understanding racial phenomena. This is not the kind of claim for which it is easy to provide definitive proof, but I will use three examples of issues involving race to motivate the idea that paying attention to matters of social hierarchy without also paying attention to how people often identify on the basis of appearance and ancestry with distinctive ways of life generally leads to confusion about what is going on.

Consider, first, the example of education. This is a topic that can be racially fraught, especially in majority-white countries with sizable non-white minorities (although I have mentioned already that racial dynamics in education have been recently controversial in South Africa). The political account of race is certainly helpful in illuminating many problems with education, such as inequality in basic access, inequality in funding, and unequal treatment of students by teachers and other staff with regard to discipline and the provision of opportunities. One will badly misunderstand mobilization over racism in education, however, if one ignores matters of curriculum design, and such matters can only be understood through attention to cultural difference. For many concerned with racism in education, it would be manifestly unsatisfactory for us to achieve equality in access, funding, discipline, and opportunities while doing nothing about the traditional privileging of white people, their accomplishments, and their perspectives in school materials and teaching methods. This traditional Eurocentric bias is viewed by many anti-racists not only as problematic in itself, but also as a significant factor in non-white students—especially black students—doing less well than others, dropping out at higher rates, and other such manifestations of inequality. Concern about these effects strongly motivates demand for the availability of black-focused schools, where emphasis on the value of black cultural heritage is an essential component of the pedagogical approach.[47]

While there can be no mistaking the centrality of cultural difference in demands for and efforts to provide black-focused education, it might be objected that this mode of dealing with the problem of racism in schools is controversial and that, if put aside, it remains possible to understand the issue at hand without any focus on cultural differences between students. After all, it seems clear that students of every racial group benefit from a curriculum that does not minimize the contributions or ignore the perspectives of non-white people. This is indeed true but, if used by a political constructionist as a reason for not paying attention to cultural difference, this is self-defeating. The only way this point could be seen as eliminating the role of cultural difference would be if the suggestion were that an inclusive curriculum benefits all students in the same way, but that would mean denying that the Eurocentric approach being targeted for change hurts non-white students differently than white students, thus denying that there is a problem of racial hierarchy here in the first place! To admit that students are placed in unequal positions by a Eurocentric curriculum is to admit that some students—white ones—are culturally affirmed by such a curriculum while others—non-white students—are not. An inclusive curriculum in a racially integrated school benefits everybody but benefits different students in different ways. Most importantly,

---

47. For an example of such a school, see the Africentric Alternative School in Toronto, Ontario: http://schoolweb.tdsb.on.ca/africentricschool/Home.aspx. Political philosopher Will Kymlicka sympathetically considers the case for black-focused schools in the United States and in Canada in his essay, "A Crossroads in Race Relations," in Kymlicka, *Politics in the Vernacular: Nationalism, Multiculturalism, and Citizenship* (New York: Oxford University Press, 2001), 177–199.

for our purposes, if it is effective with regard to non-white students, such a curriculum encourages them to positively value their racial group and what is unique about it, instead of leading them to covet whiteness as the authoritative source of goodness and progress.

Consider, second, the issue of interracial marriage. Opposition to it by white people dedicated to keeping their race pure is, by now, an uncontroversial example of irredeemable racism. But what about opposition to it by non-white people? Is this similarly worthy of automatic dismissal and disdain? A number of black philosophers have demanded that we take seriously the concerns motivating such opposition among black people, especially as expressed by black women. Anita Allen points out that many African Americans think of *Loving v. Virginia*, the Supreme Court case that struck down bans on interracial marriage, as an important blow to racial injustice while still remaining "morally troubled by marriage between blacks and whites."[48] What could explain this mix of attitudes? Notice that the attitude toward the law here is sensitive to how marking racial difference is often a matter of affirming social hierarchy. It is therefore telling and useful from my perspective that Allen foregrounds the ideal of commitment to one's cultural community as often underlying the moral concern.

To be clear, Allen does not conclude that those who hold this ideal are ultimately right to oppose interracial marriage, but she defends the moral innocence of interracial marriage not by dismissing the values invoked against it, but by outlining a position that "reconciles interracial marriages between blacks and whites with black community-centered concerns about respect and care."[49] Taylor also takes concerns that non-white people have about interracial marriage seriously, but he appears to go even further than Allen in his conclusion by not only rejecting a duty to marry within the race, but finding little justification for anyone having a *right* to "color-conscious endogamy."[50]

---

48. Anita Allen, "Interracial Marriage: Folk Ethics in Contemporary Philosophy," in Naomi Zack (ed.), *Women of Color and Philosophy: A Critical Reader* (Malden, MA: Blackwell, 2000), 183.

49. Ibid., 193.

50. Taylor, *Race*, 167. Besides Allen and Taylor, the other classic philosophical engagement with this topic is Mills's "Do Black Men Have a Moral Duty to Marry Black Women?" Of the three, Mills ends on the note most friendly to black opponents of interracial marriage, answering the question in his title by saying that there are enough at least partially strong arguments to yield a "presumptive duty," while leaving it open how easy it may be to defeat the presumption. See Mills, "Do Black Men Have a Moral Duty to Marry Black Women?" *Journal of Social Philosophy* 25 (June 1994): 150.

When rejecting arguments that rely on preserving culture, he repeats his refrain that "races aren't cultural groups."[51] Later on, however, when clarifying that he is not saying we should immediately eradicate all racial endogamy, Taylor concedes that "racial populations may serve as incubators for ethnic communities, whose members may choose to relate to each other more closely than to other groups" and, in this way, racial endogamy may be "the consequence, sign, and mechanism of some benign segregation."[52] This sounds to me like an argument from the cultural dimension of race to the permissibility of having a preference for marrying within one's race, which is support from a surprising source for my claim about the importance of culture to race.[53]

Consider, finally, stereotyping. It is undoubtedly one of the things one must understand in order to know how race works in the world at present. Simple interactions are affected, such as when acquaintances wrongfully assume that you must know how to dance because you are black or you must be good at math because you are East Asian. It is a major issue in art and media, requiring critical analysis of when, how, and to what purpose stereotypes function in individual cases and in patterns across various works, genres, and forms of representation. It is also a source of danger to people's bodies and lives, given the way that racial profiling, especially by the police, promotes the influence of stereotypes over when people are detained and how they are treated, including whether they might be subjected to deadly force. A political constructionist account of race can help us understand all of this, from the small slights to the serious harms, by pointing out how stereotypes rob us of our individuality and obscure our humanity by flattening us into caricatures on the basis of appearance and ancestry—caricatures that correspond to particular placements in a social order.

The logic of the political constructionist account, however, can lead us toward an untenable position. We are apt to respond to stereotypes by affirming our individuality—"I am not just some black guy, I am Chike, and Chike is not good at basketball"—or our humanity—"Stop portraying us in servile roles only, we are fully human and we can be heroes"—or sometimes both. These responses certainly have merit, but the more strongly we cling to our

---

51. Ibid., 161.

52. Ibid., 169.

53. Surprising but not extremely so. As I have noted elsewhere, this is not the only case of Taylor making comments about the relationship between racial and cultural identity that seem strikingly compatible with my perspective. See Jeffers, "The Cultural Theory of Race," 420 n52, and Taylor, *Race*, 114–115.

uniqueness as individuals or to our shared humanity, the more we move in the direction of wrongly suggesting that nothing of interest can be said about groups. Consider the example of someone being stereotyped as particularly in touch with nature because she belongs to one of the indigenous groups of North America. This is racial stereotyping and, like all stereotyping of individuals, involves a false, essentialist assumption. One has learned the wrong lesson, however, if one concludes that all perceptions of the first peoples of this land as distinct in how they conceive of and interact with the natural environment must be equally mistaken. Indeed, it is necessary to learn something about cultural difference in this regard in order to properly understand debates about land ownership and use, special rights to hunt and fish, and various other matters involving indigenous peoples.

Stereotypes, then, are problematic distortions, but not by virtue of representing differences in thought and behavior between races. The problems are in how they exaggerate differences, in how intrinsic to group membership they represent differences, in how they reduce groups to specific differences, thus obscuring inner complexity and diversity, and, at times, how the differences they represent are completely made up. Opposing stereotypes should not be equated, then, with opposing the representation of racial groups as having different ways of life. Sometimes a stereotype will be related to real differences between races that are political in nature, such as stereotypes about criminal behavior that can be connected to disproportionate convictions for crimes because of the disadvantaged socioeconomic status of the group and bias within the justice system. Other times, a stereotype will relate to a cultural difference with roots older than racial difference as we know it, as in the indigenous case just mentioned. Often enough, there will be relations of both kinds: stereotypes about black people being good at dancing may be related both to the significance of dance in traditional African cultures as well as a white supremacist willingness to recognize physical but not intellectual talents among black people. And, finally, some stereotypes may have nothing but the most tenuous relation to anything real, whether political or cultural. What relation or lack of relation there may be, though, cannot be predicted in advance of attention to the racial group's past and present.

Throughout the preceding discussions of education, interracial marriage, and stereotyping, a crucially important theme emerges. In each case, a political account of race can be credited with insight into the ways that the issue involves unfair distinctions and divisions between people that ought to be overcome. In each case, however, paying attention to culture is necessary for appreciating how the issue also involves legitimate forms of difference, that is, differences that need not be overcome but rather affirmed and appreciated. My claim that culture and politics are equally fundamental to race in the present can be understood as the claim that there can be no justification in assuming, before examining an issue involving racial difference, that the ways in which people are different from each other in this case will be the unfair kind or the legitimate kind, although the best bet will be that both kinds are involved. The normative implication of this view is that dedication to fighting racism requires sensitivity to racism's ability to operate in two seemingly contradictory ways: it creates and sustains difference where there ought to be none, and it disparages and suppresses difference where it ought to be respected and valued. Achieving victory over racism involves arriving at the point where the first kind of difference is no more, while the second kind of difference is uninhibited in flourishing.

This brings up my final point: my opposition to the political constructionist tenet that racial difference would no longer exist if equality were to be achieved. If races are at present partly cultural constructions, then the end of racial hierarchy has the potential to usher in a condition of racial equality, where races as cultural groups coexist in an egalitarian manner, rather than a post-racial era in which there are no more races. I do not deny that the latter outcome is possible—as a social constructionist, I accept that just as races came into existence, they may cease to exist. I deny, however, that their ceasing to exist is a necessary condition for or consequence of the end of racism. Furthermore, as someone of sub-Saharan African descent, I personally desire the indefinite persistence of black people as a cultural group.

Despite political constructionism's dominance, I take my position here to be the more intuitive one. What could make the political constructionist view true? Even if you suspect that it is *most likely* that we would need to mix together until appearance gave no clue as to ancestry before racism would end, that is not yet to say that it is simply *impossible* that we could eliminate relative advantage and disadvantage while still identifying as black, white, Polynesian, etc. The political constructionist can make the move, however, of refraining from claiming that that would be impossible and claiming instead that, under conditions of equality, identifications of these sorts would no longer count as identifications with races. Haslanger, for example, has considered the possibility that groups that are otherwise like races but are not "hierarchically organized" might be called "ethnicities."[54]

---

54. Haslanger, *Resisting Reality*, 245.

I reject this move, both Haslanger's specific version (as 'race' ought not to be confused with 'ethnicity') and the general idea that we should call races something else after the achievement of equality. I take it to be both intuitive from an everyday perspective and expressive of a social constructionist highlighting of historical development to hold that people's continued attachment to being black, for example, in a post-racist world would remain an attachment to a race. It would remain, that is, identification with a group distinguished by appearance and ancestry but made distinguishable in these ways through social significance.

3

HOW TO BE A BIOLOGICAL RACIAL REALIST

Quayshawn Spencer

3.1. Introduction

"There's an echogenic intracardiac focus (EIF) on the ultrasound image." That is what I heard during the second trimester ultrasound exam for the mother of my first child. Those are not words that any parent wants to hear. An EIF is a small bright spot on an ultrasound image that represents a calcification in the heart of a fetus. The scary thing about spotting an EIF is that EIF is correlated with having a fetus with an abnormal number of chromosomes in all or some of its cells, a state called 'aneuploidy' in medical jargon. Furthermore, aneuploidy usually (but not always) causes a genetic disorder in the child. For instance, a fetus with an extra chromosome 21 in all of its cells (a state called 'trisomy 21') usually develops Down Syndrome.[1] Other genetic disorders that arise from aneuploidy are Patau Syndrome (caused by trisomy 13), Edwards Syndrome (caused by trisomy 18), and Turner Syndrome (caused by monosomy X).[2]

The next step after spotting an EIF is to assess whether the chance of having an aneuploidal fetus is high enough to warrant doing an amniocentesis, which is a procedure where amniotic fluid is extracted from the mother and the fetal cells are tested for aneuploidy. But an amniocentesis is not risk-free. Doing an amniocentesis during the second trimester will result in a miscarriage in 2.5% of instances for women 20–34 years old (Papantoniou et al.

---

1. However, there are benign aneuploidies. For instance, a fetus with trisomy 21 in some of its cells instead of all of them will develop "mosaic Down Syndrome," which is benign if few enough cells are affected.

2. A person has *monosomy X* just in case she has one X chromosome and no other sex chromosome in all of her non-reproductive cells.

2001, 1055). So, an amniocentesis is inadvisable if the chance of having an aneuploidal fetus is lower than the chance of having a miscarriage from an amniocentesis. Here is where things got interesting. Our risk assessment was very short. The obstetrician said, "I wouldn't recommend an amniocentesis because she's Asian. EIF is a common occurrence for Asian mothers."

While I was delighted to hear the recommendation, I was also skeptical. How good was our obstetrician's reasoning? In particular, was she justified in using *race* as a relevant factor in her risk assessment? After all, what we are trying to do is assess the risk of aneuploidy in a fetus, and aneuploidy is a purely biological condition. What does that have to do with the mother's race? So I did some research. It turns out that T. D. Shipp et al. (2000) conducted a landmark study on whether there are racial differences in EIF frequencies among expectant mothers, and whether any such differences (if they exist) are caused by racial differences in having an aneuploidal fetus among expectant mothers.

Shipp et al. (2000, 461) divided mothers into Asian, Black, White, and Unknown. Next, the authors found that the EIF rates for Asian, Black, White, and Unknown mothers were 30.4%, 5.9%, 10.5%, and 11.1%, respectively, but that only one fetus had aneuploidy and it was from a White mother (Shipp et al. 2000, 461).[3] Given the sample sizes for each race, it follows that the average EIF rate for the sample was 12.1%, which is much lower than the 30.4% seen in Asian mothers.[4] Furthermore, using the definition of a conditional probability, a frequentist interpretation of the probability of an event, and the results from this study, it follows that the probability of having an aneuploidal fetus given that an EIF is observed on the mother's second trimester ultrasound image (call it '$\Pr\{Aneuploidy \mid EIF\}$') is 1 out of 59, or $\approx 1.7\%$, and that the probability of having an aneuploidal fetus given that an EIF is observed on an Asian mother's second trimester ultrasound image (call it '$\Pr\{Aneuploidy \mid EIF \cap Asian\}$') is less than or equal to 1 out of 14 ($\leq 7.1\%$).[5]

---

3. The fetus had monosomy X in some, but not all, of its non-reproductive cells and was diagnosed with mosaic Turner Syndrome.

4. Shipp et al. (2000, 461) sampled 46, 34, 400, and 9 mothers from the Asian, Black, White, and Unknown races, respectively.

5. I say "less than or equal to" instead of "less than" here because Shipp et al. were unable to follow up with one of the Asian mothers to determine whether her child had aneuploidy. See Shipp et al. (2000, 461).

Furthermore, these probabilities are not unique to Shipp et al. (2000). S. H. Tran et al. (2005) did a follow-up study on 7,480 mothers and found that $\Pr\{\text{Aneuploidy}|\text{EIF}\} = \frac{9}{309}$ ($\approx 2.9\%$) and $\Pr\{\text{Aneuploidy}|\text{EIF} \cap \text{Asian}\} = \frac{3}{83}$ ($\approx 3.6\%$). While Tran et al.'s $\Pr\{\text{Aneuploidy}|\text{EIF}\}$ value is slightly higher than Shipp et al.'s,[6] their $\Pr\{\text{Aneuploidy}|\text{EIF} \cap \text{Asian}\}$ values and the pattern that the race of the mother matters are consistent with Shipp et al.'s study.

Given that research, two things became clear to me. First, the probabilistic reasoning of our obstetrician was flawed. While our obstetrician was correct that EIF is a more common occurrence for Asian mothers compared to mothers overall, the latter is because aneuploidal fetuses are more common in Asian mothers! Moreover, it takes a large sample of expectant mothers to see that. Second, our obstetrician was correct that race matters in calculating the risk of having an aneuploidal fetus. So, I did a calculation of my own using the $\Pr\{\text{Aneuploidy}|\text{EIF} \cap \text{Asian}\}$ value from Tran et al. (2005) and determined that an amniocentesis was unwarranted, and not because of a miscarriage risk, but because of the test's false-positive rate for detecting aneuploidy!

Stories like the preceding raise the interesting philosophical question of whether race is biologically real. While I—as a concerned parent— interpreted the research as showing that race matters in medical genetics, many medical scholars would discourage such an interpretation. For instance, Michael Yudell et al. (2016, 564–565) have argued that "racial classifications do not make sense in terms of genetics," and, thus, to use race as an indicator of human genetic diversity in any way is "problematic at best and harmful at worst." In truth, there are three routes that one can take to explain the higher occurrence of aneuploidal fetuses in Asian mothers in the medical studies I discussed.

One route is to look for a purely biological explanation, such as differences in medically relevant allele frequencies between Asian mothers and mothers of other races.[7] Another route is to look for a purely social explanation. For

---

6. This might be explained by the fact that 57% of the mothers in Tran et al. sample were 35 or older, which is itself a risk factor for having an aneuploidal fetus. See Tran et al. (2005, 159).

7. For instance, one could look at the alleles that affect spindle checkpoint. *Spindle checkpoint* is a series of checks during gametogenesis that reduce the probability of chromosomal nondisjunction (the most frequent cause of aneuploidy) (May and Hardwick 2006).

instance, neither Shipp et al. (2000) nor Tran et al. (2005) report the average age of Asian mothers in their samples. Since we know that a woman's risk of having an aneuploidal fetus increases with age, the reason why Asian mothers in these studies displayed a higher risk for having an aneuploidal fetus might have been because they were, on average, getting pregnant at a much later age than mothers of all other races. Yet a third route is to look for a biosocial explanation. For instance, Shannon Sullivan (2013) has highlighted how epigenetic processes—such as inheritable DNA methylation acquired from diet, pollution, or stress—can explain some racial disparities in health.[8] So, that could be what is happening in this case.

Hence, we have an interesting and unsettled philosophical question about whether (and, if so, how) race matters in calculating someone's risk for being born with a genetic disorder. Furthermore, answering that question encourages a position on the biological reality of race.[9] If you think that race is not biologically real, then it probably would not make sense to you to include race in a calculation of someone's risk for developing a genetic disorder. For instance, people who think that race does not exist or that race is wholly socially real and not at all biologically real would be baffled by such a risk assessment. However, if you think that race is biologically real, then whether race is relevant in such calculations is a sensible question to ask. Of course, there are other good reasons for asking whether race is biologically real, but its relevance to medical genetics is sufficient to warrant philosophical attention.[10]

What does the question "Is race biologically real?" mean? Well, first, I want to engage with my coauthors, and second, I want to engage with people in the medical profession struggling with whether race should be used in genetic disorder risk assessments and in other ways relevant to medical genetics. Since both groups are interested, to some extent, in 'race' as it is used

---

8. An *epigenetic* process is any inheritable process in an organism that alters its gene activity without altering its genetic sequence (Weinhold 2006, A163). There are three paradigm examples of epigenetic processes: histone acetylation (which causes DNA to unwrap itself from histones, making genes available for expression), DNA methylation (which involves methylation at the cytosine bases in front of a gene, thus preventing that gene's expression), and mRNA silencing from microRNA (which is when non-protein-coding RNA halts gene expression by deactivating protein-coding RNA).

9. I say "encourages" instead of "presupposes" because it is possible for something to not be biologically real but to be a reliable indicator for something that is biologically real.

10. In fact, my personal interest in whether race is biologically real came from reading *The Bell Curve* and wondering whether the authors were confused when they posited a "genetic component" to the average IQ score differences among Blacks, Whites, and East Asians (Herrnstein and Murray 1996, 299).

to classify people in current, ordinary American English, that is the way I will understand 'race' in the question.[11]

For instance, in Joshua Glasgow's *A Theory of Race*, he explicitly states that he is interested in what 'race' means according to "competent English speakers in the United States" (Glasgow 2009, 3). He also focuses on "contemporary mainstream discourse" in that linguistic group (Glasgow 2009, 8). Also, in Sally Haslanger's *Resisting Reality,* she states that she is interested in the "single or dominant public meaning (or folk concept) of 'race' " as it is used among "competent users of English" (Haslanger 2012, 304). While Haslanger does not limit her focus to American English speakers, she is certainly interested in how people are "currently racialized in the United States" (Haslanger 2012, 308).

Finally, in Chike Jeffers's "The Cultural Theory of Race," he assumes a combination of Paul Taylor's and Michael Hardimon's definitions for 'race' (Jeffers 2013, footnote 62). Furthermore, Taylor (2013, 20) is upfront about his primary interest in "contemporary US conceptions of race" and its "English" roots. Also, Hardimon (2017, 27) has recently clarified that his focus is "ordinary uses of the English word 'race' and its cognates."

As for engaging with people in the medical profession, there are certainly many medical scientists and healthcare providers who do not care about how 'race' is used in American English. However, many of them do. For instance, both Neil Risch et al. (2002, 5) and Esteban Burchard et al. (2003, 1171) have argued that the racial scheme used on the "2000 US Census" is relevant to studying and treating human genetic diseases.

But there is a second ambiguity lurking here, namely, what I mean by a "biologically real" entity. All I will say right now is that I intend to use the term 'biologically real entity' in a way that adequately captures all of the entities that are used in empirically successful biology (e.g., the monophyletic group, the TYRP1 gene, the hypothalamus, etc.) and that adequately rules out all of the entities that are not (e.g., the monobaramin, the feeble-mindedness gene, the destructiveness organ, etc.).[12] However, I will offer a

---

11. For the rest of this chapter and Chapter 7, I will drop the phrase "to classify people" when talking about 'race' usage in current and ordinary American English. Instead, I'll just presuppose that the usage of 'race' in this context is about classifying people. I'll also stop modifying the noun 'American English' with "current" and "ordinary" as well for the rest of this chapter and Chapter 7, and, instead, I will just presuppose these modifiers when I talk about American English.

12. The monobaramin is the fundamental unit of classification in baraminology, which is a creation-science version of taxonomy. See Wood (2006, 151) for its definition. The

particular conception of a biologically real entity when I defend my answer to the question of interest. So, for clarity, the question I will answer is whether race is biologically real, and, more specifically, whether race—in any way that 'race' is used in American English—is real in the same way as entities like the monophyletic group, the TYRP1 gene, and the hypothalamus. My answer to this question is a highly qualified 'yes.'

3.2. OMB Race Talk as a US Race Talk

Suppose a *race talk* is a discourse that uses 'race' (or a synonym) to classify people into subgroups. Suppose the subgroups picked out in a race talk are *races* and the names of races are *race terms*. Also, for ease of discussion, I will call any race talk that occurs in American English a *US race talk*.[13] While this jargon is new, I consider it to be a thinner version of Taylor's (2013, 28) "race-talk." According to Taylor (2013, 16–18), a race-talk is any discourse that utilizes "race thinking," and race thinking is "a way of assigning generic meaning to human bodies and bloodlines," by which he means the activity of drawing "distant" inferences about a group of people from "bodily appearance and ancestry." While I like Taylor's definition of 'race-talk,' we will soon see why it is too thick to capture the diverse ways in which groups of people are called 'races' in American English.

One US race talk that is widely used by current Americans is *OMB race talk*. OMB race talk is any race talk that uses the meaning of 'race' that's currently adopted by the Office of Management and Budget (OMB), which is the largest office in the executive branch of the US government. Also, by 'currently adopted' I mean the race talk that the OMB endorses on the date that I'm writing this chapter, not the race talk that the OMB happens to endorse when this chapter is being read. In OMB race talk, the races are American Indians, Asians, Blacks, Pacific Islanders, and Whites. Hispanics are not a race in OMB race talk, but rather, are an ethnicity composed of people from

---

feeble-mindedness gene is a fictional gene that was often referred to by eugenicists. For example, see Davenport (1917, 365). The destructiveness organ is a fictional organ in animal brains that was believed to exist by phrenologists. See Combe (1853, 256–276) for a discussion of this organ.

13. Note that I am using 'US race talk' differently here than how I used it in Spencer (2014). In Spencer (2014, 1026), I used 'US race talk' to name the race talk that has the widest-used meaning of 'race' in the US that is also used by a majority of US citizens.

Table 3.1 The OMB's "Definitions" for Each of Its Races According to Federal Register Document 97-28653

American Indian or Alaska Native—A person having origins in any of the original peoples of North and South America (including Central America) and who maintains tribal affiliation or community attachment.

Asian—A person having origins in any of the original peoples of the Far East, Southeast Asia, or the Indian subcontinent including, for example, Cambodia, China, India, Japan, Korea, Malaysia, Pakistan, the Philippine Islands, Thailand, and Vietnam.

Black or African American—A person having origins in any of the black racial groups of Africa.

Native Hawaiian or Other Pacific Islander—A person having origins in any of the original peoples of Hawaii, Guam, Samoa, or other Pacific Islands.

White—A person having origins in any of the original peoples of Europe, the Middle East, or North Africa.

---

multiple races.[14] Furthermore, according to the OMB, people can belong to more than one race at a time. In Table 3.1, I have listed what the OMB calls its "definitions" for each of its race terms according to the federal register document where the OMB introduces its racial scheme; a document called "97-28653."

OMB race talk usually occurs in formal communication among Americans and usually involves one or more persons self-reporting their race(s) to another party. For example, it is not uncommon for Americans to engage in OMB race talk when applying to college, applying for a job, applying for a mortgage loan, applying for a birth certificate, filling out a health provider survey, filling out a child-care registration request form, or so forth. See the following figures for some evidence.

Figure 3.1 is a screenshot of the race and ethnicity questions on the 2016 college application for Penn State. Figure 3.2 is a screenshot of the race and ethnicity question on the 2016 registration request form for a child-care center in Pennsylvania. Figure 3.3 is a screenshot of the race and ethnicity questions on a 2016 Starbucks' job application for a barista position.

---

14. While 'Latino' is a synonym for 'Hispanic' in OMB race talk, I will primarily use 'Hispanic' to talk about Hispanics in this chapter.

8 Racial/ethnic background

Is your ethnicity Hispanic/Latino (Cuban, Mexican, Puerto Rican, South or Central American, or other Spanish culture of origin)?

☐ Yes ☐ No

What is your race? (Select all that apply.)

☐ White
☐ Black or African American
☐ Asian
☐ American Indian or Alaska Native
☐ Native Hawaiian or other Pacific Islander

FIGURE 3.1. Question 8 on Pennsylvania State University's 2016 undergraduate application.

Part 6. Participant's ethnic and racial identities (optional)

Mark one ethnic Identity:	Mark one or more racial Identities:	
☐ Hispanic or Latino	☐ Asian	☐ American Indian or Alaska Native
☐ Not Hispanic or Latino	☐ White	☐ Native Hawaiian or Other Pacific Islander
	☐ Black or African American	

FIGURE 3.2. The race and ethnicity questions on Today's Child Learning Centers' 2016 child-care registration request form.

The OMB began regulating race talk among federal agencies in 1977 with the introduction of Directive No. 15, which is a statistical policy directive that requires any federal agency in the United States that uses race talk in official business to classify people into races in a way that is translatable into OMB's racial scheme. From the Department of Education to the Centers for Disease Control and Prevention, all federal agencies in the United States must follow Directive No. 15.[15]

---

15. Incidentally, Directive No. 15 is one reason why the OMB's racial scheme is used outside of the US government. For instance, because the US Department of Education (USDE) has to comply with Directive No. 15, it requires all educational institutions that receive USDE funding to use OMB's racial scheme when reporting racial and ethnic data to the USDE. This is why many American colleges and universities use OMB's racial scheme on their college applications. See document E7-20613 in the federal register.

Are you Hispanic or Latino? (A person of Cuban, Mexican, Puerto Rican, South or Central American, or other Spanish culture origin, regardless of race)
O Yes
◉ No
O I do not wish to provide this information

Race:
O American Indian or Alaska Native – A person having origins in any of the original peoples of North and South America (including Central America), and who maintain tribal affiliation or community attachment.
O Asian – A person having origins In any of the original peoples of the Far East, Southeast Asia, or the Indian Subcontinent, including, for example, Cambodia, China, India, Japan, Korea, Malaysia, Pakistan, the Philippine Islands, Thailand, and Vietnam.
◉ Black or African American – A person having origins in any of the black racial groups of Africa.
O Native Hawaiian or Other Pacific Islander – A person having origins in *any* of the peoples of Hawaii, Guam, Samoa, or other Pacific Islands.
O White – A person having origins In any of the original peoples of Europe, the Middle East, or North Africa.
O Two or More Races – A person who identifies with two or more race/ethnic categories named above.
O I do not wish to provide this information.

FIGURE 3.3. The race and ethnicity questions on Starbucks' 2016 job application for a barista position.

In 1997, the OMB revised its race talk to include only the five races that it uses today. In that revision, the OMB clarified that the purpose of Directive No. 15 is, first, "to provide consistent data on race and ethnicity throughout the Federal Government," and second, "to enforce civil rights laws" (OMB 1997, 58782). Also, the OMB (1997, 58782) said that it revised its race talk in 1997 in order to deal with concerns about its 1977 race talk as being outdated due to a significant rise in "immigration" and "interracial marriages" in the United States since 1977. To deal with these concerns, the OMB included the people indigenous to Central and South America in its American Indian race (e.g., Maya, Pima, Quechua, etc.), recognized Asians and Pacific Islanders as two distinct races, dropped its Asian or Pacific Islander race, and allowed people to be a member of more than one race.

Despite the empirical support that I have provided for the claim that OMB race talk is a US race talk, this claim is not uncontroversial. For instance, someone might object to OMB race talk as being an *ordinary* race talk. Since a US race talk must be an ordinary race talk (given how I have defined it), the objection would imply that OMB race talk is not a US race talk. Perhaps the motivation for such an objection is that in order to be an ordinary race talk, it is not sufficient to be a race talk that occurs in ordinary discourse (which is how I have defined it in the preceding). Rather, the race talk must be "how ordinary people conceive of race," which may differ from how a group of "experts" conceive of race (Glasgow 2009, 48).

This is a good concern. It is important to distinguish between ordinary race talk and "specialist" race talk among experts because, first, the two can harbor different meanings of 'race,' and second, I am interested in exploring ordinary race talk in this chapter (Glasgow 2009, 48). Furthermore, OMB race talk is a specialist race talk. It is the default race talk that agencies in the US government use. With that said, I am not convinced that we should limit what an ordinary race talk is to only those race talks that embody "how ordinary people conceive of race," and that is because it assumes that ordinary race talk does not partake in a linguistic division of labor.

Notice that limiting what an ordinary race talk is to what ordinary people conceive about race implicitly assumes that ordinary people are the correct people to consult to find out the meaning of the terms they are using. Sometimes the latter is not a bad assumption. For instance, most English-speaking Americans should be able to define 'foot' (the unit of measurement), at least in terms of inches. However, the latter assumption is false for a large portion of terms used by ordinary people. In cases where

(3.1) ordinary speakers intend a term t to refer,
(3.2) ordinary speakers intend t to refer to the same object that a group of experts on t intends t to refer to, but
(3.3) ordinary speakers do not know or do not agree on what t means

it turns out that the meaning of t is whatever that group of experts means by t. The fact that some terms used by ordinary speakers have a meaning determined by a group of experts was first recognized by Hilary Putnam (1973, 704), and he called this sociolinguistic phenomenon a "division of linguistic labor." For example, consider the term 'DNA' in American English.

The term satisfies (3.1) because Americans do not use 'DNA' as if it is a term with no referent, like, say, 'unicorn.' Americans also talk about DNA with an intention to talk about the same stuff as biochemists, geneticists, and other scientists who are experts on DNA, thus satisfying (3.2). However, most Americans do not know what DNA is. For instance, if you think that DNA is just the genetic material of living things, you're wrong. For one, the genetic material of all living things on earth used to be RNA.[16] But also, it is possible for something to be a strand of DNA without ever having played the role of being genetic material (e.g., DNA synthesized in a lab). Rather, biochemists, geneticists, and other DNA experts define 'DNA' as 'a polymer of deoxyribonucleotides' (Stryer 1995, 75–76).

While it is true that some terms used in ordinary discourse seem to be involved in a division of linguistic labor but are not actually involved in a division of linguistic labor,[17] there is no reliable way to know which ones are and which ones are not without empirical investigation. So, as long as it is *possible* that terms used in ordinary discourse (including 'race') are involved in a linguistic division of labor, we should not require ordinary race talk to be "how ordinary people conceive of race" (Glasgow 2009, 49). Rather, we should define ordinary race talk as race talk used in ordinary discourse, and pay attention to "how ordinary people conceive of race" in an ordinary race talk only after ruling out the possibility that 'race' is involved in a division of linguistic labor. However, one interesting fact about OMB race talk is that it *is* involved in a division of linguistic labor.

3.3. The Meanings of 'Race' and Race Terms in OMB Race Talk

Remember that Putnam's conditions for a term t having a meaning that is determined by a group of experts on t, call it ' e ,' are as follows: (3.1) ordinary speakers intend t to refer, (3.2) ordinary speakers intend t to refer to the same object that e intends t to refer to, and (3.3) ordinary speakers do not know or do not agree on what t means. It turns out that 'race' and race terms in OMB race talk satisfy (3.1)–(3.3), and here is why.

First, some solid evidence that American English speakers intend 'race' and race terms to refer in OMB race talk is that the overwhelming majority of Americans self-report one or more race when queried for their race in that race talk. For example, on the 2010 US Census questionnaire, there were 299.7 million respondents, and a whopping 93.8% self-reported one or more OMB race, while just 6.2% reported "Some Other Race" (Humes et al. 2011,

---

16. This is known as *the RNA world hypothesis*, and it was independently invented by Francis Crick, Leslie Orgel, and Carl Woese in the late 1960s. See Robertson and Joyce (2012) for a discussion of the hypothesis.

17. For some examples, see Dupré (1981, 74–75).

4). That statistic would be hard to explain if American English speakers did not intend 'race' and race terms to refer in OMB race talk.

Next, there are strange patterns in how American English speakers self-report their OMB race that would be hard to explain if (3.2) were not true for 'race' and race terms in OMB race talk. First, on the 2000 US Census questionnaire—which is the most recent one that collected data on Arab ancestry—80–97% of Arab Americans self-reported 'White' (de la Cruz and Brittingham 2003, 8). This result might seem strange, but it is not strange if Arab Americans intend to use 'White' (in OMB race talk) in the same way that the OMB uses it. After all, in OMB race talk, White is not a narrow group limited to Europeans, European Americans, and the like. Rather, White is a broad group that includes Arabs, Persians, Jews, and other ethnic groups originating from the Middle East and North Africa.

Second, on the 2010 US Census questionnaire, the majority of Hispanic Americans self-reported in a way that corresponded to their primary ancestry in three continental groups.[18] The most populous Hispanic American national origin groups are Mexicans (58.7%), Puerto Ricans (15.1%), Cubans (3.3%), Salvadorians (3.0%), and Dominicans (2.7%).[19] Furthermore, we know from genetic studies that Cuban Americans, Puerto Rican Americans, Dominican Americans, and Mexican Americans have, on average, 73%, 62%, 50%, and 47% "Caucasian" ancestry, respectively (Manichaikul et al. 2012, 4).[20] Moreover, what is interesting here is that the average Caucasian ancestry of a Hispanic American national origin group nicely correlates with the proportion of that group that self-reports 'White' alone in OMB race talk.

---

18. Actually, the correct term to use here is 'genomic ancestry.' I will explain why later. Also, the continental groups I'm referencing are "Caucasian, African, and Native American" (Manichaikul et al. 2012, 1). Finally, I'm looking at how Hispanic Americans' racial self-reporting correlates with their primary ancestry in these three continental groups because just looking at racial self-reporting for Hispanic Americans as a group is likely to be misleading (due to confounding), and it's plausible to think that Hispanic Americans' racial self-reporting is correlated to this particular kind of ancestry.

19. These are all of the Hispanic national origin groups that composed ≥2.5% of total Hispanic Americans according to 2010 US Census data, including Puerto Rican residents. See Ennis et al. (2011, 14) and USCB (2010).

20. The estimate for Salvadorian Americans is missing because they have not yet been singled out in genetic studies of Hispanic Americans. Also, while I am just reporting estimates from Manichaikul et al. (2012), their estimates fall within the 95% confidence interval of estimates from other studies, such as the "European ancestry" estimates for Mexican and Puerto Rican Americans in Risch et al. (2009, 3).

For instance, on the 2010 US Census questionnaire, the proportion of Cuban Americans, Puerto Rican Americans, Mexican Americans, and Dominican Americans who self-reported 'White' alone was 85.4%, 63.2%, 52.8%, and 29.6%, respectively (Ennis et al. 2011, 14). Conducting a linear regression analysis shows that the average Caucasian ancestry of a Hispanic American national origin group positively and highly correlates (r = +0.864) with the proportion of that group that self-reported 'White' alone on the 2010 US Census questionnaire.[21] This pattern would be hard to explain if (3.2) were not true for 'race' and race terms in OMB race talk.

Now, one could worry that the statistic that I reported about the racial self-reporting of Arab Americans in OMB race talk is outdated.[22] After all, a lot has changed for Arab Americans since September 11, 2001 (or '9/11'). Most importantly, Arab Americans have experienced many more hate crimes since then due to being stereotyped as Muslim terrorists[23]—so much so that in February 2015, the Federal Bureau of Investigation (FBI) added a new uniform crime reporting bias code—code 31—to track hate crimes against Arab Americans (FBI 2015, table 1).

While a lot has changed for Arab Americans since 9/11, whether and how much those changes have affected their racial self-reporting in OMB race talk is testable. For instance, if we look at the "Some Other Race" respondents to the 2010 US Census questionnaire in the 50 states and the District of Columbia, and compare that number to the USCB's 2010 estimate for the number of Arab Americans, we can estimate that the maximum percentage of Arab Americans who wrote in some other race (e.g., Arab, Middle Eastern, etc.) on the 2010 US Census questionnaire was 36.7%.[24] For context, the

---

21. The linear regression equation I used to make this calculation is: $Y = 1.6812X - 39.761$.

22. For instance, I would expect Joshua Glasgow, Linda Alcoff, and Paul Taylor to have this concern. See Glasgow (2003, 472; 2009, 96), Alcoff (2006, 258), and Taylor (2013, 146–147).

23. What is so absurd about this stereotype is that the overwhelming majority of Arab Americans are not even Muslim! For instance, in Alia Malek's myth-busting book *A Country Called Amreeka,* she reports that just 24% of Arab Americans are Muslim (Malek 2009, ix–x). Rather, the overwhelming majority of Arab Americans are Christian (Malek 2009, x).

24. I arrived at this estimate in the following way. I started by using the USCB's 2010 American Community Survey one-year estimate for the number of Arab Americans in 2010 (1,698,570). Next, I assumed that the percentage of Arab Americans who self-reported as Hispanic on the 2010 US Census questionnaire was the same as the percentage who did so on the 2000 US Census questionnaire, which was 3.2% (de la Cruz and Brittingham 2003, 8). Thus, there should have been 54,354 Hispanic Arab Americans in 2010. Next, I assumed that the percentage of Arab Americans who self-reported as Hispanic on the 2010 US Census questionnaire had

"Some Other Race" write-in rate for Mexican Americans on the 2010 US Census questionnaire was 39.5% (Ennis et al. 2011, 14).

However, remember, the latter is a maximum estimate. In fact, it assumes that all of the non-Hispanic "Some Other Race" write-ins on the 2010 US Census questionnaire came from Arab Americans, which is almost certainly false. So, as it turns out, the aftermath of 9/11 has not affected the racial self-reporting of *most* Arab Americans ($\geq 63.3\%$) in OMB race talk. Furthermore, this result should not be too surprising. According to the Pew Research Center, 94% of Jewish Americans self-report as "non-Hispanic white," and this is despite the fact that the rate of anti-Semitic hate crimes is very high in the United States (Lugo et al. 2013, 46; FBI 2014).

So far, I have provided empirical support for (3.1) and (3.2) holding for 'race' and race terms in OMB race talk. All that remains to be done to show that OMB race talk is involved in a division of linguistic labor is to show that American English speakers do not know or do not agree on what 'race' and race terms mean in OMB race talk. But this will be easy.

While there are lots of empirical studies that are relevant for supporting the claim that Americans do not share a common meaning for 'race' and race terms when engaging in OMB race talk, my favorite study is the focus group portion of the Alternative Questionnaire Experiment (AQE), which was conducted by Elizabeth Compton et al. (2013) for the USCB. The AQE focus group study is unusually informative for three reasons. First, it uses focus groups instead of surveys, and lots of useful, qualitative information can arise in focus groups that are hard to obtain from surveys. Second, it was explicitly designed to study how Americans use 'race' and race terms in OMB race talk (Compton et al. 2013, 68–69). Last, and most importantly, it is one of the few studies on how Americans use 'race' and race terms that uses a nationally representative sample of US adults.[25] So, what did they find?

---

the same "Some Other Race" reporting rate as Hispanic Americans overall, which was 36.7% (Humes et al. 2011, 6). Thus, there should have been 19,948 Arab Americans who reported both 'Hispanic' and 'some other race' on the 2010 US Census questionnaire. Next, I assumed that all of the non-Hispanic "Some Other Race" respondents on the 2010 US Census questionnaire (a total of 604,265 people) were Arab Americans (Humes et al. 2011, 6). Next, I added 19,948 and 604,265 to obtain a maximum value for the number of Arab Americans who self-reported "Some Other Race" on the 2010 US Census questionnaire, which, of course, turns out to be 36.7% of the number of Arab Americans in 2010.

25. For instance, while Hirschfeld (1996), Glasgow et al. (2009), Morning (2011), and Guo et al. (2014) have conducted relevant empirical studies for this topic, their samples of US adults are not nationally representative. However, see OMB (2000) for another nationally representative empirical study on how Americans use 'race' and race terms in OMB race talk.

One major finding was that there was "no consensus" on the definition of 'race' in OMB race talk (Compton et al. 2013, 70). Rather, "race was defined as skin color, ancestry, culture, etc." among focus group participants (Compton et al. 2013, 70). Another major finding was that many participants expressed confusion about why the White race included Arabs and why Hispanics were not a race (Compton et al. 2013, 70). But what was most fascinating was that the participants "recommended that these terms should be defined so respondents could better understand how to report" (Compton et al. 2013, 71). The first two major findings suggest that (3.3) is true for 'race' and race terms in OMB race talk, and the last major finding removes all doubt about whether 'race' and race terms are operating by a division of linguistic labor in OMB race talk. Here, the respondents are basically saying, "We are trying to racially self-report in the way the OMB wants us to, but we need more guidance!"

Now that we have solid evidence that 'race' and race terms are involved in a linguistic division of labor when used in OMB race talk, we can move on to figuring out what 'race' and race terms mean in OMB race talk by scrutinizing what the OMB intends these terms to mean. But let me back up a bit and talk about meaning. 'Meaning' is understood in different ways by academics. However, since I am interested in linguistic meaning, linguistic meaning is a prime area of research for philosophers of language, and since 76.6% of "specialists" in philosophy of language adopt a truth-conditional approach to the linguistic meaning of a name, I will adopt the truth-conditional approach to meaning to figure out what 'race' and race terms mean in OMB race talk (Bourget and Chalmers 2014, 483).[26] The truth-conditional approach to the meaning of a name is to see a name's meaning as the "contribution" it makes to the truth-conditions of propositions in which the name occurs (Perry 2001, 18).[27]

---

26. The operational definition used for a *specialist* in philosophy of language in this study was that of a "regular" faculty member in a "leading" department of philosophy in the English-speaking or analytic philosophy world who lists 'philosophy of language' as an area of specialization (Bourget and Chalmers 2014, 468). Also, "leading" was determined by having a score of 1.9 or above in the Philosophical Gourmet Report (PGR) or by being judged to be "comparable" to such schools by the editor of PGR, which, at that time, was Brian Leiter (Bourget and Chalmers 2014, 468).

27. To be clear, Perry (2001, 17) considers *meanings* to be the rules that assign content to types of expressions or subsentential expressions (e.g., names). However, Perry (2001, 18) does say that "ordinary" meaning is the same thing as content. So, what I'm calling *linguistic meaning* is what Perry calls *ordinary meaning* or *content*, not *meaning*. However, what philosophers of race are interested in when they talk about the meaning of 'race' is the content of 'race,' not the rules for assigning content to names.

For instance, suppose I want to know what 'Fab Five' means in the specialist English discourse of NCAA basketball talk, and suppose I want to know its truth-conditional meaning. Then, what I should do is figure out what I can substitute for 'Fab Five' in all of the propositions that include 'Fab Five' in the relevant context while maintaining the same truth-values. Historically, there are two ways of going about doing this. One way is to use a set of "identifying conditions" (conditions that competent users of a term use to pick out the referent of the term) (Perry 2001, 4). For example, we could define 'Fab Five' as "the 1991 recruited class for the Michigan Wolverines men's basketball team." But another way is to use the object that the term designates. For example, we could define 'Fab Five' as the set consisting of Juwan Howard, Ray Jackson, Jimmy King, Jalen Rose, and Chris Webber. The first approach is known as *descriptivism* among philosophers of language, while the second approach is known as *referentialism*.

There is an ongoing debate in the philosophy of race about whether descriptivism or referentialism is the best way to model an ordinary meaning of 'race.'[28] However, I do not want to take sides in this debate. Rather, I will assume that both approaches are respectable options, but that the best approach to use for 'race' and race terms in OMB race talk is the one that works best for these names. For instance, it is widely acknowledged among philosophers of language that non-referring names (e.g. 'feeble-mindedness gene,' 'Santa Claus,' etc.) are poorly modeled by referentialism (Perry 2001, 6–7).[29] So, it will be prudent to model the meanings for 'race' and race terms in OMB race talk as their referents only if these names refer.

Also, it is widely acknowledged among philosophers of language that descriptivism is a poor model for a name's meaning if assuming that the name's identifying conditions are its meaning results in getting the wrong truth-values for a large number of counterfactual or modal propositions in which the name occurs (Perry 2001, 5).[30] For instance, Saul Kripke (1980, 117) argued that 'yellow metal' is not the meaning of 'gold' because taking it to

---

28. For example, see Glasgow (2009, 20–26), Haslanger (2012, 429–445), and Glasgow (forthcoming).

29. 'Feeble-mindedness gene' was a name used in eugenics for what is now known to be a nonexistent gene.

30. A *counterfactual* proposition is a conditional where the antecedent intentionally states something that is false, such as "If the Golden State Warriors had won the 2016 NBA finals, then they would have had a better season." A *modal* proposition is a proposition that says something is or is not necessary or possible, such as, "LeBron James could have been the NBA's MVP in the 2015–16 season."

be so leads to several counterfactual conditionals with the wrong truth-value. One example that Kripke (1980, 118) gave was, "If the substance in South Africa that we call 'gold' were not actually yellow due to an optical illusion brought about from the South African atmosphere, then there would be no gold in South Africa." The correct truth-value for this counterfactual conditional is *false* according to Kripke (1980, 118), but if the meaning of 'gold' is 'yellow metal,' then this counterfactual conditional is *true*. So, it will be prudent to model the meaning of 'race' and race terms in OMB race talk as their identifying conditions only if doing so captures the correct truth-values for a large number of counterfactual and modal propositions in which these names occur.

Furthermore, I will judge whether 'race' and race terms refer in OMB race talk and how well the identifying conditions and referents (if there are any) for 'race' and race terms serve as truth-conditional meanings by appealing to what the OMB presently intends to pick out with 'race' and its race terms, both in the actual world and in non-actual, accessible possible worlds.[31]

First, let's look at what the OMB calls its "definitions" for its race terms. These are the identifying conditions that many American English speakers use to figure out how to self-report in OMB race talk. However, given what the OMB intends to pick out with its race terms, these identifying conditions are anything but *meanings*. Before the OMB introduced its revised racial scheme in 1997, it adopted 13 "principles" to guide that revision (OMB 1997, 58782).[32] According to principle 4, OMB race terms should pick out "population groups" in humans that are "comprehensive in coverage" and "nonduplicative" (OMB 1997, 58783). In other words, in the OMB's racial scheme, there are not supposed to be any unnecessary races, and every single member of the human species should belong to one or more races.[33]

---

31. Thus, I am adopting Kripke's (1980, 163) view that the referent of a name is fixed by the "present intentions" of the speaker (or speakers) that control its meaning. Also, I will be using quantified modal first-order free logic with a T interpretation of necessity and necessary identity to assign truth-values to propositions in all possible worlds accessible to the actual world. See Girle (2009, 14, 107) for its syntax rules and Girle (2009, 14–15, 39, 108, 133) for the meanings of important types of expressions in the language (e.g., its propositions, its logical constants, its necessary truths, etc.).

32. These principles were developed by a committee of more than 30 federal agencies put together by the OMB in 1993 whose job it was to explore various options for changing OMB's racial scheme (OMB 1997, 58782).

33. It is easy to see why the OMB wants this. Obtaining a racial classification like this would solve the problem of how to classify any US immigrant and any child born from an interracial mating in the US.

However, given what we know about human evolutionary history, the "definition" that the OMB provides for 'Black' makes all of the other OMB races unnecessary!

Remember that the OMB claims that the "definition" for 'Black' is "A person having origins in any of the black racial groups of Africa" (OMB 1997, 58789).[34] Also, the OMB has explicitly or tacitly recognized all of the following ethnic groups as examples of Blacks: African Americans, Afro-Brazilians, Cape Verdeans, Ethiopians, Haitians, Jamaicans, Louisiana Creoles, and Nigerians (OMB 1995, 44682; OMB 1997, 58789; OMB 2000, 28).[35] However, the problem here is that it is not just African Americans, Ethiopians, Jamaicans, and the like that are Black according to this definition. Rather, *all* humans are Black according to this definition given what we know about human evolutionary history.

First, according to the widest accepted theory on the evolution of human populations, all current human populations descend from a single population (of about 1,000 people) that resided in East Africa about 100,000 years ago (Cavalli-Sforza and Feldman 2003, 270). Second, according to the most widely accepted theory on the evolution of human skin pigmentation, all humans had dark skin until about 40,000–60,000 years ago, when we first left Africa and found ourselves in environments with low ultraviolet B light (Jablonski and Chaplin 2010, 8962). Together, these two facts imply that all living humans—every single one of us—descend from black-skinned people in Africa, and, thus, all of us are *Black* according to the OMB's "definition" for 'Black.' While that result makes the OMB's racial scheme "comprehensive in coverage," it also makes all OMB races except Blacks unnecessary, which is something that the OMB does not want.

Now, we could try to fix this problem by offering a more nuanced identifying condition for 'Black.' For instance, we could add 'recent' in front of 'origins' in the OMB's "definition" in order to try to fix the problem. However, adding such tweaks creates counterfactual problems. For example, suppose

---

34. The OMB is notoriously vague about what it means by 'racial groups.' However, it does not mean 'races,' since the OMB only acknowledges five races in its racial scheme and its "definition" for 'Black' is an attempt to define one of those races. However, given how the OMB uses 'racial groups,' I will interpret it as interchangeable with 'ethnic groups.'

35. For instance, the OMB rejected requests from Cape Verdean Americans and Louisiana Creole Americans to be recognized as distinct races because they can self-report as mixed Blacks (OMB 1995, 44682; OMB 1997, 58786).

that by 'recent' we mean 'before twenty-one generations ago.'[36] Furthermore, suppose that, contrary to how events actually unfolded, the English settlers who created the thirteen colonies that would eventually become the United States brought just one installment of black-skinned people from Africa (hereafter, *black Africans*) to the colonies for slave labor and forced that population to exclusively inbreed for twenty generations up until a generation t . Suppose we call these highly inbred people *American Africans* to contrast with African Americans, who are a mixed people. Also, suppose that, just as in the actual world, all human populations in this non-actual, accessible possible world descended from a single black African population. Then, since no American African at t has "recent origins" in any black African people, no American African at t is *Black* according to our revised definition for 'Black'! But there is more. Since no American African at t has any recent origin in any OMB race at all, this tweak prevents OMB's racial scheme from being "comprehensive in coverage" as well, which is a clear violation of principle 4.

Suppose we call the possible world in the preceding *the American African world*. The American African world is not "wholly metaphysical" (Hardimon 2013, 27; 2017, 45).[37] There are lots of human populations that are similar to American Africans in the actual world. For example, there are many unmixed Aboriginal Australians who do not possess "recent origins" from any of the original people to any of the geographic regions that the OMB mentions in its race term "definitions." Instead, unmixed Aboriginal Australians exclusively descend from the original people to Sahul, who arrived in Sahul 46–60 kya (where 1 kya is equal to 1,000 years) (McEvoy et al. 2010, 297).[38] Some examples of such populations are the Karryarra people of Western Australia, the Kuranda people of Queensland, and the Gunganji people of Queensland (Bergström et al. 2016, 810). Thus, there are many Aboriginal Australians who can go back at least 1,840 generations without finding a single ancestor

---

36. This is not an arbitrary number. Assuming that an average human generation is 25 years (which is standard in population genetics), twenty-one generations back from 2017 is 1492, the year that Europeans first colonized the Americas.

37. This is a phrase that Michael Hardimon uses to respond to a thought experiment of Glasgow's that attempts to show that sharing a common ancestry is not necessary to being a race in the ordinary English sense. See footnote 13 in Hardimon (2013) and Hardimon (2017, 45).

38. Sahul was a continuous landmass including present-day Australia, New Guinea, and Tasmania from at least 100 kya to about 10 kya.

from one of the original human populations to any geographic region that the OMB mentions in its race term "definitions."[39]

The problems that I have raised for considering the OMB's identifying condition for 'Black' as a meaning can be generated in an analogous way for each OMB race term. By that I mean, each of the "definitions" that the OMB provides for its race terms are inadequate to pick out the intended referents of those terms. Furthermore, while we could continue to try to tweak these identifying conditions to avoid each concern, a simpler explanation for what is going on here is that the OMB intends to pick out *ancestry groups* with its race terms, and since everyday American English is ill-equipped to articulate the essences of ancestry groups, we are better off taking the meanings of OMB race terms to be the objects they designate and leaving the task of articulating the nature of each race in OMB race talk to the experts on ancestry: geneticists.[40]

As for 'race' in OMB race talk, the OMB does not even attempt to give a definition for that term.[41] Furthermore, when names are used without any identifying conditions, but rather, as just tags for objects, that itself is *some* evidence that the name's meaning is just its referent.[42] For instance, in the city of Philadelphia, the name 'Penn' is just a tag for the University of Pennsylvania.[43]

Now, one could object here and try to offer a descriptive definition for 'race' in OMB race talk. For instance, perhaps the OMB is assuming what Hardimon (2003, 437; 2017, 27) calls "the ordinary concept of race," which is supposed to be a very thin concept of race that captures "ordinary uses of the English word 'race' and its cognates" (at least in the dominant use of 'race' in ordinary English). However, according to the ordinary concept of race,

---

39. Here, I'm making a conservative assumption of an average Aboriginal Australian generation of 25 years.

40. The term 'ancestry group' is not mine. It was coined by Marcus Feldman (2010, 151).

41. For evidence that the OMB does not attempt to provide a definition for 'race' in any of its publications on its racial scheme, see OMB (1995), OMB (1997), Wallman (1998), and OMB (2000).

42. I'm borrowing the locution "tags for objects" from Perry (2001, 4). However, the convention of talking about names with referential meanings as merely "tags" originates with Ruth Barcan Marcus (1961, 310).

43. I learned this fact the hard way when I first moved to Philadelphia and misinterpreted the name 'Penn' as a nickname for Pennsylvania State University in a casual conversation. I was quickly corrected!

"visually indistinguishable" races are impossible, but that situation is not impossible in the OMB's racial scheme (Hardimon 2003, 442).[44]

For instance, in the OMB's racial scheme, Melanesians are a Pacific Islander subgroup (OMB 1997, 58789). However, in biological anthropology, it is well known that Melanesians, on average, share the same visible racial traits as black Africans (e.g., dark skin, black hair, very curly hair, full lips, etc.).[45] Suppose that American Indians, Asians, Blacks, Whites, and Melanesians exist in a non-actual possible world accessible to ours, but that no non-Melanesian Pacific Islanders exist in that world. Suppose we call this world *the black Pacific Islander world*.

It's worth pointing out that the black Pacific Islander world is not a world that clashes with biological facts. The world could easily be generated from non-Melanesian Pacific Islanders engaging in enough interbreeding with unmixed White people to make all non-Melanesian Pacific Islander subgroups go extinct. Now, an important observation about the black Pacific Islander world is that it contains two OMB races that are visibly indistinguishable: Blacks and Pacific Islanders. Thus, Hardimon's ordinary concept of race is not as ordinary as he thought!

While we could tweak Hardimon's ordinary concept of race to attempt to achieve an adequate descriptive definition for 'race' in OMB race talk, that strategy is no more likely to work than our previous attempt to tweak the identifying condition for 'Black.' Rather, the simplest explanation for the way the OMB uses 'race' is that the term's meaning is just its referent. But now the question arises, what is that referent? In my previous work on OMB race talk, I discovered a surprising fact about how the OMB uses 'race' (Spencer 2014, 1028). The OMB never calls race a kind or a category, but rather, always calls race a set of categories or population groups. For instance, the OMB calls race a "set of categories" six times in 97-28653. This observation leads me to believe that the meaning of 'race' in OMB race talk is just the set of five races used in that race talk.

---

44. It's worth noting that many philosophers of race besides Hardimon think that the way 'race' is used in American English requires that races are not visibly indistinguishable. Some of these other proponents are Naomi Zack (2002, 37), Lawrence Blum (2002, 132), Glasgow (2009, 33), and Taylor (2013, 16). So, what I will say next applies equally well to these philosophers' theories of race as well.

45. See Spencer (2015, 50) for a discussion of this interesting fact. Also, by a "racial" trait I mean what Glasgow (2009, 86) means, which is one's skin color, facial features, hair type, and, sometimes, hair color.

While the result that the meaning of 'race' in OMB race talk is a *set* might be surprising at first, there are lots of names in American English that are used as tags for sets. For example, consider 'Fab Five.' That name is used as a tag in sports lingo for Juwan Howard, Ray Jackson, Jimmy King, Jalen Rose, and Chris Webber. Likewise, 'Twin Towers' is a name used as a tag in sports lingo for Tim Duncan and David Robinson. But more importantly, assuming that the meaning of 'race' in OMB race talk is just the set of five races in that race talk provides us with a large number of correct truth-values for related modal propositions. For example, given the referential approach, the following modal propositions possess the correct truth-value of *true*: "It is possible for there to be two visibly indistinguishable races" and "Pacific Islanders could be visibly indistinguishable from Blacks."[46]

Even though the referential approach has been fruitful so far, its utility will disappear if the things that I have been calling "referents" for 'race' and race terms in OMB race talk do not actually exist. While it is possible to defend the view that non-referring names have referential meanings, that defense is going to be a tough sell to many philosophers of language.[47] Thus, to convincingly defend my use of the referential approach, I need to show that the relevant terms refer, and, moreover, refer to what I have claimed they refer to. So, I need to show that OMB race terms refer to *real* ancestry groups in the human species, and I need to show that 'race' in OMB race talk refers to a *real* division of humans into ancestry groups.

3.4. The Nature and Reality of Race and the Races in OMB Race Talk

Before I begin, I should say more about how I will establish the reality of race and the races in OMB race talk. I will show that all of these entities are real in virtue of being biologically real entities. Unlike many philosophers of race, I will not require a biologically real entity to "exist objectively" or "independently of human interest" (Andreasen 1998, 209; Sundstrom 2002, 93).[48] Also, I will not require a biologically real entity to be a "primary or fundamental

---

46. I am assuming that the correct truth-value for these propositions is determined by how the OMB intends to use 'race' and its race terms, not my intuitions about what these truth-values should be.

47. Nevertheless, for one attempt to do so, see Braun (1993).

48. For other proponents of this way of defining 'biological racial realism,' see Mills (1998, 45–46), Zack (2002, 4–5), and Maglo et al. (2016, 2).

category in human population genetics," or otherwise be very important to biology (Maglo 2011, 363; Hochman 2013, 347). Rather, what I will mean by a *biologically real entity* is an epistemically useful and justified entity in a well-ordered research program in biology, which I will call a *genuine biological entity*. Furthermore, I am adopting this conception of a biologically real entity not because I want to defend a version of biological racial realism. Rather, I am adopting it because I think it adequately captures the collection of entities that are actually used in empirically successful biology (e.g., monophyletic group, TYRP1 gene, hypothalamus, etc.).

For instance, if we restrict the realm of biologically real entities to only those entities that exist independently of human interest, then we would have to tell population geneticists that they are wrong that "ethnic groups" in the human species (which exist only because of human interest) are real biological populations, such as the Han people of China, the Yoruba people of Nigeria, and the Maya people of Central America (Cavalli-Sforza 2005, 338–339). Also, if we restrict the realm of biologically real entities to only those that are very important to biology, then we would have to tell molecular geneticists that trivial alleles, such as the 93C allele from the TYRP1 gene, are not real because they are not important enough to biology.[49]

While the theory of a genuine biological entity is complex, the part of the theory that I will use is the part that designates an entity *e* as biologically real if

(3.4) *e* is useful for generating a theory *t* in a biological research program *p*,

(3.5) using *e* to generate *t* is warranted according to the epistemic values of *p* to explain or predict an observational law of *p*, and

(3.6) *p* has coherent and well-motivated aims, competitive predictive power, and frequent cross-checks (Spencer 2012, 193).[50]

I will assume that population genetics satisfies (3.6). Population genetics has been such an empirically successful research program in biology, it is not worth our time to detail exactly how it satisfies (3.6). Thus, in order to show that race and the races in OMB race talk are biologically real, all

49. The only function of the 93C allele is coding for blond hair in some Melanesian people. See Kenny et al. (2012).

50. For all of the details of this theory, see Spencer (2012) or Spencer (2016).

I need to do is show that they satisfy (3.4) and (3.5) for population genetics. To do this, I will use recent results from human population structure analysis.

A common research project in population genetics is to figure out all of the ways that a species subdivides into biological populations. This is called an analysis of "population structure" for that species, and each subdivision is called a "population subdivision" of that species (Hartl and Clark 2007, 275). There are many ways that population geneticists go about conducting population structure analysis, but a common method today is to use patterns in allele frequencies across a species' organisms to detect that species' *demes* (which are its randomly mating groups of organisms), and then to use patterns in allele frequencies across a species' demes to detect all other levels of population structure in that species. In essence, the method is to use different types of "genetic structure" to infer all of the population subdivisions in a species (Cavalli-Sforza 2005, 338).

In a landmark study by Noah Rosenberg et al. (2002), which was cross-checked by Rosenberg et al. (2005), five levels of genetic structure were detected among putative human demes. Furthermore, one of those levels is relevant for us because it is where we find both a human population subdivision and the referents for 'race' and race terms in OMB race talk. In Figure 3.4 are the genetic structure results from Rosenberg et al. (2005).

In Figure 3.4, Rosenberg et al. are reporting five levels of genetic structure among putative human demes. They discovered these levels from analyzing 993 loci in the human autosome that lack protein-coding alleles from 1,048 people in 52 ethnic groups that represent our entire geographic range, using a fuzzy genetic clustering algorithm in a computer program known as *structure*.[51] Each level is named according to the number of "genetic clusters" in the subdivision (Rosenberg et al. 2005, 660). So, for example, $K = 3$ is the level with three genetic clusters. Also, *genetic clusters* (represented as colors in Figure 3.4) are nothing more than fuzzy groups of organisms (organisms are represented as colored horizontal lines in the figure) such that an organism's degree of membership in any genetic cluster is equal to the proportion of its

---

51. Any human's genome is divided into three parts. A human's *allosome* is her set of sex chromosomes. A human's *autosome* is her set of non-sex chromosomes. Finally, every human has a set of mitochrondrial DNA that composes part of her genome. Note that the autosome is what Rosenberg et al. (2002, 2005) are studying. Keep this in mind when interpreting their results.

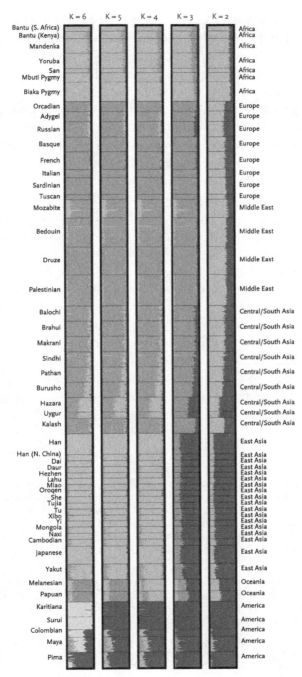

FIGURE 3.4. The genetic structure of putative human demes according to Rosenberg et al. (2005, 663).

genome that originated from that cluster.[52] Multicolored horizontal lines represent "mixed" organisms, and monochromatic horizontal lines represent unmixed organisms (Rosenberg et al. 2005, 660). Now, let us turn our attention to K = 5 genetic clusters: Africans, Eurasians, East Asians, Oceanians, and Native Americans.

While some of the K levels in the figure do not reflect a human population subdivision (e.g., K = 2), population geneticists have provided compelling evidence that K = 5 does. First, even though Rosenberg et al.'s K = 5 result does not always appear in similar studies, it is robust.[53] In particular, Rosenberg et al.'s K = 5 result has appeared in ~ 70% of all human genetic clustering studies that use a worldwide sample of human ethnic groups (Spencer 2015, 48).[54] Furthermore, these studies have used different samples of people, ethnic groups, and loci, and genetic clustering computer programs with different clustering algorithms (e.g., *structure, frappe, admixture*, etc.).

Second, even though Rosenberg et al.'s sample of ethnic groups is far from perfect due to its abundance of isolated populations and unmixed people (see Figure 3.4), there is ample evidence that Rosenberg et al.'s K = 5 result is not merely an artifact of that sample.[55] For one, Rosenberg et al. (2005, 663) have shown that even after controlling for the geographic distance among sampling locations, their K = 5 result still holds. But more importantly, Trevor Pemberton et al. (2013) have also obtained Rosenberg et al.'s K = 5 result using the largest and most diverse sample of human ethnic groups to date. They used 5,795 people from 267 ethnic groups from all over the world,

---

52. For clarity, q_k^i is a model parameter of the admixture mode of *structure* that represents the proportion of an individual's genome that originated from a cluster, where that individual is i and that cluster is k (Pritchard et al. 2000, 948). However, q_k^i can be interpreted in additional ways depending on the data set. For instance, sometimes q_k^i values are interpreted as membership grades when the clusters are plausibly viewed as biological populations or ancestry groups. For instance, in Rosenberg et al.'s (2002, 2382) study, q_k^i values are called "membership fractions."

53. For critics who worry about the variation in *which* genetic clusters appear at K = 5 given different background assumptions used in the analysis, see Hochman (2013, 348) and Barbujani et al. (2013, 157). However, I have addressed this concern elsewhere and in depth. In particular, see Spencer (2014, 1034–1035) and Spencer (2015, 48).

54. By a *worldwide* sample, I mean a sample that includes every "major area" in the United Nations' 2011 classification of countries. These areas are Africa, Asia, Europe, Latin America and the Caribbean, Northern America, and Oceania.

55. For critics who worry that Rosenberg et al.'s K = 5 result is an artifact of their sample of ethnic groups, see Kittles and Weiss (2003), Serre and Pääbo (2004), Bolnick (2008), Maglo (2011), and Hochman (2013, 2014).

including dozens of non-isolated populations and hundreds of mixed people, such as African Americans, Coloured South Africans, Latin Americans, and Polynesians (Pemberton et al. 2013, 891, 897).[56]

Finally, we have adequate reason to believe that the genetic structure at K = 5 in humans is caused by underlying human population structure because each K = 5 human genetic cluster is anchored in a region circumscribed by major geographic barriers to human interbreeding, such as "oceans, the Himalayas, and the Sahara" (Rosenberg et al. 2005, 663).

Now, even if Africans, East Asians, Eurasians, Native Americans, and Oceanians form a human population subdivision, the latter does not imply that this subdivision is biologically real. As Koffi Maglo (2010, 362) has astutely pointed out, the utility of an entity in biology does not entail its biological reality. Thus, we need to argue for the biological reality of the human population subdivision at K = 5 directly.

In the medical genetics and population genetics literature, Africans, East Asians, Eurasians, Native Americans, Oceanians, and other continent-level human populations are known as "continental populations" (Cooper et al. 2003, 1167; Zhao et al. 2006, 399). However, for ease of reference, I will call Africans, East Asians, Eurasians, Native Americans, and Oceanians, and only these five populations, *the human continental populations*. The evidence that the set of human continental populations is biologically real is the following. First, the set of human continental populations satisfies (3.4) because it is useful in population genetics for generating a theory about human population structure—namely, the theory that the set of human continental populations is the population subdivision at level K = 5 in humans.

Second, the set of human continental populations satisfies (3.5) because the theory in which the entity is posited is warranted according to the population-genetic epistemic values of empirical accuracy, completeness, and quantitative precision to predict a population-genetic observational law.[57] That observational law is that humans have K = 5 genetic structure that is largely geographically clustered in the following regions: the Americas, Sub-Saharan Africa, Oceania, Eurasia east of the Himalayas, and Eurasia west of the Himalayas and North Africa. Given our assumption that population genetics satisfies (3.6), it follows that the set of human continental populations

---

56. Also, Rosenberg et al.'s K = 5 result was replicated again by Mallick et al. (2016, 9) using the second largest and second most diverse sample of ethnic groups to date.

57. These epistemic values are discussed in Pierre Duhem's *The Aim and Structure of Physical Theory*. See Duhem (1906/1981, 19–30).

is biologically real. An analogous line of reasoning can be used to show that each human continental population is biologically real as well.

Now that we have established the biological reality of the set of human continental populations and all of its members, I think you can predict where I am headed. From looking at the set of human continental populations and the set of races in OMB race talk, it is not absurd to think that the two sets are identical, which is what I will call *the identity thesis*. In fact, several medical geneticists realized early on that the set of human continental populations and the five major races used on the "2000 US Census" were at least "aligned nearly perfectly" (Risch et al. 2002, 5–6).[58] Of course, there's a big difference between being nearly identical and identical. Nevertheless, one way to defend the identity thesis is to show that adopting it provides us with solutions to the puzzles that led us to reject the OMB's "definitions" as definitions as well as the best predictive power—which are usually marks of a true empirical theory.[59]

For one, the identity thesis solves the puzzle of how to define a person's ancestry in a way that makes the OMB's racial scheme "nonduplicative" as the OMB intends. Remember that the OMB's "definition" for 'Black' is insufficient to yield a nonduplicative racial classification of people because human evolutionary history unfolded in such a way that every living human is a Black person according to the OMB's "definition" for 'Black,' thus making all non-Black races in the OMB's racial scheme unnecessary. Also, remember that temporal qualifiers for ancestry (e.g., 'recent') don't fix this problem due to counterfactual scenarios like the American African world and actual outliers like unmixed Aboriginal Australians. But also, comparative qualifiers for ancestry (e.g., 'primary') are dead ends as well for a different reason.[60]

What solves the preceding puzzle is that racial ancestry in the OMB's racial scheme is all and only ancestry that contributes to an individual's genome,

---

58. For other medical geneticists who made this observation, see Burchard et al. (2003, 1171). For some population geneticists who made it, see Sarah Tishkoff and Kenneth Kidd (2004, S21).

59. Here and elsewhere in this book, I will be assuming a rather weak view of truth for empirical theories that comes from Arthur Fine's natural ontological attitude. The view is "referential" and simply states that "a sentence (or statement) is true just in case the entities referred to stand in the referred-to relations" (Fine 1984, 98).

60. Specifically, given what we know about the tree of life, the *primary ancestry* (understood as the majority of one's ancestors) of any human lies outside of the human species, thus making every human race-less. Furthermore, tweaking the qualifier to 'primary human ancestry' will yield unintended results, such as no Polynesian being a Pacific Islander due to the majority of any Polynesian's human ancestors not being Pacific Island natives.

called "genomic ancestry" in the population-genetic literature (Weiss and Long 2009, 707). For instance, according to the identity thesis, the meaning of 'Black' is the African population. Thus, a *Black* person is a person with genomic ancestry from the African population. That's it. In other words, if any allele in a person's genome originated from the African population, that person is Black. Furthermore, the *degree* to which a person is Black is equal to the proportion of her alleles that originated from the African population. Hence, according to the identity thesis, there are plenty of people who aren't Black.

For instance, a Taiwanese American who has 100% genomic ancestry from the East Asian population is exclusively *Asian*, and a European American who has 100% genomic ancestry from the Eurasian population is exclusively *White,* which makes the Asian and White races useful in OMB's racial scheme, just as they were intended to be. Also, an Aleutian Islander with 100% Native American genomic ancestry is exclusively *American Indian*, and a Native Hawaiian with 100% Oceanian genomic ancestry is exclusively *Pacific Islander*, which makes the American Indian and Pacific Islander races useful in OMB's racial scheme, just as they were intended to be.

Second, the identity thesis solves the puzzle of how to make the OMB's racial scheme "comprehensive in coverage." For instance, anyone from the American African population in the American African world is exclusively *Black*, since all of her alleles originated from the African population. Also, unmixed Aboriginal Australians—a group with no recent ancestors from the original people to any geographic region mentioned in the OMB's "definitions"—are exclusively Pacific Islander (McEvoy et al. 2010, 300).[61] So, solving the puzzle of which race unmixed Aboriginal Australians belong to is a concrete accomplishment of the identity thesis.

In addition, notice that there are several geographic regions that are not mentioned in the OMB's "definitions" despite there being indigenous people to these regions. For instance, in addition to Australia, the OMB neglects to mention the Andaman Islands, Central Asia, and Madagascar, to name a few. So, it's unclear how to racially classify the indigenous people to these forgotten lands. However, the OMB needs to racially classify each of these

---

61. I say "unmixed" because many Aboriginal Australians have recent European ancestors due to the colonization of Australia by European settlers. In fact, a recent genetic study by Duncan Taylor et al. (2012, 534) showed that 59% of Aboriginal Australian males possess a Y chromosome inherited from a European male. Thus, a substantial proportion of Aboriginal Australians are, at least, White.

indigenous people in order to have a "comprehensive" racial classification. The identity thesis solves this puzzle effortlessly.

According to current genetic clustering results, the Malagasy are a mixed people who, on average, belong to the African and East Asian populations (Kusuma et al. 2016, 5). As for Andaman Islanders, they are an assortment of different ethnic groups with different genomic ancestry mixture averages. For example, the Jarawa are mostly unmixed and Oceanic (Aghakhanian et al. 2015, 1210). However, some studies of the Onge show that they are mostly mixed and belong primarily to the East Asian and Oceanic populations (Mallick et al. 2016, 9). Finally, indigenous Central Asians are a mixed people that primarily belong to the Eurasian and East Asian populations. However, their primary racial membership varies by ethnic group. For instance, the Tajiks are primarily Eurasian, while the Uzbeks are primarily East Asian (Martínez-Cruz et al. 2011, 221).

Next, if the identity thesis is true, then we not only can solve lots of puzzles about OMB race talk, but we can make many predictions with "very high" accuracy (Burchard et al. 2003, 1172). For instance, if the vast majority of US adults have a primary human continental population membership, are competent in OMB race talk, self-report a single race, and racially self-report the human continental population in which they have primary membership, then using knowledge about primary human continental population membership alone, geneticists should be able to predict the self-reported OMB race of most US adults with very high accuracy. Interestingly, this is exactly what geneticists are able to do.

For example, using a nationally representative sample of US college students (N = 2,065), Guang Guo et al. (2014) tested the extent to which they could predict the self-reported OMB race of subjects who reported a single race using only each subject's primary genomic ancestry in a human continental population. After finding no self-reported Pacific Islanders and just four self-reported American Indians in the sample, the authors decided to focus on self-reported Asians, Blacks, and Whites (Guo et al. 2014, 153). Next, looking at just the subjects who reported a single race (which was 1,773 subjects) and using only *structure* and a sample of each subject's genome, the authors were able to predict each subject's race with 98.8% accuracy (Guo et al. 2014, 153).[62] While this is an amazing feat, Guo et al.'s result is not unique. Hua Tang et al. (2005, 271) were able to predict the self-reported OMB race of 2,657 US adults with 99.8% accuracy using primary human

---

62. This statistic includes the self-reported Hispanic subjects.

continental population membership alone.[63] While there are other instances of predictive power that I could talk about to lend further support to the identity thesis, perhaps I should wrap up.

3.5. Conclusion

In this chapter, I have defended a nuanced biological racial realism as an account of how 'race' is used in one US race talk. I will call the theory *OMB race theory*, and the theory makes the following three claims:

(3.7) The set of races in OMB race talk is one meaning of 'race' in US race talk.

(3.8) The set of races in OMB race talk is the set of human continental populations.

(3.9) The set of human continental populations is biologically real.

I argued for (3.7) in sections 3.2 and 3.3. Here, I argued that OMB race talk is not only an ordinary race talk in the current United States, but a race talk where the meaning of 'race' in the race talk is just the set of races used in the race talk. I argued for (3.8) (a.k.a. 'the identity thesis') in sections 3.3 and 3.4. Here, I argued that the thing being referred to in OMB race talk (a.k.a. the meaning of 'race' in OMB race talk) is a set of biological populations in humans (Africans, East Asians, Eurasians, Native Americans, and Oceanians), which I've dubbed *the human continental populations*. Finally, I argued for (3.9) in section 3.4. Here, I argued that the set of human continental populations is biologically real because it currently occupies the $K = 5$ level of human population structure according to contemporary population genetics.

Before I end, it will be interesting to see how much OMB race theory sheds light onto the problem that motivated this chapter. While I will not pretend that OMB race theory has the power to settle the debate about whether (and, if so, how) race matters in medical genetics, the theory does provide some helpful insight that may inch us closer to a resolution. For one, OMB race theory implies that medical scientists who investigate whether there are genetic explanations for racial disparities in heath are *not* making a

---

63. This statistic only includes the self-reported non-Hispanic Blacks and non-Hispanic Whites, and leaves out the Chinese, Japanese, and Hispanics in Tang et al.'s sample. I'm leaving out the Chinese and Japanese because they didn't self-report 'Asian' in the study, but rather, as 'Chinese' or 'Japanese.' See Tang et al. (2005, 269). I'm leaving out the Hispanics because it's well known that Tang et al.'s sample of Hispanics was unrepresentative. See Glasgow (2009, 95).

metaphysical mistake provided that the races they are using are OMB races. The latter is because OMB race theory gives us the result that OMB races are biological populations that are essentially genomic ancestry groups, and it is metaphysically possible for such populations to non-accidentally differ in medically relevant allele frequencies. So, for instance, Eric Jorgenson et al.'s (2004, 276) study that searched for medically relevant differences in genetic maps among "African Americans," "East Asians," and "whites" was not a metaphysically confused research project.[64]

However, my result conflicts with Yudell et al.'s (2016, 564–565) claim that "racial classifications do not make sense in terms of genetics."[65] While I am sympathetic to Yudell et al.'s claim, it turns out that *some* racial classifications do make sense in terms of genetics, namely, the OMB's racial classification. However, Yudell et al. are absolutely right that *some* racial classifications do not make sense in terms of genetics, such as any racial classification based on what Anthony Appiah (1996, 54) has called "racialism."[66]

A third result that's relevant for whether (or how) race matters in medical genetics is that OMB race theory does not *imply* that OMB races differ in medically relevant allele frequencies, and it does not imply that OMB races *don't* differ in medically relevant allele frequencies. Likewise, OMB race theory does not imply that OMB races differ in any socially important traits (e.g., intelligence, beauty, moral character, etc.), and it does not imply that OMB races don't differ in any socially important traits. Determining whether OMB races differ in any phenotypic ways requires a separate empirical investigation. Furthermore, I am not saying this out of political correctness. It turns out that the DNA evidence that supports the existence of human continental populations comes from non-protein-coding and non-functional DNA in the human genome. Nevertheless, we now know that it's metaphysically possible for some races to matter in medical genetics because *some* races are biologically real.

---

64. Note that the authors are using 'African American' in this study as a term that is synonymous to the OMB's 'Black.' Also, a *genetic map* is a map of the relative position of each gene in a genome. The first genetic map was constructed by Alfred Sturtevant in 1913.

65. For other scholars who hold the same view, see Root (2003), Graves and Rose (2006), Kaplan (2010), and Roberts (2011, 129).

66. According to Appiah (1996, 54), "racialism" is the view that humans naturally divide into a small number of groups called 'races' in such a way that the members of each race share certain fundamental, inheritable, physical, moral, intellectual, and cultural characteristics with one another that they do not share with members of any other race.

References

Aghakhanian, F., Y. Yunus, R. Naidu, T. Jinam, A. Manica, B. Hoh, and M. Phipps. 2015. "Unravelling the Genetic History of Negritos and Indigenous Populations of Southeast Asia." *Genome Biology and Evolution* 7(5): 1206–1215.

Alcoff, L. M. 2006. *Visible Identities: Race, Gender, and the Self.* Oxford: Oxford University Press.

Andreasen, R. O. 1998. "A New Perspective on the Race Debate." *The British Journal for the Philosophy of Science* 49(2): 199–225.

Appiah, K. A. 1996. "Race, Culture, Identity, Misunderstood Connections." In K. A. Gutmann (ed.), *Color Conscious.* Princeton, NJ: Princeton University Press, pp. 30–105.

Barbujani, G., S. Ghirotto, and F. Tassi. 2013. "Nine Things to Remember about Human Genome Diversity." *Tissue Antigens* 82: 155–164.

Barcan Marcus, R. 1961. "Modalities and Intensional Languages." *Synthese* 13(4): 303–322.

Bergström, A., N. Nagle, Y. Chen, ... C. Tyler-Smith. 2016. "Deep Roots for Aboriginal Australian Y Chromosomes." *Current Biology* 26: 809–813.

Blum, L. 2002. *I'm Not A Racist But . . . : The Moral Quandary of Race.* Ithaca, NY: Cornell University Press.

Bolnick, D. 2008. "Individual Ancestry Inference and the Reification of Race as a Biological Phenomenon." In B. Koenig, S. Lee, and S. Richardson (eds.), *Revisiting Race in a Genomic Age.* New Brunswick, NJ: Rutgers University Press, pp. 70–85.

Bourget, D., and D. Chalmers. 2014. "What Do Philosophers Believe?" *Philosophical Studies* 170(3): 465–500.

Braun, D. 1993. "Empty Names." *Noûs* 27(4): 449–469.

Burchard, E., E. Ziv, N. Coyle, S. Gomez, H. Tang, A. Karter, ... N. Risch. 2003. "The Importance of Race and Ethnic Background in Biomedical Research and Clinical Practice." *The New England Journal of Medicine* 348(12): 1170–1175.

Cavalli-Sforza, L. 2005. "The Human Genome Diversity Project: Past, Present, and Future." *Nature Genetics* 6: 333–340.

Cavalli-Sforza, L., and M. Feldman. 2003. "The Application of Molecular Genetic Approaches to the Study of Human Evolution." *Nature Genetics* 33: 266–275.

Combe, G. 1853. *A System of Phrenology,* 5th edition, revised, vol. 1. Edinburgh: MacLachlan and Stewart.

Compton, E., M. Bentley, S. Ennis, and S. Rastogi. 2013. *2010 Census Race and Hispanic Origin Alternative Questionnaire Experiment.* Washington, DC: US Census Bureau.

Cooper, R., J. Kaufman, and R. Ward. 2003. "Race and Genomics." *The New England Journal of Medicine* 348(12): 1166–1170.

Davenport, C. 1917. "The Effects of Race Intermingling." *Proceedings of the American Philosophical Society* 56(4): 364–368.

de la Cruz, G., and A. Brittingham. 2003. *The Arab Population, 2000.* US Census Bureau. Retrieved from http://www.census.gov/prod/2003pubs/c2kbr-23.pdf

Dupré, J. 1981. Natural Kinds and Biological Taxa. *The Philosophical Review* 90(1): 66–90.

Ennis, S., M. Ríos-Vargas, and N. Albert. 2011. *The Hispanic Population, 2010.* US Census Bureau. Retrieved from http://www.census.gov/prod/cen2010/briefs/c2010br-04.pdf

FBI. 2014. *2014 Hate Crime Statistics: Table 1.* Washington, DC: Federal Bureau of Investigation.

FBI. 2015. *Hate Crime Data Collection Guidelines and Training Manual, version 2.0.* Washington, DC: Federal Bureau of Investigation.

Feldman, M. 2010. "The Biology of Ancestry: DNA, Genomic Variation, and Race." In H. Markus and P. Moya (eds.), *Doing Race: 21 Essays for the 21st Century.* New York: W. W. Norton, pp. 136–159.

Fine, A. 1984. "The Natural Ontological Attitude." In J. Leplin (ed.), *Scientific Realism.* Berkeley: University of California Press, pp. 83–107.

Girle, R. 2009. *Modal Logics and Philosophy*, 2nd edition. Montreal: McGill-Queen's University Press.

Glasgow, J. 2003. "On the New Biology of Race." *The Journal of Philosophy* 100(9): 456–474.

Glasgow, J. 2009. *A Theory of Race.* New York: Routledge.

Glasgow, J. Forthcoming. "'Race' and Descriptivism." In Q. Spencer, *The Race Debates from Metaphysics to Medicine.* New York: Oxford University Press.

Glasgow, J., J. Shulman, and E. Covarrubias. 2009. "The Ordinary Conception of Race in the United States and Its Relation to Racial Attitudes: A New Approach." *Journal of Cognition and Culture* 9: 15–38.

Graves, J., and M. Rose. 2006. "Against Racial Medicine." *Patterns of Prejudice* 40: 481–493.

Guo, G., Y. Fu, H. Lee, T. Cai, K. Harris, and Y. Li. 2014. "Genetic Bio-Ancestry and Social Construction of Racial Classification in Social Surveys in the Contemporary United States." *Demography* 51(1): 141–172.

Hardimon, M. 2003. "The Ordinary Concept of Race." *The Journal of Philosophy* C(9): 437–455.

Hardimon, M. 2013. "Race Concepts in Medicine." *Journal of Medicine and Philosophy* 38: 6–31.

Hardimon, M. 2017. *Rethinking Race: The Case for Deflationary Realism.* Cambridge, MA: Harvard University Press.

Hartl, D., and A. Clark. 2007. *Principles of Population Genetics*, 4th edition. Sunderland: Sinauer Associates.

Haslanger, S. 2012. *Resisting Reality.* Oxford: Oxford University Press.

Herrnstein, R., and C. Murray. 1996. *The Bell Curve: Intelligence and Class Structure in American Life.* New York: Free Press.

Hirschfeld, L. A. 1996. *Race in the Making.* Cambridge, MA: MIT Press.

Hochman, A. 2013. "Against the New Racial Naturalism." *The Journal of Philosophy* CX(6): 331–351.

Hochman, A. 2014. "Unnaturalised Racial Naturalism." *Studies in History and Philosophy of Biological and Biomedical Sciences* 46: 79–87.

Humes, K., N. Jones, and R. Ramirez. 2011. *Overview of Race and Hispanic Origin 2010: 2010 Census Briefs.* Washington, DC: US Census Bureau.

Jablonski, N., and G. Chaplin. 2010. "Human Skin Pigmentation as an Adaptation to UV Radiation." *Proceedings of the National Academy of Sciences* 107(2): 8962–8968.

Jeffers, C. 2013. "The Cultural Theory of Race: Yet Another Look at Du Bois's 'The Conservation of Races.'" *Ethics* 123(3): 403–426.

Kaplan, J. 2010. "When Socially Determined Categories Make Biological Realities: Understanding Black/White Health Disparities in the U.S." *The Monist* 93(2): 281–297.

Kenny, E., N. Timpson, M. Sikora, M. Yee, A. Moreno-Estrada, C. Eng, . . . S. Myles. 2012. "Melanesian Blond Hair Is Caused by an Amino Acid Change in TYRP1." *Science* 336: 554.

Kittles, R., and K. Weiss. (2003). "Race, Ancestry, and Genes: Implications for Defining Disease Risk." *Annual Reviews: Genomics and Human Genetics* 4: 33–69.

Kripke, S. A. 1980. *Naming and Necessity.* Cambridge, MA: Harvard University Press.

Kusuma, P., N. Brucato, M. Cox, D. Pierron, H. Razafindrazaka, A. Adelaar, . . . F. Ricaut. 2016. "Contrasting Linguistic and Genetic Origins of the Asian Source Populations of Malagasy." *Scientific Reports* 6: 260–266.

Lugo, L., A. Cooperman, G. Smith, E. O'Connell, and S. Stencel. 2013. *A Portrait of Jewish Americans: Findings from a Pew Research Center Survey of U.S. Jews.* Washington, DC: Pew Research Center.

Maglo, K. 2010. "Genomics and the Conundrum of Race: Some Epistemic and Ethical Considerations." *Perspectives in Biology and Medicine* 53(3): 357–372.

Maglo, K. 2011. "The Case against Biological Realism about Race: From Darwin to the Post-Genomic Era." *Perspectives on Science* 19(4): 361–390.

Maglo, K., T. Mersha, and L. Martin. 2016. "Population Genomics and the Statistical Values of Race: An Interdisciplinary Perspective on the Biological Classifcation of Human Populations and Implications for Clinical Genetic Epidemiological Research." *Frontiers in Genetics* 7: Article 22.

Malek, A. 2009. *A Country Called Amreeka: U.S. History Retold Through Arab-American Lives.* New York: Free Press.

Mallick, S., H. Li, M. Lipson, . . . D. Reich. 2016. "The Simons Genome Diversity Project: 300 Genomes from 142 Diverse Populations." *Nature* 538(7624): 201–206.

Manichaikul, A., W. Palmas, C. Rodriguez, C. Peralta, J. Divers, . . . J. Mychaleckyj. 2012. "Population Structure of Hispanics in the United States: The Multi-Ethnic Study of Atherosclerosis." *PLoS Genetics* 8(4): e1002640.

Martínez-Cruz, B., R. Vitalis, L. Ségurel, F. Austerlitz, M. Georges, . . . E. Heyer. 2011. "In the Heartland of Eurasia: The Multilocus Genetic Landscape of Central Asian Populations." *European Journal of Human Genetics* 19: 216–223.

May, K., and K. Hardwick. 2006. "The Spindle Checkpoint." *Journal of Cell Science* 119: 4139–4142.

McEvoy, B., J. Lind, . . . A. Wilton. 2010. "Whole-Genome Genetic Diversity in a Sample of Australians with Deep Aboriginal Ancestry." *The American Journal of Human Genetics* 87: 297–305.

Mills, C. 1998. *Blackness Visible: Essays on Philosophy and Race.* Ithaca, NY: Cornell University Press.

Morning, A. 2011. *The Nature of Race: How Scientists Think and Teach about Human Difference.* Berkeley: University of California Press.

OMB. 1995. "Standards for the Classification of Federal Data on Race and Ethnicity." *Federal Registrar* 60(166): 44674–44693.

OMB. 1997. "Document 97-28653: Revisions to the Standards for the Classification of Federal Data on Race and Ethnicity." *Federal Register* 62(210): 58782–58790.

OMB. 2000. *Provisional Guidance on the Implementation of the 1997 Standards for Federal Data on Race and Ethnicity.* Washington, DC: Office of Management and Budget.

Papantoniou, N., G. Daskalakis, J. Tziotis, S. Kitmirides, S. Mesogitis, and A. Antsaklis. 2001. "Risk Factors Predisposing to Fetal Loss Following a Second Trimester Amniocentesis." *British Journal of Obstetrics and Gynaecology* 108: 1053–1056.

Pemberton, T., M. DeGiorgio, and N. Rosenberg. 2013. "Population Structure in a Comprehensive Genomic Data Set on Human Microsatellite Variation." *G3: Genes, Genomes, Genetics* 3(5): 891–907.

Perry, J. 2001. *Reference and Reflexivity.* Stanford, CA: CSLI Publications.

Pritchard, J., M. Stephens, and P. Donnelly. 2000. "Inference of Population Structure Using Multilocus Genotype Data." *Genetics* 155: 945–959.

Putnam, H. 1973. "Meaning and Reference." *The Journal of Philosophy* 70(19): 699–711.

Risch, N., E. Burchard, E. Ziv, and H. Tang. 2002. "Categorization of Humans in Biomedical Research: Genes, Race and Disease." *Genome Biology* 3(7): 1–12.

Risch, N., S. Choudhry, M. Via, M. Basu. R. Sebro, C. Eng, . . . E. Burchard. 2009. "Ancestry-Related Assortative Mating in Latino Populations." *Genome Biology* 10(11), R132: 1–16.

Roberts, D. 2011. *Fatal Invention: How Science, Politics, and Big Business Re-Create Race in the Twenty-First Century.* New York: The New Press.

Robertson, M., and G. Joyce. 2012. "The Origins of the RNA World." *Cold Spring Harbor Perspectives in Biology* 4(a003608): 1–22.

Root, M. 2003. "The Use of Race in Medicine as a Proxy for Genetic Differences." *Philosophy of Science* 70(5): 1173–1183.

Rosenberg, N., S. Mahajan, . . . M. Feldman. 2005. "Clines, Clusters, and the Effect of Study Design on the Inference of Human Population Structure." *PLoS Genetics* 1(6): 660–671.

Rosenberg, N., J. Pritchard, . . . M. Feldman. 2002. "Genetic Structure of Human Populations." *Science* 298(5602): 2381–2385.

Serre, D., and S. Pääbo. 2004. "Evidence for Gradients of Human Genetic Diversity within and among Continents." *Genome Research* 14: 1679–1685.

Shipp, T., B. Bromley, E. Lieberman, and B. Benacerraf. 2000. "The Frequency of the Detection of Fetal Echogenic Intracardiac Foci with Respect to Maternal Race." *Ultrasound in Obstetrics & Gynecology* 15: 460–462.

Spencer, Q. 2012. "What 'Biological Racial Realism' Should Mean." *Philosophical Studies* 159(2): 181–204.

Spencer, Q. 2014. "A Radical Solution to the Race Problem." *Philosophy of Science* 81(5): 1025–1038.

Spencer, Q. 2015. "Philosophy of Race Meets Population Genetics." *Studies in History and Philosophy of Biological and Biomedical Sciences* 52: 46–55.

Spencer, Q. 2016. "Genuine Kinds and Scientific Reality." In C. Kendig (ed.), *Natural Kinds and Classification in Scientific Practice*. Abingdon: Routledge, pp. 157–172.

Stryer, L. 1995. *Biochemistry*, 4th edition. New York: W. H. Freeman.

Sullivan, S. 2013. "Inheriting Racist Disparities in Health: Epigenetics and the Transgenerational Effects of White Racism." *Critical Philosophy of Race* 1(2): 190–218.

Sundstrom, R. 2002. "Race as a Human Kind." *Philosophy & Social Criticism*, 28(1): 91–115.

Tang, H., T. Quertermous, . . . N. Risch. 2005. "Genetic Structure, Self-Identified Race/Ethnicity, and Confounding in Case-Control Association Studies." *American Journal of Human Genetics* 76(2): 268–275.

Taylor, D., N. Nagle, K. Ballantyne, . . . R. Mitchell. 2012. "An Investigation of Admixture in Aboriginal Australian Y-Chromosome STR Database." *Forensic Science International: Genetics* 6: 532–538.

Taylor, P. 2013. *Race: A Philosophical Introduction*, 2nd edition. Cambridge: Polity Press.

Tishkoff, S., and K. Kidd. 2004. "Implications of Biogeography of Human Populations for 'Race' and Medicine." *Nature Genetics* 36(11): S21–S27.

Tran, S., A. Caughey, and M. Norton. 2005. "Ethnic Variation in the Prevalence of Echogenic Intracardiac Foci and the Association with Down Syndrome." *Ultrasound in Obstretrics & Gynecology* 26: 158–161.

USCB. 2010. *Race and Hispanic or Latino Origin for Puerto Rico: 2010 Census Summary File 1*. Washington, DC: US Census Bureau.

Wallman, K. 1998. "Data on Race and Ethnicity: Revising the Federal Standard." *The American Statistician* 52(1): 31–33.

Weinhold, B. 2006. "Epigenetics." *Environmental Health Perspectives* 114(3): A160–A167.

Weiss, K., and J. Long. 2009. "Non-Darwinian Estimation: My Ancestors, My Genes' Ancestors." *Genome Research* 19: 703–710.

Wood, T. 2006. "The Current Status of Baraminology." *Creation Research Society Quarterly* 43(3): 149–158.

Yudell, M., D. Roberts, R. DeSalle, and S. Tishkoff. 2016. "Taking Race Out of Human Genetics." *Science* 351(6273): 564–565.

Zack, N. 2002. *Philosophy of Science and Race.* New York: Routledge.

Zhao, Z., N. Yu, Y. Fu, and W. Li. 2006. "Nucleotide Variation and Haplotype Diversity in a 10-kb Non-Coding Region in Three Continental Human Populations." *Genetics* 174: 399–409.

4 IS RACE AN ILLUSION OR A (VERY) BASIC REALITY?

Joshua Glasgow

It was 1915, and Vaishno Das Bagai had several thousand dollars. He was educated. His high school headmaster recommended him as "a high-caste Hindu [from] a respectable family" and an individual of "very good character." But these advantages were not enough. He still needed to escape India's domination. His wife Kala would later remember him saying, "I don't want to stay in this slave country," in reference to Britain's colonial rule. "I want to go to America where there is no slavery."

After the long journey, it must have been difficult for Vaishno, Kala, and their three children to get stuck at the immigration center on Angel Island. But the officials there wanted to know how the family would provide for themselves in a new country. A few days in, the Bagais made their wealth known, which seems to be all that was needed to gain entry to San Francisco.[1] The local paper featured a piece about Kala, headlined "Nose Diamond Latest Fad; Arrives Here from India." It reported that she was "the first Hindu woman to enter this city in ten years."

In the late 1800s and early 1900s, the United States was engulfed in a flood of anti-Asian racism. Seven years before the Bagais arrived, a white mob in Marysville, California, robbed and ran out of town seventy "Hindus," telling them not to return. Whites repeatedly engaged in race riots that targeted Chinese and Filipino lives and property. Following an 1882 ban on Chinese immigrants,

---

1. One report from 1915 had the family holding $17,000 in cash; another from 1928 had them carrying $25,000 in gold, the equivalent of over half a million dollars today.

the Immigration Act of 1917 banned immigration from India, Siam, Arabia, and elsewhere.

Nevertheless, Vaishno became a naturalized citizen six years after entering the United States. Because California's Alien Land Act of 1913 said that only citizens could own land, this new membership card translated into the right to own property. Of course, legal rights are not everything. His citizenship did not prevent racist neighbors from locking the Bagais out of the house they bought in Berkeley, compelling them to return to San Francisco, where they lived above their store on Fillmore Street. Still, Vaishno's citizenship was in hand, at least for the time being.

Three years after the US Constitution was adopted, the Naturalization Act of 1790 established that only white people could become naturalized citizens, and while this policy would take different forms over time, naturalization was racially restricted until the 1940s, when the Nazi specter shamed any nation that still stained itself with racialized population policies. In the meantime, the Naturalization, Immigration, and Alien Land Acts were just a few of the many bludgeons used for racial domination and exclusion. But enforcing this system required classifying people into races, and the law buckled under this task.

A singular piece of conceptual acrobatics came from the Supreme Court of California in *People v. Hall* (1854). A white man, George Hall, had been convicted and sentenced to death for killing another man, Ling Sing. But Hall's conviction was based on the eyewitness testimony of three Chinese people, and at the time California law put racial restrictions on eyewitness testimony. Specifically, neither black people nor Native Americans were legally eligible to testify against white people. What, then, was the legal status of the eyewitnesses in Hall's case? On appeal the Court declared both that Chinese people were black, because they were not white and 'black' just meant *non-white*; and also that Chinese people were American Indians, because indigenous Americans' ancestors originally arrived via the Bering crossing from China. Legally speaking, then, the witnesses were now both black and Native American. Racist law and a contorted judgment about racial identity set free the murderer Hall.

This was just one moment in America's long legal confrontation with racial categorization. Proving your race could be the key to proving which school your child was eligible to attend, to proving that you could marry your beloved in a country infested with anti-miscegenation laws, or to proving that your parents' marriage was legitimate under those same laws, entitling you to your inheritance. Prior to the abolition of slavery, plaintiffs sought freedom by arguing that their race made their enslavement illegal. And of course lives, relationships, treasure, and freedom were not the only goods that hung in the balance. If you wanted the protections and privileges of citizenship, you had to authenticate your whiteness here, too. The proving ground was the courthouse.

Generations earlier, witch-hunters in Salem identified their prey by looking for a hidden "witch's mark." When it came time to identify people's races, things were hardly better. Admissible evidence of one's race included one's behavior, one's reputation, even the shape of one's feet. The rules about how to classify people of mixed racial ancestry were particularly notable for their sheer variety from state to state. And slotting individuals into races was not the only challenge. By the early 1900s, when events surrounding World War I sent new waves of immigrants seeking safe harbor around the world, America's courts were tasked with sorting out the racial status of entire peoples. They had to decide: legally speaking, were Arabs white? How about Syrians or Armenians? Inconsistent rulings using varying standards piled up.

Enter the Supreme Court. Takao Ozawa, a Japanese immigrant, petitioned to be legally recognized as white for the purpose of becoming a citizen. In making his case, he pointed to his light skin color. He noted that he was assimilated in education, religion, language, and style. He emphasized his love of America. Late in 1922, the Court ruled. Justice George Sutherland—himself a naturalized citizen but apparently not one who felt liberated to expand the club—wrote that from a legal perspective, 'white' meant *Caucasian*. Sutherland recognized that there was some controversy about who exactly is and is not Caucasian. But he held that Ozawa "is clearly of a race which is not Caucasian and therefore belongs entirely outside the zone on the negative side." The Supreme Court was unanimous: Ozawa was not Caucasian, so he was not white. Consequently, he was ineligible for citizenship.

By making being Caucasian the legal key to whiteness and therefore citizenship, the Court appeared to open a door for Bhagat Singh Thind. Citing scholarly authorities such as Johann Friedrich Blumenbach, Thind marshalled linguistic and other evidence to prove that Punjabis like himself were part of the Caucasian race. In fact, like Bagai, Thind had official certification that he was of "Aryan origin." Thus from a scientific perspective, it looked like Thind was Caucasian, and since it was now legally established that 'white' meant *Caucasian*, citizenship appeared to be within reach.

Just three months after the *Ozawa* ruling, Justice Sutherland again codified whiteness from the bench: for legal purposes, Thind's evidence was beside the point. In this context, the words 'white' and 'Caucasian' were to be understood as "words of common speech and not of scientific origin." Technical biological classification did not matter. Ancestral connection did not matter. Cultural assimilation and language did not matter. What mattered in this context was that common sense said that South Asians were not white. And under the Naturalization Act, that meant they were barred from citizenship. Thind lost his case.

Twelve years later, Congress allowed World War I veterans to become citizens, and due to his service Thind was naturalized. And by 1946, Congress and President Truman would create new law that Indians (and Filipinos) could become naturalized US citizens. But in 1923, the *Thind* decision stripped sixty-five Indians of their naturalized citizenship. Among them was Vaishno Das Bagai.

No longer being citizens, Bagai and others were forced to sell their real estate under California law. (Some would transfer their holdings to their children who, being born in the United States, had birthright citizenship; the Bagai kids were born in India.) And that was not the only setback. Bagai had renounced his British citizenship when he became an American citizen. Now there was no home to give him a passport. He had no way to travel to India again.

Bagai had sacrificed to tear off the cuffs of colonial oppression. Now his sanctuary had turned against him, rendering him dispossessed, legally bottlenecked, stateless, and geographically stuck. He had escaped the suffocating scope of British imperialism only to meet the relentlessness of American racism. What did it mean to trade chains for a box?

By this point he was desperate and heartbroken. Fed up, he wrote the following in a letter to the *San Francisco Examiner*:

But they now come to me and say, I am no longer an American citizen. They will not permit me to buy my home and, lo, they even shall not issue me a passport to go back to India. Now what am I? What have I made of myself and my children? We cannot exercise our rights, we cannot leave this country. Humility and insults, who is responsible for all this? Myself and American government.

I do not choose to live the life of an interned person; yes, I am in a free country and can move about where and when I wish inside the country. Is life worth living in a gilded cage? Obstacles this way, blockades that way, and the bridges burnt behind.

Bagai had settled on a plan to escape his gilded cage: he would protest, by committing suicide. To spare his loved ones, he traveled to San Jose and rented a room, paying the whole month's $35 in advance. He wrote a separate note to his family. Then he closed the windows, locked the door, and released the room's illuminating gas. On March 16, 1928, Vaishno Das Bagai was dead from self-inflicted gas poisoning.[2]

And what was this thing behind it all, race? This beam of support for the Naturalization Act? This puzzle George Sutherland tried to solve to the exclusion of Japanese and Indian immigrants? This quality that racist Berkeleans saw as some sort of reason to lock the Bagais out of their own house? This line that lay underneath twenty white Californians running seventy innocent souls out of Marysville? This thing that has been behind white people regularly forcing non-white people out of towns, and much, much worse? What kind of thing is this?

It is not obvious how to answer that question. For starters, we could easily be confused about our concept of race. After all, when people thought that the word 'whale' referred to a kind of fish, this did not mean that whales actually were fish. What we care about, ultimately, is what the word 'race' *actually* means, not what we *think* it means. We want what Sally Haslanger (2012) calls the *operative* meaning of the term 'race'—the meaning that governs our use of the term, even when we are unaware of it.[3]

Further complicating matters is that there are very likely several meanings of 'race.' What I am focused on here is how the term 'race' is used by ordinary, linguistically competent people in the contemporary United States, to describe groups of humans. Now this group of speakers brings with them a tremendously diverse set of perspectives. Still, I believe that people from these many positions have been having a collective, long-lasting, and broad conversation about race. I aim to focus on this conversation.

Although this conversation is inclusive and broad, it does exclude some communications that use the word 'race.' In particular, if some specialists or

---

2. 260 U.S. 178 (1922)—*Takao Ozawa v. United States*; 261 U.S. 204 (1923)—*United States v. Bhagat Singh Thind*; "An Indian Merchant's Suicide: Patriotic Protest against Racial Discrimination"; Bagai (n.d.); Chesnutt (1889); Franklin (2015); Gross (2008); Haney López (1996); Lambah (1920); McNish (2013); "Nose Diamond Latest Fad; Arrives Here from India." Details were also provided via personal communication with Rani Bagai.

3. That said, even mistaken beliefs about what a word means can have real consequences. An 1818 jury ruled that for the purposes of the New York City fish tax, whales are fish on the grounds that a fish, by definition, is any sea creature (Sainsbury 2014).

experts (genomists, anthropologists, psychologists, etc.) somewhere use 'race' in a way that deviates from the meaning implied by the way ordinary non-specialists use 'race,' then that usage won't be relevant to the following discussion (Glasgow 2010). They simply have their own definition, and so their own conversation. There is not necessarily anything wrong with this, it's just that it is a conversation that would not be relevant to the conversation that I am addressing.

The same goes for non-expert speakers who use the language of race in a way that semantically deviates from that broad and inclusive conversation. If I said, "A couch is a race," you would say that I mean something different by 'race' than what you mean when you use that word, assuming we mean the same thing by 'a couch.' Less unusually, some people may (some people *do*, I think) use 'race' in novel or revolutionary ways that depart from the broad conversation I'm focused on. Even narrowing the scope of our investigation to the context of ordinary usage, there is still plausibly more than one meaning of 'race.' I want to focus on whichever concept of race has the most currency—call this, for simplicity, *the ordinary concept of race.*

Again, this concept is no doubt thought of in many different ways and understood from many different perspectives. Nonetheless, to the extent that people from those different standpoints are at least sometimes having a coherent conversation about race, and at least sometimes participate in a shared system of racial identification and practice with each other, underlying that common conversation and practice is what I'm calling the ordinary concept of race. As I mean it, this is the concept that has shaped our approach to race for so many years, that has given definition to our identities and experiences, and that has been complicit in so much oppression and, for some, a key to liberation from that very oppression. In this way, by referring to the discourse surrounding the "ordinary" concept of race or "our" concept of race, I mean to refer to the same discourse that Sally Haslanger and Chike Jeffers are diagnosing. (The degree to which this is also the same discourse that Quayshawn Spencer is analyzing will be explored in subsequent chapters.)

By this idea of a 'coherent conversation,' I just mean that there must be some shared concept of race for us to even talk—even just *disagree*—about race. We can meaningfully disagree and converse about something only if we use our words in such a way that they have a shared meaning. Otherwise, we'll talk past each other, using the same words to talk about different things. If you invite me to "cut the deck of cards" and I slice each of them in half with my scissors, we're having a communication breakdown, not a genuine disagreement. In this way, shared meaning is required for communication.[4] I'm interested in whatever meaning of 'race' is presupposed by our frequent communications about race and by our use of racial categories, even when we disagree.[5]

I believe that the operative, ordinary meaning of 'race' is something like the following. This is a rough way of putting it, and it only captures part of the definition, but it's a good starting point: *Races, by definition, are relatively large groups of people who are distinguished from other groups of people by having certain visible biological traits (such as skin colors) to a disproportionate extent.*[6]

With that working definition in hand, the next question is whether there is anything in the world that fits that description. Does 'race,' so defined, refer to anything real? Do races exist?

My coauthors have argued in the first three chapters of this book that race is biological, sociocultural, and sociopolitical. I think there are substantial merits to all three of these views, and I feel the pull of the arguments that have brought us to this point. Nevertheless, next I argue for a different view. I believe that the overall balance of considerations pressures us to conclude that races are neither biologically nor socially real. And from this a pretty compelling argument by elimination follows: if races are neither biologically nor socially real, then race is an illusion. This is *racial anti-realism*, and it is a stark claim. It maintains that Vaishno Das Bagai had no race. Neither do you, neither do I, neither does anyone else. Slavery, the Naturalization Act, Jim Crow, global domination and exploitation by Europe's colonial powers, the exclusion of Ozawa and Thind, the racial biases and discrimination that shape our world today, and all the rest have been premised on a terrible confusion. Race does not exist.

Now, like any argument by elimination, it is possible that this argument for anti-realism is missing a viable but hidden option, beyond the options that race is biologically real, socially real, and not real at all. In particular, maybe

---

4. This is misleading, strictly speaking. Shared meaning is required for conversation when we "take it for granted that the contents of [our] speech acts are true or false" (Stalnaker 2002, 702). But in those conversations where we merely *presuppose* something false, we can have conversation without shared meaning (see Stalnaker 2002 for more). My arguments here implicate the former diagnosis of our racial conversation, not the latter.

5. Lionel McPherson (2015) is skeptical about our prospects for landing on one overarching meaning of 'race' to stably ground conversations about race. What follows here will suggest otherwise. To emphasize the present point, though, this does not imply that there is only one meaning of 'race.'

6. This definition is, of course, unoriginal. A very wide range of other commentators, from A(lcoff 2006) to Z(ack 2002), also identify visible traits as essential to race.

race is real in some more basic way, one that is irrelevant to the biological *and* social sciences. Toward the end of this chapter I will also explore this view— *basic racial realism*. So ultimately we'll have to choose between the idea that race is an illusion and the idea that race is real in a basic, scientifically irrelevant sense. This will turn out to be a difficult choice.

But before confronting those alternatives, return to the step that starts us down this path. It is hard not to gravitate toward the common-sense idea that race is a biological fact, and really a fairly obvious one. So we start there. Can't the biologists deliver race?

4.1. Mermaids, Werewolves, and Other Fantastical Things: On the Gap between the Biological Facts and the Concept of Race

4.1.1. The Spectrum

Races would be biologically real if—and only if—the concept of race played some legitimate role in good biological science. So if something is part of bad science or non-science, such as astrology, or if it's useful for a non-biological science like sociology, then that thing is not biologically real.[7] With this and the working definition of 'race' given earlier, our question then becomes whether it is useful for the biological sciences to divide humanity into large groups based on the relevant visible traits, like skin color. The answer is: no.

It has long been noticed that if you line up all of humanity by skin color, from darkest to lightest, you'll see a spectrum of shades. Joseph Graves puts it this way: "If we were to only look at people in the tropics and people in Norway, we'd come to the conclusion that there's a group of people who have light skin and there's a group of people who have dark skin. But if we were to *walk* from the tropics to Norway, what we would see is a continuous change in skin tone. And at no point along that trip would we be able to say, 'Oh, this is the place in which we go from the dark race to the light race'" (Herbes-Sommers 2003). The same goes for shapes and sizes of facial features. And for hair textures. And for any other visible trait that we might associate with race. Each variation transitions gradually to the next.

Call this fact *The Spectrum*. The Spectrum means that there is no principled biological reason to put one racial boundary *here* and another racial

---

7. I'm happy to adopt Spencer's (2012) way of understanding *useful to good biological science*, namely as being valid in well-ordered scientific research programs. My argument aims to be neutral on that question.

boundary *there* based on visible traits. From the perspective of (good) biological science, there is no use in carving humanity into visible trait groups one way rather than another. And so, if races just are visible-trait groupings, races are not biologically real.

Now obviously we can establish some boundaries between groups based on visible traits. Put the lines of demarcation wherever you want! All the same, biologists still will have no *scientific* reason to recognize your lines—or any others based on visible traits. The boundaries within The Spectrum could be put here, they could be put there. From the perspective of biology, each of these boundaries is arbitrary. So we can draw lines around groups of humans, which we then call 'Asian,' 'white,' or 'Latinx.' But the lines that separate those bounded categories are imposed by us onto a blurred image of humanity. This is the sense in which race is not biologically real. Skin colors are biological traits. And we can divide ourselves up according to those traits. But our lines of racial demarcation are not discovered in the biology. Which means that racial groups themselves are not in the biology. It is akin to dividing ourselves into the height categories of 'short' and 'tall'—individually, our properties (our particular skin colors and heights) are biological, but we project the *categories* (white people, short people) onto the world (Relethford 2017).

In addition, attempts to ground race on certain bio-medical conditions, like heart disease or sickle-cell trait or Tay-Sachs disease, run into the roadblock that the populations with these conditions do not correspond to ordinary races. Moreover, to whatever extent there appears to be a correlation between races and medical conditions, this correlation is ultimately best explained by social, rather than biological, causes (Diamond 1994; Herbes-Sommers 2003; Kaplan 2010; Sullivan 2013). For example, black Americans suffer heart disease disproportionally, so you might think that something biological about being black gives rise to this disease susceptibility. But black people who are recent immigrants to the United States do not suffer disproportionate heart disease, suggesting that the spike in heart disease is due not to being black itself, but rather to the experience of being black in America (plausibly, to the stress that comes from an unrelenting, intergenerational subjection to racism). To that extent, self-identified race may be worth taking seriously in a medical context, but that is because it can indicate risks due to social environment, not long-standing genetic risks. And to be sure, it is very hard to find medical conditions that correspond to ordinary races. Sickle-cell trait is an adaptation to fight malaria, so it is found in people with ancestral connections to malarial regions, including parts of Africa and southern India but excluding parts of South Africa. A coalition of some Indians and some

Africans is not a race on the common-sense understanding of race. Likewise, Tay-Sachs disease is disproportionally found among those with Northern European Jewish ancestry, but that smaller group of people is not its own race, either, on the common-sense concept of race.

This will be a recurring theme: biologically real groups of humans do not seem to line up with races, as ordinarily defined. This is the *Mismatch Objection* (Mallon 2006), and its source is that the ordinary concept of race is pegged to visible traits, but groups based on visible traits are not useful for biology.[8]

4.1.2. "Words of Common Speech"

More sophisticated biological theories of race, including Quayshawn Spencer's contribution to this book, may seem to sidestep the Mismatch Objection. To give them a broad characterization, *genealogical theories* say that races are populations produced by the breeding patterns of our ancestors. This might get cashed out in terms of the ancestral lineages themselves, or in terms of genetic populations that result today, or in terms of some other genealogical element.[9] What is crucial is that the genealogical element in question is the *only* thing distinguishing each race from the next. These are not the rac*ist* biological theories of yesteryear that held that important qualities like intelligence, virtue, and beauty were part of some inherited racial package. Race, on these accounts, is merely a matter of ancestral relations or that microscopic residue of ancestry, our genes.

I believe that genealogical theory faces its own Mismatch Objection: scientifically provable genealogical populations are not races.[10] The source of the mismatch is that genealogical populations are ultimately determined by

---

8. Variations on the Mismatch Objection can be found, for example, in Appiah (1996, 71–74); Atkin (2017); Blum (2002, 143–144); Condit (2005); Feldman et al. (2003); Glasgow (2003; 2009, Ch. 5); Hirschfeld (1996, 4); Hull (1998); Jorde and Wooding (2004); Keita et al. (2004); Keita and Kittles (1997, 538); McPherson and Shelby (2004); Millstein (2015); Montagu (1964, 7); Pigliucci (2013); Pigliucci and Kaplan (2003, 1166); Witherspoon et al. (2007); Yudell et al. (2016); Zack (2002).

9. For variations on genealogy theory, see, for example, Andreasen (1998, 2000, 2004); Arthur (2007, Ch. 2); Burchard et al. (2003); Dobzhansky (1941, 162); Kitcher (1999); Mayr (2002); Risch et al. (2002); Sarich and Miele (2004); Spencer (2014); Templeton (1998).

10. The Mismatch Objection is not the only reason to be concerned about genealogical theory. For example, some worry that the data used to back it up are not taken from globally representative samples (Witherspoon et al. 2007).

reproductive patterns, while races, again, are supposed to be determined by the way we look. The two can come apart.

For instance, Roberta Millstein (2015) points out that individuals can migrate between populations, at least on one plausible articulation of what a population is. If you descend from population A but start reproducing with people from population B, then population-wise you will have stopped being an A and started being a B, she argues. Race obviously does not work like that. When "Hindustani" men in the early twentieth century migrated to California's Imperial Valley and married and reproduced with women racialized as "Mexican" (Hart 1998), that wrinkle in mating behavior may have changed their population, but it did not amount to a literal race change, on the ordinary concept of race. So *migratability* is one difference between populations and races.

In addition, two genealogical populations could, in principle, be visibly identical, whereas two races cannot. One hundred years and four days after the Bagais arrived in San Francisco, the prosecutor's office in Cuyahoga County, Ohio, received a letter from lawyers representing Samaria Rice. The letter asked the prosecutor to pursue an aggravated murder charge against police officer Timothy Loehman for killing Samaria's 12-year-old son, Tamir. Loehman had gunned down Tamir as he played in a park while in possession of a toy weapon. With no apparent justification, Loehman jumped out of the police car before it had stopped and only let two seconds elapse before he started firing on Tamir. Two seconds to say anything to Tamir. Less than two seconds for Tamir to potentially comply with any orders. Now imagine that some activists conclude that it is time to do something radical about the police persistently brutalizing and murdering black people in this way. The activists decide that the best solution is just to make us all look the same. So they develop a chemical agent that changes the genetic makeup of anyone who ingests it such that they end up looking exactly, and permanently, like the Dalai Lama. They then infuse the global water supply with this agent, and sure enough, within a few weeks, every human being on earth looks like the Dalai Lama.

Now also imagine that at least for a few generations we keep the ancestral populations we had prior to the change: geographical and cultural forces (such as language, dress, and popular places to find potential mates) impact reproductive choices, preserving genealogical lines. But everyone *looks* like the Dalai Lama. In that world, ancestral populations have not (yet) faded away. But race *has* disappeared in that world, because we look the same. There aren't any black people in a world of only Dalai Lamas. But there are still people with recent ancestry that is entirely from sub-Saharan Africa. Here again, we have a mismatch: races must, by definition, be *visibly distinct*, but populations need not be.

Migratability and the irrelevance of visible traits are *features* of genealogical populations that diverge from what we are trying to talk about when we talk about race. In addition, genealogical theory also has a different *groups* problem: the particular racial groups we ordinarily recognize are not the same as the genealogical populations recognized by science. One part of the problem is that some individuals get classified by science in a way that they themselves, and others, may reject—a phenomenon that has been highlighted with Americans who are racialized as black but would not fit the genealogical category of 'African' (McPherson and Shelby 2004). A second part of the problem is that genealogy theory fails to recognize some common-sense racial groups altogether. In particular, categories like *Arab* or *Latinx* find no home in the flow charts of population genetics, but they are routinely racialized in the United States. Importantly, the people *in* these groups routinely racialize themselves in this way (Alcoff 2006, Ch. 10–11; Haney López 2005). Until recently, it appeared that the 2020 US Census might add *Hispanic* and *Middle Eastern or North African* to its list of races, partly because the people who fall under these labels have found no place for themselves on previous Censuses (Krogstad and Cohn 2014). That proposal has been shelved, at least for now. In any event, it looks like certain identity commitments do not answer to population science.

Now one reply to the Mismatch Objection is that it doesn't matter if science and common sense fail to map onto one another, since science can have its own concept of race (Andreasen 2005). And, indeed, some might *like* the fact that genealogical theory recognizes different races than common-sense racial thinking recognizes. Thind certainly wanted to let science dictate our legal racial categories.

There's a kernel of truth in this reply: science can have whatever concepts it wants. So can the rest of us. It is up to us how to use our words. If you want, you could use the term 'race' to refer to *window*, in which case—as long as we believe in real windows—we would want to think that race is real. And if genealogical theorists want, they can use 'race' to refer to genealogical populations.

But for our project, what 'race' refers to is constrained. Our goal is to see if the term 'race', *as it operates in ordinary talk*, maps onto anything real. And for that purpose, we have to stick with the operative, ordinary concept of race. We can't just use whatever concept we want, and in particular we can't use a technical, scientific concept that is dislodged from the ordinary concept of race. If we are more committed to ordinary racial categories than we are to conforming our racial discourse to mismatching scientific categories, then a scientific meaning that deviates from the ordinary meaning is not relevant to our project (Glasgow 2010; cf. McPherson and Shelby 2004, 187–188).[11]

In short, it looks like some of our racial identities and some features conceptually bound up with race do not map onto the populations recognized by science. The ordinary term 'race' purports to refer to something other than the genealogical lines validated by biology.

4.1.3. Surprising Referents, Take 1: Whales Are Not Fish

But wait. We used to think that 'atom' was defined as the smallest particle and therefore indivisible. Then we split the atom, and it turned out that our attempt at defining the word 'atom' was wrong. We also used to think that whales were by definition fish. Then we discovered that whales are warm-blooded and breathe with lungs. Our early attempts at defining 'whale' had failed, too. Sometimes our concepts are *opaque*. We can make mistakes in how we define terms. So why not say something similar about race, that 'race,' *even in the ordinary sense*, refers to something unexpected and contrary to common thought? Actually, haven't we already said similar things about race? For example, some argue that Italians went from being classified as non-white to being classified as white.[12] Is that really so different from what genealogical theory is requiring us to do with the category *Latinx*? Sometimes our words refer to things in ways that are surprising to us. So why not allow that 'race' is

---

11. David Ludwig (2015) argues that because each side in the race debate can adopt its own semantics of race, each side can be correct within the definition of 'race' it privileges (cf. McPherson 2015), and it has long been noted both that there are different specifications of what race is supposed to be and that each specification has its own consequences for the status of race (e.g., Appiah 1996; Glasgow 2010; Mallon 2006). But when we decide to figure out if the term 'race' *in ordinary discourse* refers to anything real in the world, then not all definitions are equal: we need the meaning operative in ordinary discourse (cf. Chalmers 2011; Sidelle 2007). And this decision matters: the ordinary meaning of 'race,' whether race in that sense is real, and if so what its nature is, are questions that are both interesting in themselves and consequential insofar as the answers impact policies, actions, and lives (Glasgow 2009, Ch. 3; Haslanger 2012, Ch. 10). However, as we will revisit below, none of this means that we are necessarily right when we try to analyze the ordinary concept of race—the contents of our concepts are often hidden to us (and see Glasgow 2010; Glasgow forthcoming a, forthcoming b; Haslanger 2012).

12. See Gross (2008) for a penetrating discussion of how, though treated differently, Italians and other groups with contested whiteness were always white legally.

one of those words—why not say that the term 'race,' like 'atom' and 'whale,' has a *surprising referent*? In particular, why not accept that the surprising referent for 'races' is the set of populations recognized by the most plausible version of genealogy theory?

Distinguish the surprising-referent view from a view that recommends that we should *change* what 'race' refers to. On the latter view, you might concede that the ordinary term 'race' is currently supposed to refer to something that is incompatible with genealogy theory; simultaneously, you might also maintain that we should improve the meaning of 'race' so that going forward it can refer to certain ancestral relations. To give this kind of view a name, let's call theories that recommend a change in a term's referent *revolutionary*. Revolutionary theory, however appealing it may be, is not applicable to our present project (though it will reappear later in our discussion). It answers the questions, what *should* 'race' refer to, and what *should* its definition be? Our present question is what the *current*, operative concept of race *is*. The surprising-referent proposal does answer this question. It says that there really are biological races in the way that whales really were mammals all along: these facts are just hidden from us. To paraphrase Ron Mallon (2017), we might call these *covert* kinds of thing. This view does not recommend that we change what racial terms actually refer to, as revolutionary theory says. Instead, we correct what we *mistakenly think* racial terms refer to. On this approach, 'race' already means that there is no Latinx race and that all races could look exactly alike; we just haven't realized it yet, since the true nature of race has been covert to date. As with 'whale,' the surprising referent of 'race' just needs to be revealed to us. Call this view *revelation* theory. On the genealogical version of revelation theory, it is surprising to learn that individuals can change races by reproducing with someone of another race, that there is no *Latinx* race, and so on. But it was also unexpected to learn that atoms could be divided and that whales were not fish, so why not accept some unanticipated aspects of race, too?

Revelation theory presents the big challenge for the race debate (cf. Glasgow 2009, 126–132). It puts us at a crossroads. On the one hand, we are inclined to preserve the phenomena we believe in, including race. This *existence commitment* pushes us toward genealogical theory and whatever surprises come along with it, if that is the most likely way to vindicate our race-talk. On the other hand, 'race' having a genealogical referent is incompatible with other commitments, as we have seen. We are committed to racial groups being organized by visible traits. We are committed to the idea that you are born with your race and cannot change it simply by having sex with someone of a different race. Many are committed to certain racial identities, including *Latinx*. Call these, collectively, our *features-and-identities commitments*. The big challenge is what to do when our existence and features-and-identities commitments conflict. If our most fundamental, stickiest conceptual commitments are the features-and-identities commitments, then we have to accept that races cannot be the ancestral populations recognized by biology. But if we're willing to negotiate on features and identities in order to preserve existence, then races could be genealogical populations, surprisingly. It all depends on which commitments are so firmly held that they get embedded into the very meaning of the word 'race.'

There is no general principle that dictates when one commitment has conceptual priority over another (Appiah 1991). Sometimes, as with 'whale' and 'atom,' we accept surprising referents. Other times, we do not. Apparently one source of the werewolf legend was that people with rabies were thought to be possessed by wolves. So we could have said that werewolves are real: 'werewolf' surprisingly refers to *person with rabies*. But we don't say that; 'werewolf' is defined by the *features* commitment that werewolves have to be human by day and wolf by night. To preserve this, we're willing to give up the existence commitment and accept that werewolves are not real. Similarly, sailors supposedly mistook manatees for mermaids. So we could have said that 'mermaid' surprisingly refers to *manatee*. But instead we stuck with the *features* commitment that mermaids, by definition, must be half-people/half-sea creatures, meaning that there are no mermaids. We could have said that phlogiston was really oxygen in disguise; but we stuck with the commitment that phlogiston is supposed to be a certain kind of substance that just does not exist.

So sometimes, as with 'atom' and 'whale,' we are willing to negotiate on our *features* commitments to preserve the existence commitment. Other times, as with 'werewolf,' 'mermaid,' and 'phlogiston,' we give up existence and favor our features-based definitions. The challenge for us is to identify which set of commitments is stronger when it comes to 'race.' What is non-negotiable for us in our shared racial discourse?

Our predicament is that there is no obvious way to figure out which commitments are stickiest. We may never satisfactorily meet the challenge. I am a fan of experimental approaches to questions about our concepts, where we poll people on what they think about race, ask them to classify test cases, and so on, as a way of exploring the definition of 'race' (Glasgow 2008; Glasgow, Shulman, and Covarrubias 2009; Shulman and Glasgow 2010). The results of such studies provide evidence about where our commitments lie. But we have to be careful here: this is just evidence; it is not a conclusion. Some say that each folk theory of race reveals a separate operative concept of race (e.g., Ludwig 2015, 255). Another possibility is that some single experiment can tell us what the content of the concept of race is (Pierce 2015, Ch. 4). I believe something else is closer to the truth: we have multiple commitments of varying strengths; our most strongly held commitments ultimately define 'race' and limit what it can refer to; and experimental studies only hint at what our commitments are and what their degree of conceptual entrenchment is.

The operative concept of race consists of the commitments people would stick to when they are forced by consistency to abandon part of a set of incompatible commitments (Carnap 1955; Chalmers 2012; Glasgow forthcoming a), and this is hard to demonstrate experimentally. Potential confounds abound, whether we poll many people or just reflect internally on our own thinking about race. Are participants really keeping *all* relevant cases in mind as they answer a prompt? Do they recognize the conflicts? How do you test the potential conflicting commitments about features and identities in a way that can rank their conceptual priority? Are there other commitments that are left out of the study? Are the experimental prompts distorting—or changing—participants' answers? So my view is that while experimental studies can be suggestive, no experiment could decisively prove which complex set we would be willing to negotiate on and which we would insist on keeping when they are thrown together into multiple inconsistent sets. (That said, I hope an experimenter proves me wrong on that one.)

In the empirical studies we do have, people regularly point to biological features like skin color as definitive of race, but though this dovetails with my argument, it really only *suggests* that race is defined in terms of biological traits and skin color in particular. Even if *everyone* prioritized biology, it still would not be decisive. After all, if a representative poll found ancient Europeans univocally saying that whales are fish, this would not decisively prove that 'whale' by their definition referred to a kind of fish. The question is what those language users would (and ultimately did) say when forced to confront evidence that the objects they call 'whales' are not actually fish. (Again, this is what Haslanger calls the *operative* meaning of the word 'whale.') Existing research does not force respondents to choose between vast and complex sets of propositions about race—and potentially cannot do this, given the confounds that are built into such choices. The most we can do is identify our commitments, map their inconsistencies, speculate as to which ones would survive attempts to reconcile them into consistent sets of beliefs, and try to partially defend our speculations with the best experiments and arguments we can find.

For now, our ongoing dialogue about race is arguably the best trial we have. This natural experiment can indicate which commitments we keep and which ones we jettison. In effect, books like this one—or the most perfect version of them, anyway—are the tests, and reader reactions are the results. But this is an inherently flawed sort of test, because it will always be possible that reader reactions constitute an online *redefinition* of 'race' rather than *revealing* our hidden-all-along definition. Revolution might overtake revelation.

So the best we can do is to interpret the data we have. The view I have tried to argue for here is that the features-and-identities commitments are stickier than the existence commitment. In essence, to say this is to predict that, if we could generate an ideal experiment, the ordinary concept of race would be shown to be inconsistent with any view that denied that Latinx identity is a possible racial identity (not least because of the tremendous stakes at play in such a denial). It will also be inconsistent with the idea that one could change races just by having children with someone from another race. It will also be inconsistent with the claim that all races could look exactly alike. As with mermaids, werewolves, and other fantastical things, we are more willing to stop believing in the existence of biological race than to abandon the idea that these core features and identities are central to race, at least when we mean 'race' in the sense in which it operates in our day-to-day lives.

Those who agree will find that biological theories of race face insurmountable problems. The most stringent version of the mismatch standard says that to demonstrate that race in the ordinary sense is biologically real, we'd have to show that it is useful for biology to recognize a Latinx race but not, say, a biological race of musicians; that there are biologically principled groups organized according to the relevant visible traits, including skin color; and that these groups cannot be entered and exited by reproducing with someone in a different group. Given what we know about biology, it seems unlikely to deliver race in that sense. Some may accept a weaker standard than this. Perhaps, for instance, you're willing to accept that *Latinx* does not need to be shown to be a biological race—you can accept that Latinx identity may not turn out to be a *racial* identity—but you also maintain that the ordinary concept of race requires that a person's race cannot change simply by virtue of her mating behavior. (Or perhaps, vice versa.) Even then, biology seems unlikely to deliver race in that sense.

4.2. Amnesia, Babies, and Equals: On the Relevance and Irrelevance of Social Facts

4.2.1. "But They Now Come to Me and Say..."

If the racial boundaries we think we see are not biological, then it seems we must have projected them onto ourselves. How we draw these borders has been a matter of choice: different societies, and the same societies in different eras, have recognized different racial lines. This behavior provides the raw materials for an alternate theory: Don't we create race by these acts of dividing humanity? We treat one another differently based on how we perceive each other's visible traits; perhaps that treatment, or perhaps the results of this treatment, are the very thing that generates races. Race, on this constructionist view, is a social rather than biological kind of thing.

The most rudimentary version of constructionism says simply that when we classify ourselves into races, we create real races, just as classifying ourselves into students and teachers creates actual students and teachers. We create the real groups of nurse, ballplayer, engineer, and dancer, so why not say we create race, too?

I do not think that this view can work, for it faces its own Mismatch Objection, in the form of a *different features* problem.[13] Imagine that we all forgot about race for a few minutes, due to some physical force—imagine the activists infused the global water supply with a different drug. The racial amnesia sets in quickly. We no longer recognize any lines of racial demarcation. We just see a spectrum of individualized traits, not groups based on them. Then after a few minutes our amnesia passes, and we resume classifying ourselves and others racially.

Rudimentary constructionism says that, because we no longer recognize racial divisions, we literally lose our races during our bout of amnesia. Jonathan Franzen goes from white to non-white to white again, in a matter of minutes. Oprah Winfrey stops being black. Sonia Sotomayor stops being Latina. Then they change back. Notice how strong the implication is. It is not merely that we stop *classifying* or *perceiving* people in these ways—that is true by hypothesis. Rudimentary constructionism implies that when we stop classifying people racially, something more substantive changes, too: people actually stop *being* Native American, Asian, black, Latinx, and white. In the way that paper money stops having monetary value if we stop classifying that paper as money, rudimentary constructionism says that if we stop recognizing race, then race itself actually *disappears*.

---

13. For elaboration, see Glasgow (2009, esp. Ch. 6).

But race does not work that way. On the operative ordinary concept of race, you cannot lose your race simply because we happen to forget what your race is. Franzen doesn't really stop being white just because of what we *think* or fail to think. It therefore looks like socially recognized groups have different features than races must have. Socially recognized groups disappear when the recognition disappears, but races are supposed to persist throughout different forms of social recognition.

Before complicating this argument, there is an important truth in constructionism that we need to capture. Let's call groups that society recognizes as races *racialized groups* (Blum 2002; Shelby 2005). Racialization, as distinguished from race, is socially real. Because differential treatment follows racialization, we bend ourselves into groups that come with their own possibilities, experiences, and identities. This racialized interaction has tremendously significant consequences for people's lives, and we have urgent responsibilities to address the massive moral failures that have historically marched in lockstep with it. In slogan form, we must *recognize racialization*. On that much we should all agree. But at the same time, constructionism posits, further, that racialized groups just are races. Against this, the amnesia thought experiment suggests that *races* and *racialized groups* have different features, because racialized groups, unlike races, disappear with changes in social recognition.

There are students and teachers, readers and authors, citizens and government officials. There are the powerful and the powerless, oppressors and oppressed. Chefs and diners, stoics and whiners, hardscrabble coal miners. And there are racialized groups. Not one of those categories is biological. The people who fall under these labels are brought together by the fact that they inhabit certain social roles, and I thoroughly agree with constructionists that such labels name realities that are explainable only from a social, rather than biological, perspective. I am just arguing that race is not one of those realities, for race is supposed to stick around even when the social facts change.

4.2.2. Sophisticated Constructionism

Most constructionist theories are more sophisticated than the rudimentary form I've just examined. You've seen two such views in the chapters by Haslanger and Jeffers.[14] Because constructionists disagree with each other about which social facts make a group of people into a race, race could be created by social facts that are more durable than the mere fact of engaging

---

14. Other constructionist theories abound. Just in philosophy this camp includes Alcoff (2006); Gracia (2005); Mills (1998); Outlaw (1996); Piper (1992); Root (2000); Sundstrom (2002a); and Taylor (2004), among others.

in racial classification. And because these more durable facts might not disappear during a bout of collective racial amnesia, a more sophisticated constructionism could avoid the amnesia counterexample. Consider the way that Ta-Nehisi Coates (2015) puts it in his penetrating reflection on blackness in America:

> the power of domination and exclusion is central to the belief in being white, and without it, "white people" would cease to exist for want of reasons. There will surely always be people with straight hair and blue eyes, as there have been for all of history. But some of these straight-haired people with blue eyes have been "black," and this points to the great difference between their world and ours. We did not choose our fences. They were imposed on us by Virginia planters obsessed with enslaving as many Americans as possible. Now I saw that we had made something down here, in slavery, in Jim Crow, in ghettoes. At The Mecca I saw how we had taken their one-drop rule and flipped it. They made us into a race. We made ourselves into a people.

Coates here positions race as essentially a matter of creating categories based on visible traits and attaching them to different positions in a power hierarchy, updating W. E. B. Du Bois's much-discussed claim that "the black man is the person who must ride Jim Crow in Georgia." Skin color for Du Bois is a "badge" that indicates which race one has been given by society, but the essence of race ultimately lies in who has power over whom. On these accounts, a white supremacist social system, be it in the form of Jim Crow laws or a one-drop rule designed to maximize the economic gains of slavery, is what imposes race on human bodies. According to Coates, whiteness in particular loses its raison d'être, if white supremacy disappears. By placing power at the center of race, Coates, Du Bois, and Haslanger (2012) could likely agree with this constructionist analysis of race from Hazel Rose Markus and Paula Moya (2010, 21):

> Race is a doing—a dynamic set of historically derived and institutionalized ideas and practices that . . . associates differential value, power, and privilege with these characteristics; establishes a hierarchy among the different groups; and confers opportunity accordingly.

Not all constructionists place power in the very definition of 'race.' Ian Haney López (1996, 14) defines race as "the historically contingent social systems of meaning that attach to elements of morphology and ancestry." This is a constructionist view, but it allows for races that do not *necessarily* involve a power difference. But whether power is thought to be essential or merely very common to racialization, racialization on all of these accounts is more complex than simply engaging in racial classification. The idea of race has been thoroughly woven into our actions and institutions, from slavery and George Sutherland's writings through the fact that a police officer wantonly killed Tamir Rice without proportionate and just consequences. Racialization shapes our family lives through inherited wealth and poverty, along with privileges and discriminations that are renewed daily. It is in a misunderstood glance and in a hiring decision that is unconsciously guided by unknown biases. It is manifested in massive inequalities and reflected in our most hallowed and influential chambers. It is in how we live and where we live. It is in our laws, and it is in our kitchens. It is incorporated into our bodies (Alcoff 2006; Haslanger 2012, Ch. 9).

Because racialized practice as a whole is more complicated and enduring than racial classification, the amnesia thought experiment is not sufficient to undermine sophisticated constructionism. Even if we collectively forget about race for a few minutes, that doesn't change the fact that Tamir Rice's perceived blackness was likely a factor in Timothy Loehman murdering him. It doesn't change the fact that Vaishno Das Bagai was ruled ineligible for citizenship. It doesn't change the way that power has been wielded and resources distributed. And so if race is created by a set of social forces that outlast mere classification, then they can explain how race can outlast a brief period of racial amnesia. That counterexample can't work against all forms of constructionism.

4.2.3. The Persistence of Race

I have learned a tremendous amount from constructionists about how we filter our lives through the lens of race. Still, I also believe that all constructionist accounts of race are exposed to counterexamples that are structurally similar to the amnesia case. For all constructionists, if the relevant social facts, the ones that they think create race, are not in place, then race would disappear. This exposes all versions of constructionism to the *different features* problem: on the ordinary concept of race, race persists even when the social facts change.

Consider the constructionist view that what makes race is inequality. It could be inequality in power, wealth, health outcomes, educational opportunities, or anything else. Regardless of the details, the problem is that these views make racial equality impossible. For power-based theories and all other inequality-based theories of race, inequality is the very *essence* of race. So if we gain equality, we lose race, on these accounts. The most that these views can deliver on the equality front is *post*-racial equality. *Racial* equality for these theories is literally a contradiction in terms. But in that way, inequality-based constructionism fails to capture our ordinary concept of race (Glasgow 2009, 120). We, and therefore our operative ordinary concept of race, are committed to the idea that racial equality is possible. It might be a long way off. It might be hard to imagine. If you are more pessimistic about the future than I am, you might think racial equality is even more unrealistic than drugs that make us look like the Dalai Lama. But racial equality is not *incoherent*. Yet inequality theories make it literally incoherent. They turn racial equality into the squared circle of social life—something that is impossible even in our dreams. And that flies against the ordinary concept of race. The ordinary concept of race—the operative one, the one we are committed to in the practices and discourses that constructionists rightly demand that we focus on—allows that racial equality is a *possibility*, a legitimate goal, an ideal that is conceptually sound. Inequality constructionism, including sociopolitical constructionism, invalidates that goal by turning it into a contradiction, and in so doing it violates the concept of race. Consequently, inequality theories of race are not actually theories of *race*. At best they are theories of *racialized groups*, or even more plausibly, *unequal* racialized groups.

Against this, Haslanger (2012, 255) has argued that there would be no *point* to society "recognizing" or "addressing" color-based categories if we get rid of racial inequality. This seems to be built on the notion that the reason to recognize race is to promote justice (Haslanger 2012, 250, 258–260). But why can't ultimate justice be the achievement of racial equality, rather than the elimination of racialization altogether (Outlaw 1996)? Moreover, what justice requires is different from what is in the world. There are people with hitchhiker's thumb—a thumb that can curve significantly away from one's fingers. Presumably there is no justice-based reason to recognize people with hitchhiker's thumbs. But even if they enjoy equality with those who lack hitchhiker's thumbs, they exist all the same. Similarly, inequality-based analyses of racialized practice are crucial to addressing injustice, but that is different from the task of identifying what exists.

All forms of constructionism say that race disappears if and when the relevant social facts, the ones that the constructionist thinks are race-making facts, disappear, be they facts of classification, inequality, or anything else. That is why all forms of constructionism are inconsistent with the ordinary concept of race: it is coherent to imagine race persisting through *any* social change, and constructionism rejects this possibility—as not just *unlikely* but downright *incoherent*.

In arguing against constructionism, I want to emphatically underscore the significance in the racialized facets of our social reality. We must attend to their impacts, in all their complex detail and history. Racialized behavior has affected lives in ways that we neglect at our moral peril, ways that arguably should draw the bulk of our attention. At the same time, no matter which social facts we attend to, we can always imagine them disappearing while race stays. And if race is conceptually able to persist across all social practices, then by definition it is not a social phenomenon.

One thought experiment challenges all constructionist views: imagine a world of only babies. Everyone else has died off. A new technology keeps the newborns alive and cares for them until they can care for themselves. Before the adults perished, they acted to prevent the terror wrought by centuries of unjust racist behavior. Wanting their children to avoid the same racial struggles with which humanity had plagued itself, the parents decided to wipe any trace of racialization. They destroyed any records that refer to our racially fraught history. In fact, just to be safe, they erased all history and culture other than what was needed to provide the babies with enough science to maximize their well-being. All babies are given equal resources. A variety of therapies become available to allow them the equal chance for equal health outcomes. And so on. Any other information is eradicated in an attempt to present the Reboot Generation with a social blank slate.

Because *every* racial practice, along with *every* result of our racialized past, dies off with the adults, constructionism is forced to say that a (racially) Asian baby stops being (racially) Asian when the last adult dies. According to constructionism, that baby was firmly Asian, but her Asian-ness somehow instantaneously vanishes at the age of four months and six days, even though the only thing that changes is that some adult, some stranger on the other side of the world, passed away. That is not how race purports to work. Surely the babies would still have their races after the adult perishes, if they have any races to begin with. This is how constructionism fails to capture race in the ordinary sense of the term.

Of course, committed constructionists will not (and do not!) share my reactions to these thought experiments. They will say that we *can* lose our races in the amnesia case, that racial equality *is* impossible (Haslanger 2012,

9), that races wholly sharing culture *is* impossible, and that the Asian baby truly stops being Asian.

The constructionist and I disagree on these points. You, reader, must judge for yourself. Interestingly, our judgments as to what would and would not make race disappear themselves determine how we *should* react. Our judgments about how to properly deploy the term 'race' give definition to that word, and in so doing they set boundaries for which judgments are correct. This conceptual bootstrapping may seem odd, bur reactions to these cases—our patterns of applying or refusing to apply the relevant term, in this case 'race'—dictate the content of the concept. If I have correctly anticipated the commitments shared by our linguistic community, then we have found a new part of the definition of 'race.' This part of the definition was not explicit in the working definition given earlier. If we are to use the language of race— which is an open question here—we have to say that on the currently operative ordinary concept of race, the British were not spontaneously made white in the early 1490s, that an Asian baby is Asian regardless of whether some random adult dies, and that people of all racialized groups could, in principle, enjoy equality and harmony. It's not just that races by definition must be organized by visible traits. In addition, races by definition must be *non-social*.

4.2.4. Surprising Referents, Take 2: Gender

Recall that sometimes our words can refer to objects in highly surprising ways. Whales are not fish, and atoms are not indivisible, despite what people thought. Such revelations are possible with social objects, too. In particular, sometimes we think we are talking about a biological thing, when really we are talking about a social thing (Haslanger 2012, Ch. 4). Consider the behaviors associated with gender. It was once common to think that biological hardwiring as males and females dictated who was most fit for taking on child-care responsibilities, changing lightbulbs, earning income, doing dishes, wearing pink. We now know differently. We invented the assignment of these behaviors to sex, just as we constructed what it means to be a 'foodie.' Boys used to wear pink and girls did not; then it was switched. We treat one another differently, which creates almost all of the gender role differences we see. For lack of a better word, we genderize.

Racial constructionists ask us to see race in the same, revelatory way. It may be true, on this revelatory theory, that race *appears* to be biological. It may also be true that race *appears* to persist across any social practice, as in the cases I have presented. But appearances can be deceiving. While it used to appear that women's biology rendered them unsuited for being medical doctors, we now know that to be false. Race is similar, on this version of revelation theory: it is revealed to be different from what we thought it was. Race is, on this account, a covert kind.

Again, I take revelation theory to bring the race debate's big challenge into relief. We could protect our commitment that race appears to be real by allowing that, to our great surprise, an Asian baby can actually lose its Asianness if a random adult dies on the other side of the planet. In that case, race could be socially real. Or we can stick with our *features* commitment, preserving the apparent semantic fact that race is supposed to be simply about our bodies and thus persist even when our social practices change, which would mean that constructionism is false. Which commitment is stickier?

Haslanger (2012, Ch. 10) holds that socially racialized groups act as a "reference magnet" for the term 'race.' Once we give up our belief in visible-trait-based biological races, we should search for the next best thing for 'race' to refer to—the 'magnet.' And, she claims, the next best thing, the magnet, is a set of social groups. Now we should be careful here: Why should we think that 'race' is drawn to a social magnet rather than some other magnet? If we need something for 'race' to refer to, why pick apparently mismatched socially racialized groups rather than, say, the biological populations on which genealogy theory focuses? What counts as the *next best thing* for 'race' to refer to? That's one gap in the constructionist reference-magnet argument. But there is also a more basic question: Why should we think that the term 'race' successfully refers to any reality at all? Why think it has *any* magnet?

Some people think that every term has a real-world referent to which it is magnetized, in which case racial terms "refer to whatever is the best candidate for reference given how we use those terms" (Pierce 2015, 60). But words do not *always* refer to the real object closest to their perceived reference. 'Werewolf' does not refer to a person with rabies. When we discovered that the people we called 'witches' did not have supernatural powers, we could have said witches are, roughly, people who are treated in socially witchized ways, in the manner that the racial constructionist thinks that white people are, roughly, people who are socially racialized as white. That would be the "best candidate" referent for 'witch' in the real world. But we remained semantically committed to a feature of being a witch, namely, they had to have the supernatural abilities to cast spells and commune with the devil. Since nothing in the world has those abilities, there just aren't any witches. (At least, this is part of the meaning of 'witch' when we say that there are no witches. Obviously, terms are ambiguous, and people sometimes use 'witch' to refer to practitioners of Wicca, who do exist. There are witches in one sense of the word but not in another.) In this way, not every word is magnetized to an object in the world. Our *features* commitments sometimes block that option.

So it is not enough to say that 'race' *could* have a surprising referent. The big challenge is to figure out whether 'race' *is* magnetically drawn to a surprising referent or instead purports to refer to some sort of entity that just doesn't exist. And as with genealogical revelation theory, the answer lies in which of our competing conceptual commitments are more entrenched, that is, which principles are most deeply rooted in our concept of race. If we find ourselves unable to accept that an Asian baby could stop being Asian when the last adult disappears, then race is not socially real.

To revisit a point made earlier, an answer to this question is out there, but it is elusive. I believe that the cases I presented earlier speak against constructionism in a way that is more powerful than the considerations constructionists call on. That said, though race is not socially real, racialization is. There are facts about inequality. There are facts about patterns of discrimination. There are facts about who is exercising power over whom. There are facts about violence, about privilege, about pain, about culture. We build the fences, and lives are consistently and unjustly taken and made worse off. Redress is required. We interact with one another on the assumption that race is real, and in that we create new realities and new moral obligations. But beyond that, constructionism adds that when we racialize, we create real *races*. If my semantic claims are accurate, then the concept of race does not work like that. Race, as opposed to racialization, is something that by definition must persist beyond the social, if it is to exist at all.

4.3. A Confusion

The arguments I have presented suggest that the biological sciences do not, and likely will not, deliver race in the relevant sense, though they might vindicate genealogical populations. The social sciences, similarly, can deliver racialized groups, but not races. What this adds up to is that the sciences cannot find race. From there it is easy to conclude that the world doesn't seem to contain anything that fits the operative, ordinary concept of race. If race is not a biological reality, and if it is not a social reality, then it looks like race just is not real. This is racial anti-realism: race does not exist. We have no races. Vaishno Das Bagai had no race, nor did Tamir Rice. Their lives were cut down early by terrible injustices multiplied by an exceptional confusion.

Some worry that anti-realism won't allow us to make sense of and deal with the lived reality of race.[15] They argue that racial anti-realism compromises people's identities, invalidates their experiences, or forces us to ignore racial injustices and neglect our voluminous racial ills by stripping us of the words needed to address them. If race isn't real, then we shouldn't talk about race— but if we can't talk about race, then how can we fight racism?

These are serious charges, and it would be a devastating problem if racial anti-realism could not answer them. So it is important to see that anti-realism does *not* require us to compromise identity, invalidate experience, or undermine progress in these ways. Anti-realism about race can capture *every* moral phenomenon that racial realism can. The difference is in how they frame the phenomena. In particular, Lawrence Blum (2002), Tommie Shelby (2005), and others have drawn attention to this solution:

We can talk about real racialized groups even if there are no races.

We can say that anti-black discrimination is discrimination that targets people who have been racialized as black. We can say that white privilege is the unequal benefit that accrues to people racialized as white. We can say that identifying as racially Asian is better understood as identifying as someone who is racialized as Asian. We can direct restorative and reparative programs toward victims of racist action. Anti-realism about race can in this way make sense of every consequence of every action that is based on the belief in race: these realities are facts of *racialization*, rather than *race*.

That said, if our belief in race is a mistake, we will have to confront the fact that lot is built on this mistake. Identities, communities, and more have been based on the premise that race is real. So the risk in anti-realism is not that we'll be unable to attend to injustice, but that once we accept our mistake, we might have to dismantle certain entrenched parts of our social lives, and not necessarily in a healthy way (Outlaw 1996). In particular, if we're not going to believe in race in the currently operative, ordinary sense, what will happen to our identities?

Early waves of racial anti-realism recommended simply eliminating the concept of race (e.g., Appiah 1985), and others have recommended replacing race with neighboring categories like socioancestry (McPherson 2015) or

---

15. See, for example, Du Bois (1897); Gracia (2005, 93, 97–99, 144); Hardimon (2003); Haslanger (2012, 199); Outlaw (1996); Sundstrom (2002b); Taylor (2004, 126).

genogroup (Montagu 1964, 23). I have argued that it would be better to re-pair the mistake and preserve something very close to our present racial iden-tities and communities, but in a new and improved way (Glasgow 2009, Ch. 7). To do this, we'd have to attend to not only the massive pain, abuse, and injustice that has been inflicted in the name of race, but also to the mistake upon which that name rests. Two pieces of the concept of race, namely that 'race' is defined non-socially and in terms of visible traits, have conspired to make our belief in race a mistake. So to fix the mistake, we must change the definition of 'race' accordingly. In particular, 'a race' should be *redefined* to mean something like *a socially racialized group*. This is one kind of revolu-tionary theory: we now ask, not what our concept of race *is*, but what we *should want it to be*. Given that our most pressing needs are to address that pain, abuse, and injustice, my view has been that we should redefine 'race' to directly and explicitly capture our social practices. I call this version of revolu-tionary theory 'reconstructionism.'

To emphasize: 'a race' does not *currently* mean *a socially racialized group*. We have seen that races are not racialized groups, because race—as presently defined—is supposed to persist even when social racialization expires. But we can always stage a semantic revolution and change our terms' meanings. If we eliminate the non-social element in the definition of 'race,' then race could be as the constructionists think it is now. On the reconstructionist picture, race-now is an illusion, and in particular it is not a social reality; but race-future could be socially real, if we redefine our words. Constructionism would be-come true, even though it is false presently.

Such a change in our definition of 'race' would require a significant shift in how we understand race, a shift so profound that it destabilizes the con-ceptual core of racial discourse. We would have to start accepting that a baby could start out Asian, and then literally stop being Asian if some adult on the other side of the world dies. We would have to accept that race would no longer persist beyond the social. But accepting tomorrow what is perplexing today is the price of revolution.

4.4. Could Race Be a More Basic Kind of Thing?

I have found this picture of anti-realism and reconstructionism compel-ling for more than a decade. I remain confident that *if* race is not real, then we ought to fix our mistaken belief in race by embracing conceptual revolution. But another theory of race has made me question whether anti-realism really is true.

Several years ago, a then-student of mine, Jonathan Woodward, asked this question: Granting that race is not a biological or social thing, why does that mean it couldn't exist? We eventually called this idea *basic racial realism*: rather than race being biologically real, socially real, or illusory, this view says that race is real in a way that is more 'basic' than what science aspires to (Glasgow and Woodward 2015).

Science, be it social or natural science, is in the business of finding out how things work and identifying what must exist in order to explain how things work. The sciences tell us that there are quarks and genes and genders, but no mermaids or phlogiston or witches. But, arguably, science is not in the business of finding *everything* that exists. For example, everyone agrees that science does not and should not focus on what we call *sundogs*—things that are either suns or dogs. No science cares about sundogs. The sciences care about suns, and they care about dogs. But there is no good reason for science to recognize sundogs as such, since that category has no role in its theories. For science, whether something is {a sun or a dog} is irrelevant. Barring a radical change in the universe, you'll never see sundogs show up in a biology or sociology textbook. Nevertheless, it sure looks like there are things that are either suns or dogs. Fido is a sundog, because Fido is a dog. So it is plausible to say that sundogs are real, even if they are scientifically irrelevant.

Now obviously *sundog* is a disunified category—dogs and suns share little in common besides being material objects. There are other categories that are more unified but still scientifically irrelevant. Take the category, *stuff around trees*. All stuff around trees has another thing in common beyond being stuff, namely being near a tree. But still, science does not care about stuff around trees any more than it cares about sundogs. The category is *closer* to being scientifically relevant than *sundog*, particularly because it significantly overlaps with categories that *are* scientifically relevant, such as *fire fuel*. But given that some stuff around trees, such as ash from a previous fire, is not fire fuel, the two categories are not the same. *Stuff around trees* itself is scientifically irrelevant. It plays no role in scientific theories.

Call kinds of things that are unified by some similarity but irrelevant to the sciences *basic* kinds of things. Because they don't rise to the level of scientific relevance, basic kinds, including *stuff around trees*, are not biological kinds or social kinds. Nevertheless, Woodward and I argue that basic kinds are real. After all, they exist. There really is stuff around trees.

You can see where this is going: If there really are basic kinds of things, like stuff around trees, why not say that there are races in this more basic sense, too? The argument for anti-realism held that, if race is neither biologically real nor socially real, nor real in any other science, then since there is no other way that it could be real, race is an illusion. But if a kind of thing can be real without being backed by *any* science, then that argument fails. Race might still be a real, basic kind of thing.

The other realist views are undermined by the conceptual fact that races are supposed to be—on the operative, ordinary definition—certain non-social groups distinguished by their visible traits. Neither biological nor social theories of race can deliver objects that fit that definition. But basic racial realism can avoid this Mismatch Objection: just make the unifying trait of race visible traits, and don't add anything social. What makes each race a race, then, will be that it has a distinctive visible profile. (What we will *identify* as races are groups that we *perceive* to have this profile.) Basic realism can deliver groups that have the exact features that are embedded in the definition of race.[16]

These visible traits are biologically real traits. Nonetheless, basic races are not biologically real, for the boundaries dividing us into races are still biologically arbitrary. And you might hesitate there. Why not just go ahead and call them biological groups, if they are based on biological traits?

It is worth keeping in mind that calling races biologically real is potentially dangerous. One study showed that prompting people to think about race in certain biological ways leads them to more broadly accept inequality between the races and to reduce interracial interaction (Williams and Eberhardt 2008); another found that biological race-thinking correlates with racist attitudes (Glasgow, Shulman and Covarrubias 2009). But not all studies reveal such dangers (Shulman and Glasgow 2010), and just because a fact is dangerous, that does not make it any less of a fact. So a more direct consideration is simply that when calling something 'real' for a science, it should somehow be useful to that science (Spencer 2012). Though basic races are unified by *traits* that considered independently of race might be useful for biology, the *ways of demarcating* within those traits, and the *groups* themselves—*races*—are not useful for biology. So there are no biological races, even if the traits that give character to basic races are biological.

---

16. You might wonder: if race is based on visible traits, how can people who have atypical traits for their group still be members of those groups? The short answer is that ancestry or some other factor could determine the racial membership of each individual even if ancestry or that other factor does not make a group of people into a race (Glasgow 2009, 79; Hardimon 2017, sec. 2.3; cf. Mills 1998).

To be sure, sometimes basic kinds can step in and act as imperfect proxies for scientifically relevant kinds of things. A firefighter might shout, "Clear that stuff away from the tree!" during a fire. She would be putting her point in terms of stuff around trees, but that's just paraphrasing. Really she would be talking about fire fuel. (If ash or a pail of water was near the tree, she wouldn't care if it was removed.) Similarly, it might be easier to gather data on people in a basic racial group than it is to find data on a significantly overlapping disease population; so to simplify, the research community might settle for using basic race as an imperfect proxy for the disease population. But this is just a proxy relationship. The basic racial group is not itself scientifically relevant. It just is easier to find than a scientifically relevant kind that it overlaps with to a significant degree.

4.4.1. Choosing Fences

The racial classifications that we ended up with sprung from a stew of ignorance and faulty human cognition, seasoned with the corrupting motivations of power, wealth, and status. In particular, as Coates emphasizes, Americans generated the one-drop rule, according to which having any black ancestors makes you black. Barack Obama, who has one black and one white parent and whose visible traits are basically right in the middle of The Spectrum, regularly ends up classified as black. This classification is the result of our perceptual capacities being trained to represent people in a way that adheres to the one-drop rule (Alcoff 2006).

We could have settled on other potential boundaries for social regulation; the one-drop rule was just the one that stuck in this one community. We could have adopted a reverse one-drop rule, as Haiti reportedly did (Mukhopadhyay et al. 2013, 170; cf. Mills 1998: 46–47). If we did—if our perception had been trained differently, with all the implications for social practice that go with that—then we would perceive Obama to be as obviously white as he is obviously black to us now. We took one way of carving humanity and made it socially *relevant*. We now seem more willing than we have in a long while to recognize mixed-race or multiple-race identity. The next time someone like Barack Obama is elected, the *New York Times* might announce that we elected a mixed-race president, not a black president (Nagourney 2008).[17]

---

17. The numbers are moving toward recognizing Obama as being mixed race (Cillizza 2014a). More generally, the one-drop rule may be losing its sway (Glasgow, Shulman, and Covarrubias 2009; Cillizza 2014b).

In this way, basic racial realism says that President Obama belongs to at least three races, which have uneven amounts of social salience. He belongs to one basic race—one collection of people organized according to one set of scientifically irrelevant defining visible traits—called 'black,' which comes into focus when we use the one-drop rule. He simultaneously belongs to another, called 'white,' which would be relevant if we used the reverse one-drop rule. And he simultaneously belongs to a third, 'mixed-race,' which is socially operational in contexts where we recognize being mixed-race. The first identity is the one that the United States has prioritized historically, but all three are equally real in the basic sense. That is, while the social adoption of the one-drop rule has had tremendous implications for the way lives go in the United States, from the perspective of basic racial realism, it does not change the fact that Obama is equally a member of all three races, and many more. There are multiple, cross-cutting ways of dividing us up by visible traits. None is better or worse from the perspective of what is *real*, though some better capture our social realities. It is therefore very likely that you, reader, are also part of multiple basic races. The one(s) you identify with is (are) just the one(s) that we have vested with social relevance.[18]

Basic races are out there in the world. We do not invent them. They are not social constructions. We have our basic races regardless of social relevance. Their lines are already drawn: we each look a certain way, and because of that we resemble some people more than others. However, we do get to choose which boundaries, which basic races, we care about. Faced with The Spectrum, we chose how to divide humanity. Many possibilities are given by the world; we decide where to put society's fences, and we could move them yet again if we like. All the way through, we'd be tracking real but basic, nonbiological, unconstructed kinds of thing. We'd just change which ones we care to track.

Because basic races exist independently of any of our social practices, basic racial realism more closely hews to the operative ordinary concept of race than

---

18. Pierce (2015) independently developed a view similar to basic racial realism that he calls "biological constructionism." The main difference is that, while basic racial realism says we have our basic races even if they are not socially relevant, Pierce's biological constructionism says that without the social relevance, those groups are not races (Pierce 2015, 85, 90). (We also disagree on terminology: he thinks that to call a view 'constructionist,' it is enough if it says that races are made socially *significant* (74, 89); I think constructionists must say that society makes races *exist*.) Haslanger (2012, 302, 306) very briefly considers a view like basic racial realism as well (and also see Haslanger 2016), but then she reiterates her constructionist view that the defining features of race are not visible traits but social facts.

constructionism does. As common sense says, if we achieve perfect equality of power, (basic) race continues to exist, because we still have our skin colors and other visible features. Likewise, if we achieve economic equality, (basic) race continues to exist. If all the adults die off and take all their racial practices with them, a baby born Asian remains Asian. And before we ever got our idea of race, way back when on the savannah and in the caves, in our ancestors' little bands where they had no idea of the amount of human variation or of the pain and division that would eventually accompany it, they had races in the basic sense, too.

So says basic racial realism, anyway.

4.5. Is Race Real?

So in the end, what is race? What is this division in which we invest so much that we need the Supreme Court to tell us where the fence is? This feature that meant Vaishno Das Bagai unwittingly traded British oppression for American oppression? This concept that says that our first mixed-race president is our first black president? This ghostly idea that hovers over Tamir Rice's two-second murder?

It is tempting to think that race might be a biological, sociopolitical, or sociocultural reality. My coauthors have demonstrated that there are real strengths to all three of these views. But I believe that the balance of arguments pushes us to conclude that race is neither social nor biological. That said, to know what race is not is not to know what race is. Is it an imagined piece of biology, or is it a real but scientifically irrelevant, basic kind of thing? The answer lies buried in the meaning of 'race,' somewhere in a partially concealed web of intentions about how to use racial terminology.

We stand again at the crossroads: Which is our deepest commitment? If, on the one hand, our racial discourse is most committed to the idea that racial *groups* are biological, non-social entities organized by visible traits, then race is an illusion. On the other hand, if the essential idea is just that racial groups are based on (biological) *traits* like skin color, then races can be real, basic kinds of things—otherwise random, intrinsically unimportant, and unscientific collections of individual people that we spin up into socially momentous entities. We need hypothetical thought experiments no longer, for the actual world has given us the test on this one: there are no visible-trait-based biological racial groups, but there are traits that could be the basis for real, basic races. Is that enough to have race?

On this question, I'm afraid that I am at a loss. All I have are weak and wavering leanings about which of these commitments is entrenched in the meaning of the word 'race.' It may be that we have some conversations in which we deploy one meaning of 'race' and other conversations where we deploy the other, allowing basic racial realism to be true for some conversations while racial anti-realism is true for others. It might be that we have not taken a stand either way, in any conversation, in which case 'race' is semantically indeterminate on this question, meaning that there simply is no fact of the matter whether basic realism or anti-realism better fits what we mean by 'race.' Or it may be, instead, that there is a determinate, decisive answer in one direction that I am not seeing. Perhaps you can do better at navigating through this particularly heavy fog.

References

Alcoff, Linda Martín. 2006. *Visible Identities: Race, Gender, and the Self.* Oxford: Oxford University Press.

Andreasen, Robin O. 1998. "A New Perspective on the Race Debate." *British Journal for the Philosophy of Science* 49: 199–225.

Andreasen, Robin O. 2000. "Race: Biological Reality or Social Construct?" *Philosophy of Science* 67(Supplement): S653–S666.

Andreasen, Robin O -. 2004. "The Cladistic Race Concept: A Defense." *Biology and Philosophy* 19: 425–442.

Andreasen, Robin O. 2005. "The Meaning of 'Race': Folk Conceptions and the New Biology of Race." *The Journal of Philosophy* 102: 94–106.

"An Indian Merchant's Suicide: Patriotic Protest against Racial Discrimination." 1928, May 22. *The Hindustan Times*, p. 5. Reproduced at: https://www.saada.org/item/20130709-2976. Last accessed August 7, 2018.

Appiah, K. Anthony. 1985. "The Uncompleted Argument: Du Bois and the Illusion of Race." *Critical Inquiry* 12: 21–37.

Appiah, K. Anthony. 1991. "Social Forces, 'Natural Kinds.'" In Abebe Zegeye, Leonard Harris, and Julia Maxted (eds.), *Exploitation and Exclusion: Race and Class in Contemporary US Society.* London: Hanz Zell, pp. 1–13.

Appiah, K. Anthony. 1996. "Race, Culture, Identity: Misunderstood Connections." In Appiah and Gutmann, *Color Conscious: The Political Morality of Race.* Princeton, NJ: Princeton University Press, pp. 30–105.

Arthur, John. 2007. *Race, Equality, and the Burdens of History.* Cambridge: Cambridge University Press.

Atkin, Albert. 2017. "Race, Definition, and Science." In Naomi Zack (ed.), *The Oxford Handbook of Philosophy and Race.* Oxford: Oxford University Press, pp. 140–149.

Bagai, Rani. n.d. "'Bridges Burnt Behind': The Story of Vaishno Das Bagai." http://www.aiisf.org/stories-by-author/876-bridges-burnt-behind-the-story-of-vaishno-das-bagai. Accessed January 5, 2016.

Blum, Lawrence. 2002. *"I'm Not a Racist, but . . .": The Moral Quandary of Race*. Ithaca, NY: Cornell University Press.

Burchard, Esteban Gonzalez, Elad Ziv, Natasha Coyle, Scarlett Lin Gomez, Hua Tang, Andrew J. Karter, Joanna L. Mountain, Eliseo J. Perez-Stable, Dean Sheppard, and Neil Risch. 2003. "The Importance of Race and Ethnic Background in Biomedical Research and Clinical Practice." *The New England Journal of Medicine* 348: 1170–1175.

Carnap, Rudolf. 1955. "Meaning and Synonymy in Natural Languages." *Philosophical Studies* 6: 33–47.

Chalmers, David J. 2011. "Verbal Disputes." *Philosophical Review* 120: 515–566.

Chalmers, David J. 2012. *Constructing the World*. Oxford: Oxford University Press.

Cillizza, Chris. 2014a. "Is Barack Obama 'Black'? A Majority of Americans Say No." *The Washington Post*, April 14. https://www.washingtonpost.com/news/the-fix/wp/2014/04/14/is-barack-obama-black/

Cillizza, Chris. 2014b. "The Next America Poses Challenges, Opportunities for Politicians." *The Washington Post*, April 13. https://www.washingtonpost.com/politics/the-next-america-presents-challenges-opportunities-for-politicians/2014/04/13/66d72e3e-c311-11e3-b574-f8748871856a_story.html

Chesnutt, Charles W. 1889. "What Is a White Man?" *The Independent* 41 (May 30): 5–6. Reprinted at the Charles Chesnutt Archive: http://www.chesnuttarchive.org/works/Essays/whiteman.html. Accessed October 28, 2015.

Coates, Ta-Nehisi. 2015. "Letter to My Son." *The Atlantic*, July 4. http://www.theatlantic.com/politics/archive/2015/07/tanehisi-coates-between-the-world-and-me/39D7619/

Condit, Celeste M. 2005. "'Race' Is Not a Scientific Concept: Alternative Directions." *L'Observatoire de la génétique* 24.

Diamond, Jared. 1994. "Race without Color." *Discover* 15(11): 82–89.

Dobzhansky, T. 1941. "The Race Concept in Biology." *Scientific Monthly* 52: 161–165.

Du Bois, W. E. B. 1987 [1897]. "The Conservation of Races." Reprinted in David W. Blight and Robert Gooding-Williams (eds.), *The Souls of Black Folk*. Boston: Bedford, pp. 228–238.

Feldman, M. W., R. C. Lewontin, and M. King. 2003. "Race: A Genetic Melting Pot." *Nature* 424: 374.

Franklin, Ruth. 2015. "Trial and Error: Three Centuries of American Witch Hunts." *Harper's* 331(1986): 89–94.

Glasgow, Joshua. 2003. "On the New Biology of Race." *The Journal of Philosophy* 100: 456–474.

Glasgow, Joshua. 2008. "On the Methodology of the Race Debate: Conceptual Analysis and Racial Discourse." *Philosophy and Phenomenological Research* 76: 333–358.

Glasgow, Joshua. 2009. *A Theory of Race*. New York: Routledge.

Glasgow, Joshua. 2010. "Another Look at the Reality of Race, by Which I Mean *Race?*" In Allan Hazlett (ed.), *New Waves in Metaphysics*. New York: Palgrave Macmillan, pp. 54–71.

Glasgow, Joshua. Forthcoming a. "Conceptual Revolution." In Teresa Marques and Åsa Wikforss (eds.), *Shifting Concepts: The Philosophy and Psychology of Conceptual Variability*. Oxford: Oxford University Press.

Glasgow, Joshua. Forthcoming b. "'Race' and Description." In Quayshawn Spencer (ed.), *The Race Debates*. Oxford: Oxford University Press.

Glasgow, J., J. Shulman, and E. Covarrubias. 2009. "The Ordinary Conception of Race in the United States and Its Relation to Racial Attitudes: A New Approach." *Journal of Cognition and Culture* 9: 15–38.

Glasgow, Joshua, and Jonathan Woodward. 2015. "Basic Racial Realism." *Journal of the American Philosophical Association* 1: 449–466.

Gracia, Jorge J. E. 2005. *Surviving Race, Ethnicity, and Nationality: A Challenge for the Twenty-First Century*. Lanham, MD: Rowman & Littlefield.

Gross, Ariela J. 2008. *What Blood Won't Tell: A History of Race on Trial in America*. Cambridge, MA: Harvard University Press.

Haney López, Ian F. 1996. *White by Law: The Legal Construction of Race*. New York: New York University Press.

Haney López, Ian F. 2005. "Race on the 2010 Census: Hispanics and the Shrinking White Majority." *Dædalus* 134: 42–52.

Hardimon, Michael O. 2003. "The Ordinary Concept of Race." *The Journal of Philosophy* 100: 437–455.

Hardimon, Michael O. 2017. *Rethinking Race: The Case for Deflationary Realism*. Cambridge, MA: Harvard University Press.

Haslanger, Sally. 2012. *Resisting Reality: Social Construction and Social Critique*. Oxford: Oxford University Press.

Haslanger, Sally. 2016. "Theorizing with a Purpose." In Catherine Kendig (ed.), *Natural Kinds and Classification in Scientific Practice*. London: Routledge, pp. 129–144.

Hart, Jayasri. 1998. *Roots in the Sand*. Hart Films.

Herbes-Sommers, Christine. 2003. *Race: The Power of an Illusion. Episode One: The Difference between Us*. California Newsreel.

Hirschfeld, Lawrence A. 1996. *Race in the Making: Cognition, Culture, and the Child's Construction of Human Kinds*. Cambridge, MA: MIT Press.

Hull, David L. 1998. "Species, Subspecies, and Races." *Social Research* 65: 351–367.

Jorde, Lynn B., and WStephen P. Wooding. 2004. "Genetic Variation, Classification, and 'Race.'" *Nature Genetics* 36(Supplement): S28–S33.

Kaplan, Jonathan Michael. 2010. "When Socially Determined Categories Make Biological Realities: Understanding Black/White Health Disparities in the U.S." *The Monist* 93: 281–297.

Keita, S. O. Y., and Rick A. Kittles. 1997. "The Persistence of Racial Thinking and the Myth of Racial Divergence." *American Anthropologist* 99: 534–544.

Keita, S. O. Y., R. A. Kittles, C. D. M. Royal, G. E. Bonney, P. Furbert-Harris, G. M. Dunston, and C. N. Rotimi. 2004. "Conceptualizing Human Variation." *Nature Genetics* 36(Supplement): S17–S20.

Kitcher, Philip. 1999. "Race, Ethnicity, Biology, Culture." In L. Harris (ed.), *Racism.* Amherst, NY: Humanity Books, pp. 87–117.

Krogstad, Jens Manuel, and D'Vera Cohn. 2014. "U.S. Census Looking at Big Changes in How It Asks about Race and Ethnicity." *The Pew Research Center*, March 14. http://www.pewresearch.org/fact-tank/2014/03/14/u-s-census-looking-at-big-changes-in-how-it-asks-about-race-and-ethnicity/

Lambah, Mool Chand. 1920. "Caste Certificate for Vaishno Das Bagai." https://www.saada.org/item/20130701-2900. Last accessed January 5, 2016.

Ludwig, David. 2015. "Against the New Metaphysics of Race." *Philosophy of Science* 82: 244–265.

Mallon, Ron. 2006. "'Race': Normative, Not Metaphysical or Semantic." *Ethics* 116: 525–551.

Mallon, Ron. 2017. "Social Construction and Achieving Reference." *Noûs* 51: 113–131.

Markus, Hazel Rose, and Paula M. L. Moya. 2010. *Doing Race.* New York: W. W. Norton.

Mayr, Ernst. 2002. "The Biology of Race and the Concept of Equality." *Dædalus* 131: 89–94.

McNish, Emily. 2013. "Rani Bagai on Vaishno Das Bagai." https://www.saada.org/item/20130821-3099. Last accessed January 5, 2016.

McPherson, Lionel K. 2015. "Deflating 'Race.'" *Journal of the American Philosophical Association* 1: 674–693.

McPherson, Lionel K., and Tommie Shelby. 2004. "Blackness and Blood: Interpreting African American Identity." *Philosophy and Public Affairs* 32: 171–192.

Mills, Charles. 1998. *Blackness Visible: Essays on Philosophy and Race.* Ithaca, NY: Cornell University Press.

Millstein, Roberta L. 2015. "Thinking about Populations and Races in Time." *Studies in History and Philosophy of Biological and Biomedical Sciences* 52: 5–11.

Montagu, Ashley M. 1964. *The Concept of Race.* New York: The Free Press.

Mukhopadhyay, Carol C., Rosemary Henze, and Yolanda T. Moses. 2013. *How Real Is Race? A Sourcebook on Race, Culture, and Biology*, 2nd edition. Lanham, MD: Rowman & Littlefield.

Nagourney, Adam. 2008. "Obama Elected President as Racial Barrier Falls." *The New York Times*, November 5. http://www.nytimes.com/2008/11/05/us/politics/05elect.html?pagewanted=all

"Nose Diamond Latest Fad; Arrives Here from India." September 1915. *The San Francisco Call & Post.* Reproduced at: https://www.saada.org/item/20130508-2734. Last accessed August 7, 2018.

Outlaw, Lucius. 1996. *On Race and Philosophy*. New York: Routledge.

Pierce, Jeremy. 2015. *A Realist Metaphysics of Race: A Context-Sensitive, Short-Term Retentionist, Long-Term Revisionist Approach*. Lanham, MD: Lexington Books.

Pigliucci, Massimo. 2013. "What Are We to Make of the Concept of Race? Thoughts of a Philosopher-Scientist." *Studies in History and Philosophy of Biological and Biomedical Sciences* 44: 272–277.

Pigliucci, Massimo, and Jonathan Kaplan. 2003. "On the Concept of Biological Race and Its Applicability to Humans." *Philosophy of Science* 70: 1161–1172.

Piper, Adrian. 1992. "Passing for White, Passing for Black." *Transition* 58: 5–32.

Relethford, John H. 2017. "Biological Anthropology, Population Genetics, and Race." In Naomi Zack (ed.), *The Oxford Handbook of Philosophy and Race*. Oxford: Oxford University Press, pp. 160–169.

Risch, Neil, Esteban Burchard, Elad Ziv, and Hua Tang. 2002. "Categorization of Humans in Biomedical Research: Genes, Race, and Disease." *Genome Biology* 3: 1–12.

Root, Michael. 2000. "How We Divide the World." *Philosophy of Science* 67: S628–S639.

Sainsbury, Mark. 2014. "Fishy Business." *Analysis* 74: 3–5.

Sarich, Vincent, and Frank Miele. 2004. *Race: The Reality of Human Differences*. Boulder, CO: Westview Press.

Shelby, Tommie. 2005. *We Who Are Dark: The Philosophical Foundations of Black Solidarity*. Cambridge, MA: Harvard University Press.

Shulman, Julie L., and Joshua M. Glasgow. 2010. "Is Ordinary Race-Thinking Biological or Social, and Does It Matter for Racism?" *Journal of Social Philosophy* 41: 244–259.

Sidelle, Alan. 2007. "The Method of Verbal Dispute." *Philosophical Topics* 35: 83–113.

Spencer, Quayshawn. 2012. "What 'Biological Racial Realism' Should Mean." *Philosophical Studies* 159: 181–204.

Spencer, Quayshawn. 2014. "A Radical Solution to the Race Problem." *Philosophy of Science* 81: 1025–1038.

Stalnaker, Robert. 2002. "Common Ground." *Linguistics and Philosophy* 25: 701–721.

Sullivan, Shannon. 2013. "Inheriting Racist Disparities in Health: Epigenetics and the Transgenerational Effects of White Racism." *Critical Philosophy of Race* 1: 190–218.

Sundstrom, Ronald R. 2002a. "Race as a Human Kind." *Philosophy and Social Criticism* 28: 91–115.

Sundstrom, Ronald R. 2002b. "'Racial' Nominalism." *Journal of Social Philosophy* 33: 193–210.

Taylor, Paul. 2004. *Race: A Philosophical Introduction*. Cambridge: Polity Press.

Templeton, A. R. 1998. "Human Races: A Genetic and Evolutionary Perspective." *American Anthropologist* 100: 632–650.

Williams, Melissa W., and Jennifer L. Eberhard. 2008. "Biological Conceptions of Race and the Motivation to Cross Racial Boundaries." *Journal of Personality and Social Psychology* 94: 1033–1047.

Witherspoon, D. J., S. Wooding, A. R. Rogers, E. E. Marchani, W. S. Watkins, M. A. Batzer, and L. B. Jorde. 2007. "Genetic Similarities within and between Human Populations." *Genetics* 176: 351–359.

Yudell, Michael, Dorothy Roberts, Rob DeSalle, and Sarah Tishkoff. 2016. "Taking Race out of Human Genetics." *Science* 351: 564–565.

Zack, Naomi. 2002. *Philosophy of Science and Race*. New York: Routledge.

HASLANGER'S REPLY TO GLASGOW, JEFFERS, AND SPENCER

5.1. Returning to the Question

Each of the four accounts of race offered in earlier chapters captures something important about the phenomenon of race and offers a credible account of what race is. How do we decide between them? Do we have to decide between them?

Philosophical disagreements are often hard to evaluate. It is easy to wonder: What are the data? What are the agreed-upon methods? What is at stake? Moreover, answers to questions such as "What is race?" can easily inherit disagreements from other related topics. For example, we saw in Chapter 1 that if we try to answer the question "What is race?" by considering what the term 'race' *means* (using what Mallon [2006] calls the "semantic strategy"), we often end up with disagreement about race because of background disagreements about meaning. And disagreements about meaning can themselves rest on disagreements about such matters as how the mind works, what we can know, and whether abstract entities exist. Do we need to have a complete philosophical account of the world in order to determine which account of race to accept? That would be discouraging!

An initial, and somewhat straightforward, way of evaluating an answer to a "What is X?" question considers if it gets the cases right: we have a pre-theoretic sense of at least core examples of X and not-X, and an acceptable answer must apply to those cases.[1] For example, suppose we answer "What is a bachelor?" by saying that a bachelor is an unmarried male. That is not good enough. The Pope is an unmarried male, but is the Pope a bachelor? What about my

---

1. This is the "Matching Criterion" that Mallon's (2006) and Glasgow's (Chapter 4 in this volume), "Mismatch Objection" relies on.

dog Sparky? I don't think so. But just getting the core cases right doesn't seem to be enough either, for the answer to such questions are supposed to give us insight not just into which things are X, but also into *what it is to be X*. Plato's classic example in the *Euthyphro* is *piety*. He points out that all and only those things that are pious are loved by the gods. But, he argued, being loved by the gods isn't *what it is to be* pious. Why not? Because piety is in some important sense prior to the gods' love: the gods love prayer, for example, *because* it is pious. So their love cannot be what makes prayer pious.

How do we answer questions about *what it is to be X*? What is this sort of question even about? Let's consider why we might ask such questions. Two kinds of contexts come to mind. One is when there is a conflict over whether something is, or is not, X. For example, I say that mold is a plant, and you disagree. We then look up what it is to be a plant and discover that plants are living organisms that produce their own nutrients through photosynthesis. This is *what it is to be a plant*. So I'm wrong. Molds are not plants, they are a kind of fungi. Cases of this kind don't actually need to involve conflict. They may be more a matter of uncertainty: Is a mold a plant or an animal? (Neither, we discover, because molds don't satisfy what it is to be a plant or what it is to be an animal; figuring this out may also require knowledge of what it is to be a mold.) Another context for asking such questions is when we want to explain why something characteristically behaves in a certain way. For example, I want to understand why the trees in my yard are dropping their leaves, and you explain what it is to be deciduous, which may, in turn, involve an explanation of what it is to photosynthesize, etc. The twofold role of *what it is to be X*—settling uncertainty over cases and seeking explanation—are both important in answering such questions.

This suggests that to answer questions about *what it is to be X*, we must situate Xs in a broader frame of understanding. The questions carry implicit contrasts, for example, is a mold a plant (or an animal or a fungi)? Why is my tree dropping its leaves (rather than keeping them all winter)? Explaining what it is to be X characterizes the phenomenon in ways that provide explanatory links to related phenomena.[2] But it is not always clear what sort of explanation is called for, or what phenomena are relevantly related.

With this in mind, it is worth considering the idea that the four chapters are asking and answering somewhat different questions. As I read them,

---

2. I want to allow here that there are different kinds of explanations, e.g., explanations in terms of composition, function, structure, etc. See Garfinkel (1981) on explanation as a response to contrastive questions.

Glasgow and Spencer focus primarily on race as a classification of humans: Is this person Black? Is that person Asian? If so, then what features underlie those attributions? Jeffers and I, however, focus on a broader range of social and cultural practices: What are racial identities? What makes a group a racial group? Race is not assumed to be an intrinsic fact about us or our bodies, by virtue of which we can be classified. *Race* is a conceptual tool for understanding the social world; race is attributed to individuals derivatively by virtue of facts about their social milieu.

Our inquiries have different starting points, so our questions about the practices in question reasonably differ. Glasgow and Spencer ask whether the practices of racial classification in question are warranted, or whether the classificatory terms fit the world. (Spencer says yes, Glasgow, no.) Jeffers and I ask whether and why certain social and cultural practices are properly thought of (and should continue to be thought of) as racial. Jeffers and I both think that some social practices are racial, but differ in which ones we take to be relevant to this determination and whether the practices we focus on should continue. How does one go about comparing and evaluating answers to different questions?

In spite of the differences, one might nevertheless think that there is a background question that we all must answer: What makes something (anything!) *racial*, for example, what makes a practice (of classification, or other social practice) a *racial* practice? And here the four of us do seem to differ. Spencer takes it at face value that the OMB is employing a racial classification: this is what it claims to be doing and what people grant it the authority to do. Glasgow takes the reliance on biological visible features to be a necessary condition for racial classification based on a careful examination of ordinary judgments, hypothetical cases, psychological studies, and reflective equilibrium. Jeffers takes a shared form of life to be necessary for a group to be a racial group, based on historical research, sociological studies, and normative considerations concerning the value of racial practices. And I take social hierarchy to be a necessary condition on racial groups based also on an interpretation of our past and present practices and normative considerations about how we might usefully deploy 'race' in political debate. It would seem that we disagree not only in our conclusions, but also in our methods. We are engaged in different projects that overlap, but shouldn't be expected to yield the same results; there is room for many projects to flourish. That being said, there are reasons why we are engaged in different projects, and it is worth considering some of those reasons. I will consider Spencer and Glasgow first, and then turn to Jeffers, whose views and methods are closest to my own.

5.2. Reply to Spencer

On Spencer's view, races are genomic ancestry groups corresponding to the OMB classification of people into American Indians, Asians, Blacks, Pacific Islanders, and Whites. He provides evidence that the OMB classification is authoritative from the point of view of ordinary Americans by reference to the census and other legal documents. He bases the claim that there are genomic ancestry groups corresponding to the OMB classification on recent population genetics.[3]

What question or questions is this theory of race answering? As he sets it out, the heart of Spencer's project lies in asking whether there are biological races that might be relevant for medical research. Is such research legitimate, or is the belief in such races misguided? More specifically, he wants to determine whether there are genetic differences between the five groups formally classified as races in the United States. The OMB classification is significant because it is the standard for medical and other governmental research; and ordinary residents of the United States, when interacting with the state, knowingly rely on it.

Spencer makes clear why his project is important: if there is even a chance that there are significant biological differences corresponding to the Rosenberg $K = 5$ genetic ancestry groups, we should be doing research that explores such possibilities. We can facilitate such research if there is a standard classification system that can be assumed across research projects, a system that individuals know and the state enforces, and that matches the Rosenberg groups. It turns out that the OMB racial classification system meets these conditions, so it has a legitimate claim to being, in some sense, ordinary and—given the potential relevance for medical research—a valuable classification system. Moreover, it is one that most Americans consider a "racial" classification system.

It seems that a social constructionist about race, myself in particular, could grant all this. It is compatible with my view that there are genetic ancestry groups corresponding to the OMB categories and that we should keep an open mind about whether there are significant medical results to be had by doing genetic research on these groups. Given the challenges of gathering data and the significance of racial identities in the United States, it may also be fruitful to continue to use the term 'race' for these categories. Such questions

---

3. I'm not going to discuss the "mismatch" between the OMB classifications and the Rosenberg $K = 5$ genomic ancestry groups. This is something that Glasgow discusses at length in his chapters.

and concerns are very different from my own, however, so if concession on these points is what he is after, I see no conflict with my view (with the substantial caution that it is an empirical question whether using the term 'race' for these categories is, on balance, politically wise in the long term, or not).

Nevertheless, there are a number of places where I find Spencer's arguments unconvincing. First, if the issue is really about promoting biomedical and other research, it is not clear to me that the Rosenberg K = 5 level of classification is the best one for research purposes (see Koenig et al. 2008; Hochman 2013); there is little evidence that the K = 5 classification is the most interesting or medically significant. On the assumption that the goal is to organize ourselves into meaningful (or potentially meaningful) biological categories for the purposes of medical research, wouldn't a more fine-grained (or differently grained) classification system be better? Why not divide up human populations along the lines of historical exposure to malaria (so linked to sickle cell disease), or those descended from pastoral tribes (so less prone to lactose intolerance), or annual exposure to sunlight (relevant to vitamin D absorption and other diseases such as multiple sclerosis), or many other possible classifications?[4] Given that the state can undertake to enforce just about any system, why shouldn't the OMB use a more obviously biologically fruitful one? Or why include racial categories on the census (and other legal documents) at all and instead leave the classification to the medical professionals?

I also find implausible Spencer's arguments that the OMB is the "expert" on race that ordinary speakers defer to. Would the general population defer to any classification tagged as "racial," by the OMB; for example, if the OMB chose the Rosenberg K = 12 classification, would that become the ordinary concept of race? (I doubt it.) It might be that such a change in the

---

4. I'm also confused about Spencer's claim that racial terms are "tags" or "names" (as in the sense of proper names) for the K = 5 continental populations. On one interpretation, the tag or name is attached to a particular—just as the name 'Sally' is attached to me. What is the particular for which 'Black' is a name? Perhaps it is the set of individuals who have a certain genetic profile. But which set is that? It isn't the set of currently existing (living) people with that profile, because someone born in 10 months of two Black parents should also be in the set. Is it the set of all future and past individuals with that genetic profile? Note that we are not in a position to determine what set that is—it may not even be determinate which set it is. Is it the set of all possible individuals who might have had that genetic profile? At this point we are nearing the second option, which is to take racial terms to be names, not for particulars, but for properties, e.g., having genetic profile G. But then it is confusing to emphasize that racial terms are names for populations, rather than just claiming that the term functions as an ordinary predicate. To say that x is Black is to say that x has a certain genetic profile. Racial populations are those who have one of the K = 5 genetic profiles.

state-mandated classifications is not in the offing anyway because the OMB is not primarily responsive to biologists or doctors, and is both historically and currently responsive to opinions of the American population (Nobles 2000).[5] Because the OMB seeks input from and defers to the general population about what race is in setting up its categories, it is hard to claim also that it is functioning as the expert.

Spencer relies on the broad use of the census and other legal documents to obtain information about race to support the claim that most Americans "defer" to the state, and in particular the OMB, to determine what race is. However, Americans are required by law to fill out forms in which they designate their race (for the census, school, employment, etc.) and are given a mandated set of options to choose from. There is considerable evidence that millions of Americans change their race and/or ethnic categories from census to census;[6] so many, at least, do not find such forms a meaningful exercise to report the facts about their ancestry (and why, if it were, would self-report be taken as sufficient?). There is a sense, of course, in which I defer to the state in determining what the state's racial$_{OMB}$ categories are, just as I defer to the state in determining what a class-A felony is (or, as in my earlier chapter, what a sheriff is).[7] But this is no evidence that I defer to the state in what racial or ethnic practices I engage in, or not. I also defer to astrologists in determining what astrological sign I am, and if I am asked to identify my sign, I give the answer based on my birthdate. But my ability and willingness to do this says nothing about how I live my life, what matters to me, or whether I take the classifications to be warranted. I take astrology to be ridiculous. If I were required by law to complete a census (or other legal document) that asks me to indicate my astrological sign, not based on my birthdate, but on self-identification, I would give an answer, but my answer would say nothing about what I mean, how I live, or to whom I grant authority. Those of us interested in racial and racializing practices see the OMB as part of the system that creates and enforces race as we know it, not a source of expertise with respect to what race is.

---

5. The Census Bureau National Advisory Committee on Racial, Ethnic, and Other Populations (previously the National Advisory Committee) includes members from diverse populations, conducts regular public meetings, and makes recommendations based on input from academic and non-academic sources.

6. http://www.pewresearch.org/fact-tank/2014/05/05/millions-of-americans-changed-their-racial-or-ethnic-identity-from-one-census-to-the-next/

7. For example, the fact that state governments use a binary sex distinction on state documents and that most people assume, as a result, that sex is binary, does not make it true. The fact that most people have either an XX or XY chromosomes does not make it true either.

There are clearly different legitimate priorities in considering the huge range of racial phenomena—biological, medical, cultural, political, legal, aesthetic, normative—and the theorist comes to them with a particular set of practices in mind, a particular set of questions, and a particular theoretical and/or political purpose (see Haslanger 2016). The social and political practices that I want to describe and explain concern patterns in human interaction, racial ideology, and durable forms of social stratification, and for this, neither the OMB classification, nor the Rosenberg research, is especially useful. Biology and the state are only some of the many factors to draw on in answering legitimate questions about race. I am happy to grant that Spencer has pointed to one way of understanding race in response to one set of questions and concerns. We should be cautious, however, in concluding that he has captured "our" concept of race, or that that we should use the term as he proposes in all (or even some) contexts.

5.3. Reply to Glasgow

Glasgow provides us with a hard choice. Either race is not real—our uses of the term 'race' are vacuous and are based on illusion—or race is real in only a "basic" sense. In the latter case, the term 'race' picks out somewhat random groups of individuals and has no meaningful role in natural or social science.

My comments here will focus on the first, anti-realist, option. In fact, I'm sympathetic to Glasgow's "basic realism," that is, a permissive ontology that allows him to say that the term 'race' has an extension, even though that extension is neither a natural or social kind (Haslanger 2012, Ch. 6). He and I disagree, however, about what constitutes a social kind. On my view, social kinds are not necessarily the subject matter of social science. For example, a city animal commission could stipulate a distinction between big dogs and little dogs (e.g., by weight) for the purposes of designating different dog parks as open to different sized dogs. Such a distinction, I believe, is a social distinction, even though it would not play a role in social science (Haslanger 2016). Nevertheless, races, as I understand them, *are* important kinds in social science. (I will say more about how I understand race as a social kind in my reply to Jeffers.) The core difference between Glasgow's view and my own lies in our methods for determining what it is to be a race. And I believe this difference can be traced back to differences in our broader projects.

How should we understand Glasgow's project and the question he is asking? As I read him, Glasgow is primarily interested in how we—understood as the general population—*think* about race. Our thinking about race, however, need not be conscious and self-aware. To elaborate this, he draws on the distinction between manifest and operative concepts. A concept is manifest to us, if we can introspect its content (e.g., by a priori reflection on application of the term to potential cases and intuited connections to other concepts). So the concept of *chair* is plausibly manifest. I don't need to conduct empirical research to figure out what a chair is, and it is unlikely that I would be surprised to find out what chairs *really* are. Operative concepts, on his view, are not fully accessible through a priori reflection. We may need empirical input, and we may be surprised about what we learn. So, for example, at one point the concept of fish seemed to involve nothing much more than an animal that swims in oceans, rivers, lakes, and such. But then we found out about whales. Whales swim in oceans, but aren't fish. That was a surprise! Similarly, it can be surprising to learn that tomatoes and avocados are fruits. The operative concept, then, takes our ordinary judgments as central, but allows for some degree of correction both to the content and the extension.

But, Glasgow argues, there is a limit to what we can learn and still be working with the same concept. If our empirical investigation yields that werewolves are just people with rabies (no magic involved), do we keep the concept of werewolf, or drop it? In fact, when this hypothesis emerged, we stopped applying the concept of 'werewolf' to actual cases, because the empirical results were incompatible with the core commitments underlying how we viewed and treated alleged werewolves. As he describes them, operative concepts are what we rely on in ordinary discourse, and consist "of the commitments people would stick to when they are forced by consistency to abandon part of a set of incompatible commitments" (Glasgow, Ch. 4).[8]

According to Glasgow, one core commitment about race is that "*Races, by definition, are relatively large groups of people who are distinguished from other groups of people by having certain visible biological traits (such as skin colors) to a disproportionate extent*" (Glasgow, Ch. 4) Since humans display a continuum of biological, visible traits, the condition is not satisfied. Not all Asians have eyelids with epicanthic folds. Not all Blacks are dark skinned or have tightly

---

8. Note that although Glasgow relies on my characterization of an operative concept (Haslanger 2012, Ch. 2), we disagree about this characterization of operative concepts. I don't think there need be a set of shared commitments that we (the general population) rely on when faced with inconsistencies or that, even if there are, that the ones we choose to hold on to in one context or at one time would have been the same in others, e.g., before we learned the relevant empirical facts. This disagreement stems, in part, from our background philosophies of language. I am a semantic externalist and Glasgow, as I understand him, is a neo-Fregean. See: https://plato.stanford.edu/entries/two-dimensional-semantics/

curled hair. Many people in the world are such that they cannot be placed into a race by virtue of appearance; but according to our pre-theoretic judgements, we all have a race. Given the inconsistency in our judgments, we have to give up something. Glasgow argues that the ordinary response is to hold on to the appearance criterion for race (the core commitment), and reject existence: races don't exist.

As I interpret Glasgow's project, the crucial issue is how to understand our classificatory practices. We are inveterate classifiers and constantly rely on classification in thought and action. On Glasgow's view, a crucial and ineliminable part of what we do when we classify by race is to classify by (visible) appearance. But it is misguided to think that there are a small number of human groups that can be differentiated by appearance, and that these map onto our pre-theoretic selection of racial groupings. It is an illusion that has had terrible consequences, and we should, on his view, disrupt the illusion and all it has produced.

I am sympathetic to Glasgow's effort to debunk our ordinary thinking about race and to find ways to convince people that their classificatory practices purporting to group humans into races are misguided. Yes, people do rely on visual cues to differentiate races and to attribute race to people (Alcoff 2005). And this is a source of much wrongdoing and injustice. If we could stop people from engaging in racial attributions based on appearance, we would be better off.[9]

I have some concerns, however, about Glasgow's arguments for his view. In particular, I think that the phenomenon of racial classification is more complex and the common practices are less consistent than he suggests. We surely attribute race to individuals based on factors other than appearance: this is why there is resistance to racial "passing." For example, there are individuals who appear and represent themselves as White, but are still considered Black (see Hobbs 2016; Ginsberg 1996); there are transracial efforts (e.g., Rachel Dolezal appeared Black but many think she remained White[10]); John Howard Griffith in *Black White Me* (1961) remained White in spite of his successful disguise; Gregory Howard Williams (who became president

---

9. My agreement with Glasgow here concerns an issue on which I disagree with Jeffers. If we understand race as culture—with no associated appearance expectations or norms—then I am not opposed to race—though I would call it *ethnicity* rather than race. But I don't trust culture that brings with it and enforces appearance and ancestry rules.

10. In 2015, Rachel Dolezal, who identifies as African American, or "trans-Black," was revealed to have White parents. For more information, see: http://www.nbcnews.com/news/nbcblk/rachel-dolezal-why-she-can-t-just-be-white-ally-n738911, also Dolezal and Reback (2017).

of the University of Cincinnati) "learned" he was Black at age 10 and to most appears White (Williams 1995).[11] More generally, in my experience, appearance is given much more importance in the White community than the African American community for determining racial membership. Given this history of the sexual exploitation of Black slaves and the one-drop rule, African Americans are well aware that there is a broad spectrum of appearance in the Black community, that some Blacks have "white" features and, more generally, that appearance is a poor guide to race. Such examples strike me as important evidence of "our" commitments and should be factored in as inputs to deliberation regarding whether and how we go on.

One strategy for managing these examples is to suggest that races (the groups) are associated with a particular set of visible traits, but race need not be attributed to *individuals* based on appearance. For example, one might count as a member of the Black race, even if one doesn't "appear" Black, by virtue of having a recent ancestor (within *n* generations?) who appears (stereotypically?) Black. This would also help address some of the mismatch caused by the spectrum of human features. But, importantly, one doesn't get to be White in the United States by virtue of having a recent ancestor who appears White. And as far as I can tell, there is no canonical appearance for Native Americans or Asians. This is partly why, in the United States, individuals who are hard to interpret visually in racial terms are often asked "Where are you from?" with the hope of eliciting a racial cue. (This is also reasonably interpreted as an insult—the implication is that if you aren't, or don't appear, White then you aren't American.) Such questions are often addressed to those who are born in the United States (and sometimes several generations before them are as well), so it isn't about birthplace or current residence.

Glasgow suggests, however, that there must be a shared concept of race—a shared set of core conditions on the application of the term—in order for us to communicate, even to disagree. One might extend his argument by suggesting that if there isn't a shared set of (consistent) conditions, then that is another reason to think there are no races. Nothing can satisfy a set of inconsistent conditions.

However, it isn't true that one must share a core set of commitments regarding the meaning of one's terms in order to communicate with others. In

---

11. For a summary of his story, and a slide show, see http://magazine.uc.edu/issues/0310/president.html. Williams's autobiography (1995) goes into more detail. Critics have questioned his narrative of identity: https://adpowellblog.wordpress.com/2014/06/14/the-problem-with-gregory-howard-williams-poster-child-for-the-one-drop-myth-of-white-racial-purity/

ordinary cases, one only needs enough common ground for the purposes at hand (Stalnaker 2002), and not for all conversations in which I might use the term in question. For example, I can talk with my colleague about the person in the next room, even though he believes that persons are essentially psychologically unified and I think they are unified by the continuity of their body. His core commitments include psychological continuity and not somatic continuity; mine are the opposite; our intuitions about hypothetical cases may diverge. Yet the people we are talking about aren't going to be transferred to new bodies, so we communicate perfectly well.[12] Most of us have no idea what our core semantic commitments are, and it is likely that we vary those commitments depending on context and with whom we are communicating. Moreover, if you and I are using a term in different ways, it is fairly easy to adjust one's use for the conversation at hand. For example, I have an articulated set of commitments with respect to the term 'race' (see Chapter 1), but I know that these are not the conventional commitments and that most others I talk to don't share those commitments. This does not prevent me from communicating with them, agreeing and disagreeing with them about empirical claims, and generally managing in (and often resisting) racial practices.[13]

Nevertheless, I agree with Glasgow that there are many errors in ordinary thinking about race, and that we sometimes think we are engaged in a meaningful classificatory process, when we aren't. We should aim to correct these errors, and doing so will be a step in promoting justice. For example, in August 2017, as I am writing this reply, the US Justice Department has announced that it will reopen an affirmative action lawsuit against Harvard University, alleging discrimination in admissions against Asian Americans.[14] In the wake of this decision, National Public Radio hosted a call-in discussion of affirmative action during which a caller, "Sean from Dayton," passionately expressed that in college admission, consideration of "the color of our skin should be non-negotiable. That shouldn't even be an admissible

---

12. For many more examples, see Williamson (2003).

13. There is much controversy over word meaning, and multiple distinctions are relevant here. Gasparri and Diego (2016) offer an excellent overview. For example, even if terms have a lexical meaning, it is not clear what determines that meaning, and lexical meaning (plus syntax) is not enough to determine a truth-evaluable proposition; moreover, semantics and syntax certainly don't determine what is said on a particular occasion (Saul 2012).

14. The recent Justice Department action is described here: http://www.thecrimson.com/article/2017/8/11/justice-department-intervene-analysis/ and useful background on the case can be found here: http://www.thecrimson.com/article/2016/11/7/harvard-admissions-lawsuit-explainer/. The *New York Times* also offers commentary: https://www.nytimes.com/2017/08/02/us/affirmative-action-battle-has-a-new-focus-asian-americans.html?_r=0

part [of the criteria for admission]."[15] This is an excellent example of how race is often equated, at least verbally, with visible features such as skin color. (Though what "skin color" is Sean from Dayton thinking distinguishes Asian Americans, who are supposedly at issue in this discussion?[16]) Like, Glasgow, I think the assumption that race is a matter of skin color (or other visible markers) should be rejected, and it would help in discussions such as the one just mentioned to point this out. But Glasgow and I differ in the next step. He argues that we should conclude that races don't exist (though racialized groups do). I maintain that there is a way of reading the history of our understanding of race such that it is apt to claim that races exist as social groups defined in part by a projection of "color" markings onto certain (assumed) lineages, and systematic subordination along those lines (see Chapter 1). What does this disagreement between us amount to? Does it really matter which approach one takes?

In fact, I think that there are costs and benefits to both an anti-realist approach and a social constructionist approach. In some contexts, one approach will be more fruitful, and in other cases, another approach will be effective. As I've emphasized, negotiation of meaning in conversation is a fluid and socially complex matter, and is not limited to insisting that one's interlocutor conform their usage of a term to the lexical or conventional definition. Context-free semantic facts, if there are any, cannot be wheeled in to settle our disagreement.

Nevertheless, let's return to Sean from Dayton's comments. As I read his comments, reference to "skin color" is not reflecting a core commitment about the visibility of race (or the "skin color" of Whites or Asians), but instead functions as a code for race that purports to reveal its moral irrelevance. Skin color, like eye color or earlobe shape, is a paradigm of something that should (in an ideal context) be morally irrelevant. If race is just skin color, then it too is morally irrelevant. But this equation with race and skin color deflects attention from what's at stake. Once skin color and other such visible markers have been used as a basis for unjust treatment, ignoring that history is either staggeringly naïve, or disingenuous.

15. See *On Point*, August 7, 2017. "Rethinking Affirmative Action," with Jane Clayson, Anemona Hartocollis, Stuart Taylor, and Nancy Leong. http://www.wbur.org/onpoint/2017/08/07/rethinking-affirmative-action In the podcast, Sean's comments occur from 23:01–24:03; the comment about skin color quoted in the text begins at 23:48.

16. One way of interpreting Sean from Dayton's points is to see him as complaining specifically about "black" and "brown" people "taking" admissions slots; this is why "skin color" is at issue. The fact that Asian Americans are also being displaced by Whites is obscured.

Glasgow's approach invites us to change Sean's thinking: your belief in races as essentially distinguished by skin color (or as visibly marked groups) is false. Instead, think of Asian Americans (etc.) as *racialized groups*. You can then see that differential racialized group treatment is warranted. Racialized groups have been treated unjustly. But racialized groups are not races.

My strategy, instead, is to focus on Sean's actions: look at what you are doing. Your awkward reaching to skin color as a proxy for race—a move that you may not be aware of or even be prepared to reflectively endorse—is part of a racializing process that creates and sustains the very racial groups we are talking about. Who are these groups? They are groups of individuals who may or may not get into Harvard (which was his concern), not by virtue of differences in skin color, but rather, due to actions like yours. Your apparently true and innocent comments about the irrelevance of skin color mask the (White) power you have to deny that race is morally significant, and this, in turn, buttresses your power. (He explicitly states in the full version of his comments that he is White.)

As I see it, my approach is focused on the actual people who will be affected by the discussion and the policies—the ones who are the subject matter of the controversy—rather than intuitions about how to apply terms in a broad range of remote possibilities. Let's talk about these people right here—you, Sean, call them a 'race'—what do they really have in common? Not skin color! You are wrong about that. And you are wrong about the moral aptness of differential treatment of races, for race isn't all about skin color (or visible biological features, more generally).

There is a sense in which I don't really care what Sean from Dayton is thinking, but who he is talking about and what his comments do to the groups being referenced (and those who make policy affecting them). Racialization does not happen elsewhere and elsewhen, but in our everyday conversations. My doubts about the importance of core semantic commitments (etc.) of the sort Glasgow explores leads me to focus more on racial practices other than racial thinking and racial classification. Racial language and concepts are not irrelevant to racial practices. However, invocation of "color"—whether it be skin color or other markers—is not an innocent classification scheme gone wrong, but is an instrument in constituting, tracking, policing, abusing, glorifying, and celebrating forms of social hierarchy.[17]

---

17. There is so much literature on this issue. A powerful example is in Lawrence Blum (2002, Ch. 6), though perhaps ironically, Blum agrees with Glasgow that there are no races, but only racialized groups. I believe that the heart of the differences between Glasgow and Blum, and

All that said, I am completely open to the idea that in some contexts, it is useful to challenge how people think about race, and assumptions they make about the necessary conditions (visible or otherwise) for being a race, or a member of a race. Intervening in political debate is like intervening in a conversation. There isn't a general strategy that will work in all contexts. My goal in this book has been to argue that the project of trying to understand what "the ordinary person" *means* by race is not really a well-defined project, given the controversies in the background about meaning, and that even if we are trying to identify what "the ordinary person" *thinks* about race, the phenomenon is more complex than Glasgow's account captures. Finally, I grant that it is not at all obvious what is at stake in distinguishing races from racialized groups, but have offered some reasons for thinking that not only do the full range of considerations suggest that races are social groups (see Chapter 1), but also that focusing on the groups that people are trying to talk *about* when they use the term 'race,' rather than supposed core commitments of their concepts, is not only semantically permissible, but also politically valuable.

5.4. Reply to Jeffers

Recall that in my discussion of "What is *X*?" questions at the beginning of this reply, I suggested that such questions, more specifically, "What is it *to be X*?" typically arise in context in which we are uncertain about (or encounter conflict in) adjudicating instances of *X*, or when we are trying to situate *X*s in an explanatory framework. As suggested earlier, I read Glasgow and Spencer as primarily concerned with *race* as a system of classification. When considering systems of classification, two sets of questions are pressing: (1) On what basis does the system differentiate between kinds of things? This helps us sort out controversies over cases. And, (2) are we warranted in using the classifications; do they give us a fruitful way to understand the range of phenomena? Are there things that fall into each of the various categories in the system? Answers to these questions help us evaluate the explanatory potential of the classifications within a broader explanatory framework.

---

me, lies in the philosophy of language. I'm attempting here, however, to articulate what is politically at stake in the linguistic controversy. In effect, what people think is not obviously accessible to us (or to them) and doesn't really capture what we are talking *about* with racial language: what we are talking about is a group of people, and what matters is how we treat *these people*, not some obscure intuitions about how we would use a term under bizarre conditions.

Jeffers and I don't deny that racial categories provide ways of classifying people. However, our discussions in this book are guided by an interest in race as a set of social practices. What does that mean?

Consider a different question. What is a family? As I understand this question, it is not about our concept of *family*, or what the term 'family' means, or how families, as a category, should fit within a broader classification system. Rather, asked in the context of the contemporary United States, it is a question about a particular social formation: the (nuclear) family. People organize themselves into families; the state recognizes families; families have effects on their members and their neighbors; families can be evaluated as functional and dysfunctional. In other words, families are part of a social ontology.

To say that families should be included in a social ontology is not to say that they are *things*. It is more illuminating to say that families are small systems that fit within bigger systems.[18] Families are made up of individuals and particular sorts of relationships between them (e.g., spouse of, parent of, child of, sibling of, pet of). They play a functional role in the society; for example, they provide a space of intimacy and lasting bonds, a site for dependent care, and a financial unit for cooperation and taxation.

When there are disagreements about what families are, the disagreements are plausibly about the sorts of relationships that constitute families (Do same-sex spousal relationships constitute a family? Are birthparents part of an adoptive family?), and the social function of families (How much dependent care should the family, as opposed to the state, be responsible for?). These questions are not best answered by consulting intuitions about possible cases or by considering the legal (OMB?) definition of a family. The question invites us to investigate a variety of families and similar groups, to come up with a model that has explanatory potential, and to evaluate whether there might be meaningful adjustments to how the formation works that would constitute an improvement (along some lines or other). For some time, the model (nuclear) family has consisted of a married heterosexual couple and their offspring. However, this model has never fully fit the facts, though the facts differ from place to place, culture to culture. Groups of individuals who live together in intimate, long-standing relationships that involve financial and material interdependence include unmarried (and now married) straight and gay couples, adopted children, extended biological family, single parents,

---

18. Note that systems are not just groups of individuals, e.g., their parts are specified in terms of functional roles and they are multiply realizable. See Epstein (2015); Haslanger (2017).

groups of unmarried (coupled or un-coupled) friends, etc. The question, "What is a family?" is too open-ended to answer on its own because the data are too complex and could be organized in different ways. We need more information about the point of the question (is there a background controversy about cases?), the relevant contrasts, the explanatory (or legislative) project to which an answer contributes, and background normative considerations (Garfinkel 1981). For example, am I a sociologist attempting to explain the racial achievement gap by reference to family structure? Or a psychologist planning a treatment plan for a depressed child? Or am I a legislator making a recommendation for revision of the tax code? Or am I deciding whom to invite to a family reunion?

When I ask "What is race?"—and I believe this is true of Jeffers as well—the goal of the project is to understand a distinctive set of social formations generally understood as racial, for example, patterns of association, stable positions within a social hierarchy, values and cultural differences (e.g., in religion, music, literature, and art). One issue is whether these social formations have a biological basis; for example, is the racial wealth gap, or the academic achievement gap, or the marriage rate, best explained by biological differences between the races? All of the authors in this book would reject this hypothesis. In short, no. A related question that also raises issues of biology is whether humans are naturally disposed to mistrust or feel hostile to others who "look different" from us (Hirschfield 1998; Mallon 2019). My guess is that the four of us all reject this hypothesis as well. (However, note that even if this is a human predisposition, that does not mean that it is inevitably expressed—socialization can override it.) On my view, the very notion of people "looking different" is socially shaped. As a mother once mentioned to me (jokingly) in commenting that I look like my (adopted, Black) son: "People say I look like my sons. But how could that be? They are boys!" Her point was to raise the question of why the judgment of "looking like" in such cases is supposed to be evaluated mainly in terms of facial features, skin color, hair texture, and other racial markers, and not by age, size, sex.

In general, social constructionists about race look to history to explain the origin of racial formations and to social and psychological dynamics to explain their persistence. In this respect, Jeffers and I are engaged in very similar projects, and as far as I can tell, I think we would agree on the broad outline of the explanations of race as we know it. But there are also some telling differences.

On Jeffers's view, race is the product of European voyages of exploration and conquest (cf. Mallon 2013). The minimal conception of race sketched by

Hardimon (2003) in terms of appearance, ancestry, and geography has been used as a basis for dividing humans into groups, and according them different social, political, and legal positions. The groups, being differently positioned in society, each developed a culture that both protected them against harms and offered affirming interpretations of their histories, their lives, and their bodies. As a result, although the origin of racial groups lies in subordination along lines of minimal race, racial formations have evolved past this and are sources of value. In effect, one might argue that a social-political conception of race, such as my own, stops the analysis too early: although it captures a stage in the history of race, it does not do justice to how races offer valuable ways of life that, although rooted in a history of subordination and injustice, have surpassed that. As a result, we should not seek to undermine the racial order, but to support and build upon the existing racial formations.

I am deeply sympathetic with Jeffers's view. I agree that racial groups have developed valuable ways of life and that racial identity is a meaningful part of many people's lives. I also do not intend, nor is my view committed to, eliminating or resisting cultural differences; I want to eliminate White supremacy and other forms of unjust social hierarchy. There are two points, however, where I think Jeffers and I diverge. The first concerns the scope of our projects. The second concerns the normative considerations that guide our different inquiries.

In undertaking to provide an account race, the task is complicated by the fact that races are formed differently in different contexts. For example, it appears that there are both different races, and different criteria for being a race, in Brazil, South Africa, the United Kingdom, the United States, and other parts of the world. As I understand the four authors in this book, we are primarily concerned with racial formations (and racial classification) in the United States. However, this does not mean that we are only concerned with African Americans, Asian Americans, Native Americans, European Americans, and Latin Americans (the last of course being a controversial case of race). Considering how race functions in the United States, I would think that an African American's distant cousin who lives in Cameroon is Black, though not an African American; a Hmong American's grandmother living in Laos is also Asian, though not Asian American. That races extend beyond the United States is, for certain purposes of explanation, important. Attitudes and decisions within the United States (e.g., concerning immigration, legal standing, stigma, and cultural appropriation) have an effect on racial formations, not only within the boundaries of the United States, but around the world. And race has always been an international matter, involving the capture, enslavement, transport, and exploitation of geographically distant peoples, justified in many cases by reference to race (and admittedly also supposed "degrees of" culture). The problem is, however, that it is not clear how to define a "way of life" that is shared by all Asians, or all Blacks, or all Whites, or all Native Americans (I mention this also in Chapter 1). Even Latin Americans, who are sometimes counted as an ethnicity rather than a race, do not share a way of life (Alcoff 2000).

So here is one issue of scope: In analyzing racial formations in the United States, are we just considering the formations that occur within US borders? In other words, are we just considering African Americans, Native Americans, etc.? In my own account of race, I do not want to restrict myself to formations that occur within the United States, but include how racial formations in the United States extend beyond our boundaries to impact the rest of the world and affect the racial formations globally. For example, Blacks, around the world, are racialized in the United States, and this affects international relations, development efforts, and global capitalism.

But suppose we restrict ourselves to racial formations within the United States. Is there a basis for claiming that those who participate in these formations "share a culture" in a very thin sense? Perhaps they are cultures of the sort discussed by Espiritu as *pan-ethnicities*. Pan-ethnic groups have a shared identity as being racialized by the dominant culture, and develop shared practices of resistance (among others). (We would have to adjust this to include Whites as a pan-ethnic group—perhaps based on dominance?) I'm not wholly convinced that US racial groups even constitute pan-ethnicities. I would guess that there are complex diasporic populations who would constitute the relevant pan-ethnicities for non-White groups (Gilroy 1993), and these aren't coextenisve with African Americans, or Asian Americans, (etc.), culturally or geographically. Nor are they coextensive with racial or racialized groups that span original and diasporic communities.

One approach to address this problem—again focusing on US racial formations—would be to start from shared cultures within American racial groups, and take whomever the members of those groups count as members as part of the race. For example, if there is an African American way of life, and those who participate in that way of life count anyone with relatively recent ancestry in Africa as a participant in that way of life, then because African Americans regard Black Africans as members of their racial group, they are.

I am not suggesting that Jeffers would endorse such an interpretation. I offer it because I think it illuminates some of the issues. In particular, it prompts the question: What counts as a shared "way of life"? If the extension of a race is determined simply by being thought of in a certain way by core members, even if there is no shared language, shared cultural traditions, or substantive contact, then it is not clear how a "way of life" within the group is a source of unity and meaning. I am a whole-hearted believer in the value of shared ways of life. I'm raising here a version of the Mismatch Objection: I don't think that meaningful shared ways of life correlate with races understood as racial formations.

But perhaps I'm still interpreting the scope of the project too widely. Perhaps we should not be thinking of all African Americans, or all Asian Americans, or all Whites, as the relevant groups, but more culturally coherent and meaningful subsets. Immigrant Haitians in the Boston area share a "way of life" that is different from the "way of life" of African Americans in rural Mississippi. Should these count as different racial groups? Among American Whites also, there are substantial differences in culture. Should we conclude that American Whites are not a single racial group? These questions raise, I think, an important question for both Jeffers and me: Is it really useful to think of *racial formations* at all? Is race a plausible way of understanding how people organize themselves across the entire United States? Perhaps this is a false presupposition at the heart of the social constructionist project.

Let's return to the analogy with the family. Families are very diverse. Even in the United States there are different ways of forming families (e.g., love marriages, arranged marriages, no marriage); there are different norms for the behavior of partners to the marriage; there are different norms for child-rearing, household and financial matters, and inclusion of non-biologically related members. Not all family members love each other. Not all families live together. Not all families involve children or even sex. What makes a family, we might say, is structural: there are certain relationships of interdependence internal to the family, and certain functional roles that the family plays in the larger society.

Races are different from families, but they can also be understood structurally. Here is one way of capturing the structure: There is set of "anchoring"-ancestors who were (or were thought to be) from a particular part of the world at a certain point in history,[19] and a set of features that these anchoring-ancestors and their "same race" descendants have (or are thought to have). Having (or being thought to have) an anchoring-ancestor of this kind, and the features that are supposed to pass through the lineage, positions one in a social hierarchy. The hierarchical structure created and sustained by referencing

---

19. Jeffers draws on Hardimon (2003, 442, 445, 447) to suggest that for American races that it is ~1492.

the anchoring-ancestors and their assumed descendants positions individuals in races. Sameness of culture within a race is not required, so we avoid the mismatch between culture and race. These structures, however, are helpful in explaining social and historical phenomena.

However, I grant that there are mismatches, unintuitive consequences, and plenty of vagueness in this sort of social-political account. For example, on my view, a group can count as a race even though it is a total fiction that there are anchoring-ancestors from a particular region. For example, race and caste hierarchies are similar, but different. In caste hierarchies, differences between groups are not linked to different geographical origins, but typically are social role or function based. So, for example, one caste may be identified with priests, another with warriors, and so on. But there is no assumption that the priests, or warriors, originated in a particular geographical region. (Sometimes caste is explained by analogy with the body: the body depends on there being hands and feet, heart and mind; likewise, society's body also depends on such distinctions.)[20] Suppose, however, that an ideology develops according to which one of the castes (or sub-castes) is imagined to have originated elsewhere and to be physically distinguishable; suppose further that social formations emerge that exploit this, for example, by questioning the group's belonging, questioning whether the members count as "one of us," or their rights to remain. Then, on my view, this group is racialized—it is in the process of becoming a race—even if the ideological claims are false. The same might occur in the case of an ethnicity, a class, or other social divisions.[21] I grant that this is does not capture how many of us think of race, but it is valuable as a tool for understanding how racial formations work: what attitudes to expect, what policy changes to be alert to, and the evolution of practices both within a group and in response to it.

Another complaint about my view is that it doesn't capture the phenomenon of "passing." If an individual has a race by virtue of being a member of a racialized group, and if racialized groups consist of those who occupy a particular social position—possibly based on misreadings of visible features, or

---

20. For example, "The body also provides metaphors that fund religious conceptions of ideal social relationships. Hinduism's Vedic literature, for example, explains that the four successively 'higher' social castes derived from a cosmic sacrifice separating a primordial being's mouth, arms, thighs, and feet" (Fuller 2015). See Rig-Veda Bk 10 (http://www.sacred-texts.com/hin/rigveda/rv10090.htm). This line of thought supports the idea that castes have been considered endogenous (in contrast to race as exogenous) and by analogy with the body.

21. Arguably, this happened in Rwanda between the Hutus and Tutsis, and in the former Yugoslavia between the Serbians and Croatians.

fictions of origin—then one who "passes" as (is viewed as, treated as, and lives as) Asian is a member of the Asian race (mutatis mutandis for other races). This consequence is one that, at least to me, seems apt for some purposes, but not all. As mentioned in my reply to Glasgow, I think that how we use language is a complicated and context-sensitive matter, and we should not attempt to legislate how a term should be used in all contexts.[22] How we want to think about "passing" and claims of being transracial are not to be decided, I think, by consulting our current intuitions, but by a reading of our past and our normative commitments.

However, one might accept my account for races, as groups, but complicate what it is to be a member of a race. For example, let races be social formations within a broader sociopolitical structure (formations that distribute rights, access to social goods, material resources and such, based on "color"), and add that to be a member requires both that one is socially positioned in such a formation, *and* that one is accepted as a member of the race by others in the group, were the facts of one's ancestry known. In cases of "passing," there would at least be some cases in which one would not satisfy this further condition (consider again Rachel Dolezal). Adding the condition would potentially contribute some explanatory power to the account, but it is also an important normative question whether we should add it, and who are the appropriate "we" to add it.

This brings us back to the second difference between Jeffers's approach and mine. Both of our projects are importantly normative. Jeffers emphasizes the value of racial solidarity and racial practices, both for those who participate in them, and for the cause of justice. He eloquently articulates the importance of maintaining races as cultural groups. I take it that this would involve not just sustaining racial cultural practices, but using the minimal conception of race as necessary conditions on membership. So the normative recommendation is that we continue to group ourselves according to the minimal conception of race (appearance, ancestry, geography), and support the development and continuity of those cultures within these groups that celebrate the distinctive histories, traditions, and bodies of their members.

I agree with Jeffers that we need, for the foreseeable future, to promote the development of racial practices that protect members of racial groups from the effects of injustice and that discourage others from perpetrating injustice. Racial solidarity is valuable under conditions of injustice, both among the

---

22. I also discuss this in my original paper (Haslanger 2012, published first in 2000).

subordinated, and also among those who reject racial privilege (Shelby 2005). Both Jeffers and I also recognize that an account of race raises questions about how we envision the world we are aiming for, and what prefigurative practices it is important to embrace (Leach 2013). A prefigurative politics embodies in the movement for social justice the values and practices it aims to achieve. What are those values and practices?

Suppose that we want to promote cultural forms and practices that provide people ways of understanding their histories, their life experiences, and their embodiment in ways that are affirming and empowering. As I see it, the question on which Jeffers and I mainly disagree is whether drawing divisions between humans on the basis of the minimal conception of race, that is, along lines of "color" in my sense of the term (marked bodies that carry the meaning of geographically framed ancestry), is valuable *in the long run*. I think it is not. And moreover, I think there are risks in treating "color" divisions between humans as an ideal, that is, as something that we should embrace not just in response to current injustices, but as something to be maintained "after the revolution," so to speak.

As some evidence that actual shared "color" is not necessary for participation in empowering cultural forms, there is no doubt that there are individuals who do not have the relevant racial ancestry for a racial group, say Asian, and do not appear to have the relevant ancestry, but nonetheless participate in racial practices and find meaning in them. For example, a child might be told incorrectly that he had an Asian grandparent (perhaps he, or one of his parents, was adopted, and was not given correct information), and that even though he doesn't appear Asian, this is part of his background. The child might make this a central part of his identity and participate fully in an Asian American community. Actual ancestry and appearance are a poor guide to who finds what meaningful, not only by "mixed"-race individuals, but even those who fall squarely within the current racial formations.

But, more generally, how do we want to "carve" histories, and distinguish bodies, and prioritize ancestry? What does it mean for me to understand "my history"? Is my history the history of White people? Why that history? Is my past reduced to my ancestral background? My maternal ancestors sided with the British in the American Revolution and fled to Canada. Does that tell me anything about myself (other than the mere fact that this is true of my great-great-great-great-grandfather)? Should I consider myself Canadian? English? Royalist? Am I less American than a descendant of a family who fought with the revolutionaries? And what of my Black children (who, as mentioned before, were adopted). Is this history not theirs, too? Is their Jewish grandfather's emigration from Poland not part of their history? Is one's history really to be traced by "blood"? Why? Even if we do find value in tracing biological ancestry, how should that factor into our identities and group formations?

Moreover, what are the cultural practices that inform my embodiment? Skin cancer runs in my family, so I apply sunblock. But I also am amazingly adept at braiding cornrows, maintaining dreadlocks, putting in extensions (either by braiding or crochet), doing Senegalese twists, and other hair techniques. (I'm not so good at doing a weave, but have managed to do so a few times.) I've studied hair designs, learned through practice the geometry of the head, can distinguish different hair products and make an informed choice. I am known for light hands. My embodiment is not just a first-person experience. It is a way of being in relation to others, in both intimate and public ways. The phenomenology of embodiment is deeply affected and enhanced by appreciation of, and being appreciated by, others (Haslanger 2012, Ch. 9). Sometimes this is achieved through encounters with sameness, sometimes encounters with difference.

More generally, why should we assume that empowering cultural practices are ones that group those of the same "color"? Shouldn't we be interested in disrupting the assumption that "color" should divide us and seek ways to be embodied and form identities across "color"? It is extremely important to note that I am not claiming that we should deny any groups of people (large or small) opportunities to construct narratives or to engage in embodied practices that celebrate their understandings of their past or their bodies. This includes groups who have the same "color." However, I reject the idea that "color"-based narratives and practices are necessarily constitutive of *what it is to be of a race*.

I am well aware that "blood" relations are valued more highly than "non-blood" relations in the contemporary United States. I'm also aware that racial markings are taken to be of great significance to identity. These are background assumptions that I believe need to be questioned and that should not be enforced through norms of racial authenticity. In the world I envision "after the revolution," we will not be bound primarily by narratives about the significance of "blood" or appearance, for I believe these narratives misguide us to focus on relationships that narrow our capacity to live together well. The narratives may be important for now and for long into the future. But I work on a daily basis to prefigure a world in which they no longer limit how we might live in justice.

5.5. Conclusion

At the beginning of this reply, I suggested that there was much right and important about all four of the accounts of race sketched in this book. I posed the question: Do we have to decide between them? I have suggested that the four authors might reasonably be read as asking different questions and as undertaking projects of different scope. To the extent that this is correct, there isn't pressure to pick one as "the right view." We are all making important contributions to the understanding of race—whether we are talking about racial classification or racial formations.

My own approach differs from Spencer's and Glasgow's because I am not, first and foremost, attempting to understand race as a system of classification, or what the term 'race' means. Instead, I am trying to understand and explain a distinctive social formation that, I believe, shapes not only how the United States is socially organized, but how the United States functions in global economic and cultural relations.

I agree with a tremendous amount of Jeffers's discussion: our views are close both methodologically and substantively. We differ, perhaps, on the scope of our inquiry, and on the normative considerations that shape our vision of justice. However, I have not argued for the vision I've just sketched here. I am prepared to believe that mine is not well-grounded in the experience of being racialized in North America, and that it is ultimately naïve about what form of justice is possible. But I also think that we are not in a position to tell, yet, what justice will involve in the long run. The best we can do is engage in a prefigurative politics that constitutes experiments in living (Anderson 2014). In effect, I doubt that philosophy can tell me I'm wrong (or right!) about what justice will be, in the long run. That is something we must learn by doing, and doing together.

References

Alcoff, Linda Martín. 2000. "Is Latina(o) Identity a Racial Identity?" In Jorge Gracia and Pablo De Greiff (eds.), *Hispanics/Latinos in the United States: Ethnicity, Race, and Rights*. New York: Routledge, pp. 23–44.

Alcoff, Linda Martín. 2005. *Visible Identities: Race, Gender and the Self*. Oxford: Oxford University Press.

Anderson, Elizabeth. 2014. "Social Movements, Experiments in Living and Moral Progress: Case Studies from Britain's Abolition of Slavery." The Lindley Lecture, University of Kansas.

Blum, Lawrence. 2002. *I'm Not a Racist, But. . . .* Ithaca, NY: Cornell University Press.

Dolezal, Rachel, and Storms Reback. 2017. *In Full Color: Finding My Place in a Black and White World.* Dallas TX: Benbella Books.

Epstein, Brian. 2015. *The Ant Trap.* Oxford: Oxford University Press.

Fuller, Robert. 2015. "Religion and the Body." *Oxford Research Encyclopedia on Religion.* http://religion.oxfordre.com/view/10.1093/acrefore/9780199340378.001.0001/ acrefore-9780199340378-e-18#

Garfinkel, Alan. 1981. *Forms of Explanation: Rethinking the Questions in Social Theory.* New Haven, CT: Yale University Press.

Gasparri, Luca, and Diego Marconi. 2016. "Word Meaning." *The Stanford Encyclopedia of Philosophy* (Spring 2016 edition), Edward N. Zalta (ed.), https://plato.stanford. edu/archives/spr2016/entries/word-meaning/.

Gilroy, Paul. 1993. *The Black Atlantic: Modernity and Double Consciousness.* New York: Verso.

Ginsberg, Elaine K. 1996. *Passing and the Fictions of Identity.* Durham, NC: Duke University Press.

Griffith, John Howard. 1961. *Black Like Me.* New York: Haughton, Mifflin, Harcourt.

Hardimon, Michael. 2003. "The Ordinary Concept of Race." *Journal of Philosophy* 100(9): 437–455.

Haslanger, Sally. 2012. *Resisting Reality: Social Construction and Social Critique.* Oxford: Oxford University Press.

Haslanger, Sally. 2016. "Theorizing with a Purpose: The Many Kinds of Sex." In Catherine Kendig (ed.), *Natural Kinds and Classification in Scientific Practice.* New York: Routledge, pp. 129–144.

Haslanger, Sally. 2017. "Failures of Individualism: Materiality." Presented at the First Annual Critical Social Ontology Workshop, St. Louis, MO. Draft on Academia. edu.

Hirschfield, Lawrence A. 1998. *Race in the Making.* Cambridge, MA: MIT Press.

Hobbs, Allyson. 2016. *A Chosen Exile: A History of Racial Passing in the United States.* Cambridge, MA: Harvard University Press.

Hochman, Adam. 2013. "Against the New Racial Naturalism." *Journal of Philosophy* 6: 331–351.

Koenig, Barbara A., Sandra Soo-Jin Lee, and Sarah S. Richardson. 2008. *Revisiting Race in a Genomic Age.* New Brunswick, NJ: Rutgers University Press.

Leach, Darcy. 2013. "Prefigurative Politics." In *The Wiley-Blackwell Encyclopedia of Social and Political Movements.* http://onlinelibrary.wiley.com/doi/10.1002/ 9780470674871.wbespm167/abstract

Mallon, Ron. 2006. "'Race': Normative, Not Metaphysical or Semantic." *Ethics* 116(3): 525–551.

Mallon, Ron. 2013. "Was Race Thinking Invented in the Modern West?" *Studies in History and Philosophy of Science Part A* 44(1):77–88.

Mallon, Ron. 2019. "Naturalistic Approaches to Social Construction", *The Stanford Encyclopedia of Philosophy*, Edward N. Zalta (ed.), forthcoming URL = <https://plato.stanford.edu/archives/spr2019/entries/social-construction-naturalistic/>.

Nobles, Melissa. 2000. *Shades of Citizenship: Race and the Census in Modern Politics*. Stanford: Stanford University Press.

Saul, Jennifer. 2012. *Lying, Misleading, and What Is Said: An Exploration in Philosophy of Language and Ethics*. Oxford: Oxford University Press.

Shelby, Tommie. 2005. *We Who Are Dark*. Cambridge, MA: Harvard University Press.

Stalnaker, R. 2002. "Common Ground." *Linguistics and Philosophy* 25(5): 701–721.

Williams, Gregory Howard. 1995. *Life on the Color Line: The True Story of a White Boy Who Discovered He Was Black*. New York: Penguin Random House.

Williamson, Timothy. 2003. "Blind Reasoning." *Proceedings of the Aristotelian Society, Supplementary Volumes* 77: 249–293.

6 JEFFERS'S REPLY TO GLASGOW, HASLANGER, AND SPENCER

Useful debate concerning the metaphysics of race seems to me to require a healthy balancing of conciliatory and critical approaches, which might be true of all philosophical debate, but I also have reasons related to this particular topic in mind. With regard to the virtue of being conciliatory, there are the general values of being charitable and avoiding nitpicking forms of disagreement, but there is also the important question of how much distance we ought to perceive between the major philosophical positions on what races are. Ron Mallon's seminal challenge in his article, "Race: Normative Not Metaphysical or Semantic," forces us to consider the possibility that metaphysical disagreement about race among philosophers is largely an illusion, as there is widespread agreement among them on what exists and on the nature of what exists, with the appearance of disagreement still sustained only by differences in defining terms.[1] Mallon concludes that this appearance obscures the real debate worth having over normative questions concerning the value of various kinds of talk of race. One lesson that can be drawn from his challenge, even if we hold that there is a substantive metaphysical debate about race to be had, is that we should not exaggerate how different anti-realism, social constructionism, and non-essentialist biological realism are when they are all united in denying the existence of the biological essences traditionally ascribed to races and it remains unclear how much they diverge with regard to those entities or relations whose existences they positively affirm.

Nevertheless, willingness to be critical, sometimes sharply so, is warranted not only by the general wisdom of proving the worth

---

1. Ron Mallon, "'Race': Normative, Not Metaphysical or Semantic," *Ethics* 116 (April 2006): 525–551.

of ideas by putting them to the test of confrontation with opposing ideas, but also by the high stakes underlying the discussion of race. Distinctions between groupings referred to as races are of massive social importance in today's world. What therefore ought to undergird a critical orientation when doing metaphysics of race is an acute sense of the social significance of getting things right—indeed, I would go so far as to say that one ought to have a conscious commitment to one's metaphysical musings on race having useful implications for figuring out problems of social life (and thus also a commitment to forthrightly opposing positions one believes will lead us astray in that enterprise). This is, to be clear, not a matter of sacrificing truth for social utility, but rather prioritizing the derivation of practical implications when thinking about a matter of social importance.

Reflecting on the need to say something useful with regard to social problems can also help us address Mallon's challenge and maintain that, despite what he says, metaphysical debate about race will necessarily continue. Ideas of race among the general public are no doubt currently in flux, but biological essentialism remains very much an important part of the mix. This means that, even assuming it is true that philosophers of race disagree on absolutely nothing concerning what exists in the world, there is still the question of how best to encourage the wider public to revise their metaphysical understandings of humankind. Consider now, in connection with this, Mallon's examples of what should be factored in when engaging in normative debate about racial discourse:

> the epistemic value of 'race' talk in various domains, the benefits and costs of racial identification and of the social enforcement of such identification, the value of racialized identities and communities fostered by 'race' talk, the role of 'race' talk in promoting or undermining racism, the benefits or costs of 'race' talk in a process of rectification for past injustice, the cognitive or aesthetic value of 'race' talk, and the degree of entrenchment of 'race' talk in everyday discourse.[2]

Philosophers who come to the conclusion that, say, the costs of racial identification outweigh the benefits must reflect on how we convince people to stop taking for granted and let go of an aspect of their lives that seems as normal and real as their occupation or height. Philosophers who decide,

---

2. Ibid.., 550.

by contrast, that the benefits outweigh the costs must reflect on how we encourage the embrace of racial identities while simultaneously encouraging the stripping away of essentialist beliefs about race. Debate between philosophers holding these two positions will thus be, in significant part, debate about how it makes sense to try to change or not change common sense metaphysical pictures of the world. Adding the other factors Mallon mentions to the conversation only multiplies the possible metaphysical positions that can be held, as someone could perhaps promote an anti-realist stance in relation to personal racial identification, a social constructionist stance in relation to rectificatory justice, a non-essentialist biological realist stance in relation to certain medical matters, and so on.

In what follows, I will engage with my coauthors' chapters, attempting to balance conciliatory and critical moves. In the first section, I will respond to Spencer's non-essentialist biological realism, suggesting that we can see biology as potentially illuminating matters of race without agreeing that races are fundamentally biological. The second section will be about Glasgow's two competing positions, arguing that both his basic realism and his anti-realism collapse into social constructionism when plausibly reconstructed. Finally, in the third section, I will address Haslanger's political constructionism, highlighting our similarity and then explaining and defending how my cultural constructionism differs.

6.1. On Spencer's Non-Essentialist Biological Realism

One motivation for non-essentialist biological realism is the fact that race has been used by biologists as a subdividing principle for species other than humans. Philip Kitcher points out, for example, that Theodosius Dobzhansky, a central figure in the development of evolutionary genetics, discussed in his classic work on that subject differences between races among beetles, fruit flies, and snails.[3] To differentiate between races of fruit flies does not imply that some fruit flies are superior to others or even that we can expect stable behavioral differences between these races beyond higher rates of endogenous mating. The thought therefore arises that biological race should be recognized as a phenomenon very distinct from both the essentialist myths and the complicated social matters many of us associate with talk of race. Kitcher,

---

3. Philip Kitcher, "Race, Ethnicity, Biology, Culture," in *In Mendel's Mirror: Philosophical Reflections on Biology* (New York: Oxford University Press, 2003), 232.

in his "Race, Ethnicity, Biology, Culture," explores the possibility that social differentiation in the United States may lead in some cases to reproductive isolation sufficient to be counted as biological racial difference. Even with his linking of biology with social matters, it is the measurable fact of mating patterns, and not the social pattern of perception of outward difference associated with differing geographical origins, that makes race a concept he is willing to employ here.

Andreasen's use of Cavalli-Sforza's tree to distinguish between cladistic races among humans, which I described in Chapter 2, severs the tie between racial differentiation and social differentiation as completely as possible. Interaction between groups thought of as races in the modern period is not only not the basis for racial differentiation on this account but such interaction is, in fact, the cause of what Andreasen takes to be the gradual disappearance of races: "Ever since the voyages of discovery, colonization and immigration have been blurring racial distinctness."[4] The reduction of reproductive isolation between different branches of the tree collapses the branches, so the massive relocations and increasingly frequent interactions of people in the modern era threaten the distinctness of races, as Andreasen understands them, in comparison to the ways in which geographical barriers fostered their distinctness over the long period of human evolution prior to the modern era. Andreasen thus argues that social constructionism and her brand of biological realism are "not in competition" but rather are "complementary" because they address two different subjects.[5] When thinking about what "race" means, we may look to social constructionism to "aid our understanding of social and political implications of current uses of the term" and to a biological realist view of the kind that Andreasen offers to help us "understand the patterns and processes of human evolution."[6]

Especially given the goal of being conciliatory, there is a tough challenge here to the idea that social constructionists must reject race as a biological reality in order to affirm that it is fundamentally social in nature. Why not simply allow that "race" is a term that can be used in different ways in different contexts of research and discussion, and thus that it sometimes refers

---

4. Robin O. Andreasen, "A New Perspective on the Race Debate," *The British Journal for the Philosophy of Science* 49 (June 1998): 215.

5. Ibid., 218.

6. Ibid., 220, 219.

to something social and sometimes something biological?[7] Despite the temptation to relent here, it strikes me as important that we resist and emphasize the confusion bound to result from encouraging among the general public the simultaneous acceptance of two strongly divergent concepts of race. Even if we imagine that the resulting confusion will be relatively minimal, the question to ask is why we should court any such confusion at all when we can choose other specialized terms to refer to the kinds of populations that non-essentialist biological realists like Andreasen have in mind.

Spencer, in Chapter 3, provides social constructionists with a different sort of challenge. By tying his defense of the biological reality of race to the social currency of the racial categories of the US Census, Spencer suggests that the task of the non-essentialist biological realist is to reveal the biological underpinning of some commonly accepted notion of what races there are, rather than offer up a novel scientific division of our species that may have no connection whatsoever to what is commonly accepted. Spencer thus meets social constructionists on their own turf, so to speak. Furthermore, by taking as his starting point the question of whether race is medically relevant, he aptly highlights the practical significance of the possibility that our common sense racial categories represent real biological diversity. This shared focus with social constructionists on what has social currency and on what makes a practical difference to people's lives makes it a powerful challenge that Spencer demonstrates significant overlap between what are counted as races by the US Census and genetic clusters among human populations as found in the research of Noah Rosenberg and colleagues.

By the same measure, though, this shared focus increases the bite in the standard objection to all forms of non-essentialist biological realism: the Mismatch Objection, according to which discrepancies between biologically respectable distinctions and common sense racial distinctions show that we should not describe the biologically respectable distinctions as racial. In Chapter 2, I used the example of a woman born in England to parents from Bangladesh finding out that South Asians ought to be in the white rather than Asian category on Spencer's account. There is, I should admit, an interesting way in which Spencer's choice of Census categories helps him deal with certain Mismatch Objections. I would argue, for example, that to think

---

7. There are, to be sure, criticisms of Andreasen's specific proposal for a biological concept of race that could lead one to reject it regardless of one's position on the relationship between biological and social concepts. For a recent example, see Zinhle Mncube, "Are Human Races Cladistic Subspecies?" *South African Journal of Philosophy* 34(2) (2015): 163–174.

of Arab Americans as white will result in a failure to understand both anti-Arab prejudice as well as anti-racist forms of Arab pride, both of which take the non-European origin of Arabs to be significant.[8] Thus I would take the fact that Arabs are the same race as those of English or German heritage on Spencer's account to be a mismatch. Spencer can respond, however, that we do not have a mismatch here between biological and social categories because, as he shows, the overwhelming majority of Arab Americans report themselves as white on the Census. My reply to this is that it is not at all odd that Arab Americans are responding in accordance with the definitions provided by the Census, and it is worth remembering that simplicity (e.g., less rather than more categories) and stability (e.g., not rushing to add or subtract categories) are valued traits of bureaucratic schemes. I therefore take the current classification of Arab Americans as evidence of weakness in the ability of the Census to track racial difference, rather than as a demonstration of no mismatch.

The South Asian mismatch, though, remains probably the clearest example, and it is important, given the point just made, that its clarity is not dependent on seeing the Census as correct in its lumping of South Asians together with other Asians. It is interesting to compare the approach of the Office of Management and Budget with that of Statistics Canada: with the exception of those counted as "Aboriginal," the demographics of non-white Canadians are captured through the category of "visible minority" and the current list of options for reporting such status are Chinese, South Asian, Black, Filipino, Latin American, Southeast Asian, Arab, West Asian, Korean, and Japanese.[9] If the OMB can be seen as misleadingly lumping too many kinds of Asians together, StatsCan arguably does too much unnecessary splitting of Asians, but both recognize the social reality that South Asians are understood to be non-white.

The lesson of this mismatch and of any other is that biological continuities and discontinuities between human populations is a subject independent of the social recognition of racial differences. This is, of course, the same point that Andreasen directly and centrally affirms. My view, then, is that some non-essentialist biological realists, like her, recognize this independence and court unnecessary confusion by advocating that we use "race" to refer to both subjects, while others, like Spencer, recognize the need to avoid such

---

8. For useful discussion of these matters, see Amaney Jamal and Nadine Naber (eds.), *Race and Arab Americans before and after 9/11: From Invisible Citizens to Visible Subjects* (Syracuse, NY: Syracuse University Press, 2008).

9. http://www.statcan.gc.ca/eng/concepts/definitions/minority01a

confusion and offer a unified account of race but then wrongfully downplay the independence of the two subjects.

Now, in the spirit of conciliation, I would say that to call these subjects independent is not to deny that they are, in some ways, closely related. Indeed, I think social constructionists should never be afraid to admit that one cannot tell the story of racial distinctions without biological diversity entering the picture. The forms of physical difference involved in racial distinctions are necessarily at least partially related to forms of reproductive isolation, whether as a result of people being geographically separated going back to the distant past or through more recent social distinctions. Once we admit this, it becomes easy to admit that study of the genetics of human populations of the kind Spencer invokes has at least the potential to be illuminating with regard to the study of race. We can also be open-minded, as he is, about what such research might uncover regarding medical matters and how we might connect what is uncovered to our usage of common sense racial categories in medical settings.

Nevertheless, race is fundamentally social and not fundamentally biological. The strength of this position—or at least the strength of my adherence to it—can be illustrated with a thought experiment. Imagine if any mismatches between the groups picked out by the study of genetic clustering and the groups known as races in everyday thought and social practice were to disappear in the following remarkable way: people with influence over education policy, media outlets, and other means of knowledge dissemination came to be convinced by Spencer's non-essentialist biological realism and, over the course of a few generations, the identification of the genetic clusters at $K = 5$ as races became common sense, at least in the United States. In this scenario, we would have not just extensive overlap with some bureaucratic categories but a tight match between a set of biologically real groupings and the ideas of what races there are in all major forms of public discourse. This is, importantly, not impossible. It is part of how social norms work that scientific and philosophical ideas can shift and reshape them. Were this to happen, would it not then be the case that biology had become the foundation of race?

My answer is no. It is not merely possible but almost certain that biological research in this scenario could provide us with interesting facts about races, but this would be completely contingent on the prevailing social situation. A subsequent shift in popular ideas could result in much less connection to anything of biological significance (for example, grouping together European and East Asian under a broad Eurasian category determined by lightness of skin while splitting off dark-skinned South Asians, etc.). This second shift would not be a move away from race toward something else, but simply a reorganization of racial designations and identifications. The previous connection to something more biologically significant would thus be revealed as inessential, for what is essential to race is that people's looks and lineages as tied to places of origin gain social significance.

6.2. On Glasgow's Basic Realism and Anti-Realism

My stance with respect to Glasgow's chapter can be described as simultaneously conciliatory and critical because I reject both of the two positions on race that he describes and defends as live possibilities while holding that both of them can be easily reconstructed and accepted as versions of social constructionism. Indeed, I think Glasgow provides us with the grounds for not merely a social constructionist but a cultural constructionist perspective, in particular! Perhaps surprisingly, it is his anti-realism that collapses much more quickly into social constructionism than his basic realism, so I will start with my criticisms of the latter.

There is no doubt that Glasgow and his former student Jonathan Woodward have provided an intriguing challenge to philosophy of race with their introduction of basic racial realism.[10] A form of realism about race according to which race is neither biological nor social? This is, if nothing else, admirably creative and bold. Important to whether one can take it seriously is one's willingness to accept Glasgow's focus on visible traits as the core of the concept of race. Spencer, as readers may recall, specifically rejects the idea that races must be distinguishable from each other on the basis of visible traits, using the case of Melanesians resembling sub-Saharan Africans as an example.

I differ with Spencer on this and see two possible ways of resisting his point. Lacking Spencer's commitment to Census categories, one could resist the idea that we are talking about two different races here, since many who use the term 'black' and apply it to sub-Saharan Africans would be completely comfortable applying it to Melanesians as well. Alternatively, as I would prefer, one could caution against diminishing to nothing the physical distinctiveness of Melanesians. While it is certainly the case that one could choose an individual Melanesian and an individual sub-Saharan African and stump people on which is which, it seems easily possible to me to gain familiarity with Melanesian traits to the point of being able to do well at picking them

---

10. See Joshua Glasgow and Jonathan M. Woodward, "Basic Racial Realism," *Journal of the American Philosophical Association* 1(October 2015): 449–466.

out when shown a number of randomly chosen comparisons (and I am not only referring here to the noteworthy high incidence of natural blondes in the Solomon Islands, although this provides a nice example). I thus remain attached to difference in appearance of some sort as a necessary component of racial difference.

I part with Glasgow, on the other hand, about whether ancestry is a necessary component. He thinks it is not and uses his thought experiment in which a chemical agent is put into the water supply that makes everyone look like the Dalai Lama to show this. According to Glasgow, a world in which we all look the same is a world without race, even if, for a few generations, geographical and cultural factors work to keep genealogical lines about as distinct as they were before. It is true that I can imagine someone saying, in that circumstance, "we are all the same race." I can also imagine someone saying, in that circumstance, "we appear to be the same but this is only true at a superficial level—it remains the case that we are divided into races and our habits of association and our continued reproduction along these particular ancestral lines demonstrate that." I think the second hypothetical reaction is the more perceptive one and it is, of course, congenial to me that Glasgow evokes culture as a means of the persistence of reproduction along the old racial lines. Note also that I am not giving up on the importance of appearance by allowing that racial difference could persist in a world in which we all look like the Dalai Lama because difference in appearance was essential in distinguishing the old racial lines. Genealogical distinctions unrelated at any point in time to difference in appearance would not, I think, count as racial.

There is an insight in basic realism, however, that can be appreciated even among those of us who maintain the importance of ancestry alongside appearance. Glasgow writes: "There are multiple, cross-cutting ways of dividing us up by visible traits" (142). Similarly, I write in Chapter 2: "given the various continuities in how we look, there are different sets based on alternative divisions possible on this basis" (65). The ways of dividing up the world racially that we are familiar with are contingent and sit alongside other possible ways that are equally real in at least one important sense: there really are differences and similarities in how humans look—based, I would add, on ancestral connections—that can be discerned and used to differentiate us into broad groupings. These differences and similarities are not imaginary, even if boundaries we draw or could draw in accord with them will always necessarily be fuzzy.

Thus, if basic realism is the view that races are real groups of people unified by similar visible traits, we have reason to acknowledge that, first of all, it identifies something real about human beings and, second, this reality is worthy of our attention when trying to understand the contingent nature of racial difference as we know it or are familiar with it. These two points can be easily incorporated into a social constructionist account of race. Here is how such an account might proceed: groups that are the same in physical characteristics to the groups we call races in this world could exist without the social practices and common modes of thought that make them races in our world. Indeed, we might even want to refrain from saying that social practices and common modes of thought brought the groups we know as races into existence, because it is reasonable to think that, when considered from the vantage point of their delimitation by physical similarities inherited biologically, most of them pre-existed these practices and modes of thought. Races are thus social groups whose racial nature is a product of social construction but whose existence as sets of similar-looking people is not dependent upon anything social.

As it turns out, such an account is not only possible but has recently been defended by Jeremy Pierce in his book, *A Realist Metaphysics of Race*. According to Pierce,

> whatever groups get organized by our conceptual scheme into races would exist apart from such social organizing, and the social practices make those groups significant in a way that they would not be if we stuck with pure biology, since the biological features that tend to be common within each race are not any more important biologically than any traits we do not see as significant markers of racial distinctions.[11]

Glasgow notes the similarity between basic realism and Pierce's view (142n18). He also points out what he takes to be a terminological difference between Pierce and himself, namely, that Pierce appears to think that, for a view to be identified as social constructionist, "it is enough if it says that races are made socially *significant*," while Glasgow holds that social constructionists "must say that society makes races *exist*" (142n18). As I see it, Glasgow is responding to a problem of equivocation in Pierce's account. Pierce writes, for example, "it is better to conceive of the racial social construction as not generating the existence of racial groups to begin with but instead as drawing attention to

---

11. Jeremy Pierce, *A Realist Metaphysics of Race: A Context-Sensitive, Short-Term Retentionist, Long-Term Revisionist Approach* (Lanham, MD: Lexington Books, 2015), 97.

already-existing groups, giving them social salience and moral importance."[12] The wording here suggests that the groups that preexist the advent of their social salience can be meaningfully referred to as races or, at least, as "racial groups." But, as Glasgow notes, it seems clear at other times that Pierce's view is that "without the social relevance, those groups are not races" (142n18).

Pierce cannot count as a social constructionist, I think, unless he believes there are no races prior to the social phenomena that generate races. I believe we ought to be charitable and take as the clearest statement of his view the claim that "social constructions single out existing entities and make them into races."[13] It is telling, however, that he takes himself to be reaffirming this very claim when, a few pages later, he writes: "I do think races exist, and I think they exist independent from the social processes that give them significance."[14] This latter claim is, as far as I can tell, indistinguishable from basic realism, which is a rejection of social constructionism. While one lesson here is the obvious point that we should avoid equivocation, I think it is a happy thing for basic realism that it is so very close to what we are taking to be Pierce's considered view that Pierce himself appears to mix them up. I say this because I take Pierce's considered view to be a credible position on the nature of race. I am hesitant to embrace it wholeheartedly, as there are challenges in thinking about the way racial concepts have played a role in influencing the social and reproductive interactions of people that complicate the idea of a set of pre-existing groups made into races only by social salience (think, for example, of a racial category like *mestizo*). It may be, however, that the position can be easily adjusted to deal with such challenges (note that, when elaborating it prior to attributing it to Pierce, I spoke of most, rather than all, of the groups we know as races pre-existing their transformation into races).

Basic realism is thus clearly very close to being a credible form of social constructionism. If not collapsed into something like Pierce's considered view, however, it is completely implausible. Glasgow attempts to make basic realism sound not only plausible but more commonsensical than social constructionism by pointing out that, according to basic realism, we are what race we are regardless of social practices. If this were really all that basic realism says about the conditions of racial membership, this would indeed be an advantage over social constructionism with regard to the need to not deviate

---

12. Ibid.

13. Ibid., 92.

14. Ibid., 95.

too far from common sense, as we social constructionists must accept that our position does deviate from this standard assumption. Basic realism does not, however, actually hold this advantage. According to basic realism, as Glasgow tells us, whatever social practices are or are not in place, Barack Obama is not just black (as he and many others would identify himself) or mixed (as some would say, perhaps even interchangeably), but rather he belongs simultaneously to at least three different races, and this is not a matter of those races being mixed within him (indeed, "mixed-race" is one of the three!) but rather a matter of the different ways the spectrum of humanity can be carved up. This evidently does not accord with common sense.

Indeed, if basic realism is true, I take it to be the case that Barack Obama and each of us are members of an infinite number of races. After all, given the point that humanity is a spectrum, are there not an infinite number of ways of carving up the spectrum? I am willing to grant basic realism the point that, however many carvings are possible, the resulting groups can be considered real groups of similar things. I am even willing to grant that we could treat each group as a possible race. To say that they are all actual races and we are right now members of an uncountable number of them seems to me simply nonsensical. It undoubtedly leaves common sense far behind, and it is not clear what advantage it seeks to achieve in compensation for this departure. Non-essentialist biological realism departs from common sense with its mismatches in order to carve up humanity in a biologically significant way. Social constructionism departs from common sense in holding that social phenomena create and sustain the existence of races in order to reveal how, here as elsewhere, we have reason to question whether what seems natural and independent of our thoughts and practices is, in fact, what it seems. What does basic realism teach us with its departure from common sense? As mentioned earlier, only when reconstructed as the social constructionist claim that there are real groups based on similarity of appearance that can become races through social salience does it teach us something useful about the contingency of our racial categories. Otherwise, as far as I can see, it drops common sense and picks up nothing of value to replace it.

Glasgow's version of anti-realism departs from common sense as well, but only in the understandable and productive way that all forms of anti-realism do, that is, by denying that there are races in light of the problems of biological essentialism that make common discourse about race so often untrustworthy. If we must choose between Glasgow's basic realism, unreconstructed, and his anti-realism, I think the choice is extremely easy. We should obviously go with the latter. The reason why, to put the point bluntly, is that when

Glasgow's anti-realism is evaluated in combination with what he calls his revolutionary reconstructionism about race, there is, in fact, no meaningful difference between what he offers us and social constructionism. The collapse is pretty much automatic.

Let us review the steps in Glasgow's argument. Races are ordinarily understood to be groups distinguished by certain visible traits. Humanity is a spectrum with regard to visible traits, and biology will not lead us to carve humanity up in this or that particular way on the basis of visible traits. Non-essentialist biological realism is defeated by the Mismatch Objection. Thought experiments show that we can imagine people still being this or that race even in the absence of any social facts that could be viewed as dividing us along racial lines, so social constructionism fails. Being neither biologically nor socially real, race is not real at all (or, at least, so we will conclude if we do not consider or are not convinced by basic realism). We have, however, built identities and communities on the mistake of believing race is real, and we should address this error not by abandoning the term 'race' but by redefining it. We should change the meaning of the term 'race' from "groups distinguished by certain visible traits" to "social groups distinguished by being differently racialized," where racialization refers to being socially recognized as belonging to a particular race. Once we make this change, race will be real.

At what point along the way here should the social constructionist protest? I think one does not capture the ordinary understanding of race when including appearance but leaving out ancestry and geographical origin, but this is not a disagreement that draws a line between anti-realists and social constructionists. The points against biological realism about race will, of course, be affirmed rather than denied. So what about the alleged refutation of social constructionism? As a social constructionist, I believe people are raceless in the absence of any social facts dividing them into groups distinguished by appearance as related to ancestral place of origin. Am I thereby disagreeing with Glasgow? No, because he is not saying this is a sentiment that would be incoherent under any circumstances. His claim is that people who conceive of race in this way do so in a manner that does not accord with the ordinary understanding of the term. This is not something a social constructionist should feel the need to protest. Why should we deny that it remains common for people to understand race as something naturally inherited and not dependent upon any social facts? To suggest that denying this is part of social constructionism is to set up a straw man.

What social constructionists believe is that ordinary discourse about race, insofar as it implies that race is biological and not social, is mistaken, but it remains the case that ordinary discourse about race refers to something real, namely, certain social distinctions. Thus social constructionists have no reason to protest against what Glasgow wrongfully presents as a refutation of their position, although we will obviously still want to disagree with his conclusion that race is not real. We should not rush to do so, however, because, as it turns out, Glasgow's position is that social constructionists are wrong about whether race is real but everyone ought to become a social constructionist and, if that happens, it will become the case that social constructionists are right. As a result of this paradoxical stance, what appears to be a meaningful difference turns out to be meaningless. This is perhaps best shown by drawing a contrast with the disagreement we have with an anti-realist like Lawrence Blum, who holds that races are not real but racialized groups are. Is there a meaningful metaphysical disagreement here? As we have seen, Mallon suggests there is not, but I think he is wrong. Why?

Blum and I have much agreement on what there is—socially distinct groups generally referred to as 'races'—and on what there is not—biologically distinct groups taken to be real by many, perhaps most, who speak of 'races'— but we disagree on how to promote change among the general public with regard to common ideas of what there is and what there is not. It is important to Blum that we speak only of "racialized groups" when trying to speak of what is real because we need to carefully avoid "the implication that the groups being referred to are actual *races* (in the classic sense)—that they possess group-specific, biologically-based inherent behavioral and psychological tendencies and characteristics."[15] It is helpful, from this point of view, that "racialization refers to a *process*, largely imposed by others (but sometimes self-generated also), that a group undergoes."[16] This is a powerful position worthy of serious consideration. As stated in Chapter 2, however, I take the position that it is unnecessary and possibly misleading to switch from talking about, say, "the black race" to talking about "the group of people racialized as black" as if those talking about the black race were or are describing something non-existent as opposed to, as I would describe it, referring to a real group while misunderstanding aspects of its nature. I view the difference between Blum and myself here as meaningful (and, contrary to Mallon, I think it counts as metaphysical).

15. Lawrence Blum, "Racialized Groups: The Sociohistorical Consensus," *The Monist* 93 (April 2010): 300.

16. Ibid.

What difference is there between what I recommend to the general public and what Glasgow recommends? None, because he proposes a "semantic revolution," namely, the redefinition of "a race" as *a socially racialized group*," which will make it possible in the future for race to be "as the constructionists think it is now" (138). If the goal is for social constructionists to be right about race in the future through promoting their position to the general public, the only possible meaningful difference could be disagreement about whether they are right in the present. But there is no meaningful disagreement here. It is not as if there are groups whose present existence social constructionists affirm but whose existence Glasgow denies. He accounts for the existence of these groups using the same language as Blum: "there are racialized groups" (129). It is not as if social constructionists are right about what we should want the concept of race to be in future, as Glasgow says they are, but wrong about what people ordinarily take it to be right now, because no social constructionist believes that social constructionism has already achieved the status of common sense. In short, there is nothing for a social constructionist to criticize but the pretense that this version of anti-realism is meaningfully different from social constructionism. Rightly understood, Glasgow's anti-realism is not only not the enemy of social constructionism—it is a plea for a concerted effort at singing its praise!

A final point I will make is that, for all I have said so far, Glasgow's anti-realism might be seen as equally compatible with both of the kinds of social constructionism I described in Chapter 2. As a matter of fact, though, I think his view supports cultural constructionism, in particular. Notice that his primary reason for encouraging the reconstruction of the concept of race involves the importance of identities and communities. In his book, *A Theory of Race*, he talks about how the embrace of racial identity can, first of all, be "a psychologically and materially healthy response to living in a racist society," and this is certainly a point that political constructionists can accept.[17] He goes on to note, though, that there are some for whom "race would be valuable even if racism were no more" and he invokes Lucius Outlaw, whom I mentioned in Chapter 2 as perhaps the most prominent example of a cultural constructionist.[18] The harm that people like Outlaw (and myself, we can add) would perceive in the elimination of racial identities is among the concerns that Glasgow takes into account in arriving at his reconstructionist position.

---

17. Joshua Glasgow, *A Theory of Race* (New York: Routledge, 2009), 134.

18. Ibid.

Now consider this telling comment in Chapter 4: "the risk in anti-realism is not that we'll be unable to attend to injustice, but that once we accept our mistake, we might have to dismantle certain entrenched parts of our social lives, and not necessarily in a healthy way" (137). Glasgow believes, it seems, that anti-realist talk of racialized groups will not fail us insofar as we wish to attend to injustice, but the implication of such talk that racial categorizations are imposed mistakes will prove unhelpful when it comes to preserving our racial identities and communities as sources of value (and, once again, he directs us to read Outlaw). It is not unreasonable, I think, to interpret Glasgow as saying that political constructionism ultimately holds little, if any, advantage over anti-realism of the kind that Blum offers, but that cultural constructionism makes it clear that anti-realism of that kind is inadequate. If I am right in claiming that this leads him to a give us a version of anti-realism that is ultimately indistinguishable from social constructionism, then it seems fair to me to say that Glasgow's anti-realism collapses into not just social but specifically cultural constructionism.

6.3. On Haslanger's Political Constructionism

Naturally, there is much in common between Haslanger's position and mine, as we represent two forms of social constructionism. Beyond our obvious agreement that racial difference is fundamentally social in nature, it is notable that we both find it important to understand this claim as a matter of trying to speak with more clarity and insight about the same phenomena that has been spoken about in biologically essentialist terms, rather than as a matter of changing the subject. Haslanger emphasizes this, first, by using the example of Aristotle on slavery. Aristotle, we can say, was speaking about something we would agree is real when he offered his account of what slaves are, but this account was "badly mistaken" and a social explanation ("to be a slave is to be owned by someone according to the laws or customs of one's social milieu") represents "an improvement on the naturalistic account that defines slaves in terms of their cognitive capacities" (22-23). This example is very instructive, given the centrality that social constructionists tend to accord slavery in the development of modern ideas of race. Haslanger also uses the examples of Hippocrates' investigations of cancer, other shifts in understanding medical conditions, and changes in how people think about various divisions between castes, classes, and ethnic groups, such as the move from theological accounts of the power of monarchs to social accounts. Do all these conceptual shifts count, in Glasgow's eyes, as revolutions? Whether they do or not, to be a social constructionist about race, as Haslanger and I understand the position, is to be actively engaged in promoting this type of shift with respect to race. If this makes us revolutionaries and he is on our side, he is welcome.

Haslanger and I part ways, of course, on the role of culture in the explanation of the social nature of race. Before dealing with this disagreement, however, I should note that we are sometimes more or less on the same page even where Haslanger takes us to be notably different. She suggests, in her conclusion, that she differs from me no less than Spencer and Glasgow in methodology, because she approaches the question "What is race?" taking into consideration not merely semantic constraints from ordinary usage but also epistemic and pragmatic standards of interpretation and, perhaps most importantly, "normative considerations about what practices we should continue and the best route for maintaining or discouraging them" (34). She defends her political constructionism as appropriate, in part, because it is "morally and politically valuable," for it helps us highlight "how our racializing practices and identities contribute to injustice" (34). The lesson she draws from Laura and François Schroeter with respect to our interpretations of terms ideally helping us to see the point or rationale of our practices reminds me of Ronald Dworkin's interpretive model of adjudication, according to which judges must combine positive law with "principles of political morality that taken together provide the best interpretation of the positive law" because they give "the best justification available for the political decisions the positive law announces."[19] I find much to appreciate in such ways of thinking about interpretation. When comparing my approach to answering the "What is race?" question to Haslanger's, I see little reason to think that consciously adopting her method would make a noticeable difference to my deliberation and no reason at all to think it would make any difference to my conclusions.

What is my method? I take Hardimon's three theses representing the logical core of race to be a relatively neutral starting point, a move which might be thought of as recognition of a semantic constraint and which Haslanger seems to agree with, since the contents of the three theses are evidently incorporated into her definition of a race (26). I then suggest that we can usefully compare different metaphysical stances on the nature and reality of race by asking what significance they accord to our differences in appearance on the basis of ancestral place of origin. My conclusion in the first section of

---

19. Ronald Dworkin, "Law's Ambitions for Itself," *Virginia Law Review* 71 (March 1985): 176.

Chapter 2 is that social constructionism best captures what significance these differences can be reasonably said to have and, by the end of the chapter, my conclusion is that cultural constructionism, in particular, is the most insightful kind of social constructionism. To investigate whether and how much I diverge methodologically from Haslanger, it must be noted that central to my notion of capturing significance is the challenge of capturing moral and political significance. When I use my South Asian British example to reveal weakness first in non-essentialist biological realism and then in anti-realism, I rely, admittedly implicitly, on moral and political imperatives, as I would say the importance of recognizing this woman as non-white and of recognizing her non-whiteness as socially significant stems most of all from the need to do justice to her vulnerability to racism and to reasons she can and should take pride in her South Asian ancestry in spite of this racism. Is this not a case of normative considerations playing a role in conceptual clarification in a manner similar to the way they do for Haslanger?

Normative considerations figure more explicitly in my criticisms of political constructionism for downplaying the importance of culture in the present and for leading us to conclude that race cannot survive the end of racism. I even claim that the reason to name my position "cultural constructionism" in the first place involves its normative implications. If I were to somehow make the goal of a moral and political value in conceiving race more explicit and central, it would only lead me to the same position. I share with Haslanger the aim of revealing ways in which "our prior thinking is false or misguided," but I foreground, among those ways, the problem of the Eurocentric devaluations of the histories and cultures of non-white peoples (33). I too hope "to disrupt our ways of thinking, to motivate a new relationship to our practices," but, unlike Haslanger, I aim not to move us away from race toward "organizing ourselves on different terms" but rather to disrupt all ways of thinking that allow those of one race to set themselves over and above or in hostile competition with those of other races and to motivate relating to practices of racial differentiation as ways of expressing and embodying diversity in all its potential innocence, fecundity, and reciprocal gain (33). I fail to see how there is methodological difference of great significance between Haslanger's approach and my own, despite our divergent conclusions.

Let us now clarify this divergence. Haslanger writes in Chapter 1 that "the cultural account requires that races, as a group, share a culture" (25). This is misleading when taken as a description of my view, for readers will recall that I do not offer a maximally robust cultural constructionism, which would indeed take cultural difference to be strictly required for racial difference. On my view, diversity in ways of life is not essential to race, but neither are imbalanced relations of power. I can even envision a circumstance in which both racial hierarchy and racial cultures have faded away but race lives on as a legal distinction that is mainly of bureaucratic significance, engendering no inequality between members of racial groups but also representing nothing of great significance to the identities of members. My point is that race, on my view, is fundamentally social and will live on as long as racial distinctions are socially recognized in some form, just as it will die if they cease to be socially recognized in any form, whether the form is political, cultural, or something else. The reason my view can be identified as a kind of cultural constructionism is because it takes culture to be fundamental from a normative standpoint, for I hold that the value of cultural difference is the reason we may value race and hope to see it live on indefinitely, rather than take its destruction to be our goal, at least in the long run.

As Haslanger further evaluates the cultural account, as she calls it, she attempts to be both conciliatory and critical. She sharply differentiates ethnicities from races, defining the former as cultural groups and denying that the latter can count as such because they are generally made up of people from multiple cultures. On the other hand, she accepts that racial identities do sometimes give rise to "pan-ethnicities," which "emerge when multiple groups are racialized and treated as one group, and form an identity and way of life as a result" (28-29). She recognizes that pan-ethnicities can involve people bonding together in "celebration and resistance" and that the "racially identified artistic movements, cultural norms, and forms of association" that can come about as a result may be valued even beyond the ways in which they constitute responses to oppression (29). I take Haslanger to be trying here to acknowledge the kinds of social phenomena I highlight while nevertheless remaining critical of my position, because it remains the case, in her view, that "pan-ethnicities are not races" (29).

I would agree with this, as Haslanger makes it clear that pan-ethnicities are often the result of local processes of racialization and may thus be restricted in scope to people in that locale. She gives Asian Americans as an example (and perhaps it is my Canadian bias showing, but when she lists peoples of Asia that would presumably fit into this pan-ethnicity, it once again strikes me as so curious—and so clearly out of accord with the idea of distinctive appearance as central to race—to think of Gujarati people from western India and Japanese people as literally the same race). She allows that this scope might widen in light of some people in Asia taking themselves to be Asian, but this self-identification in response to the racialization of Asians in the United

States and elsewhere would not widen it so far as to include all who would count as racially Asian. Pan-ethnicities therefore represent, like ethnicities, subsets of races, at least as Haslanger conceives them. This reassures me that I am not intending to talk about pan-ethnicities when I speak of races and, without meaning to doubt the usefulness of Yen Le Espiritu's work with the concept, I do not currently see any role for talk of pan-ethnicity in my own attempts to clarify race and culture.

The critical question is how I can make the claims I do for the fundamental importance of culture to race if I am not relying on a concept such as pan-ethnicity. Haslanger's idea that people in Asia may be included within an Asian pan-ethnicity if they identify as Asian in response to racialization in the United States and elsewhere seems to make sense as a model of the social construction of a cultural group. If I am not talking about this sort of connection to influential ideas and practices, then what is social, much less cultural, about how people are included within racial groups on my account? As useful a critical question as this is, the first thing to note is that it applies just as much to Haslanger's account of racial membership as it applies to my account. She writes: "An individual ethnic Hmong living in China or Laos is, I would maintain, Asian$_{us}$, even if there is nothing distinctively 'Asian' about Hmong culture, and she does not identify as Asian (and maybe has not even heard of the designation)" (29-30). What is social about this? Why should someone who has never heard of the category of Asians be classified as one if race is a social rather than natural category?

Haslanger explains: "That she counts as Asian$_{us}$ is clear, however, by how Hmong are viewed and treated within the United States . . . and how she would be viewed and treated if she came here" (30). The existence of the United States as a social context in which she would be recognized as Asian is enough to secure the inclusion of this woman in the category. There is perhaps something strange about practices in social settings you have never visited being sufficient to slot you into a social group, but I ultimately think counterfactual considerations of this sort are appropriate. Knowing how you stand in relation to others in the world involves not only what you have consciously experienced, but also what you would be likely to experience if you happened to interact with others in this or that way. I can make use of counterfactual considerations as Haslanger does, although it is important for me not to tie the existence of races to single locations like the United States. I take race to be a global phenomenon, which does not mean I ignore the way popular conceptions of which races there are can differ between different places. If we are indeed talking about race and not the variety of the world's ethnic differentiations, though, conceptions of race in different places must necessarily overlap more than they diverge because they all represent broad divisions of the world according to appearance as related to place of origin and they are all shaped by the historical force of the modern West's imperial antagonisms. What divergences there are often have to do with the conceptual flexibility that comes with the mixing of races, although there are undoubtedly also divergences that stem from the variety of ways we can carve up the spectrum of humanity.

I will admit that counterfactual considerations do less for me than for Haslanger. She might grant me that we can share a story about how people can be part of races without knowing it, but she will continue to ask how culture can be upheld as centrally important to what races are when, unlike ethnic groups, races do not "share a form of life" (28). But what does it mean to share a form of life? Must we share a language? Must we share a religion? Must we share a very particular bounded set of customs governing all the major facets of public and private life? Haslanger does not tell us what would have to be missing for us to not share a form of life. She treats ethnic groups as sharing forms of life, but would she say we cannot speak of countries sharing forms of life if they are ethnically heterogenous? What about regions made up of multiple ethnically heterogenous countries? I think we can meaningfully speak, for example, not only of Fanti (and, more broadly, Akan) culture, but also of Ghanaian culture and of West African culture. I would not stop there, though. I think we can speak meaningfully of Western culture, even though this category covers an amazing variety of ethnic, national, and regional identities. Races, understood as cultural groups, have this kind of broad scope (and, of course, Western culture is inextricably linked although not reducible to the racial category of whiteness). This broadness does not render them formless. Their forms of life derive from historical developments involving encounters between previously isolated groups, the circulation of people and ideas, and modes of interaction made possible by various technologies, all developing within the context of various attempts at establishing, protecting, or resisting white supremacy.

Jemima Pierre's historical and ethnographic work in her book, *The Predicament of Blackness: Postcolonial Ghana and the Politics of Race*, nicely exemplifies important aspects of the approach to thinking about race I am defending. Opposing the treatment of articulations of race as "exported products of the contemporary West (and the United States in particular)," she explores how Ghana's past and present involve various forms of racialization and racial projects as a result of and in response to the history of colonialism and present-day realities.[20] Referencing the work of Charles Mills, she announces that she takes "as a point of departure the interdependence of cultural, political, and economic terrains in a modern world constructed in and through the key distinctions around race and the apparatuses of global white supremacy."[21] When analyzing the racialization of Africans during the colonial period as "native," she exposes the way that policies of indirect rule in a place like the Gold Coast (as it was then called) emphasized and institutionalized ethnic differences in consequential ways, even as urban spaces were starkly segregated in ways that parallel the more widely acknowledged racial divisions of a settler colony like South Africa. Moving to the contemporary period, as she locates the persistence of a privileged position for whiteness in contemporary Ghana, examines the phenomenon of skin bleaching, considers the ambiguities of slavery-related tourism, and discusses the perception of some Ghanaians that those whose ancestors were enslaved in the Americas are lucky, we have ample opportunity to consider how the globality of race is in many ways a matter of the globality of that which political constructionists take to be fundamental: racial hierarchy.

Something like skin bleaching, however, constitutes not merely evidence of race as hierarchy but also the cultural connection between people in Ghana and black populations elsewhere, such as Jamaica, where skin bleaching is also a major issue. Not all cultural connections are healthy, and the widespread practice of glorifying lighter skin is an aspect of black culture that ought not be preserved and maintained. Pierre's chapter on skin bleaching ends, however, with discussion of a poster found in a girls' bathroom in a high school. Issued by Ghana's Food and Drug Board, it features a smiling dark-skinned woman and the message: "BLACK *IS* BEAUTIFUL. DO **NOT** DESTROY YOUR BEAUTY THROUGH BLEACHING."[22] This is black cultural resistance and pride, expressed in a way that has resonated throughout the black world, especially its English-speaking part, since the 1960s.

Black cultural enjoyment is, however, not just a matter of consciously resisting that which denigrates blackness. Among Pierre's most interesting ethnographic accounts is her discussion of First Fridays Accra. First Fridays is

---

20. Jemima Pierre, *The Predicament of Blackness: Postcolonial Ghana and the Politics of Race* (Chicago: University of Chicago Press, 2013), xi.

21. Ibid., xv.

22. Ibid., 121. Although Pierre does not discuss it, it is worth noting that the woman on the poster sports straight hair, either because she is wearing a wig or has used some hair-straightening process.

a kind of networking event aimed at black professionals that was first developed in the United States in the late 1980s. When Pierre describes the event as she experienced it in Ghana's capital, Accra, what emerges is more than just the convergence of an African American institution with a Ghanaian location:

> By the end of the evening, I have met diverse groups of Black people: Ghanaians native to Accra; those who immigrated from other parts of the country; Nigerians or Liberians who now live in Accra; Black South Africans visiting Ghana for the first time; Haitians and Haitian Americans who have moved permanently to Accra; second-generation Ghanaian Americans who are either visiting or have repatriated to their parents' home; Jamaican American and African American graduate students conducting research; and African American professionals who have either decided to set up businesses in Accra, are working for companies stationed in Accra, or are on short-term volunteer trips. Clearly, this First Fridays Accra event is where people from all over Africa and the African diaspora converge in the making of a modern Black cosmopolitanism in Ghana.[23]

This black cosmopolitanism, as Pierre calls it, demonstrates how cultural blackness is not exhausted by its relationship with white supremacy. It is true and important that First Fridays originated in large part as a response to the isolation felt by African Americans in white-dominated professions, but something like First Fridays Accra tells us not only about the role of black cultural institutions in providing a refuge from white domination but, perhaps more so, about the way black cultural institutions can serve as testaments to and celebrations of the diversity of black people without this diversity thereby seeming incompatible with unity.

In light of the themes of celebrating racial identity and cultivating racial unity just explored, it is worthwhile to consider at this point an important possible objection to my view that Haslanger hints at but does not press. She talks about how thinking of white people as a pan-ethnicity alerts us to ways in which being white offers "creative opportunities" but also "resources for domination—or even more often, escape from subordination" (29). What does it mean to think of races as cultures and of cultures as worth celebrating when we turn our focus to white people? Is it not a clear consequence of my

---

23. Ibid., 178–179. Pierre herself was born in Haiti and raised in the United States.

view that white people should cherish white culture? Does this not mean that I encourage the promotion of "white pride," thereby providing surprising but convenient philosophical support to those who are dedicated to the principle of white supremacy and who seek to deny that whiteness currently holds an unfairly privileged position? This concern is, of course, an especially pressing one in the wake of the rise of the so-called alt-right.

I take it to be obvious that my view ought to be rejected if it gives non-accidental support to white supremacist calls for white pride, that is, if taking it to support such calls involves logical implications of the view rather than misreadings based on mere appearances. I also admit that there is at least the appearance of support, because my view can indeed make sense of the notion of white pride as something worth having. While there can be no doubt that white racial identity occupies a unique position in the racial landscape relative to others, I do not hold that the end of racism requires the end of whiteness, just as I do not hold that it requires the end of any other racial category. While whiteness could fade away, my view is compatible with and can explain people holding on to whiteness as a cultural identity after the end of racism. This is why white cultural pride could be permissible on my view, although the very idea of a post-racist future makes it clear that the possible persistence of white cultural identity that I countenance is necessarily divorced from the widespread treatment of whiteness as supreme.

There is a practical difficulty here. I can envision people in the future taking pride in white European heritage in an uncomplicatedly justifiable manner because I imagine as a prior condition for a post-racist future significant amounts of white people actively working and collaborating with others over a long period time in order to destroy white supremacy in all its forms. Thus this future white pride would be partly inspired by positive feelings about the process of eradicating the kinds of institutions and sentiments that currently inspire calls for white pride. This is importantly different from the way that orienting ourselves toward a post-racist future validates rather than negates current calls for pride in non-white racial identities. How then should anti-racist white people relate to white cultural identity in the present? For example, might it not be prudent to avoid championing pride in whiteness in the present given how easy it would be for one to be taken as championing white supremacy? I do think that at least the specific term "white pride" is too deeply associated with racism at present to be used as a rallying cry, although I also nevertheless think that some forms of pride in European heritage must be permissible and even healthy in the present if, as I believe, it will be possible to affirm the value of this identity in a racially egalitarian future.

Fortunately, there has been something of a wave of work in philosophy addressing the practical difficulties of how white identity may be positively affirmed by anti-racist white people. Most prominently, Linda Martín Alcoff's *The Future of Whiteness* argues for "the need for whites to have a place in the rainbow, as whites."[24] Alcoff's central point in the book is that whiteness as a social identity must not be seen as fixed and unable to change, but rather as capable of evolving in valuable ways. Shannon Sullivan's *Good White People: The Problem with Middle-Class White Anti-Racism* advocates white self-love, but not in the kind of uncritical and reactionary way that white supremacists do: "A white person's loving herself as a white person means her critically caring enough about the effects whiteness has in the world to work to make it something different and better than what it is today."[25] We can also look to Outlaw, whose essay, "Rehabilitate Racial Whiteness?"—a question he answers in the affirmative—precedes these books by about a decade.[26]

Still, Haslanger worries about the ethical implications of holding on to racial identity as a form of cultural identity even if racism is defeated. She claims, with some justification, that I focus on "the benefits of racial cultural unity, but not the costs of racial segregation" (31). The costs she has in mind include unfair pressure on those within the race to conform to cultural expectations and unfair limitations on those outside the race with regard to their ability to participate in cultural practices. Her concerns here are understandable, but it should first be made clear that they are not concerns about things I actually endorse. Especially in a post-racist future in which there is no need to find ways to support forms of cultural resistance in the face of white supremacy's cultural dimension, it is not my view that the good of the survival of distinctive racial cultures generates a duty upon each individual member of each race to consciously aim to secure said survival. Even in the present, it is important to me that those who are committed to cultural resistance recognize that others may be equally committed to that goal even when they diverge widely with regard to what they take to be central to the culture, what they believe counts or does not count as part of

---

24. Linda Martín Alcoff, *The Future of Whiteness* (Cambridge, UK: Polity, 2015), 188.

25. Shannon Sullivan, *Good White People: The Problem with Middle-Class White Anti-Racism* (Albany: State University of New York Press, 2014), 10.

26. Lucius Outlaw, Jr., "Rehabilitate Racial *Whiteness*?" in George Yancy (ed.), *What White Looks Like: African-American Philosophers on the Whiteness Question* (New York: Routledge, 2004), 159–171.

it, and so on.[27] Also, despite the deep concern that many who seek to fight racism have about cultural appropriation, nothing I have said implies that it is wrong to be influenced by or participate in the cultural practices of those of other races.

One might worry, however, that whether or not I intend to endorse such restrictions on individuality and cultural exchange, the preservation of racial cultures that I promote makes these problems inevitable or at least very likely. One might even worry that, while the problems just mentioned could arguably arise in a world characterized by equality and mutual respect between races, it is hopeless to imagine the preservation of racial cultures without the persistence or re-emergence of negative stereotyping, chauvinism, maneuvering to achieve a higher position, and other destructive modes of thinking and interacting. In response, I would say that I reject the idea that any of these problems are truly inevitable—I cannot see why this would be the case—but I cannot deny that they would be dangers to watch for, temptations to be resisted, perhaps challenges to be overcome. They are not, however, problems unique to racial difference, but challenges related to group difference in general. We cannot avoid facing them.

Thinking of how a critic might respond to this, I would reject the idea that humans should seek to rid themselves of all forms of group difference as too implausible and clearly undesirable for serious consideration (think, for example, of the implication concerning linguistic difference), but a more plausible claim might be that we should seek to minimize how many forms of group difference we have and that something with the track record of badness that racial difference has definitely ought to be abandoned. I disagree. I think we recognize the value of our shared humanity best when we treat every form of group difference that is meaningful to at least some of its members and which could possibly be benign as an opportunity to prove our ability to benefit from rather than be torn apart by group difference. Whenever we shrink from taking on the challenges of group difference, opting not to promote equality in diversity and unity without uniformity, but rather treating sameness as the only guarantee of peace, we demonstrate a demoralizing lack of faith in ourselves and a fear of complexity that is bound to inhibit our progress as moral and social beings. Racial identities are meaningful to many of us and are not reducible to positions in a hierarchy. Their preservation should be—and, I believe, is—possible.

---

27. For more on this, see my "The Ethics and Politics of Cultural Preservation," *The Journal of Value Inquiry* 49 (March 2015): 205–220.

As a final point, Haslanger is not mistaken in thinking that races as cultural groups, on my understanding, are not "porous" in the sense that you can be of any ancestry whatsoever and just make the choice to join (31). Once it is clear that my view does not imply the wrongness of individuals being influenced by and participating in the cultures of others, I do not see this as a problem. Freedom to learn from and engage in many of the cultural practices of others is not only compatible with my view, but essential to its claim that cultural diversity ought to be valued. Freedom to be considered a full-fledged member of any cultural group if one so chooses is a kind of luxurious freedom the desire for which I do not really understand. Cultural constructionism as I conceive it does not offer this latter kind of freedom, but I think what it offers instead is more attractive.

Take, for example, the difference between political constructionism and cultural constructionism regarding how we might think in a post-racist future about mixed-race families. On a political constructionist view, what would be considered a mixed-race family in the present will not only be unremarkable but completely indistinguishable from other families in a post-racist future because racial difference will no longer exist. Cultural constructionism, as I conceive it, holds that, in a post-racist future, such a family will be distinct but in a way that is worth appreciating, for it will exemplify within itself diversity, which is valuable, and, at that point, it will also symbolize the way that racial difference, while still real, is no longer a source of antagonism. This symbolic power is dependent on the continued social relevance of distinctions of appearance as related to ancestral place of origin, and it is true that this means that valuing as much mixing as possible would have the negative effect of leading directly to the end of racial difference. It is no part of my view, however, that mixing as such should be vilified or forbidden and, again, even beyond the importance of freedom of choice in family construction, it is possible to value mixed families on a cultural constructionist view in a way that political constructionism makes impossible by pointing us toward making mixing itself impossible.

7 SPENCER'S REPLY TO GLASGOW, HASLANGER, AND JEFFERS

7.1. Introduction

So far you've read four philosophical views on race. You've also read Haslanger's reply to Glasgow, Jeffers, and myself. And you've read Jeffers's reply to Glasgow, Haslanger, and myself. In this chapter, I will provide my reply to Glasgow, Haslanger, and Jeffers. I will also clarify the race theory I presented in Chapter 3. The outline of this chapter is as follows. First, I'll clarify the race theory I presented in Chapter 3. Second, I'll address one major concern that two of my coauthors have about my race theory. Third, I'll advance an objection that applies to Glasgow's, Haslanger's, and Jeffers's race theories. Fourth, I'll advance an objection aimed only at Glasgow's and Jeffers' race theories. Finally, I'll provide conclusive remarks.

7.2. A Few Clarifications

In Chapter 3, I used the pressing situation of apparent racial disparities in genetic disorders—such as the higher incidence of fetal aneuploidy among Asian mothers—to motivate a metaphysical investigation of what race is and whether it's real given how 'race' is used to classify people in current and ordinary American English.[1] What I discovered was that there is a way that American English speakers talk about race such that race is a biological and biologically real thing. I discovered that there's a widely and frequently used race talk in American English that was started in 1997

---

1. Like in Chapter 3, I will refrain from using the modifiers "to classify people," "current," and "ordinary" from now on for convenience. However, note that I'm always presupposing these modifiers in this chapter when I talk about 'race' and American race talk.

by the US Office of Management and Budget (OMB) that uses a biological thing that's also biologically real as its meaning of 'race'—where *meaning* was understood referentially.

From further investigation, I discovered that *race* in *OMB race talk* (as I call it) is nothing more than a specific set of five biological populations in the human species that I dubbed *the human continental populations*. The human continental populations are the following groups, and their OMB aliases are in parentheses: Africans (Blacks), East Asians (Asians), Eurasians (Whites), Native Americans (American Indians), and Oceanians (Pacific Islanders).[2] In other words, I argued that what 'race' *means* in OMB race talk is just the set of human continental populations, and what each race term *means* in OMB race talk is just the biological population it picks out. For instance, according to OMB race theory, what 'Black' means is the African population. Also, since it's sufficient to have genomic ancestry from the African population in order to be a member of that population, it follows from OMB race theory (and substitution) that it's sufficient to have genomic ancestry from the African population in order to be *Black* in the OMB's use of 'Black.'[3]

In Chapter 3, I didn't delve into any deep metaphysics about the essences of the human continental populations. However, following the population geneticist Marcus Feldman (2010, 151), I did say that each one is an "ancestry group" (Spencer, Chapter 3, 92). I also said that each population is capable of having partial members, or, to put it more precisely, each human continental population consists of a fuzzy set of people at any given time.[4] At this point, I should

---

2. Just like in Chapter 3, I'll use 'Caucasian' interchangeably with 'Eurasian.' This is common in human genetics, but more common in medical genetics than population genetics.

3. However, I didn't argue that having genomic ancestry from a human continental population is *necessary* in order to be a member of that population. This is because that membership condition doesn't work for the first members of a human continental population. For instance, how can the first people in the Native American population possess genomic ancestry from the Native American population if that population didn't exist before those people? For how I think membership conditions work for all members of a human continental population and other biological populations like them, see Spencer (2016). Nevertheless, I do think that possessing genomic ancestry from a human continental population is a necessary and sufficient membership condition right now and since the last time that each human continental population was entirely composed of unmixed members, which some geneticists put at 1492, but the date could have been in the more distant past (Ramachandran et al. 2010, 606).

4. Suppose *crisp sets* are the objects called 'sets' in Zermelo-Fraenkel set theory. Let an *object space X* be a crisp set of objects. Suppose a *membership function* μ is a function such that $X \xrightarrow{\mu} [0,1]$. Then, a *fuzzy set A* is a pair $\left(X_{\tilde{A}}, \mu_{\tilde{A}} \right)$. Unlike crisp sets, '$\in$' has no meaning for fuzzy sets. The analogous relation is *belonging*. Suppose $\mu_{\tilde{A}}(x)$ is x's *grade of membership* (or

clarify that I intended those claims to be claims about the essential properties of human continental populations.[5] However, while I said that each group of people that currently belongs to a human continental population is "geographically clustered" (Spencer, Chapter 3, 99), I didn't say that each one, necessarily, has a distinctive geographic origin. Furthermore, I'm still thinking about what the essential geographic properties of human continental populations are.[6]

So, my view is that each human continental population (and thus each OMB race), by its very essence, originated as a fuzzy set of people somewhere in the world. For example, Blacks originated in sub-Saharan Africa, and Asians originated in East Asia. Furthermore, at every point in time after each human continental population originated, each population, by its very essence, consisted entirely of people who formed a fuzzy set, and the whole population itself (which exists through time) formed an ancestry group based on common genomic ancestry. Given this view of what an OMB race is, it should be obvious that I believe in *racial essences*, but not the kind of essences that involves intrinsic properties and other tenets of *racialism*, which has been widely refuted by philosophers of race as untenable for any folk race that exists (Mallon 2006, 528–529).[7] Rather, I believe that the essential properties of OMB races are all relational and extrinsic.

---

strength) in A. Then, *x belongs* to A just in case $x \in X_{\tilde{A}}$ and $\mu_{\tilde{A}}(x) > 0$. These definitions are from Zadeh (1965). Also, notice that while these definitions imply that objects can partially belong to fuzzy sets, they don't imply that any object that belongs to a fuzzy set must partially belong to that set. Rather, these definitions allow for objects to wholly belong to fuzzy sets as well.

5. Interestingly, a philosopher of social science, Brian Epstein, thinks about (human) social groups in a similar way that I think about OMB races. In a fascinating book, Epstein (2015, 149) argues that social groups are, essentially, things that coincide with a "set of people" at any given time. Since I'm arguing that OMB races are, essentially, biological groups that coincide with a fuzzy set of people at any given time, there's an interesting parallel in our independently developed views which may, I think, reveal a deep connection between human social groups and human biological groups.

6. Nevertheless, see Hardimon (2017, 27–31, 93) for a philosopher who thinks that the human continental populations and the OMB races do, necessarily, have a "distinctive" geographic location of origin. However, one reason why I'm hesitant to make this claim is that it's not clear that every human continental population has a distinctive geographic location of origin. For example, at this point, it's still unsettled whether the Oceanian population originated in Southeast Asia and moved to Oceania or originated in Oceania (McEvoy et al. 2010, 303). If the former occurred, then East Asia would not be the *distinctive* geographic location where East Asians originated. Rather, it would be the shared location where both East Asians and Oceanians originated.

7. For review, *racialism* is the view that humans naturally divide into a small number of groups called 'races' in such a way that the members each race share certain fundamental, inheritable,

For clarity, by a *relational property* I mean a property that must hold between two or more things when it's instantiated, such as having a certain weight. For example, when ordinary English speakers say that a person weighs 110 pounds on Earth, what we actually mean is that this person is gravitationally accelerating toward Earth with a specific magnitude. On the other hand, when a physicist says that a person has a rest mass of 49.9 kilograms, she's attributing a non-relational property to that person.[8]

By an *extrinsic property* of a thing I mean a property of that thing that doesn't arise entirely from that thing itself. It contrasts with an *intrinsic property*, which arises entirely from the thing itself.[9] For example, having (naturally) blond hair is an extrinsic property that some people have. It's extrinsic because *blond* is a color, and all colors arise from interactions between observers, surfaces, light, the light medium, and a few other factors (Hatfield 2003). However, having negative electric charge is an intrinsic property that some fundamental particles possess, such as electrons, muons, and strange quarks.

Another fact I discovered in Chapter 3 was that the set of human continental populations is *biologically real*, at least in the sense of being an "epistemically useful and justified entity in a well-ordered research program in biology" (Spencer, Chapter 3, 95). In particular, I showed that the set of human continental populations is useful as a human population subdivision in population genetics (a well-ordered research program in biology) to explain why humans subdivide into five genetic clusters that correspond to five major geographic regions whose boundaries (e.g., the Sahara, the Himalayas, oceans, etc.) are significant obstacles to human interbreeding (Spencer, Chapter 3, 99). Also, the set of human continental populations is justified for this use because the aforementioned five genetic clusters have been reproduced in genetic clustering studies that have used a worldwide sample of human ethnic groups, and in the largest and most comprehensive human genetic clustering study to date (Spencer, Chapter 3, 98-99).

Next, I should clarify that the evidence for OMB race theory (as I call it) is entirely abductive. In other words, I take OMB race theory to be the

---

physical, moral, intellectual, and cultural characteristics with one another that they do not share with members of any other race (Appiah 1996, 54).

8. Notice that I'm talking about *rest mass*, which is an invariant quantity of bodies in physics. The mass that ordinary people measure is known as *relativistic mass* in physics, which is another relational property.

9. These distinctions are from Weatherson and Marshall (2017).

theory that *best explains* both what the OMB means by 'race' and various phenomena in population genetics. One rival I considered was Michael Hardimon's theory of what 'race' means in OMB race talk, which is what he calls 'the ordinary concept of race.' This race concept, among other things, bars races from being "visually indistinguishable" (Hardimon 2003, 442).[10]

One way in which I said OMB race theory was "best" was insofar as it solves more puzzles than any of its rivals about what race is and what races are in OMB race talk. Some examples are being able to define 'Black' using ancestry and without making every living person Black (Spencer, Chapter 3, 100-101), and being able to racially classify unmixed Aboriginal Australians (Spencer, Chapter 3, 100). Another way in which I said OMB race theory was "best" was insofar as it's more predictively powerful than any of its rivals. For example, I discussed how geneticists can predict with 98.8%–99.8% accuracy the OMB race self-reports of US adults (when they report a single race) using one's primary human continental population membership (Spencer, Chapter 3, 102). But also, I used OMB race theory to predict the truth-values of relevant modal propositions with greater accuracy than Hardimon's ordinary concept of race and other similar rivals. Some examples are: "It is possible for there to be two visibly indistinguishable races" and "Pacific Islanders could be visibly indistinguishable from Blacks" (Spencer, Chapter 3, 93). Now, I'll offer a further clarification about the membership conditions for belonging to an OMB race according to OMB race theory since I know OMB race theory is probably counterintuitive.

To be clear, a person with any genomic ancestry from a human continental population is a member of that race. So, for example, a person's parents need not be entirely Caucasian and entirely African in order to be partially White and partially Black. Also, OMB race theory, together with some well-confirmed genomic and demographic data, entails that millions of people in the United States are racially mixed according to the OMB's racial scheme.

For instance, there are 42 million African Americans in the United States, and they're, on average, 73.2% African, 24% Caucasian, and 0.8%* Native American.[11] Also, there are 32 million Mexican Americans in the United

---

10. Also, remember that in Chapter 3, I mentioned that since visible distinguishability is part of the US race theories developed by Naomi Zack (2002), Lawrence Blum (2002), Paul Taylor (2013), Joshua Glasgow (2009; this volume), and, I should include, Chike Jeffers (this volume), these are all also rivals to OMB race theory for explaining what 'race' means in OMB race talk.

11. Here and for the rest of the chapter, I'll use asterisk superscripts to flag statistics that are not statistically significant (at 95% confidence) according to the authors' assessment of survey or sampling error. Also, I'll use dagger superscripts to flag statistics with no error bounds provided

States, and they're, on average, 48% Native American, 47% Caucasian, and 4%[†] African.[12] Another racially mixed group of Americans are South Asian Americans. There are about 3.8 million South Asians in the United States, and they're, on average, 68.4% Caucasian, 26.5% East Asian, and 5.1%[†] African.[13] Here are two more examples. There are 1.4 million Dominican Americans in the United States, and, on average, they're 50% Caucasian, 43% African, and 6%[†] Native American.[14] Finally, our good friends the Native Hawaiians, who total 180,000 people in the United States, are, on average, 56% Oceanian, 30% East Asian, and 14% Caucasian.[15]

With that said, some ethnic groups of Americans are, on average, very nearly racially unmixed, and so there are almost certainly millions of racially unmixed people in the United States as well. Most racially unmixed people in the United States are likely to be non-Hispanic European Americans. There are currently 195 million non-Hispanic European Americans in the United States, and, on average, they're 98.6% Caucasian, 0.19%[*] African, and 0.18%[*] Native American.[16] There are also at least 12.8 million Eastern Asian Americans in the United States, and they're, on average, 95.5% East Asian,

---

from the authors and that are low enough that one should be skeptical as to whether they're statistically significant (at 95% confidence). These demographic data are from Rastogi et al. (2011, 6), and the ancestry data are from Bryc et al. (2015, 42).

12. These demographic data are from Ennis et al. (2011, 14), and the ancestry data are from Manichaikul et al. (2012, 4). It's also worth clarifying that the 95% confidence intervals for most of these statistics are so wide that sometimes geneticists don't know which genomic ancestry is the primary one. For example, Risch et al. (2009, 4) obtained statistically indistinguishable genomic ancestry results from Manichaikul et al. (2012, 4) for Mexican Americans. Furthermore, Risch et al.'s 95% confidence intervals for Mexican Americans' Caucasian and Native American ancestries, respectively, were (49.4%, 64.9%) and (50.5%, 65.8%). So, we really don't know whether Mexican Americans are, on average, primarily Caucasian or primarily Native American.

13. These demographic data are from Hoeffel et al. (2012, 15), and the ancestry data are from Guo et al. (2014, 155).

14. These demographic data are from Ennis et al. (2011, 14), and the ancestry data are from Manichaikul et al. (2012, 4).

15. These demographic data are from Hixson et al. (2012, 14), and the ancestry data are from Kim et al. (2012, 4).

16. The genomic ancestry facts cited are from Bryc et al. (2015, 42). Also, I estimated the current number of non-Hispanic European Americans by subtracting current counts of US Arabs, US Iranians, US Jews, and US Hispanic Whites from a current count of US Whites. The counts for US Whites and US Hispanic Whites are from Hixson et al. (2011, 3). The count of US Jews is from Tighe et al. (2013, 1). Finally, the counts for US Arabs and US Iranians are from the "Total Ancestry Reported" file from the 2010 American Community Survey (1-year estimates), which is available at http://factfinder.census.gov.

4.0%[†] Caucasian, and 0.5%[†] African.[17] Another group of Americans with low racial mixture is American Jews. There are currently 6.8 million American Jews in the United States, and, on average, they're 96% Caucasian and 4% African.[18]

What's interesting here is that even though millions of Americans are racially mixed, the majority of Americans are probably racially unmixed due to demographic and genealogical facts. For one, the overwhelming majority of Americans (63.1%) are non-Hispanic European Americans.[19] Second, as I mentioned previously, non-Hispanic European Americans are, on average, 98.6%(±1.4%) Caucasian. These two facts alone provide strong evidence that most Americans are racially unmixed, which, if true, undermines the myth that the US is a "melting pot" as opposed to a "mixed salad."[20]

At this point, I should say that even if my theory of OMB racial membership seems strange, it's the right result. Remember, the OMB (1997, 58789) embraces the existence of people with "more than one race" and starts off attempting to define each of its race terms with the phrase "A person having origins in . . ." Although OMB race theory tweaks the OMB's focus on "origins" to a focus on genomic ancestry, the OMB's idea that people can have lots of racial memberships and to differing degrees as a function of one's ancestry is maintained in OMB race theory. So, this result may seem strange if, for example, one thinks the OMB's racial scheme is supposed to be capturing Americans' racial self-identifications instead of their racial memberships in an ancestry-based racial scheme. However, while the OMB (1997, 58782) wants their racial scheme to receive "broad public acceptance" for practical reasons (since they want to use self-reporting as the default method of collecting racial membership data), they're simply not in the business of trying to pin down Americans' racial self-identifications. This is for two reasons.

---

17. These demographic data are from Hoeffel et al. (2012, 15), and the ancestry data are from Guo et al. (2014, 155). Also, by *Eastern Asians* I mean people with Northeast Asian descent (e.g., Chinese, Japanese, Taiwanese, etc.) or Southeast Asian descent (e.g. Cambodians, Filipinos, Thai, etc.).

18. These demographic data are from Tighe et al. (2013, 1), and the ancestry data are from Moorjani et al. (2011, 6).

19. I calculated this percentage from dividing my count of non-Hispanic European Americans by the US Census Bureau's 2010 count of US residents, which is close to 309 million. See Hixson et al. (2011, 3).

20. These sayings are from a former student of mine from Canada who told me that she was shocked to hear these statistics because she had been taught in Canadian schools that the US is a "melting pot" and Canada is a "mixed salad."

First, the OMB was not able to find a consensus (or even a near consensus) among Americans on what race is and which groups are races (OMB 1995). Second, and as I discussed in Chapter 3, OMB race talk was invented to serve the interests of the US government, not the American people's racial self-identification desires. In particular, it was invented to prevent communication breakdown when federal agencies share racial data and to enforce civil rights legislation (OMB 1997).

One final clarification that I'll make before moving on is clarifying how I see myself as disagreeing with my coauthors. At this point, even if you are convinced that OMB race theory is true, you may be wondering how on earth OMB race theory contradicts any other race theory defended in this book. To be specific, Sally Haslanger (Chapter 1, 25, 27) defends the "racialized group" (a sociopolitical construct) as the "dominant" meaning of 'race' among English speakers in the United States, and she argues that the racialized group is real as well. Joshua Glasgow (Chapter 4, 117) argues that the most "frequent" meaning of 'race' used in ordinary communications among competent English speakers in the United States is a "concept" that requires races to be "*relatively large groups of people who are distinguished from other groups of people by having certain visible biological traits (such as skin colors) to a disproportionate extent,*" and, furthermore, that because of this requirement, race (in this sense) is a biological thing but "neither biologically nor socially real." Finally, Chike Jeffers (Chapter 2, 39) argues that races are real sociocultural groups according to the meaning of "the English word 'race' and its etymologically related cognates."[21]

So, Haslanger, Glasgow, and Jeffers all believe that there's a single dominant meaning of 'race' among (at least) American English speakers, and they focus their efforts on articulating what race is and whether race is real assuming that dominant meaning of 'race.'[22] Given these facts, one could rightly worry that I am not disagreeing with any of my coauthors because I have not

---

21. While Jeffers emphasizes that races (for users of the English word 'race' and its cognates) originated through "the global sociopolitical system of White supremacy," races are not essentially political groups according to Jeffers (like they are for Haslanger) because races according to Jeffers can survive the end of racism by being merely cultural groups (Jeffers, Chapter 2).

22. Of course, Haslanger and Jeffers claim they are capturing more than just the dominant meaning of 'race' among American English speakers. They're also both interested in other relevant English speakers (e.g., British, Canadian, etc.) and other linguistic communities with cognate terms (e.g., some European linguistic communities). However, for now, I'll focus on the common core among us, which is American English speakers.

argued that the OMB's meaning of 'race' is the single dominant meaning of 'race' among American English speakers.

To this concern, I will say up front that OMB race theory does not contradict any of my coauthors' race theories.[23] However, OMB race theory, together with a few empirical facts, implies a race theory that does contradict every other race theory in this book because the theory has a *radically pluralist* form. But before I sketch what that theory looks like, I will say a bit about what I think the common ground is among Glasgow, Haslanger, Jeffers, and myself with respect to what a *dominant* meaning of 'race' is.

First of all, a dominant meaning of 'race' need not be the only meaning of 'race' that a linguistic community uses. Furthermore, it would be imprudent to require it to be so, since, given the empirical data we already have on how American English speakers use 'race,' a debate about what race is and whether it's real given the only meaning of 'race' that American English speakers use would be over the minute we started the debate! That's because there's ample empirical evidence that American English speakers do not use a single meaning of 'race' for all of their communications about race. Since I discussed this research in section 3.3 of Chapter 3, I won't repeat it here. However, I will say that, in my opinion, the sociologist Ann Morning summarizes the empirical data best when she says:

> Perhaps the clearest theoretical proposition to emerge from this research is that we cannot assume that individuals hold a single definition of race. Instead, they may carry around a "tool kit" (Swidler and Arditi 1994) of race concepts from which to draw depending on their reading of the situation to be deciphered. (Morning 2009, 1186)

Now, even though 'race' is undoubtedly polysemous in American English, there still may be a single dominant meaning of 'race' among American English speakers that Americans default to when engaging in race talk in order to prevent communication breakdown. Here's an analogy using language to illustrate how this situation is possible.

While US residents who are five years old or older speak 381 distinct languages, 95.2% of them speak English "very well" or "well" (Shin and Kominski 2010, 1–2). Furthermore, the second most widely spoken language

---

23. However, in the past, I have defended the set of human continental populations as the single dominant meaning of 'race' among American English speakers. See Spencer (2014).

among US residents who are five years old or older is Spanish, but only 8.7% of US residents who are five years old or older speak Spanish "very well" or "well" (Shin and Kominski 2010, 2). These statistics show that while English is not the only language that Americans speak, English is, plausibly, the single dominant language spoken among Americans—where, roughly, that means it's the language that's the widest and most frequently spoken among Americans that's spoken by at least a majority of Americans and has a commanding margin of victory compared to its closest rival. So, if 'race' use among American English speakers is analogous to language use among US residents, then it's appropriate to say that there's a single dominant use of 'race' among American English speakers.

However, there's another live possibility for how American English speakers use 'race,' and this is that there are multiple, distinct, and dominant meanings of 'race' in American English. This possibility can also be captured with another language use analogy. For example, while Republic of China (Taiwan) residents speak multiple languages (e.g., Mandarin Chinese, Taiwanese, Hakka, English, etc.), there are two that most Taiwan residents speak: Mandarin and Taiwanese. Among Taiwan residents six years old or older, 83.5% of them speak Mandarin and 81.9% of them speak Taiwanese.[24] Also, no other language is spoken anywhere near as widely as Mandarin and Taiwanese in Taiwan. The next closest fluently spoken language in Taiwan is Hakka at 6.6% frequency. So, it's not obvious at all that Taiwan has a single dominant language. Rather, it's more appropriate to say that Taiwan has two dominant languages. One (Mandarin) is dominant in formal communications (e.g., government, school, etc.), whereas the other (Taiwanese) is dominant in informal communications (e.g., speaking with friends and family). The question now becomes whether 'race' use among American English speakers is more like language use among Americans or language use among the Taiwanese?

For reasons that I will provide later in this chapter, I believe that 'race' use among American English speakers is more like language use among the Taiwanese than language use among Americans. In any case, the appropriate

---

24. I should clarify that these data are actually for Taiwan resident nationals, not all Taiwan residents. However, I'll drop the 'national' qualifier for ease of communication. Also, the data actually report the frequency of languages spoken at home. But, of course, if you can speak a language at home, you can speak that language. Finally, these data and all language use data for Taiwan that I'm citing in this chapter are from the "General Statistical Analysis Report" that Taiwan published online after analyzing the data from its 2010 Population and Housing Census. The report is available at https://eng.stat.gov.tw.

way to view OMB race theory is not as a theory about what race is and whether it's real given that the OMB's meaning of 'race' is the single dominant meaning of 'race' in American English. Rather, the appropriate way to view OMB race theory is as a part of a larger radically pluralist theory about what race is and whether it's real in the American English context. In other words, I think that the OMB's meaning of 'race' is *one* dominant meaning of 'race' among American English speakers, but not the only one, because there is no such thing as the only one. I'll wrap up this section by clarifying what I mean by a *radically pluralist* race theory.

I'll say that a *pluralist* race theory is one that presupposes there to be no single correct answer to the question of what race is and whether race is real in the relevant context, but that presupposes there to be at least one correct answer to this question.[25] For instance, given what Glasgow says at the beginning of Chapter 4, it's accurate to say that he's defending a pluralist race theory with respect to how American English speakers use 'race.' Of course, that doesn't stop Glasgow from defending a single dominantly correct answer to the question of what race is and whether it's real for American English speakers.[26]

This brings me to radical pluralism. I'll say that a *radically pluralist* race theory goes further than a pluralist race theory by accepting pluralist tenets and adding that there isn't even a single dominantly correct answer to the question of what race is and whether it's real in the relevant context, but there's still at least one dominantly correct answer to this question. So, to be crystal clear, my race theory for what race is and whether it's real relative to how 'race' is used in American English is radically pluralist, but one crucial part of that theory is OMB race theory. Admittedly, this is a complex US race theory, but at least now you see how I'm disagreeing with my coauthors.[27]

7.3. Addressing the South Asian Mismatch Objection

So far, all I've done is clarified OMB race theory, its evidence, and how it fits into a larger US race theory that contradicts the race theories of my coauthors.

---

25. My characterization of a pluralist race theory is intended to be similar in form to Gilbert Harman's definition of 'moral relativism.' See Harman (2000).

26. Another example of a US race theory like Glasgow's is Michael Hardimon's. For evidence of Hardimon's embrace of pluralism, see Hardimon (2017, 173).

27. By a *US race theory* I mean a theory about the nature and reality of race according to how 'race' is dominantly used in American English.

Now, I'll do my best to reply to one major objection that two of my coauthors offered me. I fully acknowledge that there's plenty more objections against OMB race theory that are worth a reply. However, due to space limitations, I can only address one with care, and this objection is a good one.

A historically popular objection against any attempt to biologically vindicate a folk racial classification is to claim that there's a *"mismatch"* between the groups called 'races' in the biological theory of race and the groups called 'races' in the folk discourse (Mallon 2006, 533). If the mismatch is serious enough, it shows that the meaning of 'race' in the biological theory and the meaning of 'race' in the folk discourse are different meanings. Both Jeffers and Glasgow offer unique Mismatch Objections to any attempt to define ordinary race terms in American or British English in a biological way.

In Chapter 2, Jeffers uses a thought experiment involving a dark-skinned Bangladeshi English woman to show that "it conflicts with common sense" to racially classify her with Whites (Jeffers, Chapter 2, 44). In Chapter 4, Glasgow brings up the concern that Hispanics and Arabs "find no home in the flow charts of population genetics, but they are routinely racialized in the United States" (Glasgow, Chapter 4, 122). Also, elsewhere, Glasgow has raised doubts about South Asians being correctly racially classified with Whites in other attempts to defend biological racial realism relative to a folk meaning of 'race.'[28]

Now, as you may have guessed, I don't find the Arab or Hispanic Mismatch Objection challenging. This is because OMB race theory only claims that the OMB's meaning of 'race' is biological, and the OMB is very clear that Arabs are White and Hispanics are not a race. Also, this isn't a hollow victory because, as I showed in Chapter 3, OMB race talk is an ordinary race talk in American English. It's just that this particular ordinary race talk operates by a division of linguistic labor whereby the OMB fixes the meanings of 'race' and race terms. So, even if there are contexts in current American life where Arabs and Hispanics are treated as races by ordinary people, there are also contexts in current American life where Arabs and Hispanics are not treated as races by ordinary people, namely, when ordinary people use OMB race talk.

South Asians, on the other hand, are another story. Given everything that the OMB has written about its racial scheme, it's not clear at all that it's correct to say that South Asians are, on average, part White and part Asian instead

---

28. For example, see Glasgow (2009, 96). However, Glasgow hints at this objection again in this book. See Glasgow (Chapter 4, 114).

of Asian alone, at least in the OMB's racial scheme. Rather, the OMB always talks about South Asians as paradigm Asian people. So, one challenging mismatch concern is whether it's the case that the OMB truly intends 'Asian' to be synonymous with 'East Asian'?

The seriousness of this concern is immediately obvious once one scrutinizes a few facts about how the OMB uses the term 'Asian.' First, when the OMB introduced 'Asian' as an OMB race term in 1997, it explicitly named "India" and "Pakistan" as examples of countries that many Asian people live in (OMB 1997, 58786). Second, in the OMB's attempt to define 'Asian,' the "Asian" geographic range includes "the Indian subcontinent" (OMB 1997, 58786). Furthermore, South Asian Americans tend to follow the OMB's lead and racially self-report 'Asian' instead of 'White' in high numbers. However, you wouldn't know this from looking at what geneticists report.

For instance, Tang et al. (2005) didn't sample any South Asians, and Guo et al. (2014) sampled South Asians but separated them from the remaining self-reported Asians before attempting to predict racial self-reports! In truth, if one were to have added South Asians to the rest of the self-reported Asians in Guo et al.'s sample, their accuracy for predicting self-reported Asians would have fallen from 97.7% to 66.1% (Guo et al. 2014, 153). All of these facts together suggest that there's a *mismatch* between what 'Asian' means in OMB race talk and what 'East Asian' means in OMB race theory.

Suppose we call this *the South Asian Mismatch Objection* for ease of reference. For clarity, the South Asian Mismatch Objection states that what 'Asian' means in OMB race talk and what 'East Asian' means in OMB race theory are different because the group of people that the OMB intends to pick out with 'Asian' (Chinese, Japanese, Filipinos, Indians, Pakistanis, etc.) is simply different from the group of people that count as East Asian (Chinese, Japanese, Filipinos, etc.). While the South Asian Mismatch Objection is formidable, it's not a fatal objection to OMB race theory.

First, I should clarify that, according to OMB race theory, almost all living South Asians *are* East Asian. This is because South Asians are, on average, a very racially mixed people. For example, remember that in the United States, South Asian Americans are, on average, 26.5% East Asian. That's not nothing! So, the OMB is not wrong to racially classify almost all living South Asians with Asians. Also, note that the OMB cannot, on pains of inconsistency, deny that almost all living South Asians are White as well. Remember, the OMB (1997, 58789) wants it to be the case that any person with "origins in any of the original peoples of Europe, the Middle East, or North Africa" is White. However, we know from the Out of Africa theory of human migration history that all South Asians descend from the original peoples of the Middle East (Cavalli-Sforza and Feldman 2003, 270).

So far so good. However, we can see the real problem when we look at how the OMB racially classifies unmixed South Asians. From everything the OMB has written, it's reasonable to think that the OMB would racially classify unmixed South Asians as Asian instead of White. And that's the real challenge of the South Asian Mismatch Objection. Here's a concrete example to illustrate the challenge. From recent human genetic clustering studies, geneticists have discovered that the Kalash people of Pakistan are a very unmixed group of people. For example, Rosenberg et al. (2002) found that, on average, Kalash Pakistanis are 99% Caucasian.[29] So, there's bound to be hundreds of unmixed Kalash people out there whom the OMB would racially classify as Asian alone, while OMB race theory would racially classify unmixed Kalash people as Caucasian alone. That's a mismatch! Furthermore, it's hard to imagine how the OMB could be wrong here. How can the OMB be wrong about who its own race terms pick out in the world? If the OMB truly intended to pick out all South Asians with 'Asian,' including unmixed South Asians, how can the OMB be wrong about classifying unmixed South Asians with Asians?

While it may be counterintuitive, the OMB can be wrong about who its own race terms pick out in the world. This is because, sometimes, when we fix the referents of English terms, we get *some* of what that term picks out wrong. This was always part of the referential theory of (English) name meanings.[30] Also, there are plenty of examples of this happening in the English language. Here's one.

In botany, it's widely acknowledged that the initial sample of the species that botanists now call 'watermelon,' and, officially, '*Citrullus lanatus*,' consists of the plants in the Mediterranean that Carl Linnaeus named '*Cucurbita citrullus*' in 1753, and the plant in South Africa that Carl Thunberg, a student of Linnaeus's, named '*Citrullus lanatus*' in 1773. Since Linnaeus left no remnants of *C. citrullus*, but Thunberg preserved some of his *C. lanatus* plant, in the 1930s, botanists placed the remnants of Thunberg's plant in a museum as a paradigm member of *C. lanatus* to settle all disputes about the watermelon's characteristic genomic and phenotypic properties. These special paradigm members of species are known as *type specimens* in systematic biology.

---

29. This statistic is from supplementary Table 2 in Rosenberg et al. (2002).

30. For example, see Kripke (1980, 136).

However, interestingly, in 2014, two botanists decided to run a phylogenetic analysis on the type specimen of *C. lanatus*. What they found was puzzling. They found that the watermelon's type specimen is not closely related to Egusi melon (*Citrullus mucosospermus*), even though all other phylogenetic analyses of *C. lanatus* plants place the Egusi melon as a sister species to the watermelon.[31] They also found that the watermelon's type specimen is distantly related (a first cousin) to all other samples of watermelon they studied (which were from Benin). It was a real head scratcher. The researchers could have interpreted their results in two different ways.

First, the researchers could have concluded that *C. lanatus* is not a genealogically tidy species (or perhaps not a species at all!) since the term '*C. lanatus*' must, at least, pick out its type specimen as a species member. Alternatively, the researchers could have concluded that *C. lanatus* is a genealogically tidy species, but it just so happens that the watermelon's type specimen isn't a watermelon plant! Interestingly, the researchers concluded the latter, not the former, and the community of botanists have not rejected this conclusion, but rather, have embraced it.[32]

Since English-speaking botanists can reject a type specimen for a species as a member of that species, it's simply not true that the OMB cannot be wrong about racially classifying unmixed South Asians with Asians instead of Whites. The question now becomes, what evidence is there (beyond what's presented in Chapter 3) that the OMB really did intend to pick out the set of human continental populations with 'race' as opposed to a different classification of people that's similar to the set of human continental populations, but that classifies *all* South Asians with Asians.

This is a good concern, so here's some additional evidence that the OMB intended to pick out the set of human continental populations with 'race' in 1997. In 2013, the director of the US Census Bureau from 1998 to 2000, Kenneth Prewitt, came out and said that the OMB's 1997 racial classification was a deliberate attempt to mimic "Blumenbach's racial taxonomy" (Prewitt 2013, 17). In Prewitt's (2013, 17) words, "An extraordinary thing happened two hundred years after Blumenbach announced that the world's population

---

31. In systematic biology, two species *A* and *B* are *sister species* iff each one immediately descended from the same species. Thus sister species in systematic biology are analogous to siblings in ordinary English.

32. These researchers were Guillaume Chomicki and Susanne Renner, and this story comes from Chomicki and Renner (2015).

should be divided into five race groups distinguished by skin color. The United States government agreed." Prewitt (2013, 18) even calls the OMB's races "Blumenbachian races."

Furthermore, Prewitt should know what the OMB's true intentions were in 1997 because he worked closely with the OMB demographers who revised the OMB's race talk in 1997. It was Prewitt's responsibility to figure out how to best incorporate the OMB's new racial scheme into the 2000 decennial census. But let me back up a bit and talk about Blumenbach's racial classification and its link to the OMB's racial scheme.

J. F. Blumenbach was an eighteenth-century physical anthropologist who, in 1795, published a new, fivefold way of classifying people into races using mostly visible physical features of the face and body, but also linguistic attributes. Blumenbach's five races were Americans, Caucasians, Ethiopians, Malays, and Mongolians. Table 7.1 is a summary of Blumenbach's description of each race and the groups of people he thought belonged to each race.

What was truly original about Blumenbach's racial classification was its comprehensiveness. Somehow, Blumenbach managed to classify every living human into a race, which no race scholar before him had accomplished. According to Prewitt, OMB demographers liked this feature of Blumenbach's racial scheme and decided to adopt a racial scheme very similar to Blumenbach's in order to be able to racially classify any potential US immigrant. In Prewitt's words,

> Blumenbach's taxonomy was universal and totally inclusive. Every living person on earth could be assigned to one of its five categories. A consequence of employing a universal classification system in the American census is that *any* new immigrant arriving from *any* corner of the world will be put into this preexisting taxonomy—whether or not he or she seems to fit. Recently arrived Ethiopians, for example, are counted in the census as African American, though the former are Nilotic in ways unfamiliar to the African Americans (Prewitt 2013, 18).[33]

---

33. In the preceding quote, Prewitt is, unfortunately, using 'African American' in two different ways. In the first occurrence, 'African American' is a race term that's synonymous with 'Black.' In the second occurrence, 'African American' names the largest ethnic group of Blacks in the US.

Table 7.1 A Summary of Blumenbach's Five Races

Race	Description	Members	Textual Evidence
American	Copper-colored skin, black and stiff and straight hair, broad faces, chiseled cheeks, etc.	All indigenous people of the Americas except Eskimos	Blumenbach (1795/2000, 29)
Caucasian	White-colored skin, rosy cheeks, brown or chestnut-colored hair, oval faces, straight and narrow noses, etc.	Europeans (except the Sami and Finns), North Africans, South Asians, West Asians, and Western Siberians west of the Obi River	Blumenbach (1795/2000, 28)
Ethiopian	Black-colored skin, black and curly hair, thick noses, puffy lips, etc.	Aboriginal Australians, sub-Saharan Africans, Melanesians, etc.	Blumenbach (1795/2000, 28–29, 37)
Malay	Tawny-colored skin, black soft and thick hair, full and wide noses, . . . , and use "the Malay idiom"	Malayo-Polynesian language speakers except non-Papuan Melanesians (e.g., Filipinos, Malagasy, Micronesians, Sunda Islanders, Polynesians, etc.)	Blumenbach (1795/2000, 29, 36–37)
Mongolian	Yellow-colored skin, black and stiff and straight hair, broad faces, small noses, narrow eyelids, etc.	All remaining East Asians (except Malays), Eskimos, Finns, and Sami	Blumenbach (1795/2000, 28)

Of course, the OMB wanted its races to be ancestry groups instead of phenotypic and linguistic groups like Blumenbach's races. As a consequence, the OMB's races do not perfectly align with Blumenbach's races. For instance, the OMB's *Black* race lacks the Aboriginal Australians and Melanesians that fall into Blumenbach's *Ethiopian* race, because while Aboriginal Australians, Melanesians, and sub-Saharan Africans look very similar, it's been known since at least the 1980s that Aboriginal Australians and Melanesians are distantly related to sub-Saharan Africans.[34]

In any case, even though Blumenbach's races and the OMB's races do not perfectly align, there's definitely a one-to-one correspondence between the two sets of races (e.g., American corresponds to American Indian, Caucasian corresponds to White, etc.). Furthermore, the OMB (1997, 58782–58783) did say that it wanted a "comprehensive in coverage" racial scheme and a racial scheme that can deal with "growth in immigration." So, Prewitt is probably right that the OMB wanted to adopt a human classification scheme very similar to Blumenbach's racial scheme.

Now, given that Prewitt is right that the OMB wanted to adopt a human classification scheme very similar to, but not identical to, Blumenbach's racial scheme, and given that the OMB wanted to adopt a human classification scheme based on ancestry instead of phenotype and language like Blumenbach's racial scheme, and, furthermore, given that the set of human continental populations is an ancestry-based Blumenbach-like human classification scheme, it's hard to deny that the thing in the world that the OMB intended to pick out with 'race' in 1997 was, in fact, the set of human continental populations.

7.4. The Empirical Adequacy Objection for Glasgow, Haslanger, and Jeffers

I will now turn my attention away from OMB race theory and toward the race theories of my coauthors. Remember that Glasgow, Haslanger, and Jeffers are all offering a theory about what race is and whether it's real relative to the single dominant meaning of 'race' in, at least, American English—but in other linguistic contexts as well in Haslanger's and Jeffers's cases. However, now it's time to seriously question whether modeling dominant race talk in American English as stemming from a *single* dominant meaning of 'race' provides us with a more empirically adequate US race theory than a radically pluralist US race theory.

The term 'empirical adequacy' was coined by the philosopher of science Bas van Fraassen in 1980 as a minimal condition for accepting a scientific theory. Without using any of van Fraassen's jargon, very roughly, we can say that a theory is *empirically adequate* relative to all of the phenomena that the

---

34. For example, see Cavalli-Sforza et al. (1988, 6003).

theory is designed to explain or predict just in case the theory, in fact, explains or predicts all of that phenomena (van Fraassen 1980, 12). Van Fraassen is careful to note that a theory doesn't achieve empirical adequacy just for explaining all of the relevant *observed* phenomena, but rather, *all* of the phenomena (observed and unobserved) that the theory is supposed to account for. While it's true that no scientific theory has ever been shown to be empirically adequate, scientists have used closer proximity to empirical adequacy (or what I'll call *the empirical adequacy standard*) as a useful way to select one theory out of a group of rivals. For example, biologists who studied heredity eventually accepted Mendel's theory of genes after it became obvious that all of its serious rivals (esp. Spencer's theory of physiological units, Darwin's theory of gemmules, and Weismann's theory of ids) simply failed the empirical adequacy standard relative to Mendel's theory (Morgan 1926, 26–31).[35]

In addition to being a constraint on theory acceptance that's widely adopted in science, the empirical adequacy standard is also widely accepted among philosophers of science as being a minimal condition for reliably picking one scientific theory over another as being true or closer to the truth.[36] It's important to note that van Fraassen didn't construe his empirical adequacy standard as being truth-tracking because he was a scientific anti-realist. However, scientific realists and scientific non-realists other than scientific anti-realists have embraced the empirical adequacy standard as being *at least* what's required to reliably say that one scientific theory is true or more true than another.[37] Also, while the term 'empirical adequacy' was coined by van Fraassen, the idea of empirical adequacy and its important link to reliably accepting true scientific theories has been known by philosophers of science since at least as early as Pierre Duhem's idea of "complete" scientific theories in 1906.[38]

Now, since philosophical race theories (or at least the ones offered in this book) are types of scientific theories (given that they're descriptions about

---

35. Of course, ironically, after genetics got started in the early 1900s, it was quickly realized that Mendel's theory had to be revised considerably in order to account for genetic linkage, chromosomal recombination, chromosomal non-disjunction, and other hereditary phenomena that Mendel's theory didn't account for.

36. By a *reliable* pick I mean one that's arrived at from an inferential method with low false-positive and low false-negative error. This notion of epistemic reliability is widely accepted among philosophers of science. See, for example, Godfrey-Smith (2003).

37. Some examples are Longino (1990, 93–94) and Fine (1999).

38. See Duhem (1906/1981, 19).

what race is and whether race is real given a specific linguistic context), it's appropriate to hold them up to the same minimal epistemic standards as scientific theories, including the empirical adequacy standard. So, let's see whether the race theories that Glasgow, Haslanger, and Jeffers have offered us are closer to being empirically adequate compared to a radically pluralist US race theory, such as one that includes OMB race theory.

Remember in Chapter 3 when I said that 93.8% of US residents self-reported an OMB race on the 2010 US Census questionnaire (Chapter 3, 83), and that geneticists can predict US adults' OMB race self-reports with 98.8%–99.8% accuracy given a few reasonable background assumptions (Spencer, Chapter 3, 102). It turns out that these statistics can be used to estimate the extent to which US residents are competent in using OMB race talk. The estimate turns out to be that, approximately, 92.7% of US residents are competent in using OMB race talk.[39] Also, while this estimate assumes that almost everyone who provides at least her primary human continental population membership as her race on an official form (e.g., US Census questionnaire) is competent in using OMB race talk, this assumption is not that risky.

Remember that the overwhelming majority of Americans are people with a single and clearly primary human continental population membership, such as non-Hispanic European Americans (63.1% of US residents, 98.6% Caucasian on average), African Americans (13.6% of US residents, 73% African on average), Eastern Asian Americans (4.4% of US residents, 95.5% East Asian on average), American Jews (2.2%, 96% Caucasian on average), and so forth. Given these demographic and genealogical facts, it should not be surprising that so many Americans are competent in using OMB race talk. It's not a hard language game for most Americans to play!

Now, couple the fact that about 92.7% of US residents are competent in using OMB race talk with the additional fact that OMB race talk is the default

---

39. This calculation was made by simply multiplying 0.988 by 0.938 and converting the product to a percentage. I say 'suggest' and 'approximately' because it's debatable whether everyone who has self-reported her primary OMB race (according to genomic ancestry estimates) is *competent* in using OMB race talk. For one, some of these respondents could have made a lucky guess. Second, it's unclear how many US Census racial self-reports were self-reports in the ordinary sense. Many people don't know this, but 'self-reported' (at least with respect to 2010 census data) is jargon for the US Census Bureau. It includes reports made by the respondent (who may not be the person whose race is being communicated) and assignments from the US Census Bureau itself when data are missing (a.k.a. imputations) (Humes et al. 2011, footnote 8). Third, and finally, there's the matter of error. The US Census Bureau sometimes counts people more than once, counts dead people (who will have imputed census data), omits people, etc., which adds up to a small amount of error for any statistic that the US Census Bureau reports.

race talk on any form in the US that has US government oversight or any form in the US that for some reason is tethered to the OMB's racial scheme, and we have a reasonable basis for saying that the OMB's meaning of 'race' is, at least, *one* dominant meaning of 'race' among American English speakers. Some examples of these forms are mortgage loan applications, birth certificate applications, food stamp applications, college admissions applications, day-care enrollment forms, health provider enrollment forms, health insurance enrollment forms, job applications at colleges and universities, federally funded or administered scholarship and fellowship applications, and so forth.[40]

Now, given that OMB race talk harbors one dominant meaning of 'race' among American English speakers and given our presupposition of what a dominant meaning of 'race' is, it turns out that Glasgow's, Haslanger's, and Jeffers's race theories fail the empirical adequacy standard when compared to a radically pluralist US race theory, and especially one that includes OMB race theory. In particular, the race theories that Glasgow, Haslanger, and Jeffers have offered us are empirically inadequate in two important respects. First, each of these race theories *misdiagnose* what, essentially, race is or what, essentially, the races are in situations where the OMB's racial scheme is being presupposed. Second, each of these race theories *oversimplifies* the complexity of American communications about race. Here are two examples that nicely illustrate my points.

Remember that I said the OMB's racial scheme is the default racial scheme used by American colleges and universities to collect racial data on their college applicants.[41] Well, this fact has consequences because it makes it highly

---

40. Some of these examples have interesting histories. For instance, the reason why OMB race talk is dominant on American day-care enrollment forms is because American day cares usually offer parents the option of applying for the US Department of Agriculture's Child and Adult Care Food Program and that application always uses the OMB's racial scheme to ask about the applicant's race. Also, as of December 2007, American colleges and universities are legally required to collect and report the racial and ethnic data of their students and employees to the US Department of Education if they want any funding from the department, and you can guess which racial scheme that racial data must be reported in. Also, while health care and health insurance providers are not legally required to report any racial data to the US government, they are, nevertheless, anchored into using the US government's racial scheme. In short, the enormous database of health information that the US government has (e.g., data from the NIH, CDC, NCHS, etc.) is only useful if you're using a racial scheme that's at least compatible with the US government's. Obviously, the easiest thing to do here is simply use the US government's racial scheme. I must thank Ronald Copeland for the last insight, who's the chief diversity officer for Kaiser Permanente.

41. However, there are a few US colleges and universities that don't use the OMB's racial scheme when collecting racial data on their applicants. Some states legally ban the consideration of race in the admissions decisions of their public colleges, which has led to the public

likely that any particular discussion or dispute among Americans about the lawfulness of race-based preferential affirmative action in college admissions today presupposes the OMB's racial scheme, whether Americans know it or not.

For example, as I'm writing this chapter, the US Department of Justice (DOJ) is reconsidering a complaint against Harvard University that was originally submitted to the US Department of Education (ED) and the DOJ in May 2015 by the Coalition of Asian-American Associations (or "the Coalition"). The complaint was dismissed under the Obama administration, but the Trump administration is reconsidering the complaint on the grounds that "[t]he Department of Justice is committed to protecting all Americans from all forms of illegal race-based discriminations" (Chakraborty 2017).[42]

In the complaint, the Coalition accuses Harvard of engaging in racial discrimination for years that has been repeatedly upheld by the US Supreme Court to be unlawful.[43] In particular, the Coalition accuses Harvard of using a "de facto racial quota" on Asian admits to Harvard College (Coalition 2015, 41). Since Harvard has been using the OMB's racial scheme to collect racial data about its applicants since 2010, this particular national discussion about race is anchored by the OMB's racial scheme whether Americans know it or not.[44]

---

colleges in these states not asking for their applicants' OMB race(s) in the admissions process. For example, since California is one of these states, no University of California campus (e.g., UC Berkeley, UCLA, UCSD, UC Davis, etc.) asks about their applicants' race(s) in the admissions process. However, Caltech, Claremont McKenna, Harvey Mudd, Pepperdine, Pomona, Scripps, Stanford, USC, USD, USF, and just about every other private college or university in California ask about their applicants' race(s) in the admissions process and use the OMB's racial scheme to do it.

42. Interestingly, the Coalition filed a second and similar complaint with the DOJ and ED against Brown, Dartmouth, and Yale in May 2016. However, I'll focus on the Harvard complaint since it's currently getting reinvestigated by the Trump administration.

43. Given how I've worded this sentence, you might be wondering what kind of racial discrimination federal courts consider to be lawful. Well, lots! In federal courts, *racial discrimination* is understood to be any differential treatment based on race. So, for example, a person who chooses to only intra-racially date would be racially discriminating according to federal courts. In addition, unlawful racial discrimination, for federal courts, is not just any racial discrimination that violates a federal law or the US constitution. If that were the case, race-based preferential treatment in college admissions would be obviously unlawful since it violates Title VI in the Civil Rights Act of 1964. Rather, federal courts consider racial discrimination that violates a federal law or an article of the US Constitution to be merely *presumptively* unlawful. However, such discrimination can be lawful if it passes a threefold test known as *strict scrutiny*.

44. I should clarify that Harvard used the OMB's 1977 racial scheme (which had no Asian race) to ask about race on its college applications before 2010. This actually raises an interesting

So, now the question is, what is the correct way to understand the nature and reality of the Asian race relative to this particular national debate about affirmative action? Is it correct to say that the Asian race, in this context, is, essentially, a *visible-trait grouping* as Glasgow (Chapter 4, 119) would say? I don't think so. In this context, Asians roughly divide into South Asians ~ 1.8 billion people) and Eastern Asians (~ 2.3 billion people).[45] But these two groups of people do not form a *visible-trait grouping* at all. Rather, about half of them (South Asians) look like moderately or darkly pigmented Europeans and the other half (Eastern Asians) possess a different distinctive look (e.g., light to moderate skin pigmentation, epicanthic folds, round noses, etc.).[46]

Is it correct to say that the Asian race, in this context, is, essentially, a *cultural group* as Jeffers would say (Chapter 2, 58)? I don't think so. Again, in this context, Asians roughly divide into South Asians and Eastern Asians, but these two groups of people do not share a cultural essence. There's no combination of language, religion, food, music, literature, or other cultural property that unites South and Eastern Asians into a distinctive cultural group.[47]

Finally, is it correct to say that the Asian race, in this context, is, essentially, a "racialized group," as Haslanger would say? Again the answer is 'no.' Even if it's true that the group of people consisting of, mostly, South Asians and Eastern Asians is currently racialized in the United States, the latter is merely a contingent fact about the group, not a necessary fact—and thus not an essential

---

semantic point. Harvard cannot be guilty of unlawful *racial* discrimination against Asian applicants before 2010 because they didn't recognize *Asian* as a race before 2010! Nevertheless, Harvard could have been engaging in unlawful racial discrimination against Asian applicants in 2010 and after.

45. These population estimates are from the United Nation's 2015 world population estimates. See United Nations (2017). Also, notice that I left out Central Asians. I did this for two reasons. First, they make up just 1.7% of Central, Eastern, and South Asians according to the United Nations (2017). But also, Central Asians are about evenly split with respect to how they look. Some of them (e.g., Tajiks) look more Caucasian due to their primarily Caucasian genomic ancestry, while the rest (e.g., Uzbeks) look more East Asian due to their primarily East Asian genomic ancestry (Martínez-Cruz et al. 2011, 221).

46. It's important to note that here and elsewhere in this chapter, I'm not assuming that the act of naming or attributing properties to an object commits one to the actual existence of that object. So, for example, when I said earlier that Glasgow's theory of race commits him to the claim that Asians form a visible-trait grouping if they're a race, that claim does not commit Glasgow to Asians existing if they're a race (which is a good thing since Glasgow is sympathetic to racial anti-realism). This might sound bizarre, but remember, I said in Chapter 3 that the background logic that I'm adopting in my chapters is a free logic, and all free logics reject that naming an object or attributing a property to an object commits one to that object's actual existence.

47. A generic version of this point has been made before by Anthony Appiah. See Appiah (1985, 36).

fact—about the group. The reason why is because, as Jeffers (Chapter 2, 71) and Glasgow (Chapter 4, 132) have pointed out earlier, "racial equality" is impossible if races are racialized groups. However, the OMB talks about its races in such a way that it's at least *possible* for racial equality to come about.

For example, remember that one of the two main reasons why the OMB (1997, 58782) created its race talk was to help federal agencies "enforce civil rights laws." Also, after the OMB revised its racial scheme in 1997, it published a long document detailing exactly how its new racial scheme would be useful in detecting racial gerrymandering, monitoring equal employment opportunity, protecting equal opportunity in education, enforcing Title VI of the Civil Rights Act of 1964, and improving FBI hate crime statistics (OMB 2000, 62–70, 83). That doesn't look like the behavior of an agency that rejects the possibility of racial equality.

As you might have guessed by now, I think the most plausible way to define 'Asian' in this particular national affirmative action debate is as an *ancestry group*, and, specifically, the genealogical population of East Asians (as OMB race theory does). In this way, one can make sense of all of the phenomena discussed in the preceding, plus many more, such as why the Coalition itself claims that Harvard is discriminating against Asian applicants in virtue of their "Asian ancestry" (Coalition 2015, 31).

In addition to misdiagnosing what, essentially, race is or what, essentially, the races are in particular American communications about race, the race theories that Glasgow, Haslanger, and Jeffers have constructed also oversimplify the complexity of some American communications about race. An excellent example of this oversimplification is the 2015 American obsession with Rachel Dolezal's race.[48]

Dolezal is an American citizen who, in her own words, "was biologically born white, to white parents," but who began presenting herself as Black and self-identifying as Black in every facet of her life sometime after she graduated from graduate school in 2002.[49] For example, before she garnered media attention in June 2015, Dolezal was a former Africana Studies instructor at Eastern Washington University (EWU) and the former president of Spokane's chapter of the National Association for the Advancement of Colored People (NAACP). Dolezal also filed complaints with Idaho police

---

48. Although Rachel Dolezal has legally changed her name to 'Nkechi Diallo,' she still uses her former name for her public persona. As such, I will use her public persona name in this chapter.

49. This quote is from Dolezal's November 2, 2015, interview on *The Real*, which I'll talk about in detail very soon.

about being a victim of anti-Black hate crimes. She graduated from Howard University, which is a historically Black college or university (HBCU). Her ex-husband is African American. She marked 'Black/African American' on her job application to Spokane's Office of Police Ombudsman Commission. And the icing on the cake was that she curled her hair and suntanned enough to look like a lightly pigmented African American!

Dolezal came to local media attention in Spokane after she filed anti-Black hate crime complaints with Idaho police. However, Dolezal came to national media attention when a local Spokane news reporter, Jeff Humphrey of KXLY, interviewed her on camera about her hate crime complaints. In the course of Humphrey's interview, he asked her directly, "Are you African American?" Dolezal was caught off guard and said, "I don't understand the question." Then, Dolezal quickly walked off camera and ended the interview. As you can imagine, Dolezal's response drew immediate suspicion from other news reporters. In particular, ABC news (the parent company of KXLY), quickly found Dolezal's birth parents and interviewed them. In that interview, Dolezal's parents said, "There seems to be some question of how Rachel is representing her identity and ethnicity. . . . We are definitely her birth parents. We are both of Caucasian and European descent—Czech, German and a few other things" (Capehart 2015).

When Dolezal was invited to explain herself in several national television interviews, she repeatedly said she was 'Black' or 'African American,' and, sometimes, 'not White.' However, Dolezal eventually admitted on camera that she was "biologically born white," as I mentioned earlier. One fact about the Dolezal case that's relevant for philosophical race theory is how complicated the national discussion was about Dolezal.

One debate was about whether Dolezal could accurately claim to be racially Black without possessing what was called *Black ancestry* in the conversation.[50] Furthermore, this debate was at least partially motivated by a genuine concern about whether Dolezal was taking away educational or employment opportunities that were intended for people with Black ancestry. For example, during Dolezal's interview on *The Real,* co-host Loni Love said that she didn't care about how Dolezal racially identified, but she did care about whether Dolezal marked 'Black' on her college applications because that act could have taken away scholarship money from a student with Black

---

50. For example, this was the term that YouGov used on its June 17–19, 2015, national survey about Dolezal.

ancestry.[51] Interestingly, Dolezal said that Howard's college application didn't ask about race, but she did say that she marked 'Black' on her job application to Spokane's Office of Police Ombudsman Commission. Furthermore, Dolezal said she marked 'Black' because "we all have human origins in the continent of Africa."[52]

Some of the debate was about whether Dolezal could accurately claim to be racially Black when underneath her artificially constructed Black appearance (esp. her light brown skin color and curly hair), she looked like a typical Caucasian woman. Furthermore, this debate was motivated by a serious concern that Dolezal was participating in blackface, which, if true, would make Dolezal a participant in a long history of racist imagery. For example, in a widely read op-ed on the Dolezal case for *The Washington Post,* Jonathan Capehart said, "Blackface remains highly racist, no matter how down with the cause a white person is" (Capehart 2015).

In addition, some of the debate was about whether Dolezal could accurately claim to be racially Black without having gone through the so-called Black experience. Furthermore, this debate was motivated by a genuine concern that Dolezal was exercising White privilege by pretending to be Black when it was convenient, but reverting back to identifying as White when that was convenient. This became an increasing concern once the media found out that Dolezal actually had sued Howard for racially discriminating against her because she was White! An example of this debate can be found once again during Dolezal's interview on *The Real.* In that interview, co-host Tamar Braxton expressed exactly this concern when she asked whether Dolezal thought she had "walked the walk of a Black woman." Interestingly, Dolezal responded, "Absolutely," and followed that up with, "the police mark 'Black' on my traffic tickets."

---

51. *The Real* is a daytime talk show with the same format as *The View* and *The Talk* (all women hosts who discuss the daily news), but with one big difference: all of the hosts on *The Real* are racial or ethnic minorities in the US. One host (Jeannie Mai) is Asian American, another host (Adrienne Houghton) is Hispanic American, and the remaining three hosts (Loni Love, Tamar Braxton, and Tamera Mowry) are all Black American. Actually, Braxton is no longer a host on the show, but she was a host when Dolezal was interviewed.

52. I should clarify that it was actually Jeannie Mai, not Loni Love, who got Dolezal to reveal which race(s) she marks on "applications." Also, notice that we can use OMB race theory to pinpoint exactly why Dolezal's answer here is incorrect. Remember, according to OMB race theory, OMB racial membership is about genomic ancestry, not ancestry simpliciter. So, while it's true that all living humans have African ancestry, it's not true that all living humans have African genomic ancestry.

And that's just three debates Americans were having. I didn't even discuss the so-called transracial debate! But we can stop here because it's clear to see that the national discussion about Dolezal was complicated, and so complicated that any attempt to simplify it to a discussion about a single meaning of 'race' would not accurately capture what was going on. For example, is it more plausible to say that Loni Love, Tamar Braxton, and Jonathan Capehart were somehow, covertly, and unknowingly, using the same meaning of 'race'? Or, is it more plausible to say that Love was using whatever meaning of 'race' is frequently used on American college and job applications (which is the OMB's), Capehart was using a Glasgow-style visible phenotype meaning of 'race,' and Braxton was using a Haslanger-style racialized group meaning of 'race'? I think the latter position is far more plausible than the former because we can better make sense of the extreme complexity of the conversations that Americans had about Dolezal. Nevertheless, here are two potential replies to my empirical adequacy objection.

One reply can be extrapolated from something that Glasgow says in Chapter 4. At the beginning of Chapter 4, Glasgow says:

> there must be some shared concept of race for us to even talk—even just *disagree*—about race. We can meaningfully disagree and converse about something only if we use our words in such a way that they have a shared meaning. Otherwise, we'll talk past each other, using the same words to talk about different things (Glasgow, Chapter 4, 116).

Glasgow (Chapter 4, 117) uses the preceding fact about how to prevent "communication breakdown" to motivate his search for "one overarching meaning of 'race.'" Also, Glasgow's research isn't entirely aspirational. Elsewhere he has also said that he thinks it's "implausible" that we Americans are "simply babbling past one another when we talk about race" (Glasgow 2009, 75).

I think this is a clever reply. And while I agree that a shared meaning of 'race' must be held in order to have a disagreement about race, I don't think this reply assuages the empirical adequacy concern I've offered in the preceding. For one, it's not implausible at all that, sometimes, Americans do "talk past each other" when discussing race. For example, there was definitely some cross-talk going on among Americans when discussing whether Dolezal was Black. But also, there's no need for there to be "one overarching meaning of 'race'" in order to prevent communication breakdown in national discussions about race. This is because Americans could know how to competently use more than one meaning of 'race' and utilize whichever meaning is appropriate given the situation at hand.[53] In short, just like a Taiwanese person can use *context* to decipher whether her interlocutor is speaking Taiwanese or Mandarin, Americans can use *context* to decipher which 'race' meaning her interlocutor is using. In fact, Dolezal's interview on *The Real* provides us with an example of how we do this.

Even though Dolezal was nervous on her interview with the hosts of *The Real*, she demonstrated an extraordinary skill in listening to her interviewers and responding to their questions using the way of thinking about race that was presupposed in the question that the interviewer asked. For example, remember that Dolezal responded to Braxton's question (which presupposed that races were Haslanger-like racialized groups) with evidence that she had taken part in the so-called Black experience by being treated as a Black person by the police. Also, remember that Dolezal responded to Love's and Mai's question about whether she marks 'Black' on college and job applications (which presupposes that races are ancestry groups) by explaining how she (and all humans) possess Black ancestry. So, even if you didn't like Dolezal's answers, we all can at least agree that Dolezal was *disagreeing* with her interviewers because she skillfully picked up on the appropriate race talk to use to answer each question that was asked. So, given that it's possible for Americans to disagree about race without holding a single dominant meaning of 'race,' Glasgow's observation that Americans often disagree in their discussions about race does not assuage the empirical adequacy concern that I've advanced.

However, another reply to this objection may stem from my assumption that philosophical race theories (at least the ones advanced in this book) are *descriptions* of what race is and whether race is real given a specific linguistic context. But Haslanger and Jeffers could reply that their race theories are not mere descriptions. For example, in Chapter 2, Jeffers (Chapter 2, 58) says, he does not "draw a very sharp distinction between ethics and metaphysics," and as a consequence, he thinks it's important to pay attention to "values and ideals" when "thinking about the nature and reality of race." In fact, in his response to Paul Taylor's (2013, 100–101) generic objection against cultural constructionist views about race in the US context—which is that they're confusing a "prescriptive" race theory for what should be a "descriptive" race theory—Jeffers (Chapter 2, 60) replies that his race theory, as well as that of other cultural constructionists like DuBois, is committed to both prescriptive and descriptive content.

---

53. I'm getting this response from Ann Morning's (2009, 1186) "tool kit" quote.

In addition, Haslanger (Chapter 1, 6) explicitly says in Chapter 1 that the "adequacy" of her race theory "is not to be judged simply by reference to 'the facts.' . . ." Haslanger (Chapter 1, 6) even distances herself from scientists such as "anthropologists" when clarifying what kind of race theory she's engaging in. Instead, Haslanger (Chapter 1, 8) views her race theory as an instance of critical social theory, which, in her view, is not merely a descriptive, but is also a prescriptive, exercise insofar as it recommends how to "improve" "ordinary social practices." So, in sum, both Jeffers and Haslanger might object to the empirical adequacy objection I've offered because it seems to presuppose that all a philosophical race theory is trying to do is accurately describe as opposed to, also, helpfully prescribe.

This is a wonderful concern. However, notice that I never said that philosophical race theories are *completely* descriptive theories. In fact, this would be hypocritical of me since OMB race theory uses a definition of 'biologically real' that's partly normatively justified.[54] Rather, all I said was that philosophical race theories are, in fact, descriptive theories about what race is and whether race is real relative to a specific linguistic context. This statement is compatible with philosophical race theories being more than just descriptive theories. Nevertheless, insofar as any philosophical race theory is descriptive at all, its adequacy is bound by the empirical adequacy standard just like any other scientific theory.[55] In other words, if you want to say that races are cultural groups or racialized groups given the predominant way that American English speakers use 'race,' then your theory needs to be better able than its most serious rivals to explain or predict all of the relevant phenomena.

Also, upon closer inspection of what Jeffers and Haslanger have to say, I think that they would agree with me that the adequacies of their race theories are bound by the empirical adequacy standard. For instance, Jeffers (Chapter 2, 61) explicitly says that his and other cultural constructionists' "prescriptions" about race (e.g., DuBois's prescriptions) have always been

---

54. For evidence, see Spencer (2012).

55. It's also important to note that scientific theories are often not entirely descriptions as well, and philosophers of science have known this fact since at least when Duhem (1906/1980, 208–212) observed that natural scientists often use stipulative definitions for key terms in scientific theories. For example, you might think that the claim "*Homo sapiens* immediately evolved from the species *Homo ergaster*" is a purely descriptive claim. But it isn't. It's a descriptive claim about an evolutionary relationship between two species given a preferred definition of 'species'—namely, the phylogenetic species concept (PSC). For example, Joseph LaPorte (2005) has shown that if you switch the definition of 'species' from the PSC to the biological species concept (BSC), then this evolutionary statement is false. Rather, under the BSC, the true statement would be, "*Homo sapiens* immediately evolved from the species *Homo erectus*."

"inseparable from an understanding of the race being exhorted as already a cultural group in some sense. . . ." Also, Haslanger (Chapter 1, 16) has the following to say about her race theory: ". . . the goal is to provide an interpretation of what has plausibly been at issue . . . 'all along,' as evidenced not only by what we say, but what we do, such as the practices we engage in, the laws we pass, and social scientific explanations of these." So, since both Jeffers's and Haslanger's race theories are, in large part, descriptions about what race is and whether race is real given, at least, American English speakers' usage of 'race,' both of their race theories are in just as much trouble as Glasgow's when it comes to being closer to empirical adequacy than a radically pluralist US race theory that includes OMB race theory.

7.5. A Methodological Concern for Glasgow and Jeffers

While my primary concern with Haslanger's race theory is that it's simply not as empirically accurate as a radically pluralist US race theory that includes OMB race theory, I have an additional concern about Glasgow's and Jeffers's race theories. It's about methodology. Notice that both Glasgow and Jeffers crucially rely on thought experiments whose experimental results are drawn entirely from their own intuitions, or, at least, some small group of philosophers' intuitions. For ease of communication, I'll call such thought experiments *intuition-based thought experiments*. While I have no universal worry about the reliability of intuition-based thought experiments in philosophy, I do have a serious worry about their reliability in philosophical race theory.[56]

In particular, I'm skeptical that intuition-based thought experiments can yield any reliable information about what 'race' means when the linguistic community is large and diverse, like, for example, American English speakers, or, even more so, English speakers. If I'm right that an evidential method that both Glasgow and Jeffers crucially rely on is unreliable under the very circumstances in which it's being used, then we should be worried that both Glasgow's and Jeffers's race theories aren't true, at least not given the way these theories are currently formulated. But let's explore this concern in more detail.

---

56. However, for a criticism of using intuition-based thought experiments in philosophy at all (esp. metaphysics and epistemology), see Machery (2011). For another criticism of using intuition-based thought experiments in philosophical race theory, see Haslanger and Saul (2006). What I am about to say is basically an extension of what I said in Spencer (2015, 52).

First, suppose we call any race that's part of the correct US race theory a *US race*. In that case, note that both Glasgow and Jeffers crucially rely on intuition-based thought experiments in order to evidentially support their claims about what is part of (or not part of) the essence of a US race. Glasgow does this directly with lots of intuition-based thought experiments. His Dalai Lama thought experiment is supposed to show that "races must, by definition, be *visibly distinct*," which, if true, is a problem for all theories of US races as genealogical populations (Chapter 4, 122). Glasgow's racial amnesia thought experiment is supposed to show that "race persists even when the social facts change," which, if true, is a problem for all social constructionist US race theories (Chapter 4, 132). Glasgow (Chapter 4, 132) also cites his previous Utopia thought experiment from *A Theory of Race,* which is supposed to show that "racial equality is not *incoherent*," which is a problem for social inequality–based US race theories.

To be clear, I'm not saying that Glasgow's race theory is supported solely by intuition-based thought experiments. He also uses relevant observations to support his theory, such as his observation that biological populations possess the essential property of "*migratability*," which is the property that one's members can immigrate into and emigrate from the group (Glasgow, Chapter 4, 121).[57] Rather, what I'm pointing out is that the evidence for Glasgow's race theory crucially involves intuition-based thought experiments. For example, the only evidence that Glasgow provides for his key claim that "races must, by definition, be *visibly distinct*," is the result from his Dalai Lama thought experiment.

Similarly, Jeffers's race theory crucially relies upon intuition-based thought experiments for evidence. For one, remember that Jeffers (Chapter 2, 44) uses one thought experiment (the dark-skinned Bangladeshi British woman) as a key source of evidence for rejecting "biological realism" as a "reasonable . . . description of race." But to get his result, all Jeffers (Chapter 2, 44) appeals to is his intuition that "it conflicts with common sense" and that it's less "illuminating" to describe this woman as "Caucasian" or "Caucasoid." Also, remember that Jeffers (Chapter 6, 192) adopts Michael Hardimon's "logical core" for what an ordinary race is as being a central element of his race theory. However, Hardimon's "logical core" for what an ordinary race

---

57. Notice that this constraint doesn't apply to genealogical populations like monophyletic groups or the human continental populations. Members of genealogical populations are born into them and are not able to migrate in or out.

is depends crucially—though not exclusively—on intuition-based thought experiments for evidence.

For instance, in Hardimon's (2017, 48) most recent defense of his common ancestry requirement for what an ordinary race is, he relies crucially on what's called "the permuted world" thought experiment in order to reply to an objection from Glasgow. Without that thought experiment, the common ancestry requirement of his "logical core" would be left wide open to Glasgow's objection.[58] So, now that I've shown that intuition-based thought experiments are crucially relied upon for evidence by both Glasgow and Jeffers, I'll move on to what's so problematic about relying upon intuition-based thought experiments for evidence in philosophical race theory.

Well, in short, standard statistical theory advises against using a small and non-random sample size in order to estimate the parameters of any statistical population when both the variance in the sought-after parameter and the statistical population size are large (Samuels and Witmer 2003, 57–64). In our case, the target population is not the complete group of American English speakers, English speakers, or so forth. Rather, it's the group of *ideas* about race that these latter groups of people hold. Also, we're not looking at an unchanging collection of ideas, but rather, a changing collection of ideas stretching from the present day to as far back in the past as we need to go to reach a semantic shift in what 'race' means in its dominant meaning in the relevant linguistic community (if there is a single dominant meaning). However, we can put a lower bound on this statistical population's size in the case of American English speakers.

During the 2010 US Census, the USCB counted 312,684,568 US residents and citizens in the fifty US states, the District of Columbia, Puerto Rico, Guam, and the Northern Mariana Islands (Humes et al. 2011, table 1; Guam State Data Center 2012, table GU1).[59] If we assume that each American English speaker holds some idea about what race is, then the relevant statistical population size is at least 312 million. To think that we can sample the thoughts of a single American English speaker—even if they are from insightful people like Joshua Glasgow and Michael Hardimon—and arrive at

---

58. For Hardimon's most recent discussion of Glasgow's objection to his common ancestry requirement for being an ordinary race, see Hardimon (2017, 48).

59. I include the citizens of Puerto Rico, Guam, and the Northern Mariana Islands because they are part of the American English-speaking community given their histories as US territories. Also, the Puerto Rico and Northern Mariana Islands counts are from the American FactFinder, which is available at http://www.factfinder.census.gov.

any "core" semantic content in the widest shared meaning of 'race' among American English speakers is extremely optimistic.

However, perhaps Jeffers and Glasgow will point out that my objection is deficient in the following way. I said that a small and non-random sample size is bound to lead to unreliable inductions about the parameters of a statistical population if *both* the variance in the sought-after parameters and the statistical population's size are large. But all I've done so far is shown that the relevant statistical population's size is large. So, it doesn't follow yet that there's any problem with using intuition-based thought experiments in philosophical race theory.

In fact, Peter Godfrey-Smith (2003, 583) has recently clarified that there are at least two distinct types of "reliable inference" with respect to induction. One must be based on a random and large sample of the statistical population, but the other need not be. In the other type of reliable induction, a sample of one might be okay! What's relevant in the second case is that the statistical population of interest has very low variance in its values for the relevant parameter. Godfrey-Smith (2003, 585) points out that when the latter event occurs, we are likely dealing with a "natural kind"—by which he means a kind whose members do not vary that much in the properties they exemplify. The following is an example that illustrates Godfrey-Smith's point.

Despite the fact that we know that our solar system makes up only a tiny portion of the total mass-energy of the universe, all inductions in chemistry about atoms are based on small and non-random samples of atoms from our solar system. For instance, chemists infer that, at standard temperature and pressure, *all* hydrogen ion pairs spontaneously react with electron pairs to form hydrogen gas simply because that's how hydrogen behaves in our solar system (McMurray and Fay 1995, 123). However, according to Godfrey-Smith, inductions about the chemical reactivity of hydrogen that are based on the admittedly small and non-random sample of hydrogen in our solar system are not unreliable because hydrogen atoms form a *natural kind*. That is, we can expect any hydrogen atom in the universe to behave like the ones in our solar system because hydrogen atoms themselves do not vary that much in the properties they exemplify. So, much like chemists do, why can't philosophers of race appeal to a small and non-random sample of ideas about race (their own) to make a reliable induction about what 'race' means for the community of American English speakers based on the assumption that American English speakers' ideas about race form a *natural kind?*

While this is a possible way to justify intuition-based thought experiments in philosophical race theory, I think you can guess what my response is to it. The

Table 7.2 Glasgow et al.'s (2009) Results for Average Frequency of Using Five Common Criteria for Racial Membership among 449 US Adults

Criterion	Average Frequency of Use	Scale Correction
One-Drop Rule	25.1% (2.01/8.00)	+1
Ancestry	54.3% (2.17/4.00)	0
Social Relations (i.e., Culture)	48.9% (1.96/4.00)	+2
Ψ-Essence	64.5% (2.58/4.00)	0
Visible Phenotype	48% (0.48/1.00)	0

Notes:

The scale correction is the value added to the maximum and minimum value of the original scale to mathematically translate the scale to have all positive values with a minimum value of zero.

The scale minimum and maximum values are in parentheses.

presupposition that American English speakers' ideas about race form a natural kind is itself highly suspect and almost certainly false. In fact, we can quantify how variant American English speakers' ideas about race are using a recent experiment by Joshua Glasgow et al. (2009).

Using a new psychological instrument called "the Racial Classification Questionnaire" (RCQ) and a diverse sample of 449 US adults, Glasgow et al. (2009) explored the average frequency with which ordinary Americans use five often-discussed criteria for racial membership when actually classifying other people: the one-drop rule, ancestry, social relations (e.g., culture), ψ-essentialism, and visible phenotype.[60] If one adds an appropriate correction to make each scale of the RCQ composed of all positive values with zero as the minimum value, then Glasgow et al.'s results can be summarized in Table 7.2.

It's important to remember that it's incorrect to read Glasgow et al.'s results as reporting the percentage of subjects who used each criterion.[61] Rather, the correct way to read the results is as reporting the average frequency with

---

60. Glasgow (2009, 66–67) clarifies that features are part of a *ψ-essence* just in case they are "heritable, unchangeable racial features that are fixed no later than the moment one is born."

61. The exception is the result for visible phenotype, since the scale for this criterion consisted of a single item.

which each criterion was used across all subjects. With that said, one obvious result from Glasgow et al.'s study is that Americans vary considerably in their ideas about what race is. We can quantify how much by using the coefficient of variation, which is a statistic that quantifies the dispersion of a frequency distribution as the quotient of the sample standard deviation divided by the sample mean (Samuels and Witmer 2003, 44).

If we look at Table 7.2, we can see that the coefficient of variation in the average frequency with which each criterion was used is 0.30. In other words, the standard deviation in US adults' use of the five criteria for racial membership that Glasgow et al. studied was 30% of its average use, which is a very high variation in use! Furthermore, Glasgow et al.'s result is not a fluke. Glasgow et al.–like results have been reproduced by Morning (2009, 2011), Compton et al. (2013), Guo et al. (2014), and Citrin et al. (2014), to name a few.

What all of this implies is that, according to modern statistical theory and the experimental studies that we've already done on American race-thinking, we have enough evidence to say that using intuition-based thought experiments is unreliable in philosophical race theory, at least when theorizing on American English speakers' dominant meaning(s) of 'race.' Furthermore, by extension, intuition-based thought experiments are also unreliable when theorizing on English speakers' dominant meaning(s) of 'race.' In fact, when we look at dominant race talk in English-speaking countries outside North America, this point becomes obvious.

For example, in Singapore, the national government uses a fourfold racial classification that does not respect Hardimon's requirement that ordinary English races must be visibly distinct. In particular, the Singapore government classifies people into Chinese, Indian, Malay, and Other (Kim 2010, 35). Other! That means Africans, non-Indian Caucasians, Native Americans, and Pacific Islanders form a single race in a dominant race talk in an English-speaking country. Even more amazing is that Niue's government uses the following threefold racial classification: Niuean, Part-Niuean, and Non-Niuean (Vaha 2012, 45, 119). Non-Niuean! That race is even more visibly diverse than Singapore's Other race. So, while I find Glasgow's and Jeffers's race theories interesting and potentially accurate in highly contextualized race talks (e.g., races are probably visible-trait groupings in American law enforcement race talk), their race theories are not based on a reliable evidential method when applied to American English (or English) speakers as a whole. As a result, we should be highly skeptical that these race theories are accurate given their intended scope.

7.6. Conclusion

To close, I will reiterate what I take myself to have done throughout Chapters 3 and 7, and then I'll share a few final remarks. What I take myself to have done throughout Chapters 3 and 7 is to have developed and defended a specific race theory for a specific race talk: OMB race theory for OMB race talk. The theory was that OMB race talk houses an ordinary meaning of 'race' in American English whose meaning is its referent, and, is, in fact, a set of five biological populations in the human species: Africans (or Blacks), East Asians (or Asians), Caucasians (or Whites), Native Americans (or Americans Indians), and Oceanians (or Pacific Islanders).

I used contemporary human population-genetic studies and a particular meaning of 'biologically real' to defend the view that race, in OMB race talk, is a biologically real division of people as well. I consider OMB race theory to be a nuanced and contemporary way to defend biological racial realism.

Nevertheless, I clarified in this chapter that OMB race theory is not a stand-alone race theory. Rather, it is part of a larger radically pluralist race theory about the dominant uses of 'race' in American English. So, unlike my coauthors, I did not argue for a monistic US race theory because I don't believe that the reliable empirical data we have (e.g., well-designed and well-executed surveys but not intuition-based thought experiments) support a monistic US race theory. Before I close, I should address one potentially concerning aspect of OMB race theory. The concern is not about its truth, but about its potentially negative impact on society.

As many philosophers of race have brought up in the past, one serious concern that race scholars tend to have about any defense of biological racial realism is that it possesses a potential to negatively impact society in unique ways. For example, Lisa Gannett (2001, S489) has argued that "population thinking"—such as thinking that OMB races are genealogical populations— is not "inherently anti-racist," and, in fact, such thinking makes it possible for people to engage in a more sophisticated form of racist stereotyping that happens to be statistical. Gannett (2001, S490) names this new type of racist that population thinking allows "statistical racists."

Also, Bernard Boxill (2004, 223–224) has argued that ancestry-based racial classifications tend to decrease our "compassion" for those who are not members of our race, and he also suspects (though does not argue) that ancestry-based racial classifications make us prone to "foolish rationalizations" and to be "gullible enough" to believe these rationalizations. Next, Philip Kitcher

(2007, 314–316) has expressed a deep concern that any positive consequences that result from recognizing a biological racial scheme in American society (e.g., utility in "race-based medicine") will be far outweighed by the negative consequences that follow in American society from that recognition (e.g., reinforcing "racial stereotypes"). Finally, Charles Mills (2014, 91) has expressed a sincere concern that modern versions of biological racial realism might fuel new forms of "extrinsic racism," and, as a result, add extra support to preexisting social hierarchies.[62] Furthermore, empirical social science findings have only supported these philosophers' concerns.

For instance, we now know from various psychological studies that, for some people, believing in the existence of biological human races is highly and positively correlated with having racist attitudes (Morning 2009, 1169–1170). We also know that, for some people, just reading genetic data in racial terms (e.g., 'African,' 'Caucasian,' 'White,' 'Black,' etc.) makes one more likely to develop not only racial bias, but slide into believing a *racialist* concept of race (Donovan 2014).[63]

Of course, these philosophical concerns and empirical facts are worrisome. However, I stand with Bernard Boxill (2004, 224) and Daniel Kelly et al. (2010) in taking a scientifically informed approach to addressing these concerns and facts. In short, it's not obviously true that not publishing academic defenses of biological racial realism will be an effective method of preventing any statistically significant rise in American society's statistical and extrinsic racists, racial bias, racist attitudes, etc. So, instead, let's do more empirical social science to figure out enough about how these causal links actually work to be able to disrupt these causal links in a way that efficiently and significantly reduces racial bias, racist attitudes, etc.

For instance, in Donovan's study, the link between reading genetic data in racial terms and developing a racialist concept of race turned out to be significantly negatively correlated with one's comprehension of Mendelian genetics (Donovan 2014, 481–482). In other words, the more you knew about genetics, the less susceptible you were to developing a racialist concept of race just from reading genetic data in racial terms. So, perhaps one morally respectable way

---

62. An individual is *extrinsically racist* when she treats people of a certain race differently based on a belief that membership in that race is contingently correlated to morally relevant properties (Appiah 1990, 216).

63. I should say that neither of these correlations have been shown to hold for a nationally representative sample of Americans. For example, Donovan's sample consisted of 43 eighth grade private school students in the San Francisco Bay Area (Donovan 2014, 469).

to do philosophical race theory is not to suppress research on biological racial realism, but rather, to improve the public's understanding of genetics.

Just in case the latter is a morally respectable way to do philosophical race theory, I will reiterate the disclaimer I made at the end of Chapter 3. If I'm right that the OMB races are the human continental populations and that the human continental populations form a biologically real human population subdivision, then it's not a metaphysically confused research project to search for medically relevant alleles or any other phenotypic differences among OMB races. Nevertheless, OMB race theory all by itself does not imply that OMB races differ in any socially important traits (e.g., drug-metabolizing enzymes, intelligence, beauty, moral character, etc.) or in any phenotypic ways whatsoever. Furthermore, OMB race theory doesn't imply that OMB races don't differ in any phenotypic ways either. Rather, determining whether OMB races differ in any phenotypic ways requires a separate empirical investigation. Furthermore, I am not saying this out of political correctness. It's simply a fact that the DNA evidence that supports the existence of human continental populations comes from non-protein-coding and non-functional DNA in the human genome.

References

Appiah, A. 1985. "The Uncompleted Argument: Du Bois and the Illusion of Race." *Critical Inquiry* 12(1): 21–37.

Appiah, K. 1990. "Racisms." In D. Goldberg (ed.), *Anatomy of Racism*. Minneapolis: University of Minnesota Press, pp. 3–17.

Appiah, K. 1996. "Race, Culture, Identity, Misunderstood Connections." In A. Gutmann and K. Appiah (eds.), *Color Conscious*. Princeton, NJ: Princeton University Press, pp. 30–105.

Blum, L. 2002. *I'm Not A Racist But . . . : The Moral Quandary of Race*. Ithaca, NY: Cornell University Press.

Boxill, B. 2004. "Why We Should Not Think of Ourselves as Divided by Race." In M. L. Pataki (ed.), *Racism in Mind*. Ithaca, NY: Cornell University Press, pp. 209–224.

Bryc, K., E. Durand, J. Macpherson, D. Reich, D., and J. Mountain. 2015. "The Genetic Ancestry of African Americans, Latinos, and European Americans across the United States." *The American Journal of Human Genetics* 96(1): 37–53.

Capehart, J. 2015, June 12. "The Damage Rachel Dolezal Has Done." *The Washington Post*. Retrieved September 23, 2017, from https://www.washingtonpost.com/blogs/post-partisan/wp/2015/06/12/the-damage-rachel-dolezal-has-done/?utm_term=.ae19663876fd

Cavalli-Sforza, L.A., and Feldman, M.W. "The Application of Molecular Genetic Approaches to the Study of Human Evolution." *Nature Genetics* 33(Suppl.): 266–275.

Cavalli-Sforza, L., A. Piazza, P. Menozzi, and J. Mountain. 1988. "Reconstruction of Human Evolution: Bringing Together Genetic, Archaeological, and Linguistic Data." *Proceedings of the National Academy of Sciences* 85: 6002–6006.

Chakraborty, B. 2017, August 2. "NY Times Story on Affirmative Action 'Inaccurate,' DOJ Says. Retrieved September 23, 2017, from FoxNews.com: http://www.foxnews.com/politics/2017/08/02/justice-department-reportedly-going-after-affirmative-action-programs.html

Chomicki, G., and S. Renner. 2015. "Watermelon Origin Solved with Molecular Phylogenetics Including Linnaean Material: Another Example of Museomics." *New Phytologist* 205: 526–532.

Citrin, J., M. Levy, and R. Van Houweling. 2014. "Americans Fill Out President Obama's Census Form: What Is His Race?" *Social Science Quarterly* 95(4): 1121–1136.

Coalition of Asian-American Associations. 2015. *Complaint against Harvard University and the President and Fellows of Harvard College for Discriminating against Asian-American Applicants in the College Admissions Process.* Washington, DC: The Chronicle of Higher Education. Retrieved September 23, 2017, from http://www.chronicle.com/items/biz/pdf/Final%20Aisan%20Complaint%20Harvard%20Document%2020150515.pdf

Compton, E., M. Bentley, S. Ennis, and S. Rastogi. 2013. *2010 Census Race and Hispanic Origin Alternative Questionnaire Experiment.* Washington, DC: US Census Bureau.

Donovan, B. 2014. "Playing with Fire? The Impact of the Hidden Curriculum in School Genetics on Essentialist Conceptions of Race." *Journal of Research in Science Teaching* 51(4): 462–496.

Duhem, P. 1906/1981. *The Aim and Structure of Physical Theory.* New York: Atheneum.

Ennis, S., M. Ríos-Vargas, and N. Albert. 2011. *The Hispanic Population, 2010.* US Census Bureau. Retrieved from http://www.census.gov/prod/cen2010/briefs/c2010br-04.pdf

Epstein, B. 2015. *The Ant Trap: Rebuilding the Foundations of the Social Sciences.* New York: Oxford University Press.

Feldman, M. 2010. "The Biology of Ancestry: DNA, Genomic Variation, and Race." In H. Markus and P. Moya (eds.), *Doing Race: 21 Essays for the 21st Century.* New York: W. W. Norton, pp. 136–159.

Fine, A. 1999. "The Natural Ontological Attitude." In R. Boyd, P. Gasper, and J. Trout (eds.), *The Philosophy of Science.* Cambridge, MA: MIT Press, pp. 261–277.

Gannett, L. 2001. "Racism and Human Genome Diversity Research: The Ethical Limits of 'Population Thinking.'" *Philosophy of Science* 68(3): S479–S492.

Glasgow, J. 2009. *A Theory of Race.* New York: Routledge.

Glasgow, J., J. Shulman, and E. Covarrubias. 2009. "The Ordinary Conception of Race in the United States and Its Relation to Racial Attitudes: A New Approach." *Journal of Cognition and Culture* 9: 15–38.

Godfrey-Smith, P. 2003. "Goodman's Problem and Scientific Methodology." *The Journal of Philosophy* 100(11): 573–590.

Guam State Data Center. 2012. *Guam Demographic Profile Summary File*. Hagåtña, Guam: Bureau of Statistics and Plans.

Guo, G., Y. Fu, H. Lee, T. Cai, K. Harris, and Y. Li. 2014. "Genetic Bio-Ancestry and Social Construction of Racial Classification in Social Surveys in the Contemporary United States." *Demography* 51(1): 141–172.

Hardimon, M. 2017. *Rethinking Race: The Case for Deflationary Realism*. Cambridge, MA: Harvard University Press.

Hardimon, M. 2003. "The Ordinary Concept of Race." *The Journal of Philosophy* 100(9): 437–455.

Harman, G. 2000. "Moral Relativism." In G. Harman and J. Thomson (eds.), *Moral Relativism and Moral Objectivity*. Oxford: Blackwell, pp. 3–19.

Haslanger, S., and J. Saul. 2006. "Philosophical Analysis and Social Kinds." *Proceedings of the Aristotelian Society* 106(1): 89–118.

Hatfield, G. 2003. "Objectivity and Subjectivity Revisited: Colour as a Psychobiological Property." In R. Mausfeld and D. Heyer (eds.), *Colour Perception: Mind and the Physical World*. New York: Oxford University Press, pp. 188–202.

Hixson, L., B. Hepler, and M. Kim. 2011. *The White Population: 2010, 2010 Census Briefs*. Washington, DC: US Census Bureau.

Hixson, L., B. Hepler, and M. Kim. 2012. *The Native Hawaiian and Other Pacific Islander Population: 2010, 2010 Census Briefs*. Washington, DC: US Census Bureau.

Hoeffel, E., S. Rastogi, M. Kim, and H. Shahid. 2012. *The Asian Population: 2010, 2010 Census Briefs*. Washington, DC: US Census Bureau.

Humes, K., N. Jones, and R. Ramirez. 2011. *Overview of Race and Hispanic Origin 2010: 2010 Census Briefs*. Washington, DC: US Census Bureau.

Kelly, D., L. Faucher, and E. Machery. 2010. "Getting Rid of Racism: Assessing Three Proposals in Light of Psycholgoical Evidence." *Journal of Social Philosophy* 41(3): 293–322.

Kim, S., C. Gignoux, J. Wall, A. Lum-Jones, H. Wang, C. Haiman, . . . I. Cheng. 2012. "Population Genetic Structure and Origin of Native Hawaiians in the Multiethnic Cohort Study." *PLoS One* 7(11): e47881.1–10.

Kim, W. 2010. *Census of Population 2010 Advance Census Release*. Singapore: Republic of Singapore Department of Statistics.

Kitcher, P. 2007. "Does 'Race' Have a Future?" *Philosophy & Public Affairs* 35(4): 293–317.

Kripke, S. A. 1980. *Naming and Necessity*. Cambridge, MA: Harvard University Press.

LaPorte, J. 2005. "Is There a Single, Objective Evolutionary Tree of Life?" *The Journal of Philosophy* 102(7): 357–374.

Longino, H. 1990. *Science as Social Knowledge*. Princeton, NJ: Princeton University Press.

Machery, E. 2011. "Thought Experiments and Philosophical Knowledge." *Metaphilosophy* 42(3): 191–214.

Mallon, R. 2006. "'Race': Normative, Not Metaphysical or Semantic." *Ethics* 116: 525–551.

Manichaikul, A., W. Palmas, C. Rodriguez, C. Peralta, J. Divers, . . . J. Mychaleckyj. 2012. "Population Structure of Hispanics in the United States: The Multi-Ethnic Study of Atherosclerosis." *PLoS Genetics* 8(4): e1002640.

Martínez-Cruz, B., R. Vitalis, L. Ségurel, F. Austerlitz, M. Georges, . . . E. Heyer. 2011. "In the Heartland of Eurasia: The Multilocus Genetic Landscape of Central Asian Populations." *European Journal of Human Genetics* 19: 216–223.

McEvoy, B., J. Lind, . . . A. Wilton. 2010. "Whole-Genome Genetic Diversity in a Sample of Australians with Deep Aboriginal Ancestry." *The American Journal of Human Genetics* 87: 297–305.

McMurray, J., and R. Fay. 1995. *Chemistry*. Englewood Cliffs, NJ: Prentice-Hall.

Mills, C. 2014. "Notes from the Resistance: Some Comments on Sally Haslanger's *Resisting Reality*." *Philosophical Studies* 171(1): 85–97.

Moorjani, P., N. Patterson, J. Hirschhorn, A. Keinan, L. Hao, . . . D. Reich. 2011. "The History of African Gene Flow into Southern Europeans, Levantines, and Jews." *PLoS Genetics* 7(4): 1–13.

Morgan, T. 1926. *The Theory of the Gene*. New Haven, CT: Yale University Press.

Morning, A. 2009. "Toward a Sociology of Racial Conceptualiztion for the 21st Century." *Social Forces* 87(3): 1167–1192.

Morning, A. 2011. *The Nature of Race: How Scientists Think and Teach about Human Difference*. Berkeley: University of California Press.

OMB. 1995. "Standards for the Classification of Federal Data on Race and Ethnicity." *Federal Registrar* 60(166): 44674–44693.

OMB. 1997. "Document 97-28653: Revisions to the Standards for the Classification of Federal Data on Race and Ethnicity." *Federal Register* 62(210): 58782–58790.

OMB. 2000. *Provisional Guidance on the Implementation of the 1997 Standards for Federal Data on Race and Ethnicity*. Washington, DC: Office of Management and Budget.

Prewitt, K. 2013. *What Is Your Race?* Princeton, NJ: Princeton University Press.

Ramachandran, S., H. Tang, R. Gutenkunst, and C. Bustamante. 2010. "Genetics and Genomics of Human Population Structure." In M. Speicher, S. Antonarakis, and A. Motulsky (eds.), *Vogel and Motulsky's Human Genetics: Problems and Approaches*. New York: Springer-Verlag Berlin Heidelberg, pp. 589–615.

Rastogi, S., T. Johnson, E. Hoeffel, and M. Drewery. 2011. *The Black Population: 2010, 2010 Census Briefs*. Washington, DC: US Census Bureau.

Risch, N., S. Choudhry, M. Via, M. Basu, R. Sebro, C. Eng, . . . E. Burchard. 2009. "Ancestry-Related Assortative Mating in Latino Populations." *Genome Biology* 10(11), R132: 1–16.

Rosenberg, N., J. Pritchard, . . . M. Feldman. 2002. "Genetic Structure of Human Populations." *Science*, 298(5602): 2381–2385.

Samuels, M., and J. Witmer. 2003. *Statistics for the Life Sciences*, 3rd edition. Upper Saddle River, NJ: Pearson Education.

Shin, H., and R. Kominski. 2010. *Language Use in the United States: 2007.* Washington, DC: US Census Bureau.

Spencer, Q. 2012. "What 'Biological Racial Realism' Should Mean." *Philosophical Studies* 159(2): 181–204.

Spencer, Q. 2014. "A Radical Solution to the Race Problem." *Philosophy of Science* 81(5): 1025–1038.

Spencer, Q. 2015. "Philosophy of Race Meets Population Genetics." *Studies in History and Philosophy of Biological and Biomedical Sciences* 52: 46–55.

Spencer, Q. 2016. "Do Humans Have Continental Populations?" *Philosophy of Science* 83(5): 791–802.

Tang, H., T. Quertermous, . . . N. Risch. 2005. "Genetic Structure, Self-Identified Race/Ethnicity, and Confounding in Case-Control Association Studies." *American Journal of Human Genetics* 76(2): 268–275.

Taylor, P. 2013. *Race: A Philosophical Introduction*, 2nd edition. Cambridge: Polity Press.

Tighe, E., L. Saxe, R. Magidin de Kramer, and D. Parmer. 2013. *American Jewish Population Estimates: 2012*. Waltham, MA: Brandeis University.

United Nations. 2017. *World Population Prospects: The 2017 Revision, CD-ROM Edition*. New York: United Nations.

Vaha, K. 2012. *Niue Census of Population and Households 2011*. Alofi, Niue: Government of Niue.

van Fraassen, B. 1980. *The Scientific Image*. Oxford: Clarendon Press.

Weatherson, B., and D. Marshall. (2017, Fall). "Intrinsic vs. Extrinsic Properties." In E. Zalta (ed.), *The Stanford Encyclopedia of Philosophy*. Retrieved from https://plato. stanford.edu/archives/fall2017/entries/intrinsic-extrinsic/

Zack, N. 2002. *Philosophy of Science and Race*. New York: Routledge.

Zadeh, L. 1965. "Fuzzy Sets." *Information and Control* 8: 338–353.

8 GLASGOW'S REPLY TO HASLANGER, JEFFERS, AND SPENCER

In this book I'm concerned with the concept of race that has the most currency in ordinary discourse. This concept lurks behind our racial conflicts. We implicitly use it when we racially identify ourselves and others. We deploy it when we worry about righting racial wrongs and achieving a better future. While various people no doubt use the term, 'race,' in various ways, we also have an ongoing, broad conversation about race and a vast set of practices that implicate race, and that is the sense of 'race' I hope to be exploring. With that as the backdrop, a good deal of common ground has emerged between my coauthors and me. At the same time, some disagreement remains. In what follows I first clear up three potential misconceptions about racial anti-realism (leaving basic racial realism aside for the moment), in order to lay bare a broader framework for agreement among the four theories advanced here. I then take up some lingering issues of contention.

8.1. Preliminaries

8.1.1. Is Anti-Realism Always Based on the Idea That Race-Thinking Is Inextricably Essentialist or Racialist?

Chike Jeffers suggests that the argument for racial anti-realism rests on the semantic premise that ordinary race-talk is committed to the existence of some sort of biobehavioral racial essence, where skin color is (mistakenly) supposed to reflect a suite of biologically based traits like intelligence or virtue. Now we all agree—here's our first point of consensus—that *if* ordinary race-talk presupposed that sort of classical racialism, then race in the ordinary sense would be an illusion. But, as Haslanger and Jeffers rightly point out, while old-school racialism was heavily featured in early waves of race-thinking, the word 'race' is not *defined* in terms of biobehavioral essences. I agree here, as well—our second point of consensus. Some anti-realists have argued in the way that Jeffers describes, but my argument proceeds differently. In fact, my analysis of 'race' is even more minimal than Jeffers's analysis. On his view, race is conceptually intertwined with three features (and more): visible traits, geography, and ancestry. On my analysis, visible traits are the only element of that three-part formula that is actually implicated in the conceptual core of race. So on my view, not only is it coherent to talk about race without talking about biobehavioral essences; in addition, it is also coherent to talk about race without invoking geography or ancestry.

If we imagine earth being exactly duplicated in some freak four-dimensional photocopying accident, we would judge that Hillary Clinton's *doppelgänger* is no less white than Hillary Clinton even though Twin Hillary has no racial (or even human) ancestry. And it would not violate the definition of 'race' to talk about Twin Hillary as white while knowing full well that she was created from scratch in the same geographic location (Twin New York City) as lots of non-white people. This shows that, because we can successfully talk about races under the stipulation that those races have neither distinct ancestries nor distinct geographic homes, neither ancestry nor geography is part of the *definition* of 'race.' Of course, it is a contingent, empirical fact that we regular humans have inherited our racially relevant traits like skin color from our ancestors, and that those traits developed independently in certain geographical regions due to local environmental pressures. Historical fact is one thing; what's part of the definition of the term 'race' is another.[1]

Once we strike these properties, along with biobehavioral essences, from the definition of 'race,' we are left with the idea that races are defined in terms of visible traits. The anti-realist argument only has to start with that point. (And then, if we also find that race is by definition non-social, we'll have ruled out racial constructionism.) In this way, all of the views being examined in this book can agree that race-talk does not necessarily presuppose classical racialist essences.

8.1.2. Does Anti-Realism Reject Important Social Realities?

Although they acknowledge that anti-realists recognize racialized groups, both Haslanger and Jeffers also portray anti-realism as out of step when it

---

1. For more on this argument, see Glasgow (2009, Ch. 2; 2010).

comes to explaining our social lives. Only constructionism, they say, can fully capture the race-laden ways in which we have treated one another differently.

I believe this underestimates non-constructionist views. In fact, all of the views discussed in this book can explain social reality in ways that are exactly equally adequate. Our four views do disagree: we believe that different words are more apt for capturing these explanations, and we have different views about what there is in the world. But all four views can explain all elements of our social lives in one fashion or another.

Consider Haslanger's objection to anti-realism (or error theory): if race is not real, then we cannot use race to explain group differences like cultural practices or health outcomes, and we'd have to abandon seemingly sound race-based reasons for making choices, such as trying to improve unequal educational opportunities. After all, if race is not real, then it looks like race can't correctly explain anything or give any justifiable reason for acting.

However, as noted in Chapter 4, something race-*related* can explain and be a reason for acting, namely *racialized groups*. These are real, even if race is not. This is our next point of consensus, and it may be the most important one: all sides in the race debate can agree that people have treated one another differently based on the belief in race—in other words, that we have racialized ourselves. We all agree that this treatment has impacted real lives in enormous and morally significant ways. And we all agree that racialization continues today and will likely continue for the foreseeable future. So I believe, with Haslanger, that there are racialized groups. I believe, with her, that this system of racialization is implicated in massive injustices that require repair. I believe, with her, that ignoring these facts would be both factually ignorant and ethically disastrous. Similarly, I agree with Jeffers that genuine social and historical phenomena have led to both awful realities and meaningful practical identities. Racialization explains different educational opportunities and outcomes. Racialization explains disparities in housing. Both constructionism and anti-realism agree that these disparities are best explained by how we treat one another on the premise of race. Similarly, both views agree that our reasons to remedy such disparities demand that we change how we treat one another on the premise of race.

So we agree broadly on the social facts of racialization. Constructionists then add the pivotal contested claim that racialization is sufficient for race: if racialized groups are real (as they are), then, they claim, race is real. It is here, not in explaining social life, where the debate lies. According to anti-realism, races and racialized groups are different. But while we can and do disagree about this, accepting a distinction between races and racialized groups does not hamper our ability to explain or correct racialized injustices, for that explanation and action comes in the prior step where we (all) recognize racialization.

Consider an analogy from K. A. Appiah (2007): to explain why some people were (and still are, in places) persecuted for being witches and why activists worked against that persecution, you don't have to believe that witchcraft is real. You just have to believe that *people believed* that witchcraft is real. The fact that we 'witchized' people-that we treated them as if they were witches—explains oppressive behavior and generates a reason to remedy it. Similarly, racialization explains our race-related behavior, and so we must recognize the reality of racialization. We live in a racialized world, and our actions and theories should account for that fact. This is not a reason to be a social constructionist about race, since anti-realists and biological realists can (and usually do) recognize racialization as well.

8.1.3. How Does Anti-Realism Aid the Fight against Injustice?

Haslanger is also concerned that anti-realism weakens our ability to tackle race-related injustice. "For example," she writes, "the waning of racial essentialism is not sufficient to undermine the legacy of economic deprivation" surrounding race (p. 21 above). This gets us to our final preliminary question: Even if all views can equally *explain* racialized injustice, how can the views debated in this book help us *repair* racialized injustice? Is one of them better than the others at tackling this all-important task?

I am frustrated that I have few ideas about what it will take to end racial injustice. But I do believe that anti-realism is neutral on this question. By itself, racial anti-realism neither helps nor hinders that reparative project. (I agree with Haslanger that denying that races are real is not enough to get people to stop thinking and acting racially. Parts of western Europe have excluded race from public statistics like censuses for decades, but that has hardly reduced discrimination, inequality, or coalition-building based on race [Simon 2012].) Importantly, the same is true of Haslanger's SPR understanding of race: to define 'race,' as her SPR theory does, in terms of hierarchy and subordination by itself neither helps nor hinders the project of undermining racial inequality. For that reason, neither Haslanger's SPR theory nor anti-realism is going to steer us to a morally better place.[2]

---

2. That said, recall that there is some evidence that certain biological views of race may correlate with and even reinforce racist attitudes (Williams & Eberhard 2008; Glasgow, Shulman,

Undermining racial inequality requires two steps: recognizing inequality, and fighting it. As noted earlier, all four theories discussed here can equally *call attention to* racialized inequality. Rather than packing the injustice all the way into the *definition* of 'race', as SPR does, non-political theories of race can just say that it is an (extra-semantic) *fact* about racialization that racialized groups are unequal. Either way, though, all of these views can recognize injustice. But calling attention to racialized inequality—be it inside or outside the definition of 'race'—is only part of the reparative job. All the attention in the world will not increase the urgency with which we confront and reduce racialized inequality. After all, a white supremacist might look at Haslanger's SPR theory of race and celebrate rather than condemn the inequality it captures. It would be an understatement to say that this is not the desired outcome. The task of eliminating racial inequality therefore ultimately hangs on us being *motivated* to end it, not just on recognizing it. No theory of what race is, including the views discussed in this book, will itself contain such a motivation to end racial inequality. That has to come from somewhere else.

The views being debated in this book are closer than they might appear at first glance, as Ron Mallon (2006, 2009) has argued. We agree that it is coherent to talk about race without talking about biobehavioral essences. We agree that it is unlikely that biology will vindicate race based on visible traits like skin color. We agree that racialization is real. We agree that racialization has been paired with injustice, and we agree that this injustice must be resisted. All four of our theories are compatible with that consensus. And I argue in the Appendix to this chapter that we occupy a vast amount of shared methodological ground as well—one that is vaster than is sometimes recognized. With that in mind, let's return to our central question to find where the remainder of variance lies: What is race?

8.2. Constructionism's Mismatch

Haslanger's theory of race says that racialized groups—and so races, on her analysis—must *by definition* be privileged or subordinated. While we all agree that racialized groups are *as a matter of fact* slotted into unequal social positions, Haslanger's semantic position builds that inequality up into the very essence of race: a group cannot be a race, according to her, if it is equal to

---

& Covarrubias 2009; Phelan et al. 2013). At the same time, not every study on this subject points to this risk.

another group. As we saw in Chapter 4, this would mean that racial equality is an impossibility, a contradiction in terms, an incoherent ideal. I believe that this account therefore violates one of our core commitments about race—in fact, one of the *most* cherished and *most* central inputs for many people—namely that if there are races, then racial equality is a valuable goal and so, by extension, a coherent one. It is possible to talk, for example, about black liberation, where that means that in principle a person could be both black and fully liberated from racial subordination at the same time. Haslanger's theory of race makes this goal unattainable: on her view, if a person does not occupy a subordinate social position, then by definition that person is not black. As soon as one is liberated from anti-black oppression, one loses one's blackness as well. My view, in contrast, is that the dream of racial equality means that racial groups are not *defined* by this fact of hierarchy—they *could* exist on equal ground. Liberation need not mean the end of black racial identity in particular or of race in general.

I won't belabor the point any more. At the same time, I also argued in Chapter 4 that this objection to political constructionism follows a formula that works against every form of constructionism. So can it also apply to Jeffers-style cultural constructionism?

Here again it is worth blanketing our disagreements in the warmth of consensus. I appreciate the positive value of cultural difference that Jeffers highlights. I agree that we must attend to cultural difference in designing educational curricula or responding to stereotyping. And we agree that distinctive ways of life have historically been associated with different racialized groups.

That said, when Jeffers claims that racial diversity should be preserved as a mechanism for preserving distinctive cultural traditions, I pause. Race is not *required* to preserve those distinctive ways of life. Theoretically, anyway, it seems like we could preserve diverse cultural practices without tying them to race. Instead we would have to (continue to) redistribute our cultural practices in a way that is untethered to particular racialized groups. (In other words, we'd have to pursue cultural integration without cultural homogenization, cultural erasure, cultural imperialism, or unjust cultural appropriation.) There is risk in this, of course. Humanity could easily fail at it. But it appears to be possible.

That cosmopolitan possibility brings us back to the formula: What would happen to race in such a world, on the ordinary concept of race? What if there were no longer any correlations between cultural practices and the groups commonly recognized as racial? Now, we'll have to modify this question to fully apply to Jeffers's view, since he holds that cultural race can coexist with political equality, and political race can coexist with cultural equality. The modified question is therefore this: What would happen if all racialized power hierarchies and all racialized cultural differences disappeared simultaneously? What if the only differences left were differences in visible traits?

Jeffers's version of constructionism entails that without cultural or power differences, race disappears. But I believe that on the ordinary concept of race, race persists through such changes. Even if tomorrow all groups currently recognized as racial had equal power and participated equally in eating the world's foods, dancing its forms of dance, playing its kinds of music, and so on—even in such a world, I do not think we'd say that on the ordinary concept of race Hillary Clinton somehow loses her whiteness or that Jeremy Lin stops being Asian because of *those* points of equality.

Similarly, recall the babies-only world that we imagined in Chapter 4. The babies—one who ordinarily would be recognized as Asian, another as black, and so on—are sealed off from the racialized culture and power struggles of their ancestors. The adults have all died and cleared every trace of racialization from the limited resources they left with the babies. These last humans share the only surviving culture and power equally. Does that mean they lose their races?

To answer this, we must peel off a few related questions in our conceptual centrifuge. Do the babies *recognize* race? No. Are the babies' supposed racial identities *relevant* to their lives? No. When they grow up, would it be *useful* for the babies to one day re-institutionalize the notion of race for themselves? Arguably not, but we can remain undecided on that. The decisive question is this: Do the babies stop *being* Asian or black, simply because the previously uneven distribution of power and culture has been evened out? Not on the ordinary concept of race, I believe: on our ordinary concept of race, an Asian baby doesn't stop being Asian at the exact moment when the last adult dies. And that means that racial difference is neither cultural nor political difference.

Jeffers recognizes the version of this argument as it applies to sociopolitical views of race, that is, he agrees that we could achieve power-equality without that amounting to the end of race. I think we also must recognize that cultural difference can be redistributed without that amounting to an end to race. And if the broader analysis is sound, race won't be found in any social fact at all. This is how constructionism fails to match the ordinary concept of race: ultimately the only essential ingredients for race, on the ordinary concept, are certain distributions of visible traits. Power can change hands.

Culture can come and go. Material well-being, health, education, and any other socially determined possibility might fluctuate. In the face of all such social transformations, if we continue to *look* the way we do now, then on the ordinary concept of race, race remains throughout. And reasoning in the opposite direction, if we became enduringly visibly uniform, with everyone looking like the Dalai Lama, that is when race would disappear.

8.3. Biological Racial Realism's Mismatch

In Chapter 3, Quayshawn Spencer uses the US Census as a sort of bridge between the ordinary concept of race and the biological facts, thereby promising to avoid the Mismatch Objection: the OMB-derived Census categories are an ordinary concept of race, and the OMB categories match real biological populations, so race in one ordinary sense is biologically real. To evaluate this theory, I focus first on the Mismatch Objection and then move on to a concern about what Spencer's theory means for cross-cultural communication.

In my view, we can have our Census or OMB or any other bureaucratic categories fit the common-sense concept of race, or we can have them fit the populations vindicated by biology, but they won't fit both at the same time.[3] Consider how categories like *Middle Eastern* and *Latinx* (or *Hispanic*) are absent from Spencer's list of five races. Spencer notes that Hispanic Americans can usually locate a place for themselves in the OMB system by self-identifying as white or black in accordance with "their most prevalent ancestry." Similarly,

---

3. Early in chapter 3 above, Spencer points out that ordinary people can be mistaken about the meanings of their terms and that there is a linguistic division of labor. Just for clarification, I agree, as explained further in the Appendix (and see Glasgow 2010; forthcoming a; forthcoming b). Spencer in this passage seems to suggest that my view is that we ask ordinary people what they think 'race' means and that whatever they answer will constitute the meaning of race in the ordinary sense. He writes: "Notice that limiting what an ordinary race talk is to what 'ordinary people conceive about race' implicitly assumes that ordinary people are the correct people to consult to find out the meaning of the terms they are using" (p. 82 above). In one sense, ordinary people have to be consulted—how else can we know what terms they are even using? But in another sense, I would reject that interpretation, because how ordinary people *explicitly understand* a term is not decisive in determining the meaning of that term: consulting ordinary people does not mean that they always correctly account for the meanings or referents of their terms. As I have suggested, we might even *all* be wrong about the meaning of some term! The way I see it, such consultations only generate defeasible evidence as to what the content of the ordinary concept of race is. This includes, as Spencer himself tries to show, whether ordinary people defer to experts on a term. In these cases what's at issue is when the experts have identified a meaning for *our* race-talk—race-talk in the sense *relevant* for our debate. To figure this out, we have to look at how we use ordinary race-talk; there is no other option (see also McPherson & Shelby 2004). Consequently, I think that our views on how to analyze racial or any other terms are not that far apart.

Arab Americans can use the OMB system by classifying themselves as white. But the ability to choose from a menu of options given by the OMB does not mean that this menu corresponds to the menu that we use or otherwise recognize in the rest of our lives. Spencer suggests that being able to use the OMB's categories on documents guided by the OMB (e.g., the Census, or a college application) means that people intend to refer to the same object that the OMB intends to refer to. While this may be evidence that we defer to the OMB *when using OMB-guided documents* (and more on that momentarily), it is not evidence about race as we live it outside of OMB-governed contexts. It may well be that people just want to fill out the forms the way the form-designers intended, and that they don't think it really means anything about race, in the ordinary sense. And to be sure, there is a gap between the OMB's 1997 categories and common sense. This gap is so broad that the OMB has *itself* considered changes that would threaten Spencer's argument. Citing some of the same data Spencer cites, the OMB (2016) reports the following about the 1997 Census standard:

> Although many respondents report within the race and ethnicity categories specified by the standard, recent censuses, surveys, and experimental tests have shown that its implementation is not well understood and/or is considered inadequate by some respondents. This results in respondents' inability and/or unwillingness to self-identify as the standard intends. For a growing segment of respondents, this situation arises because of the conceptual complexity that is rooted in the standard's definitional distinction of race from ethnicity. Nearly half of Hispanic or Latino respondents do not identify within any of the standard's race categories. . . . With the projected steady growth of the Hispanic or Latino population, the number of people who do not identify with any of the standard's race categories is expected to increase.

This gap between self-identification and the Census options is why the Census has considered using an expanded list of options that includes *Hispanic/Latino* and *MENA (Middle Eastern or North African)*. This is evidence that the relevant government agencies defer to ordinary usage, not the other way around.[4] In any event, the broader lesson here is clear. If, on

---

4. The Census Bureau, and separately the OMB, might ask us the question one way and then reclassify our answers according to their own standard. If this ends up happening, that will be

the one hand, the OMB is aligned with biological fact, it fails to match the ordinary concept of race, as others have observed (Compton et al. 2013; Haney López 2005; Krogstad & Cohn 2014; Navarro 2003). On the other hand, if the OMB chooses to align with (what it recognizes as) common sense, then it will no longer represent something biologically real, since biology has not vindicated a set of seven races that includes both *Latino* and *MENA*. The data from Rosenberg et al. (2002) yield as the sixth 'race' the Kalash—a small population in Pakistan that has experienced reproductive isolation from other groups. Once we go to seven categories, Li et al. (2008) found this set: {African, Middle Eastern, European, Central/South Asian, East Asian, Oceanian, and Indigenous American}. I have not seen any biological data of sufficient quality that demonstrate the existence of a Hispanic/ Latinx population that exists at the same level of partition as other purported races. Whether common sense matches biology floats free of whatever is on the Census.[5]

Now, as I wrote in Chapter 4, some might be willing to give up one or another identity (such as *Latinx/Hispanic*) in order to preserve the biological reality of race. But there are other complications on the *different groups* front, not about which identities we invalidate but about what people belong to which groups.[6] The biological populations revealed in the biological data have wide bands of fuzzy boundaries. One consequence of this is that many individuals will need to be slotted into a race not simply by their ancestry, but also by us choosing what fraction of which ancestry is sufficient for which racial membership. Various sorting principles are open to us. For example, if we were to say that having *any* of a population's ancestry made one eligible for membership in a population—as Spencer suggests regarding black ancestry—then most people in Spencer's data (his Figure 3.4 in Chapter 3)

---

evidence that the OMB is *not* deferring to ordinary usage; that would not tell us one way or the other whether ordinary language users defer to *it*, though. I sometimes hear people say that mismatch arguments won't work for reasons having to do with semantic deference and direct reference theory. For an explanation why this is not true, see the Appendix to this chapter and Glasgow (2010; forthcoming a; forthcoming b).

5. Shortly before this book went to press, it was decided that the 2020 Census would not add *Hispanic/Latino* or *MENA*. It remains an open question whether this decision will be revisited in a decade. Ultimately, though, what the *actual* OMB or Census Bureau practice is doesn't really matter. The fact that we *could conceivably* change our Census categories in this way is enough to highlight the key point: our government categories can map onto common sense, or they can map onto biology, but either way what remains to be seen is whether common sense and biology line up.

6. I am grateful to Shani Long Abdallah for helpful discussion on these points.

are going to be eligible for membership in more than one race (Atkin 2017, 146).[7] If we instead used the criterion he says Hispanic Americans follow—go with your *most prevalent* ancestry—then people will get classified differently. These sorting criteria have different implications for Spencer's theory of race. Either the number of people in just one race is substantially smaller than we currently recognize; or a large subset of people with mixed ancestry will be sorted into races other than the one that we ordinarily assign them to and that they ordinarily identify with; or a large number of people will have no race at all—which is not to say that they have a race that's hard for us to *identify*, but that they literally are *raceless*.

Now one worry is that these options all flirt with the Mismatch Objection. Ultimately, though, Spencer can insist that some revisions to common sense are acceptable and do not rise to the level of violating the very definition of 'race.' (Basic racial realism essentially says this about the first option—that we have memberships in many races, only some of which we pay attention to.) How much, and which, revision we can allow until we depart from the ordinary concept of race is a matter of interpretation, as this book has shown. But my main concern at the moment is that it is not clear how Spencer's theory secures the biological credentials of race, if this account of race selects a sorting principle in an extra-biological way. That is, whatever choice we make with these criteria, the point is that it's a *choice*, and it is hard to see where *biology* is what is dictating the choice. If multiple ways of sorting people with mixed ancestry are equally well credentialed by good biology (using Spencer's criteria for what makes something biologically real), then we're choosing which sorting principle to use in a way that is arbitrary from the perspective of the biological sciences—in which case, where is the biological, scientific backing for this?

Spencer might make a move here. He might say: well, all that I really care about is that the choice plays some role in good biological science (or something like that—I'm blurring important details in his view in the hopes of painting a broader picture). This courts questions all its own, though. If biology can only best use *one* sorting principle, then we need to know how this will get all the right results—roughly matching both common-sense and biological assignments, via the OMB's categories—for Hispanic people, black people, people from across South and Southeast Asia, and so on. I believe

---

7. Spencer clarifies in the beginning of Chapter 7 that this is indeed the principle he adopts for all races.

that has not yet been demonstrated. If, instead, multiple principles are equally usable for biology—*most prevalent ancestry, any ancestry*, etc.—the questions multiply. We still need to see that match. And also we now need to know what to do when more than one sorting principle applies to us. Which wins, and why? Finally, isn't it more sensible to say that, if multiple principles are consistent with biology, then they are not biological principles? Consider a politically disputed territory, like Northern Ireland or Alsace-Lorraine. Biology doesn't care which nation-state these lands belong to: any resolution to the political dispute is consistent with any biological facts. It seems like having multiple biologically consistent principles for sorting people into races, like sorting territories into countries, means that we've left the realm of biological fact.[8]

Finally, again, there seems to be a distinctive gap between the concepts of race and population. Most obviously, genealogical groups are not required to stay visibly distinct, unlike races. Spencer objects to this argument on the grounds that it misunderstands the relevant concept of race: two distinct races, such as Pacific Islanders and black Africans, can share the same visible traits, he argues. But as he acknowledges elsewhere (Spencer 2015), the relevant visible traits are not shared to the *exact* same degree. And all that is required for racial distinctiveness on the ordinary concept of race is *some* differentiation in visible traits, not necessarily a *lot* of differentiation (Alcoff 2006; Pierce 2015, 109). Spencer evidently disagrees with this judgment. Readers must in the end determine whether they think that two groups that are *perfectly identical* in visible traits could be racially distinct.[9]

Let's now pivot from the Mismatch Objection to a separate worry. Recall an observation from Chapter 4: semantic meaning sets a conversational boundary, such that if we use one word with different meanings, we are not truly dialoguing. We are not even disagreeing. We are just talking past each other. As Mark Sainsbury (2014, 4) puts it, "Substantive disagreement requires agreement in meaning. There needs to be some proposition that one

---

8. This is a variation on Philip Kitcher's (2007, 304–306) point that in order to carve humanity into races, we have to make an extra-biological choice about how *many* races to look for, such as Spencer's preferred K = 5 level. (Kitcher understands this choice to come down to pragmatics.) I'm suggesting here that in addition to wondering how many races to look for, we also have to figure out how to sort individuals into whatever number of racial groups we select. Both choices appear to happen outside the realm of principled biological science.

9. And recall a related problem: if Roberta Millstein (2015) is right, we can move between biological populations in a way that we cannot move between races, namely by reproducing with people in the new group.

party affirms and the other denies." You instruct me to cut the deck of cards, by which you mean that I am to take some cards off the top of the deck and place them next to the bottom portion. But I don't know that this is what you mean, so interpreting you as best I can, I get out my scissors and start cutting each card in half. If we were then to get into a heated discussion about whether I cut the deck of cards, we don't agree about how to cut a deck of cards, but we don't disagree, either. We simply miscommunicate. There is no proposition that you affirm and I deny. We talk past each other. Quite unintentionally, I simply *mean* something different by "cut the deck" than what you meant. Our attempt at a conversation failed.

On Spencer's view, the relevant meaning of 'race' is the set of five races that the OMB recognized in 1997. This entails that when Americans operate with this race-talk, they cannot communicate about race with people who use other sets of categories. (And similarly for those many countries that have *no* racial categories on their censuses.) Instead, on Spencer's view, Americans simply talk past people in those other countries when using the language of race. To choose just one example,[10] Canadians can select *Arab, Latin American, Filipino*, and *Chinese* on their Census, whereas those in the United States cannot. So if the *meaning* of the term 'race' were OMB-derived Census racial categories, there would be no meaning of 'racial' that crosses the US-Canadian border. In that case, we couldn't even say that Canada and the United States recognize different racial categories. Spencer's semantic assessment blocks us from comparing the two sets of categories at all—it removes any words we might use to do so. There's just race-in-the-US-sense and race-in-the-Canadian-sense, and there's no translating between the two senses of 'race' any more than in the 'cut the deck' case. Canadians and Americans literally would be *unable to talk with each other* about race, on this account. This has a particularly peculiar implication for us. As a Canadian, when Chike Jeffers talks about race, he would mean something different than Spencer, Haslanger, or I (as US citizens) do, which would make our book akin to the kind of miscommunication in the 'cut the deck' exchange. But this seems to be the wrong diagnosis. Our book is not a gigantic exercise in miscommunication. Unlike the 'cut the deck' exchange, Jeffers and Spencer are not talking past each other. They are genuinely dialoguing! To do so, they must share some common meaning of 'race.' They might not know what that common

---

10. For more, see http://www.understandingrace.org/lived/global_census.html.

meaning is, and they certainly disagree about it, but it must be one that is shareable.[11]

Temporal shifts present a similar problem. Spencer's view implies that it is impossible for us today (when using OMB race-talk) to reflect on and evaluate theories of race that were written prior to 1997. On this view, Taylor (2000), Sundstrom (2002a; 2002b), Blum (2002), Glasgow (2009a), and Haslanger (2012) are not disagreeing with Appiah (1985, 1996), Zack (1994), or Outlaw (1996), contrary to their own claims that they are disagreeing. In fact, Spencer's view means not only that those race theorists are not in a dialogue with one another, but also that Appiah (2007) and Zack (2002) are not even speaking continuously with their earlier selves. This is a problem. We take these discussions to be continuous— we think that post-1997 race theorists talk *with* pre-1997 race theorists. If we take Spencer's theory to be a theory of the ordinary concept of race, we make this conversational continuity impossible. Similarly, if Americans add *Hispanic* to the relevant lists of races in 2030, they will again be replacing the current meaning of 'race' with a new one, according to Spencer's analysis.[12] In that case, in 2031 Americans will not able to react to 2029 writings about race. This, too, is jarringly counterintuitive. In short, Spencer's analysis renders us unable to unequivocally talk about a single thing across that moment in time, not even to disagree.

These points suggest that we should not let any given set of racial categories—Census or otherwise—constitute the very *meaning* of the term 'race.' Americans can react to what previous generations said about race, and they can talk with Canadians about race, regardless of what particular racial categories their censuses recognize. Spencer's approach to the semantics of race would mean that we end up equivocating on the word 'race,' if we try to have a conversation about race across different racial classification schemes. His view turns what is clearly a dialogue into a series of covertly isolated monologues.[13]

---

11. To clarify, I'm still focused on the ordinary concept of race in the United States. I'm just claiming that one feature of that concept is that it is supposed to be consistent with widespread, though perhaps not universal, cross-cultural comparison and dialogue.

12. Or, for that matter, consider that "Mexican" was a US Census race category in 1930 (Gratton & Merchant 2016).

13. It might be tempting to deviate from Spencer's view and say that 'race' just *refers* to his five populations without 'race' actually *meaning* those five populations. That would avoid the miscommunication problem, but it would revive the mismatch problem.

Although I don't think that a specific set of racial categories *constitutes* the very meaning of 'race,' I do think that we can use our racial categories as *evidence* about what 'race' means. But even then we have to be careful about what this evidence shows. 'Race' is supposed to be usable in both the United States and Canada and indeed much of the world. It is supposed to be something talked about both before and after 1997. These phenomena suggest that it is defined in such a way as to be consistent with multiple systems of racial classification. It is supposed to apply to two siblings in Brazil, who get categorized into different races because they look different, even though they have identical ancestries; and it is supposed to apply in the United States where ancestry is given more weight; and we are supposed to be able to *compare* these systems of classification (Chen et al. 2018; Fish 2011). To make such cross-context communication and comparison possible, rather than tying the meaning of 'race' to one highly localized set of racial categories, we need a definition of 'race' that holds across all of these contexts. If you've made it this far, you won't be surprised to see me say that one such solution is to define racial groups as groups of humans that are supposed to be visibly distinctive in certain ways.

That said, I don't doubt that people sometimes use 'race' in special ways. The OMB may well have a specialized definition of 'race'—though given its writing and practice, I suspect that the OMB actually semantically defers to ordinary usage, sometimes misdiagnosing it in the process.[14] We might also find specialized definitions at an Atlanta church, a forensics facility in Chicago, an immigration center in Los Angeles, or a conference of anthropologists in Mexico City. And ordinary people in ordinary contexts might well carry around their own "portfolios" of racial schemas, deploying different schemas in different contexts (Roth 2012). Sometimes we just stipulate, "What *I* mean by this word is . . ." In the process we change the subject from the mainstream conversation and put our little conversation into a silo. But in addition to specialized, siloed understandings that have only local range or authority, ordinary people also have many conversations about race where they are *not* talking past one another or changing the subject or using a cloistered language, where they can talk *across* a multitude of social contexts and a variety of classification systems. This broad, social conversation uses the most common ordinary concept of race.

---

14. Not only was the US Census considering adding *Hispanic* and *MENA* in response to ordinary use, but also starting in 2000 the Census began allowing individuals to choose multiple races to align with complex and mixed heritage, as a response to political activists highlighting the complexity in everyday identities.

This suggests a more ecumenical way to think about Spencer's analysis. If it is meant to capture racial discourse *only* when certain people use OMB-directed documents (as Spencer intends it to be); and if, contrary to what I have argued, the OMB is not interested in capturing our ordinary discourse about race; then this view might be more insulated from the Mismatch Objection—it's just a specialized language with very restricted application. In this case, though, it would not capture the more extensive concept of race that stretches across cultures and moments in history and specific classification systems. It would not capture the concept of race that most of us use most of the time. In short, it would not be very relevant to our lives. (Except every once in a while when you fill out a form, and only if you're not just playing the bureaucrat's game, and only if the bureaucrats weren't themselves trying to capture something relevant to the rest of our social lives . . . and even then it is unclear that it will be a truly biological concept at work.) To speak to the broader cross-context use of 'race,' that is, to the discourse that has done tremendous damage and that demands that we make sense of it and that motivates my inquiry, at least, we must recognize a different concept of race, one that is not *defined* by a specific and local set of categories but that instead has spanned the centuries and the globe.

In my view, this concept of race has races being groups that have certain visible traits to a disproportionate extent. As it happens, it's hard to show that this concept is biologically fruitful. But it is worth noting how flexible it is. It can account for individuals who have atypical traits for their race—while the racial *group* must have a distinctive pattern of traits to count as a race on this analysis, it is not the case that every *individual* in the group needs to have some specific set of visible traits (Glasgow 2009a: 79; Hardimon 2017: §2.3; cf. Mills 1998). (This is what makes 'passing' possible.) It can explain why we recognize different cultures' varying sets of racial categories *as* racial. And it can account for the fact that different people can have very different representations of race while also having meaningful conversations about race with one another. Capturing all of those facts at the same time is, in my view, the main advantage that the visible-traits analysis has over Spencer's OMB-based semantics of 'race.'

8.4. The Racial Categories with Which We Live

Soon after Justice Sutherland wrote that Bhagat Singh Thind was not racially white, even if he was biologically Caucasian, the United States forcibly deported or "repatriated" over one million people to Mexico. Roughly half were

US citizens, and for many this racialized "repatriation" was their first time on Mexican soil (Balderrama 2015). Three decades later, in 1954, riding the same civil rights wave that crested with *Brown v. Board of Education*, the Supreme Court took up the question of Mexican identity in *Hernandez v. Texas*. For years Mexican defendants faced all-white juries in Jackson County, Texas. The state defended this practice on the grounds that Mexicans were recognized as white. Chief Justice Earl Warren responded by writing that Mexicans were treated as a group apart and therefore were their own class, legally speaking:

> The petitioner's initial burden in substantiating his charge of group dis-crimination was to prove that persons of Mexican descent constitute a separate class in Jackson County, distinct from 'whites.' One method by which this may be demonstrated is by showing the attitude of the com-munity. Here the testimony of responsible officials and citizens contained the admission that residents of the community distinguished between 'white' and 'Mexican.' The participation of persons of Mexican descent in business and community groups was shown to be slight. Until very recent times, children of Mexican descent were required to attend a segregated school for the first four grades. At least one restaurant in town promi-nently displayed a sign announcing 'No Mexicans Served.' On the court-house grounds at the time of the hearing, there were two men's toilets, one unmarked, and the other marked 'Colored Men' and 'Hombres Aqui' ('Men Here'). No substantial evidence was offered to rebut the log-ical inference to be drawn from these facts, and it must be concluded that petitioner succeeded in his proof....
>
> Circumstances or chance may well dictate that no persons in a cer-tain class will serve on a particular jury or during some particular pe-riod. But it taxes our credulity to say that mere chance resulted in there being no members of this class among the over six thousand jurors called in the past 25 years. The result bespeaks discrimination, whether or not it was a conscious decision on the part of any individual jury commissioner.[15]

Another six decades later, in late 2016, the Supreme Court again heard a dis-crimination case in *Peña Rodriguez v. Colorado*. One notable current running underneath the oral arguments was that the Justices seemed to grant that it was obviously a case of *racial* discrimination—"the best smoking-gun evidence

---

15. 347 U.S. 475 (74 S.Ct. 667, 98 L.Ed. 866).

you're ever going to see about race bias in the jury room," as Justice Elena Kagan put it (Barnes 2016). (The dispute was whether the significance of racial discrimination overrides other legal principles at stake, not whether there was any racial discrimination.)

These cases illustrate a fact repeatedly borne out not only by studies done on the Census, but also by other sociological research (e.g., Roth 2012), by our day-to-day practices, and by a mountain of anecdotal data: Latinx people are regularly treated and self-identify as a racially distinct group. We need a theory of race that can account for this and the full range of racial practice. There is a sense of 'race' that denies whiteness to Vaishno Das Bagai and Bhagat Singh Thind. It also structures blackness differently than the biological population 'African.' It forbids people from changing races merely by visiting another society or by reproducing with someone from a different group. It requires racial groups to bear some distinctive portion of visible traits. If we're trying to understand the sense of 'race' with which we live, we must identify something that captures these experiential realities and conceptual constraints.

It is these lived categories that invigorate our discussion. They are the categories where we hoard resources. They are where meaningful identities are found. We discriminate. We repatriate. We go to war. We change lives, we improve lives, we damage lives, and we end lives, all based on racialization.

The fences of racialization are meant to wall off biological traits like skin, hair, and eye color. Because these traits are biological, our categories are going to reflect our ancestors' migrations, separations, and reproductions. But the reflection has all the fidelity of a funhouse mirror. Ancestral patterns that figure in biological explanation run through different valleys than those that cradle the racial categories with which we live. We racialize humanity in ways that float free of what biologists do. And in this lies a mistake in ordinary race-thinking that cannot be repaired by simply paying better attention to the science: *we apparently believe that there is some fact about us that can be read right off of our skin.* In turn, that belief filters how we treat one another, both across and within the fences of racialization, resulting in weighty and disturbing effects on life chances.[16] When disadvantage lasts the full course of your existence; when stress and heart disease reflect not a bump on your journey but rather an integral feature of the life-paths made available to you by a white supremacist social architecture; when the prices paid are death for

---

16. Social scientists continue to document not only that we racialize but also that we treat individuals differently *within* their racialized groups based on visible traits. For recent work on colorism and 'pigmentocracy' see, e.g., Bailey, Saperstein, and Penner (2014); Monk (2014, 2015, 2016); Telles (2014).

many, a lower ceiling on reasonable hope for more, and unjust relations for all; and when this whole moral mess stubbornly attaches to categories unbroken by multiple generations of scientific correction—when that is what needs explaining, the chasm between biology and social practice yawns wider than our best bridges.

This is where we find the constructionist's truth: we need to decode the concept of race that we utilize in everyday life. As a separate matter, constructionists also conclude that our ways of using and abusing this concept can conjure race out of nothing: our practices, our identities, our power hierarchies, and our cultures are said by constructionists to be the very building blocks of race. Against this we also must take seriously the truth in biological racial realism: those social facts are not what we are purporting to talk about when we talk about race. What we are trying to do, a task that we seem to have charged to the very concept of race, is to find something biological. And yet that thing keeps eluding the biologists.

The traits that are supposed to distinguish the races—those visible traits like skin color—are bequeathed to us by our ancestors and made significant by social forces. But as we have seen, the sense of 'race' with which we live is defined neither by genealogy nor by social ties. Which leaves us with two choices. 'Race' in the sense with which we live either tries to latch onto biological kinds that end up being illusory, or onto a more basic, non-social, and non-scientific kind of thing.

Appendix on Philosophical Method: Using Intuitions about Fictional Cases

The arguments I have made use certain methods that I want to briefly defend. In particular, I have repeatedly called on thought experiments to generate a partial 'definition' of 'race,' where a definition here is, roughly, a set of properties that something must have to be what our term 'race' refers to. These properties include, on my arguments: being a group of humans, being organized by certain visible traits (as a group, not for each individual), and being non-social. To get to this list of properties, I have imagined worlds where there are no adults or where we all look like the Dalai Lama, societies that are fully culturally integrated, and situations of perfect equality and mass amnesia. How we judge such possibilities—whether or not we say that races would exist in these worlds—is pivotal in identifying what we mean by 'race.' I claim that our intuitions or judgments about these hypothetical cases suggest that the ordinary concept of race requires both that race persists even when social facts change and that races are organized according to visible traits rather than genealogy, calling into question the rival views presented in this volume.

Using intuitive reactions to thought experiments is a widely accepted method for analyzing concepts, and race theory is no exception (e.g., Appiah 1990; Mills 1998; cf. Glasgow et al. 2009). But as it happens, my three coauthors have all taken issue with this method here and in other places. And some readers may have similar hesitations. How relevant are outlandish thought experiments—don't we care about the real world rather than imaginary worlds? And why do we care about our intuitions, anyway—don't the facts of the world override whatever we might think our words refer to, like when we mistakenly think that fool's gold is real gold? And who am *I*—who is *any* individual—to decide whether *we* would say that race exists in these fictional worlds?

In a previous exchange, Jeffers (2013a, 2013b) objects to my use of *fictional* thought experiments. These objections, along with some of Haslanger's comments in Chapter 5 here, suggest a question: How can a situation about some *possible* world tell us anything helpful about race in *this* world?

The answer, in short, is that fictional scenarios can tell us about the limits of our real concepts. These thought experiments do not speak to our biology, of course. Instead, they reveal how words can and cannot attach to the world around us. Sometimes we learn about conceptual possibilities through *actual* experiments. We confirmed that it was conceptually possible for atoms to be divided when Rutherford split the atom a century ago. We didn't continue insisting that atoms were by definition indivisible, in which case he must have split something else, the *shmatom*; instead, we called it an 'atom,' indicating that it was possible to coherently talk about a divisible atom. In similar ways, real-world discoveries taught us, to our surprise, that whales are not actually fish and that fool's gold is not gold: real-world information told us what our terms actually refer to. For the purposes of mapping *conceptual* boundaries, there is no relevant difference between Rutherford's actual experiment and a fictional thought experiment: possible and actual cases allow us to identify when a term can and cannot be successfully applied. To use an example of an unrelated concept, many people believed that an agent is morally responsible for some action she performed only if she had had the ability to not perform that action. Then Harry Frankfurt (1969) presented a fictional case of an agent who could *not* have done anything other than what he did, but where his responsibility seems undiminished. We don't need to agree with Frankfurt here (and, to be sure, the ensuing discussion has not been univocal). The point is merely that his *method* is legitimate: it tests when we will and will not deploy the concept of responsibility. And of course this example is just the tip of a very large iceberg. We use thought experiments, often far removed from the actual world, to map the contours of our concepts.

Because these cases test conceptual possibility, there is nothing wrong with them being (very) unlikely. In fact, Jeffers deploys one of the fictional scenarios that I use : the possibility—the goal—of social equality between races means that the concept of race cannot be defined by power inequality (Glasgow 2009a, 120). A world of ideal racial equality is no less fictional than the other cases I've imagined—it is *very* far removed from the real world—but nothing is wrong with using it to question whether political theories of race are consistent with the ordinary concept of race. The same goes for any other relevant thought experiments. These fictional stories are supposed to tell us when we are, and are not, willing to use a term, which provides evidence as to what the term could and could not refer to.

Once we open the door to thought experiments, how should we judge them? We now know that our intuitions sometimes are not probative—they can fail to be representative, and even if they are representative, what they represent may be the product of cognitive distortion (e.g., Machery et al. 2004). In this spirit, Spencer (2015, 52) has objected that marshalling one's *own* intuitions about thought experiments is "merely clarifying an idiosyncratic idea of race." (He elaborates on this objection at the end of Chapter 7; and in Chapter 5 Haslanger questions whether some interpretations of thought experiments might be local to certain subgroups of the broader linguistic community.)

I agree that we should consult data from other sources besides just ourselves—ideally we would use a wide variety of tests to systematically gather intuitions from a large and representative sample of people who competently use the term 'race' to help establish what 'race' means (Glasgow 2009a, Ch. 3–4). But at the same time, we can reasonably have different degrees of confidence about whether some of our own intuitions are representative; and intuitions from one person can at least generate predictions that are starting points for systematic experiments. After all, most theorists aren't *that* isolated from real life. If our intuitions turn out to be wildly inconsistent with the reactions of other ordinary language users, we will need to explain the discrepancy. Moreover, recall that we should not overestimate the value of systematic and representative data: the best, largest, and most representative study on how we use a term only delivers evidence, not conclusions, about the contents of our concepts. Even a representative and *unanimous* poll can reveal mistaken results about the meanings of our words, as we would find if we traveled back in time and asked whether whales are fish.[17]

As I see it, the tricky step is not in using your own intuitions, as long as we are modest about what those intuitions might show. *Every* method uses someone's intuitions somewhere. Haslanger classifies Aung San Suu Kyi as Asian; Jeffers judges that there can be politically equal races; Spencer makes claims about how much visible-trait overlap is required to be included in a race. These are intuitions, and they are unavoidable in philosophical analysis. The trick isn't to avoid intuitions; rather, the trick is deciding what to do when inconsistent intuitions result from various tests of a concept. (One reason why we debate race is that we tap into inconsistent elements of ordinary race-thinking.) Sometimes one individual's intuition is idiosyncratic, as Spencer notes. But sometimes it is the canary in the coal mine, indicating a rift in our conceptual framework that requires eliminating a much more widely held belief, such as, way back when, the belief that the earth is flat, or that whales are fish, or that races have biobehavioral essences.

So how should we bring inconsistent intuitions into equilibrium? There is no formula to apply in advance to decide which of our conceptual commitments is stronger in any particular case. As I argued in Chapter 4, all we have is conversation and analysis, and that starts with individual judgment. There is no one person who represents the ordinary point of view or represents all language users. As I also said at the outset of Chapter 4, an incredibly diverse set of people are part of the conversation about race, and our job is to account for the concept that makes that conversation possible. No one intuition occupies a privileged position in this conversation, but then no intuition is irrelevant, either.[18] Our task is to systematize these judgments.

---

17. Relatedly, for contested categories like race, intuitions might be unstable (Atkin 2017, 142). This might mean either that there is no concept of race, or that we are working with multiple, shifting concepts of race, or that the content of the concept is underdetermined.

18. Readers might wonder whether different self-identified racial groups come up with different understandings of race. The evidence does sometimes bear this out, such as one study that found that whites scored higher than non-whites on a measure of whether individual racial identity is socially determined (Glasgow et al. 2009). Again, though, the conclusion from these differences is not—or at least not necessarily—that different folks have different concepts of race. After all, another key data-point is that people across these different groups seem to be having coherent conversations about race. What in combination this suggests is that we need to dig deeper to identify the concept of race behind those conversations, the minimal commitments required to make those exchanges possible.

For these reasons, I think we are warranted in rendering provisional, tentative, and guarded conclusions based on our (speculative) judgments about what the intuitive thing to say is when confronted with a surprising thought experiment.

Haslanger (2012) also questions the use of intuitions when addressing socially pressing phenomena like race. Now here again there is a strong consensus worth emphasizing. The field has benefited from Haslanger insisting that good race theory must respect several key principles, including the following:

- *Semantic externalism*: meaning or reference can be partly determined by the physical world and social context; consequently, intuitions *alone* are not always *sufficient* to determine what a term refers to.
- *The division of linguistic labor*: within certain constraints, we defer to some experts to tell us what some of our terms refer to.
- *Scientific essentialism*: some objects have essences tracked by our words.
- *Terminological opacity*: we do not always know what our words mean or refer to.
- *Ambiguity and context*: words often have multiple meanings, and which one is operative depends on conversational context.

I believe that all sides in the race debate can, should, and (usually) do agree with this analytical framework. Although I am sometimes interpreted by others as disagreeing with one or another element of this framework, I actually *assume* it throughout my arguments. The main question is where the data point us within Haslanger's framework, not what framework to adopt.

Haslanger and Spencer emphasize that we can be wrong about what our terms refer to, be it 'water' or 'cancer,' 'atoms' or 'werewolves,' or 'race.' This is true, obviously. But that point leaves intact our main question: At what point in revising our usage of the term 'race' have we changed the subject with 'race,' away from race in the ordinary sense and toward something else (perhaps something better)? While sometimes we can fix our mistakes without changing the subject—when our words are magnetically drawn to a surprising referent—other times we *do* change the subject, and our words simply fail to refer. Marathons aren't races in the relevant sense, and talking about people with rabies is not really talking about werewolves in the ordinary sense. This is Haslanger's point in requiring even the most surprising interpretations of 'race' to converge on sameness of reference and shared linguistic and epistemic practice. [19]

What we are looking for here is the boundary of the tradition we are trying to interpret, ordinary racial discourse. To identify this boundary, we can't just *want* or *try* to refer to the same thing, and we can't just *have an interest* in referring to the same thing. Marco Polo had an interest in trying to refer to the same thing that a community of East Africans was referring to with the term 'Madagascar.' He famously failed: while that community was using it to refer to part of continental Africa, he mistakenly used the name to refer to that big island off the coast. His mistake stuck, and so the referent of the term eventually shifted; but in the short term, shared desires and interests were not enough to help Polo and his interlocutors refer to the same thing. To succeed in co-referring, we also have to have sufficiently overlapping usage. Otherwise we talk past one another.

Even when we defer to the experts to tell us what our folk terms refer to, the experts must leave a portion of semantic authority in ordinary people's hands: folk intentions about what their terms refer to limits the range of what the experts can legitimately identify as the referent of those terms, if those experts are to deliver the referent not just for a cloistered, specialized language but for ordinary discourse. If experts start claiming that the ordinary term 'table salt' refers to H_2O rather than NaCl, they will have changed the subject, because ordinary usages of 'table salt' limit the range of what 'table salt' might refer to—it has to be something like the white-ish, granular, salty-tasting stuff that we season our food with, if we're talking about table salt in the ordinary sense (Glasgow 2010).

So when do we overlap? When do we stay on subject? What determines when we succeed in sharing meanings and referents for our terms? How do we know when someone is talking about race in the relevant sense, and when they have started a cloistered conversation using the same old words but with new meanings?

---

19. Herein lies my concern with Haslanger's 'person' analogy in Chapter 1. The case she describes is one in which we have false definitions of 'person,' and so rather than becoming anti-realists about persons, we would just give up those false definitions and try to find a better way of capturing our (opaque) definition instead. In my view the case of 'race' is different, and the analogy buckles: it's hard to give up defining 'race' in terms of visible traits (rather than social facts) without it seeming like changing the subject. This is what pressures us to become anti-realists about race but not personhood. In this respect, 'race' is more like 'witch' or 'were-wolf' than 'person'—the apparently *accurate* definition of 'race' is inconsistent with reality.

The key factors are the ways we would and would not be willing to use the terms in question—that is, how we would use the word when presented with surprising (actual and counterfactual) cases (Glasgow forthcoming a). The only indicator that we've made a mistake about what one of our words means is some *other* semantic intuitions and intentions. The only way that 'water' or 'gold' or 'cancer' or 'race' turns out to refer to something surprising or counterintuitive is if we are willing to call that surprising referent 'water' or 'gold' or 'cancer' or 'race'—that is, when *another* intuition or intention says that the referent is a surprise. One set of intentions and intuitions vetoes another set, but whichever set prevails, either way our intentions and intuitions fix what our terms can refer to. These semantic intentions just are among the inputs about race that Haslanger asks us to consider. Haslanger's input, "Aung San Suu Kyi is Asian," is an intuition about how those words can be used. Whether that input is secure (or non-negotiable) depends in part on our other commitments about how to use those words.

Elsewhere, Haslanger (2012, 305–307) holds that rather than appealing to intuitions about various cases, we should instead identify the meaning of 'race' by looking for paradigm cases and seeing what unifies those cases. I believe this is a choice we don't have to make. Really, we *can't* make it (cf. Chalmers 2011, 538–539; Glasgow 2009b). We cannot look to "what the cases in fact have in common" (Haslanger 2012, 396) until we know which cases are the relevant cases to consider, and identifying those cases is a job for intuition. That is, to identify paradigm cases is to use intuitions, as we see in the externalist tradition to which Haslanger belongs—see Burge (1979) on 'arthritis,' Kripke (1972) on 'Gödel,' Putnam (1975) on 'water.' We need to say that a coffee cup does not count as Asian and that Aung San Suu Kyi does; these are just intuitions.

Happily, I think the foregoing just expands the consensus: we can add to Haslanger's analytical framework that we must (somehow) consult intuitions and intentions when identifying what our terms refer to and mean. At that point the difference-making questions become *which cases* we consider; *what intuitions* we have in those cases; *whose intuitions* count in rendering verdicts; and *how to systematize* the intuitions when they are collectively inconsistent. In this way, while we have some lingering disagreements about whether we can and should analyze racial terms using descriptive definitions like I am doing here (Haslanger 2010; Glasgow 2017, forthcoming b), I think we actually occupy a vast methodological common ground.

So as I see it, the choices that make a substantial difference to answering this book's question are relatively limited. In particular, the issues of dispute are usually not methodological. The live choice is not whether to use intuitions or paradigms. Nor is it whether to use actual or merely possible cases as evidence of what we mean by 'race.' Nor is it whether to go with one person's intuitions or a rigorous survey of many people's intuitions. Nor is it a choice between different theories of meaning or reference. We can and must use all of the tools and evidence at our disposal. The difference-making choice, as I see it, is how to reconcile the rival sets of clashing intuitions and semantic intentions that we find ourselves with—different sets of judgments that have been marshalled by each of the four authors in this book. When faced with these incompatible judgments, the project is to identify which ones we hold on to and which ones we compromise on, to find those core commitments so that we can try to find out whether there is something in the world that captures them. To determine what race is, the first question will always be: What do we mean by 'race'?

References

Alcoff, Linda Martín. 2006. *Visible Identities: Race, Gender, and the Self.* Oxford: Oxford University Press.

Appiah, K. Anthony. 1985. "The Uncompleted Argument: Du Bois and the Illusion of Race." *Critical Inquiry* 12: 21–37.

Appiah, K. Anthony. 1990. "But Would That Still Be Me?" *The Journal of Philosophy* 87: 493–499.

Appiah, K. Anthony. 1996. "Race, Culture, Identity: Misunderstood Connections." In K. A. Appiah and A. Gutmann (eds.), *Color Conscious: The Political Morality of Race* (Princeton, NJ: Princeton University Press), pp. 30–105.

Appiah, K. Anthony. 2007. "Does Truth Matter to Identity?" In Jorge Gracia (ed.), *Race or Ethnicity: On Black and Latino Identity* (Ithaca, NY: Cornell University Press), pp. 19–44.

Atkin, Albert. 2017. "Race, Definition, and Science." In Naomi Zack (ed.), *The Oxford Handbook of Philosophy and Race* (Oxford: Oxford University Press), pp. 140–149.

Bailey, Stanley R., Aliya Saperstein, and Andrew M. Penner. 2014. "Race, Color, and Income Inequality across the Americas." *Demographic Research* 31: 735–756.

Balderrama, Francisco. 2015. Interview with Terry Gross, *Fresh Air*, "America's Forgotten History of Mexican-American 'Repatriation.'" http://www.npr.org/2015/09/10/439114563/americas-forgotten-history-of-mexican-american-repatriation

Barnes, Robert. 2016. "Supreme Court Hears Case Concerning Biased Comments in Jury Room." *The Washington Post*, October 11. https://www.washingtonpost.com/politics/courts_law/supreme-court-hears-case-concerning-biased-comments-in-jury-room/2016/10/11/f82de46c-8f2a-11e6-9c52-0b10449e33c4_story.html. Accessed October 21, 2016.

Blum, Lawrence. 2002. *"I'm Not a Racist, but . . ."*: *The Moral Quandary of Race*. Ithaca, NY: Cornell University Press.

Burge, Tyler. 1979. "Individualism and the Mental." In P. A. French, T.E. Uehling, and H. Wettstein (eds.), *Midwest Studies in Philosophy*, IV. Minneapolis: University of Minnesota Press, pp. 73–121.

Chalmers, David J. 2011. "Verbal Disputes." *Philosophical Review* 120: 515–566.

Chen, Jacqueline M., Maria Clara de Paula Couto, Airi M. Sacco, and Yarrow Dunham. 2018. "To Be or Not to Be (Black or Multiracial or White): Cultural Variation in Racial Boundaries." *Social Psychological and Personality Science* 9: 763–772.

Compton, E., M. Bentley, S. Ennis, and S. Rastogi. 2013. *2010 Census Race and Hispanic Origin Alternative Questionnaire Experiment*. Washington, DC: US Census Bureau.

Fish, Jefferson M. 2011. "What Does the Brazilian Census Tell Us about Race?" *Psychology Today*, Dec. 6. https://www.psychologytoday.com/blog/looking-in-the-cultural-mirror/201112/what-does-the-brazilian-census-tell-us-about-race

Frankfurt, Harry. 1969. "Alternate Possibilities and Moral Responsibility." *The Journal of Philosophy* 66: 829–839.

Glasgow, Joshua. 2009a. *A Theory of Race*. New York: Routledge.

Glasgow, Joshua. 2009b. "In Defense of a Four-Part Theory: Replies to Hardimon, Haslanger, Mallon, & Zack." *Symposia on Race, Gender, and Philosophy* 5(2): 1–18.

Glasgow, Joshua. 2010. "Another Look at the Reality of Race, by Which I Mean *Race*." In Allan Hazlett (ed.), *New Waves in Metaphysics*. New York: Palgrave MacMillan.

Glasgow, Joshua. 2017. "A Metatheory of Race." In Naomi Zack (ed.), *The Oxford Handbook of Philosophy and Race*. Oxford: Oxford University Press, pp. 170–179.

Glasgow, Joshua. Forthcoming a. "Conceptual Revolution." In Teresa Marques and Åsa Wikforss (eds.), *Shifting Concepts: The Philosophy and Psychology of Conceptual Variability*. Oxford: Oxford University Press.

Glasgow, Joshua. Forthcoming b. "'Race' and Description." In Quayshawn Spencer (ed.), *The Race Debates*. Oxford: Oxford University Press.

Glasgow, J., J. Shulman, and E. Covarrubias. 2009. "The Ordinary Conception of Race in the United States and Its Relation to Racial Attitudes: A New Approach." *Journal of Cognition and Culture* 9: 15–38.

Gratton, Brian, and Emily Klancher Merchant. 2016. "*La Raza*: Mexicans in the United States Census." *The Journal of Policy History* 28: 4.

Haney López, Ian F. 2005. "Race on the 2010 Census: Hispanics and the Shrinking White Majority." *Dædalus* 134: 42–52.

Haslanger, Sally. 2010. "Language, Politics, and 'the Folk': Looking for 'the Meaning' of 'Race.'" *The Monist* 93: 169–187.

Haslanger, Sally. 2012. *Resisting Reality: Social Construction and Social Critique*. Oxford: Oxford University Press.

Hardimon, Michael O. 2017. *Rethinking Race*. Cambridge, MA: Harvard University Press.

Jeffers, Chike. 2013a. Untitled comment. http://peasoup.typepad.com/peasoup/2013/06/ethics-discussion-at-pea-soup-chike-jefferss-the-cultural-theory-of-race-yet-another-look-at-du-bois.html?cid=6a00d83452b89569e2019103efe4a3970c#comment-6a00d83452b89569e2019103efe4a3970c

Jeffers, Chike. 2013b. Untitled comment. http://peasoup.typepad.com/peasoup/2013/06/ethics-discussion-at-pea-soup-chike-jefferss-the-cultural-theory-of-race-yet-another-look-at-du-bois.html?cid=6a00d83452b89569e20192ac22ccf7970d#comment-6a00d83452b89569e20192ac22ccf7970d

Kitcher, Philip. 2007. "Does 'Race' Have a Future?" *Philosophy & Public Affairs* 35: 293–317.

Kripke, Saul. 1972. *Naming and Necessity*. Oxford: Blackwell.

Krogstad, Jens Manuel, and D'Vera Cohn. 2014. "U.S. Census Looking at Big Changes in How It Asks about Race and Ethnicity." *The Pew Research Center*, March 14. http://www.pewresearch.org/fact-tank/2014/03/14/u-s-census-looking-at-big-changes-in-how-it-asks-about-race-and-ethnicity/

Li, Jun Z., Devin M. Absher, Hua Tang, Audrey M. Southwick, Amanda M. Casto, Sohini Ramachandran, Howard M. Cann, Gregory S. Barsh, Marcus Feldman, Luigi L. Cavalli-Sforza, and Richard M. Myers. 2008. "Worldwide Human Relationships Inferred from Genome-Wide Patterns of Variation." *Science* 22: 1100–1104.

Machery, E., R. Mallon, S. Nichols, and S. P. Stich. 2004. "Semantics, Cross-Cultural Style." *Cognition* 92: B1–B12.

Mallon, Ron. 2006. "'Race': Normative, Not Metaphysical or Semantic." *Ethics* 116: 525–551.

Mallon, Ron. 2009. "Commentary on Joshua Glasgow's *A Theory of Race*." *Symposia on Race, Gender, and Philosophy* 5(2): 1–8.

McPherson, Lionel K., and Tommie Shelby. 2004. "Blackness and Blood: Interpreting African American Identity." *Philosophy and Public Affairs* 32: 171–192.

Mills, Charles W. 1998. "'But What Are You *Really*?' The Metaphysics of Race." In Mills, *Blackness Visible: Essays on Philosophy and Race*. Ithaca, NY: Cornell University Press.

Millstein, Roberta L. 2015. "Thinking about Populations and Races in Time." *Studies in History and Philosophy of Biological and Biomedical Sciences* 52: 5–11.

Monk, Ellis P. 2014. "Skin Tone Stratification among Black Americans, 2001–2003." *Social Forces* 92: 1313–1337.

Monk, Ellis P. 2015. "The Cost of Color: Skin Color, Discrimination, and Health among African-Americans." *American Journal of Sociology* 121: 396–444.

Monk, Ellis P. 2016. "The Consequences of 'Race and Color' in Brazil." *Social Problems* 63: 413–430.

Navarro, Mireya. 2003. Going Beyond Black and White, Hispanics in Census Pick 'Other'. *New York Times*. https://www.nytimes.com/2003/11/09/nyregion/going-beyond-black-and-white-hispanics-in-census-pick-other.html

Office of Management and Budget (OMB). 2016. "Standards for Maintaining, Collecting, and Presenting Federal Data on Race and Ethnicity." https://www.regulations.gov/document?D=OMB-2016-0002-0001

Outlaw, Lucius. 1996. *On Race and Philosophy*. New York: Routledge.

Phelan, Jo C., Bruce G. Link, and Naumi M. Feldman. 2013. "The Genomic Revolution and Beliefs about Essential Racial Differences: A Backdoor to Eugenics?" *American Sociological Review* 78: 167–191.

Pierce, Jeremy. 2015. *A Realist Metaphysics of Race: A Context-Sensitive, Short-Term Retentionist, Long-Term Revisionist Approach*. Lanham, MD: Lexington Books.

Putnam, Hilary. 1975. "The Meaning of Meaning." *Philosophical Papers*, Vol. II: *Mind, Language, and Reality*. Cambridge: Cambridge University Press.

Rosenberg, N., J. Pritchard, . . . M. Feldman. 2002. Genetic Structure of Human Populations. *Science* 298(5602): 2381–2385.

Roth, Wendy D. 2012. *Race Migrations: Latinos and the Cultural Transformation of Race*. Stanford, CA: Stanford University Press.

Sainsbury, Mark. 2014. "Fishy Business." *Analysis* 74: 3–5.

Simon, Patrick. 2012. "Collecting Ethnic Statistics in Europe: A Review." *Ethnic and Racial Studies* 35: 1366–1391.

Spencer, Quayshawn. 2015. "Philosophy of Race Meets Population Genetics." *Studies in History and Philosophy of Biological and Biomedical Sciences* 52: 46–55.

Sundstrom, Ronald R. 2002a. "Race as a human kind." *Philosophy and Social Criticism* 28: 91–115.

Sundstrom, Ronald R. 2002b. "'Racial' nominalism." *Journal of Social Philosophy* 33: 193–210.

Taylor, Paul. 2000. "Appiah's Uncompleted Argument: W.E.B. Du Bois and the Reality of Race." *Social Theory and Practice* 26: 103–128.

Telles, Edward. 2014. *Pigmentocracies: Ethnicity, Race, and Color in Latin America*. Chapel Hill: University of North Carolina Press.

Williams, Melissa W., and Jennifer L. Eberhard. 2008. "Biological Conceptions of Race and the Motivation to Cross Racial Boundaries." *Journal of Personality and Social Psychology* 94: 1033–1047.

Zack, Naomi. 1994. *Race and Mixed Race*. Philadephia: Temple University Press.

Zack, Naomi. 2002. *Philosophy of Science and Race*. New York: Routledge.

INDEX

CPSIA information can be obtained
at www.ICGtesting.com
Printed in the USA
BVHW031538180820
586670BV00005B/21